D0930368

Pollution for Sale

INTERNATIONAL STUDIES IN ENVIRONMENTAL POLICY MAKING

General Editor: Frank J. Convery, *Heritage Trust Professor of Environmental Studies and Director of the Environmental Institute at University College Dublin, Ireland*

This important series makes a significant contribution to the development of policies to combat environmental problems. It is the result of a Europe-wide study of the use of market based instruments to formulate environmental policy and reduce degradation. International in scope, it addresses issues of current and future concern across the globe, in both East and West and in developed and developing countries.

This series provides a forum for the publication of a limited number of innovative, high quality volumes which extend and challenge the current literature. It demonstrates how economic analysis can make a contribution to understanding and resolving the environmental problems confronting the world in the twenty-first century.

Titles in the series include:

International Competitiveness and Environmental Policies
Edited by Terry Barker and Jonathan Köhler

Pollution for Sale
Emissions Trading and Joint Implementation
Edited by Steve Sorrell and Jim Skea

The Market and the Environment
The Effectiveness of Market Based Policy Instruments for Environmental Reform
Edited by Thomas Sterner

Pollution for Sale

Emissions Trading and Joint Implementation

Edited by

Steve Sorrell and Jim Skea

SPRU, Science and Technology Policy Research, University of Sussex

INTERNATIONAL STUDIES IN ENVIRONMENTAL POLICY MAKING

Edward Elgar

Cheltenham, UK • Northampton, MA, USA

363.7387
P 777

© Steve Sorrell and Jim Skea, 1999

All rights reserved. No part of this publication may be reproduced, stored in a retrieval system or transmitted in any form or by any means, electronic, mechanical or photocopying, recording, or otherwise without the prior permission of the publisher.

Published by
Edward Elgar Publishing Limited
Glensanda House
Montpellier Parade
Cheltenham
Glos GL50 1UA
UK

Edward Elgar Publishing, Inc.
6 Market Street
Northampton
Massachusetts 01060
USA

A catalogue record for this book
is available from the British Library

Library of Congress Cataloguing in Publication Data
Pollution for sale : emissions trading and joint implementation /
  edited by Steve Sorrell and Jim Skea.
    (International studies in environmental policymaking)
    Includes bibliographical references.
    1. Emissions trading—Europe.   2. Pollution—Government policy–
–Europe.   3. Emissions trading—United States.   4. Pollution–
–Government policy—United States.   I. Sorrell, Steve, 1963–
II. Skea, Jim.   III. Series.
HC240.Z9P557   1999   98–42885
                                                 CIP

ISBN 1 84064 010 3

Printed and bound in Great Britain by
MPG Books Ltd, Bodmin, Cornwall

Contents

University Libraries
v
Carnegie Mellon University
Pittsburgh, PA 15213-3890

List of figures

List of tables

List of contributors

Elizabeth M. Bailey	Center for Energy and Environmental Research, MIT, Cambridge, MA, USA.
Peter Bailey	Stockholm Environment Institute, University of York, UK.
Peter Bohm	Department of Economics, University of Stockholm, Sweden.
Dallas Burtraw	Resources for the Future, Washington DC, USA.
Christine Cros	Centre International de Recherche sur l'Environnement et le Developpement (CIRED), Paris, France.
Chris Dekkers	Air & Energy Directorate, Ministry of Housing, Spatial Planning and the Environment, The Hague, The Netherlands.
Tim Denne	Environmental Resources Management, Oxford, UK.
A. Denny Ellerman	Center for Energy and Environmental Research, MIT, Cambridge, MA, USA.
Robin Faichney	Department of Environmental Science, University of Stirling, UK.
Olivier Godard	Centre International de Recherche sur l'Environnement et le Developpement (CIRED), Paris, France.
Nick Hanley	Department of Economics, University of Stirling, UK.
David Harrison, Jr.	National Economic Research Associates, Cambridge, MA, USA.
Geir Høibye	Confederation of Norwegian Business and Industry, Oslo, Norway.
Tim Jackson	Centre for Environmental Strategy, University of Surrey, Guildford, UK.
Paul L. Joskow	Department of Economics, MIT, Cambridge, MA, USA.
Ger Klaassen	International Institute for Applied Systems Analysis, A-2361, Laxenburg, Austria.
Juan Pablo Montero	Escuela Ingenieria, Santiago, Chile.
Alistair Munro	Department of Economics & Social Studies, University of East Anglia, Norwich, UK.

Andries Nentjes   Department of Economics & Public Finance,
                         University of Groningen, The Netherlands.
Bernd Schärer   Umweltbundesamt, Berlin, Germany.
Richard   Center for Energy and Environmental Research,
Schmalensee   MIT, Cambridge, MA, USA.
James S. Shortle   Department of Agricultural Economics and Rural
                         Sociology, The Pennsylvania State University, PA,
                         USA.
Jim Skea   SPRU, Science and Technology Policy Research,
                         University of Sussex, Brighton, UK.
Steve Sorrell   SPRU, Science and Technology Policy Research,
                         University of Sussex, Brighton, UK.
Rolf-Ulrich   Institut fur Wirtschaftsforschung (IFO), Munich,
Sprenger   Germany.
ZhongXiang Zhang   Department of Economics & Public Finance,
                         University of Groningen, The Netherlands.
Tomasz Zylicz   Economics Department, Warsaw University, Poland.

Preface

This book has been developed from the proceedings of a workshop on 'Tradable Permits, Tradable Quotas and Joint Implementation', held at the Institute of Development Studies, University of Sussex in April 1997. The workshop was organized by the Science Policy Research Unit (SPRU), University of Sussex as part of a Concerted Action on 'Market Based Instruments for Sustainable Development', funded by the European Commission under the Programme 'Human Dimensions of Environmental Change'. This project is co-ordinated by Professor Frank Convery of University College, Dublin, and brings together researchers from a network of institutions throughout the European Union. The chapters in the book have been revised and, with the exception of Chapter 19, were delivered to the editor before December 1997.

The SPRU workshop came at a time when emissions trading was attracting increasing attention. While relatively unfamiliar in Europe, the concept dates back more than thirty years and was first introduced in a practical form in the United States in 1975. Since that time the US has accumulated substantial experience with trading schemes at local and regional levels, and in 1990 introduced an ambitious scheme for controlling sulphur dioxide emissions at a national level. The success of these schemes has led the US to promote the use of trading for the international control of greenhouse gases.

During 1997, the subject became a topic of intense debate in the run up to the 3rd Conference of Parties to the Framework Convention on Climate Change, held in Kyoto in December. The aim of this conference was to agree a Protocol to the Convention, incorporating legally binding targets to reduce greenhouse gas emissions. In a draft protocol, the US suggested that countries should be allowed to trade emissions, to reduce the cost of reaching an agreed target. Despite substantial opposition, and some intense debate during the marathon final negotiating session, the outcome of the conference was a victory for the advocates of emissions trading. The Kyoto Protocol provides the framework for an international system of greenhouse gas trading between countries with agreed emission targets, together with the provision for 'emission credits' from projects that reduce greenhouse gas emissions in countries without targets. The flexibility and cost savings offered by trading allowed the US to sign up to an emissions target, thereby ensuring the integrity of the Convention was maintained. Following Kyoto, emissions trading has become a central feature of the global efforts to control climate change.

The chapters in this book were completed before the Kyoto agreement, but nevertheless have important lessons for the future development of greenhouse gas trading. The chapters provide a comprehensive overview of the theory and practice of emissions trading, including the lessons learnt, the problems faced and the prospects for their extended use. The chapters cover both national experience with trading schemes in the US and Europe, together with international trading of carbon dioxide and sulphur dioxide. A particular focus is the problems of practical implementation, including institutional feasibility and political acceptability in different national contexts. An additional chapter has been added to summarize the outcome of the Kyoto conference and to suggest how international carbon trading may develop in the future.

Steve Sorrell and Jim Skea
Brighton

April 1998

NIA

BR Title:
Frank. J. Convery

Foreword

With his usual sagacity, Adam Smith pointed out that 'Man is the only animal that makes bargains; one dog does not change bones with another dog'.

This sentiment gets to the heart of the work of a network of research institutions co-ordinated by the Environmental Institute, University College, Dublin, and devoted to the study of the design and use of market based instruments for sustainable development. The network is supported by the Environment and Climate research programme of the European Commission (DG XII), and operates as follows. A number of themes have been identified, and a workshop has been, or will be, organized on each of these. Scholars, policy practitioners and others come together, a number of keynote papers on the theme are presented, these are discussed at some length, and then in most cases, the organizers of the theme in question bring together the revised papers into an edited volume. Themes which have been, or will be, addressed include: non market valuation, voluntary agreements, international trade, environmental effectiveness, institutional aspects, tradable permits, green tax commissions, and competitiveness. In addition to books, a series of Research Policy Briefs, synthesizing key findings for policy in regard to the use of each instrument are published by the Environmental Institute.

This volume is the second in the series on International Studies in Environmental Policy Making, and is the product of a highly successful workshop on tradable permits and joint implementation, organized and hosted by the Science Policy Research Unit (SPRU), University of Sussex.

Economists have long argued the merits of two alternative approaches to the integration of market forces in the management of environmental endowments. One approach calls for the introduction of prices – in the form of emission charges and environmental taxes – for the use of the environment. Such a pricing approach would signal the scarcity value of the asset in question, and the quantity 'consumed' would be adjusted downwards accordingly. The government would assert de facto ownership of the environment, and its scarcity value would be reflected in the price charged for its use. There is a wide range of practical experience with this approach in Europe. For more than thirty years, the application of charges for emissions to water have been part of freshwater management in countries such as the Netherlands, Germany and France. In more recent years, Scandinavian countries have introduced a number of charges related to emissions to air.

The second approach is to assign permits, analogous to property rights, for the limited use of the environment. These permits could be for resource extraction, such as fishing quotas, or environmental externalities, such as pollution. Since the total number of permits is fixed, the total quantity of pollution or resource extraction is also fixed. Permit holders are allowed to trade amongst themselves such that a market price reflecting the scarcity value of environmental endowments emerges. Once the overall allowable limit has been set and the permits have been allocated, then government can step aside and allow the market to do its work. While it is in Europe that the use of charges and taxes has been most widespread, it is in the US that tradable permits have emerged as the market mechanism of choice. This is exemplified by its use in California to control emissions to air of sulphur dioxide and nitrogen oxides (the RECLAIM initiative) and its use nation-wide to control sulphur dioxide emissions from power stations (the Acid Rain Program). The focus on pollution has led to the term 'emissions trading'.

This book is devoted to an exploration of the use and potential of emissions trading in general, and in Europe in particular. It reports on the 'state of the art' in 1997, just prior to the 3rd Conference of Parties to the Framework Convention on Climate Change, held at Kyoto in December of that year. This conference marks a watershed in the history of emissions trading. For the first time, emissions trading, and the related mechanism of joint implementation (JI), has become a central feature of an international environmental agreement. The inclusion of emissions trading proved a key factor in gaining political agreement at Kyoto and created the possibility of a global market in carbon dioxide and other greenhouse gases.

All Parties to the Climate Convention must now grapple with the opportunity offered by greenhouse gas trading, but for most European countries there is little first hand experience on which to draw. It is timely therefore for this volume to bring together studies by experts and practitioners from both sides of the Atlantic. The contributions explore the theory and practice of emissions trading in some detail and pay particular attention to lessons from practical experience. These allow the conditions for the successful implementation of trading schemes to be identified.

For policy makers, it is important to reduce as much as is feasible the risk of adopting, or inventing, a policy approach which doesn't work, or is counter productive. In the same spirit, but in another context, Thomas Alva Edison observed: 'Anything that won't sell, I don't want to invent.' This book is for those in the policy process who wish to be effective, who want to invent policy which will do the job and which can be sold to the stakeholders and to the public at large.

Frank J. Convery
Series Editor

|US, Europe|

1- 24

BK Title:>   425
428
H 23

1. Introduction

Steve Sorrell and Jim Skea

1. WHAT IS EMISSIONS TRADING?

Emissions trading schemes allow participants to exchange permits to emit pollution so as to reduce the cost of meeting an overall environmental goal. Alternatively, a more ambitious environmental goal may be achieved for a given level of expenditure. While emission permits may change hands, the total number in circulation is kept fixed, thereby guaranteeing compliance with the environmental target.

Almost all experience of emissions trading has been in the US and has involved companies trading at the local, regional and national level. This experience shows that significant gains in economic efficiency are possible compared to traditional regulatory measures such as uniform emission limits. It also demonstrates the importance of 'learning-by-doing' in order to build effective market institutions and trading arrangements. The US now has more than twenty years of experience with trading mechanisms and has actively promoted their use at an international level for the control of greenhouse gases. This paid off in December 1997, when emissions trading was included as a key element of the Kyoto Protocol to the Framework Convention on Climate Change (FCCC). With this Protocol, emissions trading has come of age. All signatories must now consider trading as part of their strategy for meeting greenhouse gas emissions targets. Trading is now on the agenda of countries who have little previous experience with the idea.

This book provides a comprehensive overview of the experience gained with emissions trading, with a focus on the practical problems of implementation. It aims to show both the real opportunities that exist for reducing the cost of pollution control, and the difficulties faced when introducing the instrument in widely different national contexts. It covers both national and international trading schemes and pays particular attention to the uneven attempts to reconcile trading with European regulatory traditions. The studies in the book were all completed prior to the Kyoto agreement, but an additional chapter has been added to assess how greenhouse gas trading may develop in the future.

The following sections provide a non-technical introduction to the concept of emissions trading. This includes a classification of the different types of trading scheme, an identification of the conditions most suitable for trading and an assessment of the requirements for designing a successful scheme. Section 8 provides an overview of the contents of the book.

Box 1 Key terms

> The terminology of emissions trading is varied and sometimes inconsistent. The generic term for the unit of trade is an emissions *permit*. Permits fall into two broad categories. Emissions *allowances* are allocated to plants and must cover *all* of the emissions from the plant, while emissions *credits* are generated when a plant reduces emissions below an agreed emissions baseline. Allowance schemes allow all emissions to be traded, while credit schemes only allow emission reductions to be traded.
>
> In an allowance scheme, an emissions *cap* refers to an aggregate emissions limit applied to a group of polluters for a given period. An annual cap is commonly referred to as an emissions *quota*, while a cap covering a period of several years is termed an *emissions budget*. Quota is also used to refer to the annual emission limit for an individual source.
>
> Permit *banking* refers to retaining surplus permits for subsequent use, while permit *borrowing*, refers to using permits from subsequent compliance periods to cover current emissions. *Grandfathering* is a colloquial term for the allocation of permits on the basis of historic emissions or previous regulatory controls.
>
> *Joint implementation (JI)* refers to international trading and is used in two senses. The European definition refers to informal co-operation between two or more countries to meet a joint emissions target. The more specific definition under the Framework Convention on Climate Change (FCCC) refers to one country funding an individual greenhouse gas reduction project in another country and thereby gaining an emissions credit. *Activities Implemented Jointly (AIJ)* refers to a pilot phase of JI under the FCCC with no crediting.

2. THE RATIONALE FOR EMISSIONS TRADING

Emissions trading has its origins in both the theoretical contribution of economists and the pragmatic search for increased flexibility within traditional regulatory practices.

One branch of environmental economics has focused on the use of taxes to reflect the cost of environmental damage. The alternative approach is to assign 'property rights' to carry out actions which may have harmful environmental consequences (Coase, 1960). Emissions trading is a particular form of this approach, but the concept has a wide range of application including tradable rights for harvesting natural resources (e.g. fishing quotas). Early exponents of the idea include Dales (1968) and Montgomery (1972).

In its simplest form, the operation of an emissions trading scheme is straightforward. Once the political process has determined that a particular level of emissions is socially acceptable, a fixed number of emission permits can be allocated to the plants responsible. This allocation may decline in time in a phased manner. Each plant must ensure that its emissions are equal to or less than its current permit holdings. If permits can be traded, those who face high pollution abatement costs can continue to pollute by buying additional permits. Those facing low costs can take abatement action and sell their surplus permits for a profit. In this way, each plant can trade off the cost of controlling pollution with the cost of buying or selling permits. This flexibility allows each plant to minimize its overall abatement costs. A similar result could not be achieved by a regulator who would not have access to the detailed cost information that is required.

In an ideal – and unattainable – world where there is perfect information, no barriers to trading and where the actions of buying and selling are themselves cost-free, trading should result in the overall emission target being achieved at the lowest possible cost. Also, in this ideal world, the operation of economic incentives would mean that the way in which permits were distributed initially would have no effect on the final pattern of emissions and abatement.

In the real world, polluters will not have full information about opportunities for trading and there will be costs associated with identifying, implementing and monitoring trading activity. As a result, the initial allocation of permits will influence the ultimate pattern of emissions and abatement as well as having significant economic consequences for individual emitters. For this reason, the initial distribution of permits has proved to be one of the most challenging aspects of developing emissions trading schemes.

If permits were sold in an auction, emitters would be required to pay for the damage caused by their pollution. However, this may not be politically acceptable where rights to emit have been established under an existing regulatory regime and where substantial revenue transfers would be entailed. The more practical alternative is to allocate permits free on the basis of historic emissions or previous regulatory controls.

3. EXPERIENCE WITH EMISSIONS TRADING

Emissions trading developed in an incremental fashion in the United States, as a means of introducing flexibility into an extremely rigid regulatory framework. The origins of emissions trading lie in the *offset policy* which was introduced in 1976. This allowed new plants to set up in areas which exceeded air quality standards, provided they paid for offsetting emission reductions elsewhere in the region.

The program developed further with the introduction of the *bubble policy* in 1979. This allowed plants with multiple emission points to be controlled as a group, rather than specifying individual requirements for each point source (effectively placing a bubble over the plant). The flexibility this offered was extended further by allowing for multi-plant bubbles and for the purchase of *emission reduction credits* (ERCs) from other plants as an alternative to controlling pollution directly. The offset and bubble policies were later combined with other measures to form the *Emissions Trading Program* which was agreed in 1986 (Box 2).

The flexibility offered by emissions trading has led to considerable cost savings, but the program is handicapped by the constraints inherited from the original regulatory framework (Tietenberg, 1985). However, the lessons learnt have been embodied in a new generation of trading schemes which promise to be more successful as a result. A common feature of these schemes is that the unit of trade is an emissions allowance rather than an emissions credit.

The flagship US scheme is the federal Acid Rain Program which allows any power station in the continental United States to trade sulphur dioxide (SO_2) allowances with any other power station (Box 3 and Chapters 2 and 3). The clear success of this scheme has encouraged the adoption of trading in other contexts.

A scheme of similar level of sophistication but focused upon local air pollution problems is *RECLAIM* in Southern California (Box 4 and Chapter 4). This allows 400 of the largest plants in the region to trade emissions of sulphur dioxide (SO_2) and nitrogen oxides (NO_x). A notable feature of both schemes is that the flexibility offered by trading was an important factor in gaining political acceptance of a stringent emission target. A third scheme involves eight states in the north-eastern US which are co-operating in developing a program for trading nitrogen oxides between electric utility plants.

3.1. European experience

European experience with emissions trading has been very limited. Germany has introduced offset and bubble provisions similar to the US, but

Box 2 The US Emissions Trading Program (ETP)

The Emissions Trading Program (ETP) is a credit based trading scheme for seven pollutants affecting local air quality in 247 control regions across the United States. It coexists with a complex mix of technology-based standards administered at both the federal and the state level The program developed incrementally, reaching its final form in 1986.

The program is implemented by means of four separate policies linked by a 'permit' termed an Emission Reduction Credit (ERC). These are created when a source reduces its emissions below the level currently required by state regulations. The *offset* policy provides a means for new sources to locate in heavily polluted areas provided they offset their emissions by buying ERCs. The *bubble* policy is aimed at existing plants undergoing expansion or modification and allows the source to offset increases in emissions from one emission point within the bubble by either reducing emissions from another emission point or purchasing ERCs. Bubbles may cover either single plants with single or multiple emission points or multiple plants. The *netting* policy is similar to the bubble but is aimed primarily at single plants wishing to remain below a certain size in order to avoid tighter control requirements; also, ERCs cannot be used in netting. Finally, *banking* allows firms to store ERCs for subsequent use.

Empirical studies have indicated that the program has achieved capital cost savings in excess of $10 billion, with thousands of cost saving trades being completed (Tietenberg, 1991). However, this probably represents only a small fraction of the potential. Netting has been the most popular option, but the take-up of bubble and offset opportunities has been disappointing. Furthermore, most trades have been internal to individual companies, the external ERC market has been thin, and there has been limited use of banking.

There are several reasons for this qualified success. The spatial dependence of local pollutants has presented an obstacle, since dispersion modelling is required and trades between distant sources have been discouraged. Baseline emission levels have been uncertain, leading to disputes over 'paper' emission reductions and the validity of reductions created by plant closure. The program has also been plagued by uncertainty, with frequent changes to the rules and a lack of clarity over the legal status of an ERC. The lack of a liquid market in ERCs has made it difficult to find buyers and sellers, and perceived risk has reinforced the preference towards internal trades. Finally, the administrative procedures for gaining approval for a trade are lengthy, complex and expensive.

The difficulties encountered by the ETP have provided a valuable lesson. The design of subsequent US schemes were strongly influenced by this experience, with measures being taken to avoid many of the above problems.

Box 3 The US Acid Rain Program

The US Acid Rain Program is the largest, most ambitious and most successful tradable permit scheme yet introduced. It began in 1995 and aims to reduce sulphur dioxide (SO_2) emissions from US power stations by more than a half. The program is in two stages: Phase 1 runs from 1995 to 2000 and requires 110 of the largest power stations to cut emissions by 3.6 million tons/year. Phase 2 expands the program to include 800 power stations and requires a further cut of 5 million tons/year. From 2000, total emissions are not allowed to exceed a 'cap' of 8.95 million tons/year.

The program is implemented through tradable permits known as sulphur dioxide allowances. One allowance is worth 1 ton of SO_2. Each year program participants are allocated a fixed number of allowances in accordance with their baseline fuel consumption. Allowances may be freely traded on a one-to-one basis with other participants and unused allowances may be banked for future use. Compliance with the program is ensured through continuous emission monitoring, computerized allowance tracking and stringent penalties.

Early results from the program are highly encouraging. Emission reductions in Phase 1 have exceeded the target by some 3.4 million tons, creating surplus allowances which are being banked for use in Phase 2. The allowance market has grown steadily, with allowances currently trading around $90/ton – as against earlier predictions of as much as $1000/ton. Emission reductions have been achieved through retrofitting desulphurization equipment and switching to low sulphur coal, both of which are significantly cheaper than was earlier forecast. Coal prices have fallen through deregulation of rail transport and allowance trading has allowed these benefits to be distributed over a wider area. Similarly, the incentives created by the allowance market has stimulated performance improvements and cost reductions in desulphurization equipment.

Overall, the flexibility offered by allowance trading is estimated to have reduced total compliance costs by a third to a half, with 45 per cent of allowances being used for cost saving in some form.

---

these have achieved few cost savings as a result of their limited range of applicability and restrictive rules on their use. Germany is about to introduce a trading scheme for volatile organic compounds (VOCs) emitted by smaller industrial facilities such as paint shops. Belgium, Denmark, the Netherlands and the UK have all used bubble provisions for existing power stations to implement EU limits on sulphur dioxide emissions (Chapter 5). In practice, this trading has been informal with no financial transactions being involved and has generally been between power stations belonging to a single company.

Box 4 RECLAIM

The Regional Clean Air Incentives Market (RECLAIM) is an innovative trading scheme designed to tackle the severe air quality problems in Southern California. The scheme came into force in January 1994 and applies to facilities emitting more than 4 tons of either nitrogen oxide (NO_x) or sulphur dioxide (SO_2) a year. The 390 NO_x and 41 SO_2 RECLAIM facilities represent, respectively, 65 per cent and 85 per cent of total stationary source emissions.

RECLAIM follows the stringent targets in the original 1991 air quality management plan, which it replaced. Total stationary source emissions are capped, with the cap declining each year until targets are met. Each year, participating facilities receive emission allowances denominated in lb/year and valid for one year. Allocations are based on peak fuel consumption over the baseline period multiplied by an emission factor, which depends on the fuel type.

Facilities can trade allowances but they cannot be banked. To avoid facilities having either a surplus or shortage of allowances at the end of the year, the allocation is staggered in two cycles separated by six months. Also, the risk of trading leading to high pollutant concentrations is minimized by dividing the region into two zones. Plants in the upwind zone cannot purchase downwind allowances.

Cost reductions from trading are forecast to be 42 per cent over the period 1994–2000 (Fromm and Hansjürgens, 1997). Little trading was anticipated in the first two years as most facilities can already meet their targets. Nevertheless, a market has steadily developed, with brokers offering both bilateral transactions and private auctions. A total of 32 facilities took part in the August 1995 auction and 8.6 million credits were traded. Two thirds of these were for allowances valid in 1998 or after.

RECLAIM embodies the lessons of the earlier emissions trading program and extensive consultation of interest groups has helped its public acceptability. While it is too early to judge the program a success, all the indications to date are highly positive.

There have been many scoping studies and provisional schemes which have not as yet come to fruition. The UK developed plans for a formal trading scheme for sulphur dioxide emissions, but these were abandoned on the grounds that trading was unnecessary to meet current obligations (Chapter 11). The Confederation of Norwegian Business and Industry has also proposed a sulphur trading scheme in which permits would be allocated to both sulphur emitters and producers of oil products (Chapter 6). The *quid pro quo* for this scheme would be the removal of an existing tax on sulphur dioxide.

3.2. International experience

Prior to 1998, there was one example of a scheme for emissions trading between companies located in different countries. Under the 1987 Montreal Protocol which controls substances which deplete the ozone layer, parties may transfer CFC production and consumption quotas in order to help rationalize industrial production or to achieve economic efficiency (Chapter 5). In 1992–93, 20 transfers involving EU companies took place. Owing to commercial confidentiality, very little information is available about the nature of these transfers.

The possibility of emissions trading is built into the Second UNECE Sulphur Protocol through provisions allowing two or more parties to implement their emission obligations jointly. Despite extensive studies on the scope for trading under this Protocol (Chapters 14 and 15), the rules covering such arrangements have yet to be fully articulated.

The greatest potential for emissions trading lies with greenhouse gases under the FCCC. The Kyoto Protocol, agreed in December 1997, assigns 'quantified emission limitation and reduction commitments', or QELRCs, to OECD countries and economies in transition (Annex I countries). To meet these targets, Annex I countries are allowed to trade greenhouse gas allowances measured in tonnes of carbon dioxide equivalent. While the parties to the Protocol have the legal responsibility of meeting the targets, the Protocol provides scope for individual companies to participate and for the establishment of domestic trading regimes. Such arrangements can develop only as fast as reliable monitoring, tracking and verification systems are put in place, but the rules for these have yet to be agreed.

The Protocol also allows for project-level joint implementation involving countries which have not established QELRCs (the Clean Development Mechanism). With this, one party finances and perhaps carries out a project which reduces emissions in a second country, and receives some credit for the reductions achieved. This is analogous to emissions credit trading, but it faces the challenge of defining the counterfactual emissions scenario – what would have happened to emissions in the absence of the project.

4. TYPES OF TRADING SCHEME

Permit schemes can be classified by: a) the characteristics of the pollutant; b) the permit lifetime and distribution strategy; and c) the choice between allowances and credits.

4.1. Pollutant characteristics

The nature of the pollutant is a critical element in the design of a trading scheme since the quantities traded must have a comparable environmental impact. Pollutants vary both in the importance of geographical location (a spatial dimension) and in the degree to which they can be assimilated by the environment (a temporal dimension). In the spatial dimension we can distinguish between 'uniformly mixed' pollutants, where pollutant concentration is independent of the location of the sources; and 'non-uniformly mixed' pollutants where source location matters (Tietenberg, 1985). Similarly, in the temporal dimension we can distinguish between pollutants that accumulate in the environment and those that are assimilated. Combining these gives four broad categories of pollutant:

- uniformly mixed, assimilative
- uniformly mixed, accumulative
- non-uniformly mixed, assimilative
- non-uniformly mixed, accumulative

In practice, this classification is oversimplified. For example, the environment has a limited capacity for assimilating many pollutants, up to a threshold level of emission or deposition. Similarly, the degree of spatial dependence can vary widely.

A key point is that a trading scheme becomes much more viable if the pollutant can be treated as uniformly mixed. In this instance, the trading scheme can be based on emission permits for individual sources who can trade with each other regardless of their location.

In contrast, for non-uniformly mixed pollutants, the freedom to trade is constrained. In this instance, the theoretical solution is to denominate permits in terms of pollutant concentrations at particular locations (Tietenberg, 1985, pp. 22–27). Emissions trading in this type of system implies becoming involved in as many separate permit markets as there are defined locations. In practice, the complexity entailed in such a system makes it impractical and simpler solutions must be devised.

To accommodate the temporal dimension, permits can be classified into two general categories – *flow* permits and *stock* permits. A flow permit refers either to a rate measure, where the time dimension is explicit (e.g. lbs/hour), or to a concentration measure where the time dimension is incorporated in the averaging period (e.g. hourly average ppm). In contrast, stock permits refer simply to total quantities, such as tons of emissions. The key difference between the two is that stock permits are used up as they are applied to quantities of emissions, while flow permits are not. Stock permits will deplete unless they are replenished periodically, while flow permits will not.

Combining these spatial and temporal considerations leads to a general classification of permit denomination, summarized in Table 1.1.

Table 1.1 Pollutant characteristics and permit denomination

Spatial characteristics	Temporal characteristics	Permit denomination	Permit type	Example unit
Uniformly mixed	Assimilative	Rate	Flow	lbs/hour
Non-uniformly mixed	Assimilative	Concentration	Flow	ppm (+ av time)
Uniformly mixed	Accumulative	Quantity	Stock	tons
Non-uniformly mixed	Accumulative	Deposition	Stock	tons/km^2

Source: Sorrell, 1994

4.2. Lifetime and distribution

In practice, some pollution problems may be dealt with through either stock or flow permits. For example, a source could be allocated a single flow permit to emit N tonnes/year of carbon dioxide, valid for a specified period of time. Alternatively, it could be allocated N stock permits each year, with each permit worth 1 tonne of carbon dioxide. These considerations lead to two other dimensions of permit classification:

- *Permit lifetime*: This may either be *finite* – where the right of use expires at the end of a specified period – or *indefinite*, where no termination date is defined. Stock permits may have an indefinite life in terms of 'right of use', even though their actual use results in expiry.
- *Distribution strategy*: This may either be *once-off* at the initiation of a scheme, or *periodic* at regular intervals over the duration of the scheme. Periodic distribution is most appropriate for stock permits and allows a declining pollution target to be easily accommodated.

4.3. Allowances and credits

To complete the classification of permit schemes it is necessary to distinguish between an emissions *allowance* and an emission reduction *credit*. The differences between the two are summarized in Table 1.2.

Table 1.2 Allowances versus credits

Emission reduction credit	Emission allowance
Scheme: 'Baseline and credit'	Scheme: 'Cap and trade'
Applies to emission reductions below defined baseline	Applies to all emissions
Only emission reductions can be traded	All emissions can be traded
Credits are generated when a source reduces its emissions below an agreed baseline	Allowances are allocated by the regulatory authority
May develop incrementally as a means of introducing flexibility into existing regulatory structure	Trading must be built into the regulatory structure from the beginning
Participation in the credit market is voluntary – sources can just meet existing standards	Participation in the program is mandatory – the overall emission cap still applies even if sources do not trade

The emissions baseline in a credit scheme can be identical to the emissions cap in an allowance scheme. Thus both schemes can be used to implement an emissions cap. However, the two approaches have very different implications for the extent and timing of regulatory involvement. Allowance schemes may require a great deal of investment at the inception of the scheme, but relatively little oversight during operation. In contrast, credit schemes require less initial design work, but the regulator must be involved in certifying individual trades. Allowance schemes represent a 'purer' form of emissions trading, but credit schemes may be easier to implement. The Kyoto Protocol includes both allowance trading between countries with agreed targets and the generation of credits from individual projects in countries without targets.

To illustrate these different dimensions of permit classification, Table 1.3 compares the US Emissions Trading Program with the US Acid Rain Program.

5. BENEFITS OF EMISSIONS TRADING

5.1. Economic gains

As with all market-based instruments, the central claim for emissions trading is that it will lower the costs of meeting a given environmental goal. The

Table 1.3 Permit classification in two US schemes

Dimension	Emissions Trading Program	Acid Rain Program
Basis	Credit	Allowance
Type	Flow	Stock
Spatial	Most pollutants non-uniformly mixed	Treated as uniformly mixed
Lifetime	Indefinite	Indefinite
Distribution	Once off	Periodic
Name	Emission Reduction Credit	Sulphur Allowance

extent of the cost gains which can be achieved depend on: a) the underlying cost structures for abating pollution; b) the nature of the regulatory arrangements against which trading is compared; and c) the degree to which permit markets approach conditions of perfect competition.

Trading will yield the greatest benefits where plants have a diverse pattern of abatement costs. Hence, for international carbon trading there is interest in joint implementation between developed and developing countries. However, Bohm has demonstrated that significant cost savings could be achieved through the international trading of carbon quotas between apparently similar countries (Chapter 16).

Under some traditional regulatory systems, emission limits are set uniformly across different plants. If these vary significantly in abatement cost, trading may offer considerable economic benefits. Other systems are much more flexible in 'differentiating' emission limits between different types of plant. Here, the gains of trading may be less because flexibility is captured when permits are negotiated, rather than when they are subsequently traded.

There are also several intrinsic features which may inhibit the effectiveness of permit markets: a) the costs associated with identifying and engaging with prospective trading partners; b) the costs of monitoring emissions, tracking trades and verifying compliance; and c) the difficulties of market dominance by one or a small number of large plants. In the latter case, major players may be tempted to hoard permits, either to drive up prices or to prevent new companies entering the market. This was one reason why, in the Acid Rain Program, the US authorities auctioned some permits as well as 'grandfathering' them out to existing plants.

5.2. Innovation incentives

Emissions trading is claimed to provide a continuous incentive for technological innovation. Whereas traditional regulations simply require compliance, permit schemes provide an incentive to exceed the target as a profit can be made from the sale of surplus permits. Also, if economic growth leads to an increase in the demand for permits the price will rise, creating an escalating incentive to reduce emissions.

Evidence for innovation is available from the US Acid Rain Program (Burtraw, 1996). The performance and reliability of flue gas desulphurization equipment has improved and costs have fallen significantly. Similarly, several companies have developed innovative techniques for blending low and high sulphur coals.

5.3. Responding to policy needs

Tradable emission permits are particularly attractive when there is a need to constrain total emissions to a given level. In the US acid rain debate, there was a strong focus on the aggregate level of emission reductions which might be required. The promise of cost savings through emissions trading was a key factor in gaining political support for a stringent emission target.

International environmental obligations are often formulated in terms of national emission quotas. Examples include the UNECE Protocols on SO_2, NO_x and VOCs. One of the reasons that tradable sulphur permits were given serious consideration in the UK is that they could guarantee compliance with international obligations in a transparent way.

Legal and cultural incompatibilities with existing regulatory arrangements can be a major obstacle to the introduction of emissions trading. Adherence to strict standards of 'best available technology' has prevented emissions trading from gaining much support in Germany (Chapter 9), while in the UK proposals for sulphur trading sat uncomfortably with the prevailing style of informal negotiation between operators and regulators (Chapter 11). It is still unclear whether trading is compatible with existing European Union legislation, such the Directive on Integrated Pollution Prevention and Control.

5.4. Permits versus taxes

The guarantee of achieving a given environmental goal is a key reason for the choice of permit schemes over environmental taxes. Taxes cannot do this, unless they are adjusted in the light of progress towards the goal. In addition, permit schemes can avoid the politically difficult issue of revenue transfers and, unlike taxes, the price of permits is responsive to changing market conditions.

6. FACTORS DETERMINING SUCCESS

6.1. Spatial issues

As discussed above, emissions trading can best address environmental problems where the geographical distribution of emissions does not matter. In this sense, emissions trading is ideally suited to abating emissions of gases, such as carbon dioxide, which contribute to global climate change. At the other end of the spectrum, emissions trading is unsuited to dealing with local environmental problems which arise in the vicinity of individual plants.

If location is important yet trading is unrestricted, there is a risk that individual trades will lead to negative environmental consequences at specific locations. For example, a plant close to a sensitive ecosystem may attempt to buy emission permits. This problem has been dealt with in some cases by requiring environmental impact assessments for individual trades. This will obviously push up costs and inhibit trading. A simpler alternative is to specify an absolute emission ceiling at each plant to reflect local environmental considerations. Trading can take place as long as that emission ceiling is not exceeded. Alternatively, trading could be allowed only within designated zones, or be permitted between zones provided an offset ratio is used (e.g. 1.5 to 1). While more complex arrangements could be conceived, it is unlikely they would be workable in practice. Whatever restrictions are made, there will be a trade off between environmental protection and maximizing the potential economic gains.

6.2. Timescales and banking

For participants to have confidence in trading, it is essential that the permit has a firm status and that the scheme remains stable for a sufficient period of time. However, regulators will wish to retain some flexibility in the issuing of permits to take account of new information about environmental damage or changed public expectations. For this reason, emission allowances in the US are specifically *not* defined in terms of 'property rights' as this would protect them from subsequent confiscation.

Under the Acid Rain Program, unused permits may be 'banked' for use in subsequent years, thereby giving participants an extra dimension of flexibility. In practice, many permits have been banked as operators undertake low-cost abatement measures at an early stage, thus avoiding later investment in high-cost measures. Banking can offer significant economic benefits, but does create the possibility that subsequent annual emissions will exceed the annual allocation. This is one reason why banking is not permitted in RECLAIM.

More controversial is the concept of 'borrowing' forward from future permit allocations. The US proposed borrowing, on a discounted basis, in its draft protocol to the FCCC, but this was rejected at Kyoto. Borrowing brings no environmental gains and risks deferring non-compliance with environmental obligations.

6.3. Distributing permits

The most intractable problem associated with establishing an emissions trading scheme is the initial distribution of permits. This must be perceived to be fair, but perceptions of equity may differ between participants. The scale of the problem depends on the diversity of the plants involved. Distribution difficulties were one of the major obstacles which blocked the introduction of quota switching in the UK (Chapter 11).

In order to gain a sufficient degree of acceptance from existing polluters, it has generally been necessary to *grandfather* most permits, i.e. distribute them according to a formula based on historic emissions or existing regulatory requirements. This was the case under the US Acid Rain Program, although many exceptions and adjustments were required to build adequate political support. One major problem with this approach is that it may penalize plants that have reduced emissions in the past. Giving credit for such reductions is one of many considerations that may complicate the distribution rule.

6.4. Enforcement and monitoring

The credibility of any permit scheme is critically dependent on emissions being monitored accurately, permit holdings being tracked and non-compliance punished. Since a profit can be made by selling permits, there may be a greater incentive to under-report emissions. However, a trade off may be necessary between the effectiveness of enforcement and its cost. The Acid Rain Program adopted continuous monitoring arrangements, but the cost of these may substantially reduce the gains from trade. The high cost of monitoring was the main reason smaller plants were excluded from RECLAIM.

6.5. Market institutions and actors

In general, emissions trading will operate successfully only when market players are large and sophisticated and have a strategic interest in reducing the cost of emissions abatement. Electric utilities are obvious targets, particularly as the flexibility of emissions trading may help in the adjustment to electricity market liberalization.

In principle, emissions trading can operate on the basis of bilateral deals struck between individual operators. However, comprehensive trading schemes such as the Acid Rain Program have resulted in a much richer set of institutional arrangements and actors. These include: brokering firms which will identify and arrange bilateral trades; auction houses dealing with both publicly distributed permits and those offered for sale privately; and futures markets which lower risk by creating stability over time. These schemes also allow third parties, such as environmental groups, to purchase permits.

6.6. Learning

Schemes such as the Acid Rain Program are built upon twenty years of experience with more limited credit trading. While some of this experience is transferable, successful adoption of trading schemes will require a process of institutional learning and the development of pilot projects. Schemes may also be built bottom-up, using credit trading to add flexibility to an existing regulatory framework. The negative perception of permits as 'rights to pollute' may hinder the adoption of trading schemes.

7. POLICY DESIGN

In summary, emissions trading is most likely to be successful where:

- The pollutant or good is readily quantifiable and easily measurable.
- The environmental objective is clearly defined; sufficiently stringent to pose a challenge to the regulated parties; and unlikely to be modified for a reasonable period of time.
- There are a large number of point sources of pollution, where the organizations involved are sufficiently large and sophisticated to deal with the contractual requirements of permit trade.
- The environmental problem is not tied too closely to the location of the source, thereby allowing a large number of sources from a wide geographical area to participate in trade.
- There is variation in abatement cost between sources, thereby providing significant scope for cost saving through permit trade.
- The market is not dominated by one or a small number of sources who hold the majority of the permits and are therefore in a position to exercise market power.
- There is a pre-existing institutional basis for regulatory control, providing a structure for monitoring and communication.

- There is a perceived need for greater flexibility in regulation, so permit trading can act as a cheaper means of meeting a binding target.
- The use of alternative policy instruments, notably the imposition of taxes or charges, is not politically feasible.

The success of a scheme will depend on the details of design and implementation, but key criteria for policy design can be identified as in Box 5.

Box 5 Key criteria for policy design

- *Simplicity* – the simpler the system, the more likely it is to succeed. This implies minimal restrictions on trade and streamlined administration and enforcement procedures.
- *Permit allocation* – this is the most intractable issue. The allocation rule should be simple, it should be based in part on historic data (grandfathering) and it should be perceived to be fair. Auctions of a small portion of the permits may have a useful role in stimulating the market and providing a means of acquiring permits for new entrants.
- *Data* – there must be accurate data on the baseline for permit allocation, together with reliable and accurate systems of emission monitoring and permit accounting.
- *Certainty* – permits must be protected from confiscation or arbitrary modification in value and there must be confidence in the stability of the scheme for a reasonable period of time. Without this, participants will not trade.
- *Banking* – flexibility and confidence in the system may be significantly increased by allowing permits to be banked.
- *Enforcement* – there should be strong penalties for evasion together with a high probability of detection.
- *Compatibility* – the scheme must be compatible with existing regulatory requirements and these should not unduly restrict the scope for trade.
- *Commitment* – there should be a strong policy commitment to the system and its objectives. The constituency of political support should include the affected parties, NGOs and the implementing agency.

---

8. COVERAGE OF THE BOOK

This book is divided into six parts:

1. review of recent US experience;
2. national trading schemes in Europe;

3. compatibility of trading with national regulatory traditions;
4. application of trading to water pollution and waste;
5. international sulphur trading; and
6. international carbon trading.

Apart from Part 4, all chapters discuss the use of trading for the control of air pollution. European experience is covered in both Parts 2 and 3, but the particular focus of Part 3 is how trading may conflict with established regulatory practices.

8.1. US experience

Chapter 2 by Denny Ellerman et al. summarizes the recent experience of the US Acid Rain Program. They estimate that in 1995 the flexibility provided by allowance trading led to cost savings of $225–$375 million, or up to half the cost of meeting the targets without trading. While the program has held its share of surprises, Ellerman et al. conclude that on balance it has been a 'refreshingly positive experience', with very few problems of design and implementation.

Chapter 3 by Dallas Burtraw presents projections of the long run cost savings of the Acid Rain Program, and estimates that efficient allowance trading would save about 35 per cent of the cost of the 'command and control' alternative. While not all the potential savings are currently being captured, there are good reasons for optimism about its long term future. Burtraw also examines the substantial loss in economic efficiency that results from grandfathering rather than auctioning sulphur allowances, and recommends a hybrid mix of allocation methods for future allowance schemes. Finally, Burtraw presents a monetary valuation of the benefits of the Acid Rain Program and finds them to be an order of magnitude greater than the costs.

The RECLAIM scheme in Southern California is the subject of Chapter 4 by David Harrison. This provides an account of the design of the scheme and the trade-offs that were made to gain political acceptance. Decisions were required on: the type of scheme, the coverage of plants and sectors; the rules for initial allocation; the geographical and seasonal constraints; and the administrative requirements. Harrison shows how, despite a wide diversity of sources and stringent emission targets, a politically acceptable and workable solution was devised.

8.2. Introducing trading in Europe

Part 2 turns to the less successful experience of European countries with trading schemes. In Chapter 5, Ger Klaassen provides an overview of

European experience, followed by a discussion of the potential for extending their use. He emphasizes the role of the EU in creating scope for trading when drafting environmental legislation and identifies the most promising areas for the future introduction of both national and international trading schemes.

Chapter 6 by Geir Høibye describes a proposed scheme for sulphur trading in Norway, which may well become the first national trading scheme in Europe. The scheme, which is intended to be introduced in 1999, covers nearly all Norwegian sulphur emissions and includes both large industry and fuel suppliers as permit holders. Political acceptability will be facilitated by the removal of an existing sulphur tax.

In Chapter 7, Chris Dekkers describes the policy options for achieving the stringent targets for NO_x and SO_2 in the Netherlands National Environmental Policy Plan (NEPP). A government study suggested that an NO_x trading scheme could reduce abatement costs by some 40 per cent. However, Dutch industry has proposed an alternative voluntary cost sharing scheme, in which industry as a whole would subsidize the investment costs of individual plants. Voluntary approaches represent a potential alternative to trading schemes that may be accommodated more easily in a European context.

The Polish experience with emissions trading forms the subject of Chapter 8 by Tomasz Zylicz. The potential for trading has been demonstrated by successful pilot projects, such as that at Chorzów, and detailed feasibility studies, such as the Opole project. This has raised awareness and led to attempts to include trading in revisions to the Environmental Protection Act. These have foundered, however, due to continued scepticism and competing political priorities. The fact that trading is not widely used in the EU has compounded these problems.

8.3. Trading and national regulatory traditions

Part 3 continues the examination of European experience, but places particular emphasis on how trading may challenge established regulatory traditions. In Chapter 9, Bernd Schärer presents a sceptical view of the scope for trading in German clean air policy. Germany relies heavily on technology based standards for pollution control, including the principle of 'state of the art'. Schärer argues that the application of this principle significantly reduces the scope for cost saving trades. Emissions trading is argued to prioritize economic efficiency at the expense of environmental protection.

Chapter 10 by Christine Cros examines the compatibility of sulphur trading with the French doctrine of public service. Cros highlights the differing perspectives of economics and political science on this topic and the presumed incompatibility between emissions trading and French regulatory traditions. In countering this, Cros argues that there are no major legal or institutional obstacles to the introduction of trading in France; that mechanisms similar to trading have already developed; and that institutional frameworks are evolving in a direction which should increase the scope for trading. However, key actors are insufficiently mobilized in favour of a new approach and public hostility to the idea of 'rights to pollute' presents a major obstacle.

In Chapter 11, Steve Sorrell provides a detailed examination of why attempts to introduce sulphur trading in the UK were ultimately unsuccessful. At one level the reason was simple: the switch to gas following liberalization of energy markets meant that a trading scheme was no longer needed. However, Sorrell argues that sulphur trading was doomed to failure even if the changes in energy markets had not occurred. The reasons were: a fundamental conflict of regulatory principles; a conflict of regulatory culture; difficulties in resolving the equity issue of quota allocation; persistent regulatory uncertainty; and inadequate political support. These are important lessons as similar problems are likely to be encountered elsewhere within Europe as countries consider the scope for carbon trading after Kyoto.

8.4. Scoping studies: water and waste

Part 4 shifts the focus to feasibility studies on the use of trading for water pollution and waste. While air pollution has dominated the literature on emissions trading, the concept is equally applicable, though less tried, in other contexts. In Chapter 12, James Shortle et al. examine the use of trading to meet water quality targets in the Forth Estuary in Scotland. The study combines economic modelling of pollution abatement at key pollution sources with physical modelling of pollutant transport and water quality. Shortle et al. show how explicit treatment of uncertainty in meeting water quality targets changes both the nature of the efficient solution and the likelihood of a permit market achieving the efficient solution. Such stochastic treatment of pollution problems is new and may have wide applicability.

Chapter 13 by Rolf Sprenger presents a novel examination of the design of a tradable permit system for non-returnable beverage containers. The German Packaging Ordinance sets stringent targets for the recycling rates of various types of packaging and mandates take-back obligations and deposit-refund schemes if the targets are not met. Tradable permits are investigated as an alternative to such requirements and are shown to guarantee attainment of the target while offering significant improvements in static and dynamic efficiency. The scheme should be politically acceptable provided grandfathering is used for permit allocation.

8.5. International sulphur trading

Part 5 moves to an international level and examines the scope for sulphur trading under the second Sulphur Protocol to the UNECE Convention on Long Range Transboundary Air Pollution.

In Chapter 14, Bailey and Jackson discuss the problems faced in devising rules for sulphur trading under this Protocol and the relevance of these for carbon trading after Kyoto. The principal difficulty with the UNECE Protocol is the spatial nature of the pollution – emissions from one country are not equivalent to those from another. Unlike in the US Acid Rain Program, this problem cannot be ignored. Bailey and Jackson examine the use of exchange rates to guide trading between countries and demonstrate that the magnitude of these severely restricts the potential gains from trade. Furthermore, since the magnitude of exchange rates increases with the level of abatement, trading becomes less attractive as time goes on. The attraction of trading for carbon dioxide is that such constraints do not apply.

In Chapter 15, Olivier Godard presents some alternative mechanisms for sulphur trading under the UNECE Protocol. These do not use exchange rates, but confine trading to within 'macro zones' defined by similar levels of environmental sensitivity. The chapter examines how the two types of constraint in the UNECE Protocol – national emissions ceilings and deposition constraints on individual geographic zones – may be simultaneously met. This leads to two proposals for trading schemes: a system of two types of allowances working in parallel, and an integrated system in which a single allowance embodies both emission and deposition constraints.

8.6. International carbon trading

Part 6 examines the international trading of carbon dioxide emissions, the area which offers the greatest potential for the future development of emissions trading.

In Chapter 16, Peter Bohm presents the results of an economics experiment in which negotiating teams from four Nordic countries engaged in quota trading to meet a joint target for stabilizing carbon dioxide emissions. The teams included experienced public officials appointed by the Energy Ministries of the participating countries and each team based their negotiating strategy on estimates of their own country's marginal abatement costs. The result was that, through quota trading, the countries succeeded in reducing total abatement costs by 50 per cent, which represented 97 per cent of the maximum potential savings. The results demonstrate that substantial savings can be made even where the participating countries are very similar.

In Chapter 17, ZhongXiang Zhang and Andries Nentjes explore the design and constituting elements of both national and international schemes for tradable carbon permits. They discuss such issues as the definition of the commodity; budget periods and the use of banking; distribution of permits to domestic entities; monitoring and compliance; institutional requirements; administrative costs; and international trade rules. As with any trading scheme, success depends heavily on the details of the design. The chapter outlines the options that are available and the choices that should be made to achieve a feasible, efficient and politically acceptable solution.

Chapter 18 by Tim Denne addresses the operational aspects of carbon trading and identifies the issues which are important to the implementation of such a scheme both domestically and internationally. A key issue for a domestic scheme is how small sources can be included without incurring excessive administrative costs. This could be achieved through issuing permits to fuel suppliers. At the international level, an important issue is the relationship between allowance trading and credit trading through individual joint implementation projects.

The final chapter by Jim Skea was completed after the Kyoto conference in December 1997 and describes the contents of the Protocol and the opportunities this creates for a global system of greenhouse gas trading. The Protocol introduces three separate forms of trading: a) allowance trading between Annex I countries; b) project based joint implementation (credits) within Annex I countries; and c) project based joint implementation in countries without targets (the Clean Development Mechanism). In addition it covers six greenhouse gases, rather than just carbon dioxide; it allows for the generation of credits through carbon 'sinks', such as forests; and it provides explicit provision for an EU bubble. In all, the Protocol represents an enormous leap forward in the scale and scope of trading schemes. At present, however, there is considerable uncertainty over the future evolution of trading as the rules governing each mechanism will take several years to develop. The chapter explores the implications of these various provisions and suggests how cost effective trades may begin to evolve. It pays particular attention to the development of rules for trading, the potential 'actors' in a trading regime and the problem of 'hot air' trading between the US and Russia.

9. SUMMARY

The overall message of this book is mixed. On the one hand, there is clear evidence that the second generation of US trading schemes have been highly successful. The experience gained with these represents a substantial body of knowledge that can inform the design of subsequent schemes. The Kyoto

Protocol provides a unique opportunity to capture the benefits of trading at a global level and to substantially reduce the cost of tackling climate change. This is important as the biggest obstacle to agreeing more ambitious targets for greenhouse gas reduction is the argument that reducing emissions is expensive. This is vigorously asserted by opponents to the FCCC, such as the Global Climate Coalition. Carbon trading not only creates an opportunity to reduce abatement costs, it also provides a real measure of those costs in the permit price. If costs are discovered to be low, as many suspect, this should make it easier to agree more stringent targets in the future.

On the other hand, the difficulties faced in introducing trading schemes in Europe suggest a note of caution. To date, the literature on emissions trading has been dominated by the US and there has been a tendency to assume that the instrument can work equally well in other contexts. The studies in Parts 2 and 3 of this book demonstrate that this is not the case. While trading may have much to offer, there are major obstacles to be overcome. Attention must be paid to the compatibility of the instrument with existing national traditions and to processes of institutional learning. It is possible that the range of environmental problems for which trading is appropriate is relatively small and its effectiveness compared to alternatives needs to be demonstrated in each case.

It is clear, however, that climate change is one area where trading is manifestly appropriate. The policy challenge over the next decade is to devise mechanisms whereby the opportunities offered by Kyoto can be fully exploited.

REFERENCES

Burtraw, D. (1996), 'The SO_2 emissions trading program: cost savings without allowance trades', *Contemporary Economic Policy*, **XIV**, 79–94, April.

Coase, R. (1960), 'The Problem of Social Cost', *The Journal of Law and Economics*, **3**, 1–44, October.

Dales, J. H. (1968), *Pollution, Property and Prices*, University of Toronto Press, Toronto.

Fromm, O. and Hansjürgens, B. (1997), 'Emissions trading in theory and practice: an analysis of RECLAIM in Southern California', *Environment & Planning C: Government & Policy*, **14**, 367–384.

Montgomery, W.D. (1972), 'Markets in Licenses and Efficient Pollution Control Programs', *Journal of Economic Theory* **5**(4), 395–418, December.

Sorrell, S. (1994), *Pollution on the market: the US experience with emissions trading for the control of air pollution*, Science Policy Research Unit, University of Sussex, Brighton.

Tietenberg, T.H. (1985), *Emissions Trading: An Exercise In Reforming Pollution Policy*, Resources for the Future Inc, Washington DC.

Tietenberg, T.H. (1991), 'Economic instruments for environmental regulation', *Oxford Review of Economic Policy*, **6**(1), 17–33.

PART I

The US Experience

2. Summary evaluation of the US SO_2 emissions trading program as implemented in 1995

A. Denny Ellerman, Richard Schmalensee, Paul L. Joskow, Juan Pablo Montero and Elizabeth M. Bailey[1]

1. INTRODUCTION

Title IV of the 1990 Clean Air Act Amendments (CAAA) introduced the first large-scale program using tradable emission permits to achieve an environmental goal. The approach adopted by Title IV, often called 'cap and trade', establishes an aggregate emissions limit, distributes the limited number of permits to sources more or less in proportion to historical heat input, and lets the individual sources trade the permits with any party or bank them for later use. The only requirement for a source is to have, and to give up, a valid permit, called an allowance, at the end of the year, for each ton of SO_2 emitted during the year.

Title IV imposes a 50 per cent nation-wide reduction of acid-rain precursor emissions by electric utility sources, primarily sulphur dioxide (SO_2), from 1980 levels. The emission reduction is implemented in two phases: Phase I comprising the years 1995-99 and Phase II from the year 2000 on indefinitely. In Phase I, each of 263 large generating units with high SO_2 emission rates[2] are annually issued permits, called allowances, approximately equal to the product of average 1985-87 (baseline) heat input times a target emission rate of 2.5 pounds of SO_2 per million Btu (hereafter #/mmBtu). In Phase II, all generating units with capacity larger than 25 MWe are issued allowances that will limit aggregate SO_2 emissions to approximately 8.9 million tons, or the product of baseline heat input times the lesser of the target emission rate of 1.2 #/mmBtu or the unit's actual 1985 emission rate.[3] Although the legislation offers incentives for the early installation of flue gas desulphurization ('scrubbers'), no specific technology or emission rates are mandated at any individual unit.

Title IV's cap and trade system marks a fundamental departure from the regulatory framework that has governed SO_2 emissions from electric utility sources in the United States. The pre-existing regulatory structure was created by legislation in 1970 and 1978 to eliminate local health and other secondary effects of 'criteria'[4] pollutants, including SO_2. It imposes source-specific emission rate limitations on existing (as of the early 1970s) units and effectively mandates flue gas desulphurization for all new sources, and it can only be described as 'command-and-control.' The reduction imposed by Title IV, which aims at the elimination of regional effects that are not adequately addressed by the 1970 and 1978 legislation, must be implemented within the source-specific constraints imposed by this pre-existing regulatory structure. However, by the 1980s, virtually all areas of the country were in compliance with the National Ambient Air Quality Standards (NAAQS) for SO_2, and actual emission rates at many sources were already below the source-specific limits imposed by the State Implementation Plans (SIPs) that implement the NAAQS. Although effectively superseded by Title IV, the prior structure remains as a guarantee that local health and secondary standards will not be violated as a result of emissions trading.

2. THE 1995 REDUCTION OF EMISSIONS

The first year in which Title IV became effective, 1995, was marked by significant over-compliance. A total of 8.70 million allowances were issued to 58 electric utilities for 445 generating units with a total capacity of 130 GWe. These units had emitted 10.68 million tons of SO_2 emissions in 1985, but their emissions in 1995 were only 5.30 million tons: about 3.9 million tons less than what emissions would have been without Title IV and 3.4 million tons below the 1995 cap.

More units participated in Phase I than was required by the legislation due to the operation of various substitution provisions. These allowed Phase II units to voluntarily opt-in to Phase I and to substitute for generation from mandated units. The motivation for substitution is either that actual emissions from the unit are below historic emissions and hence below the allowance allocation, or that marginal control costs at the unit are below current allowance prices.[5] In each case, opt-ins can be economically beneficial. A total of 182 units opted-in to the program, leading to a 42 per cent increase in Phase I generating capacity and an 18 per cent increase in allowance allocations. The emissions cap for 1995 is then 8.7 million tons of SO_2.[6] The details are summarized in Table 2.1.

Table 2.1 Statistics of Phase I units

Variables	Table A units[1]	Substitution units	Total Phase I
No. of units	263	182	445
Total capacity (MWe)	88007	41643	129650
Coal fired units	257	154	411
Pre 1990 scrubbers	1	25	26
Title IV scrubbers	26	0	26
Retired units	7	6	13
Baseline heat input (10^{12}Btu)	4365	1740	6105
Heat input 1993 (10^{12}Btu)	4396	1719	6115
Heat input 1995 (10^{12}Btu)	4708	1932	6640
SO₂ emissions 1985	9.30	1.38	10.68
SO₂ emissions 1993	7.58	0.97	8.55
SO₂ emissions 1995	4.45	0.85	5.30
Counterfactual emissions 1995[2]	8.13	1.06	9.19
Av. SO₂ rate 1985 (#/mmBtu)	4.24	1.58	3.48
Av. SO₂ rate 1993 (#/mmBtu)	3.30	1.67	2.63
Av. SO₂ rate 1995 (#/mmBtu)	2.10	1.21	1.74
1995 allowances (10^6)	7.22	1.33	8.55

Notes:
1. Units that were mandated to participate in Phase I.
2. Estimates of the counterfactual are based on summing the products of 1995 heat input and 1993 emission rate for every Phase I affected unit. The 1993 emission rate reflects changes in SO₂ emissions not related to Title IV, while the 1995 heat input reflects actual demand for SO₂ emitting fuels in 1995.

Source: Ellerman et al., 1997

Figure 2.1 depicts the basic relation between aggregate emissions and the Phase I and Phase II caps for the 445 generating units that were subject to Phase I in 1995. The sharp reduction in emissions in 1995 is the more remarkable in that the 1995 cap required only a slight reduction because, contrary to expectations, emissions had continued to decline in the years following 1990. The principal cause was the deregulation of railroads, which had the effect of making distant, low sulphur coal from the western states of Wyoming, Montana and Colorado more competitive with local, predominantly high sulphur coals in the Midwest where many Phase I generating units are located.[7]

The 1995 reduction of SO₂ emissions was achieved about equally by scrubbers, and by switching to lower sulphur coal, as shown by Table 2.2. Only 26 units with a total generating capacity of 13 GWe chose to reduce emissions by retrofitting a new scrubber; however, these few large units contributed nearly half of the total emission reduction in 1995.

Figure 2.1 SO₂ emission caps and forecasts for Phase I units

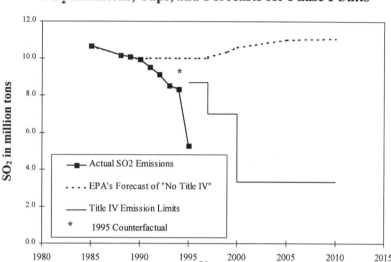

SO₂ Emissions, Caps, and Forecasts for Phase I Units

Switching to lower sulphur coals occurred at a much larger number of units, and the coals to which these units switched originated mostly from two low sulphur coal-producing regions: Central Appalachia and the Powder River Basin (PRB) in the West. A notable feature of the reduction due to switching is the amount occurring in the predominantly high sulphur coal-producing regions of the Midwest and North Appalachia. In these cases, the switching of coals did not involve a distant low sulphur coal, but a local mid or even high sulphur coal that was nevertheless of lower sulphur content than the coal previously in use at the same unit.[8] It is also notable that natural gas accounted for very little of the aggregate reduction and that, where used, it substituted for residual and distillate fuels, not coal.

Most of the 1995 reduction in SO₂ emissions occurred at the 263 units which were mandated to be part of Phase I. The 182 substitution units accounted for only 213,000 tons of the 3.89 million ton reduction in 1995 SO₂ emissions – 5.5 per cent of the total.[9]

Table 2.2 1995 SO₂ reduction at Phase I units

Method/Region	Tons SO$_2$ removed (x10^3)	% of total
Scrubbing Total	1,754	45.1
New Title IV Scrubbers	1,734	44.6
Other Scrubbers	21	0.5
Switching Total	2,133	54.9
North Appalachia	205	5.3
Central Appalachia	756	19.5
South Appalachia	60	1.5
Midwestern	406	10.4
Powder River Basin	518	13.3
Other Western Coal	146	3.8
Imported Coal	22	0.6
Natural Gas	20	0.5
TOTAL	**3,888**	**100.0**

Source: Derived from EPA Emissions Tracking System, USEPA (1996), Pechan (1993 and 1995), FERC Form 423, and Fieldston (1994)

3. THE DEVELOPMENT OF AN ALLOWANCE MARKET

Emissions trading has been long advocated as a cost effective way to achieve environmental goals; however, with a few exceptions, when it had been tried prior to the 1990 CAAA, the results had not been particularly encouraging.[10] Because of the earlier, more limited experiments, there was considerable doubt that this feature of Title IV would be any more successful. Concern focused not only on the effect of mis-informed early publicity, which labelled the first publicly announced trades 'licenses to pollute',[11] but also whether cost-of-service public utility regulation would provide electric utilities with the incentive to take advantage of the cost- saving flexibility provided by Title IV's emissions trading provisions.[12] Also, after March 1993, when the first EPA auction cleared at a price about half the then consensus estimate of allowance value, fears were voiced that particular features of the auction were biasing prices downward and discouraging trading.[13]

Despite these doubts and fears, a robust market for allowances with visible prices and low transaction costs has developed as electric utilities have made increasing use of the flexibility afforded by Title IV to reduce compliance costs. As shown in Table 2.3, very few allowances were traded outside of a mandated EPA auction in the first years after allowances were issued;

Table 2.3 Allowances sold in EPA auctions and in the private market

	Number of allowances sold in EPA auction	Number of allowances sold in the private market	Total allowances sold
Through March 1993	150,010	130,000	280,010
April 1993- March 1994	176,200	226,384	402,584
April 1994- March 1995	176,400	1,466,996	1,643,396
April 1995- March 1996	275,000	4,917,560	5,292,560
April 1996- March 1997	300,000	5,105,924	5,405,924
Total:	**1,077,610**	**11,846,864**	**12,924,474**

Notes: The number of allowances sold in the private market includes inter-utility trades, trades between utilities and third parties, and trades between two non-utility parties. This number excludes intra-utility trades (including intra-holding company trades), reallocations, and options to trade which have not been exercised.

Source: MIT/CEEPR based on EPA's Allowance Tracking System

however, beginning in mid-1994, the volume of allowances traded privately increased notably.

At the same time, what had been fairly disparate indicators of the market price of allowances converged to a relatively tight range. This convergence of price can also be observed in the reduced spread between the average bid price and the lowest winning bid in the annual EPA auction, as shown in Table 2.4.

As further evidence of the emergence of a well-functioning allowance market, various derivative instruments – options, swaps, forwards and futures – have emerged and are being used increasingly. As the private market for allowances has developed, the mandated EPA auction has receded in importance, but it did play an important early role, perhaps in stimulating the development of a functioning allowance market, but certainly in providing early, transparent – and as it turned out – reliable indicators of the market value of allowances.

The reconciliation of emissions and allowances for 1995 provides further evidence of the extent to which utilities engaged in emissions trading. Of the 8.69 million allowances issued for 1995, 5.30 million were used to 'cover' emissions in 1995. The remaining 3.39 million allowances were banked, that

Table 2.4 Percentage differences between average winning bids and lowest winning bids in EPA auctions

Year	Spot auction	6-year advance auction	7-year advance auction
1993	20.6	-	11.5
1994	6.0	5.7	6.4
1995	1.5	2.3	1.6
1996	3.2	1.9	1.9
1997	3.4	0.3	2.0

Source: MIT/CEEPR based on EPA auction data

is, reserved for later use, presumably in Phase II when higher costs will be incurred to meet the more stringent Phase II cap. Of the 5.3 million allowances used in 1995, 534,000 covered emissions in excess of the allowance allocation at 98 units that had to acquire these additional allowances by purchase or internal transfer. In all, about 45 per cent of the 1995 allowance issuance was used in a manner that implied the pursuit of cost savings through the trading of emissions, intertemporally or spatially.

4. THE COST OF COMPLIANCE AND ALLOWANCE PRICES

Table 2.5 presents our estimate of the appropriately annualized total cost of compliance with Title IV in 1995. At a total annualized cost of $726 million, average cost works out to be $187 or $210 per ton of SO_2 removed, depending on whether 425,000 tons of apparently costless emission reductions are included. The costless reductions are instances where Phase I units have switched to lower sulphur fuels, mostly Western coal, that are also lower in cost than the higher sulphur coal previously in use.[14]

This estimate of the cost of compliance with Title IV is at the lower bound of earlier predictions, even though the actual reduction was within the expected range. For instance, earlier studies of the cost of compliance with Title IV predicted an early Phase I emissions reduction of between 3.1 and 4.4 million tons at an average total cost ranging from $180 to $307 per ton of SO_2 removed.[15]

Table 2.5 1995 cost of compliance with Title IV

Method	Reduction	Total cost of compliance (million 95 $)			Av. Cost
	$(10^3$ tons)	Fixed	Variable	Total	($/ton SO$_2$)
Scrubbing	1754	375.0	89.3	464.4	265
Switching	1709	57.2	204.1	261.3	153
SUB TOTAL	3462	432.2	293.5	725.7	210
No cost PRB	425	0	0	0	0
Total	**3888**	**432.2**	**293.5**	**725.7**	**187**

Source: Derived from MIT/CEEPR Questionnaire, Federal Energy Regulatory Commission (FERC) Form 423, EPRI (1993 and 1995), EPA Emissions Tracking System, USEPA (1996), Pechan (1995), Fieldston (1994), and Pasha (1993 and 1995).

Scrubbers have proved to be a more expensive means of compliance on an average total cost basis, but that cost has been much lower than predicted. The retrofitted scrubbers achieved emission reductions in 1995 at an average cost of $265 per ton of SO$_2$ removed, in marked contrast to earlier studies that had estimated average total costs of between $450 and $500 a ton. Most of this reduction in compliance cost has been due to lower than predicted operating cost and significantly greater than expected utilization of the scrubbers (+30 per cent), which reflects, at least in part, the performance incentives created by Title IV for scrubbers to 'produce' allowances. As a result, the initial capital cost has been spread over more tons of SO$_2$ removed and the unit cost of abatement has been reduced commensurately.

While total costs have been on the low side but within the range of earlier estimates, the price of allowances has been dramatically lower than any earlier estimate. Early estimates of allowance prices were typically not very precise with respect to the year or whether stated in current, constant or future dollars, but it was not infrequent to find estimates of allowance value as high as $1000. Nevertheless, once the legislation was passed and utilities with Phase I units had performed more detailed engineering estimates of compliance cost, a consensus tended to form around values for early Phase I ranging between $250 and $300.[16] This consensus was challenged by the results of the first EPA auction, which cleared at a price of $131 for vintage 1995 allowances; however, the auction price was believed by many to be artificially low, due either to a reluctance of utilities to enter this new market or to defects in the auction itself. According to this view, the market price of allowances would increase as utilities began to comply with the Title IV emission mandate in 1995. In fact, as shown by Figure 2.2, the price of allowances did not increase in 1995. It declined steadily throughout the year until it hit a low of about $70 in March 1996, from which it increased to

Figure 2.2 Allowance prices 1992-97 (1995 or current vintage)

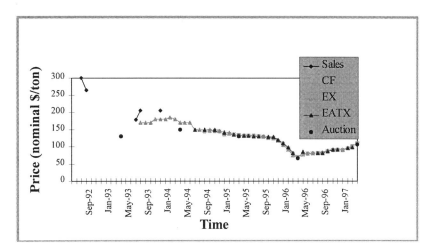

$115 in the spring of 1997 and, as we write (June 1997), the price has fallen to $95.

The primary reason for the significantly lower than expected price of allowances has been over-commitment to compliance, in the form of both over-investment in scrubbers and commitment to long-term low sulphur coal contracts. The over-commitment to scrubbers and contracts causes the observed market price to reflect short-run marginal cost, but not the long-run marginal cost, of the abatement currently supplied.[17]

Most decisions to invest in scrubbers were made in 1992-93, either before the first indications appeared that allowance prices might be lower than had been predicted, or in response to explicit incentives in Title IV and state regulation to encourage the building of scrubbers in Phase I.[18] At the time, the relatively high average total cost of scrubbing could be justified by some combination of expected high allowance prices and federal and state incentives; however, the continued operation of these units requires only that the allowance price be greater than the variable cost of scrubbing, which is about $65/ton, lower than any allowance price yet observed. As a result, a relatively fixed amount of abatement is supplied by scrubbing, and the variable cost of scrubbing forms a floor for allowance prices.

The expectation of higher Phase I allowance value also led many utilities to contract early for low sulphur coal in order to avoid a feared run-up of low sulphur coal prices when Title IV took effect in 1995. Although these contracts locked in the current price for low sulphur coal, they also reduce the buyer's ability to switch to higher sulphur coal bundled with allowances which will be (and has been) a cheaper means of compliance when allowance prices are lower than the equivalent premium between high and low sulphur coals. Like scrubbers, these contracts create a relatively inflexible supply of allowances, and they remove potential bidders from current markets, with consequent effect on allowance prices.

5. THE COST SAVINGS FROM EMISSIONS TRADING

The promise of emissions trading – and the underlying reason for advocating it to attain environmental goals – is the lower cost of compliance that can be achieved by providing participants with the flexibility and incentive to seek out low-cost emission reductions to sell to those who face more costly reductions. All earlier studies of the cost of compliance with Title IV predicted cost savings from emissions trading, although judgements of how much trading would occur – and therefore how large the cost savings would be – differed considerably. In general, the studies that expected more trading predicted lower average total costs of compliance. Our estimates of cost saving apply to a reality that included a significant volume of trade. The agreement of our estimates with these earlier predictions provides a first indication that cost savings from emissions trading have been realized.

Cost savings from emissions trading are also indicated by the observed behaviour of electric utilities and associated phenomena in compliance markets. Figure 2.3 depicts the extremely heterogeneous response of generating units to the new SO_2 emission requirements. All Phase I units are arrayed in the figure by the emission rate that would have prevailed had there been no emissions trading, as shown by the solid line. Units that were constrained by the allowance issuance would have reduced to this level, but no more; and units where emissions were already below the allowance issuance would have made no change. The columns indicate the actual 1995 emission rates at these same units. For about a quarter of the approximately 400 active units[19] the actual emission rate varied by less than +/- 10 per cent from the 'no trading' emission rate. For the remaining 300 units, the variation was greater than 10 per cent. Ninety-eight of these units acquired a total of 540,000 additional allowances to avoid the costs associated with reducing emissions to what would have been 'permitted' by the issuance of allowances to those units. The other 200 units reduced emissions by 2.4 million tons more than what would have occurred with no emissions trading. This extra reduction may be seen as providing the 540,000 allowances that were used in 1995 by units needing more allowances than they were issued,

Figure 2.3 Effect of emissions trading in 1995: actual emission rates versus lesser of counterfactual or allowance rate by unit

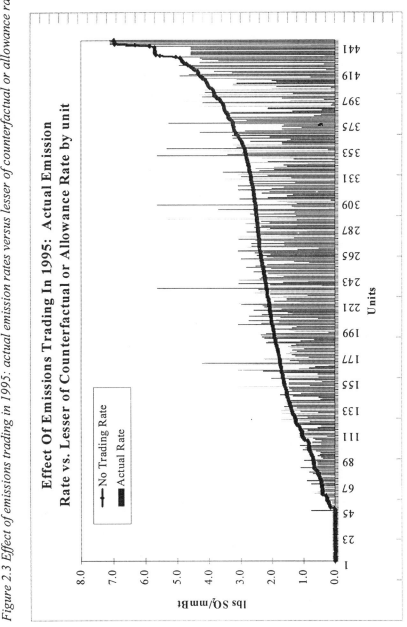

37

and the balance was banked, presumably to avoid more costly reductions in Phase II.[20]

Cost-saving behaviour is also indicated by the 50 per cent decline in the premium paid for low sulphur coals in the primary coal-producing region of Central Appalachia at the beginning of 1995. This premium fell because it was out of line with the value established for lower sulphur content in the allowance market. When compliance became actual in 1995 and allowance prices did not increase as expected, there was no alternative but to reduce the premium for low sulphur coal since bundling higher sulphur coal with allowances was a cheaper compliance option. This convergence of the real and paper price for SO_2 abatement would not have been observed if compliance managers for electric utilities had not been alert to the cost saving opportunities made available by emissions trading.

Estimation of the cost savings from emissions trading in 1995 is fraught with conceptual and empirical difficulties that cause us to demur from offering a figure in which we would place great confidence. We believe that cost savings have been achieved, as uniformly predicted by earlier studies, but that those savings are less than some of the more exuberant claims for market-based instruments.[21] Our very rough estimate lies between $225 and $375 million. This estimate implies that the cost of Title IV would have been a third to half again as costly had the flexibility offered by Title IV's emissions trading provisions not been available. It is also possible that further gains from emissions trading will be achieved as electric utilities become more accustomed to this new means of meeting environmental goals.

6. CONCLUSION

Title IV has held its share of surprises, but it has demonstrated that large-scale emissions trading programs can work, more or less as described in textbooks, and without adverse environmental consequences. Judging by the experience of 1995, utilities did take advantage of the cost-saving flexibility provided by emissions trading – perhaps to a surprising extent, although expectations were low to begin with. The experience with Title IV has also shown that efficient, competitive private markets for tradable permits can develop. As in any real program, there are features of design and implementation by both public and private parties that, in retrospect, would have been better done differently, but these defects are more the exception than the rule in what has been on the whole a refreshingly positive experience with a market-based alternative to the conventional command-and-control approaches to environmental regulation. That being said, it bears stressing that textbook perfection was not attained and that no breakthroughs in SO_2 abatement technology have been revealed. The experience with Title IV supports the argument that market-based approaches to environmental regulation will be less costly than those that ignore markets.

NOTES

[1]   This article is a summary of a more detailed report by the same authors (Ellerman et al., 1997). The underlying research has been funded by the National Acid Precipitation Assessment Program (NAPAP) and MIT's Center for Energy and Environmental Policy Research (CEEPR).

[2]   A unit is defined as a 'fossil fuel fired combustion device' in section 402 of the CAAA and corresponds to a single generator and associated boiler. Units with generating capacity greater than 100 MWe and 1985 emission rates greater than 2.5 lbs. of SO2 per million Btu of heat input were mandated to be a part of Phase I. This gives a total of 263 units at 110 power stations.

[3]   The legislative process created many exceptions to the basic principle of allocation for Phases I and II. See Joskow and Schmalensee (1998) for a more extensive discussion and analysis of the process by which the actual allocations were determined.

[4]   Criteria pollutants are common substances, such as SO2 and hydrocarbons, that create a variety of health effects at high concentrations. These are distinct from hazardous pollutants, such as mercury and radio nucleides, that have serious health effects at low concentrations.

[5]   The substitution provisions were the subject of a successful legal challenge by the Environmental Defense Fund and the Natural Resources Defense Council. This led to the EPA tightening the rules for allowance allocation to minimize the extent to which emission reductions that would have occurred anyway at Phase II units are substituted for real reductions at Phase I units. For a full analysis of the substitution provisions, see Montero (1997a) and (1997b).

[6]   The size of the cap in Phase I depends on the number of units that have opted-in to the program. In contrast, the cap in Phase II is fixed at approximately 8.9 million tons, with all units above 25 MWe participating.

[7]   See Ellerman and Montero (1996) for a discussion and analysis of the reasons for the pre-1995 decline in aggregate emissions. This analysis provides the basis for the estimate of what 1995 emissions would have been without Title IV (the counterfactual) that is shown on Figure 2.1.

[8]   There is no standard, uniform definition of a low, mid or high sulphur coal. In practice, a coal of 1.2 #/mmBtu or less is a low sulphur coal, while any coal above about 3.5 #/mmBtu would be considered a high sulphur coal.

[9]   Montero (1997a and 1997b) concludes that the substitution provisions did not compromise the emission reduction goal of Title IV and had only a minimal effect on allowance prices The wide participation suggests low transaction costs. See Atkeson (1997) for a discussion of the very different response to the industrial opt-in provisions.

[10]   The exceptions are the lead phase-down and CFC trading. See Hahn (1989), Hahn and Hester (1989) and NERA (1994) for a review of the limited results as of 1990.

[11]   Early reports of trades can be found in the *Wall Street Journal* (11 May 1992 and 1 July 1992), the *New York Times* (11 May 1992), *Energy Daily* (13 May 1992 and 1 July 1992) and various issues of *Compliance Strategy Review*.

12   See Bohi and Burtraw (1991, 1992) on the effect of public utility regulation. In the only
      empirical examination of this issue, Bailey (1996) finds widely varying regulatory
      provisions, but no significant negative effect on utilities' use of allowances.

13   Title IV required EPA to withhold 2.8 per cent of the allowances allocated to individual
      units and to sell those allowances at an annual auction with no floor price and with the
      proceeds of the auction returned pro-rata to the utilities that otherwise would have
      received the allowances. The EPA auction is a discriminating price auction in which each
      successful bidder pays his bid price instead of the lowest clearing bid as is the more usual
      case. This feature of the auction has been criticized as exerting a downward bias to
      allowance prices. See Cason (1993, 1995) and Cason and Plott (1996) for an exposition of
      this argument. Joskow, Schmalensee and Bailey (1997) point out that the emergence of an
      effective private market limits the practical effect of this feature of the auction. Hausker
      (1992) and GAO (1994) raise broader concerns about the design of the auction and about
      what was perceived to be the lack of emissions trading at the time of these writings.

14   The explanation for this phenomenon lies both in the changing economics of coal in the
      Midwest and in the rigidities introduced by long-term coal supply contracts. In general,
      see Appendix One of Ellerman et al. (1997) for an explanation of the data sources and
      methodology for the cost estimate presented here.

15   See EPRI (1993, 1995), ICF (1989, 1990) and GAO (1994).

16   The most careful and respected estimate was made by EPRI (1993) at \$250 in 1992
      dollars.

17   Intertemporal arbitrage, as evidenced in the development of futures and other forms of
      forward trading, implies that the current price reflects the (discounted) long-run marginal
      cost of abatement in Phase II, not necessarily that supplied in Phase I. This future cost is
      itself lower than earlier thought both because of the intrusion of Western low sulphur
      coals independently of Title IV and the lower than expected cost of scrubbing.

18   Federal incentives included extensions to compliance deadlines and bonus allowances.
      Midwestern states attempted to encourage scrubber construction by offering pre-approval
      of utility compliance plans which included protection of local high sulphur coal.

19   Forty-two Phase I affected units had no heat input in 1995.

20   The balance of the 3.4 million ton bank in 1995 is accounted for by about 1.0 million
      allowances issued to Table A units in excess of those units' 1995 counterfactual
      emissions and about 0.5 million allowances from the issuance of allowances to
      substitution and compensation units. It is likely that some of the 3.4 million allowances
      'banked' are the result of over-commitment to scrubbers, low sulphur fuel contracts and
      the issuance of 'excess' allowances rather than the result of a calculated decision not to
      sell. The latter is viable as the 1995 allowance price is less than the discounted, expected
      cost of a ton reduced in Phase II.

21   For instance, some of the studies cited in Tietenberg (1992), page 403.

REFERENCES

Atkeson, Erica (1997), *Joint Implementation: Lessons from Title IV's Voluntary
    Compliance Programs*, working paper 97-003, MIT Center for Energy and
    Environmental Policy Research, May.
Bailey, E.M. (1996), *Allowance trading activity and state regulatory rulings:
    Evidence from the US Acid Rain Program*, working paper 96-002, MIT Center for
    Energy and Environmental Policy Research, March.

Bohi, D.R. and D. Burtraw (1991), 'Avoiding Regulatory Gridlock in the Acid Rain Program', *Journal of Policy Analysis and Management* **10**, 676–84.

Bohi, D.R. and D. Burtraw (1992), 'Utility Investment Behavior and the Emissions Trading Market', *Resource and Energy Economics,* **14**, 129–153.

Cason, T.N. (1993), 'Seller incentive properties of EPA's emissions trading auction', *Journal of Environmental Economics and Management* **25**, 177–195.

Cason, T.N. (1995), 'An experimental investigation of the seller incentives in EPA's emissions trading auction', *American Economic Review,* **85**, 905–922.

Cason, T.N. and C.R. Plott (1996), 'EPA's new emissions trading mechanism: a laboratory evaluation', *Journal of Environmental Economics and Management,* **30**, 133-160.

Electric Power Research Institute, EPRI, (1993), *Integrated Analysis of Fuel, Technology and Emission Allowance Markets: Electric Utility Responses to the Clean Air Act Amendments of 1990*, EPRI TR-102510, Palo Alto, CA.

Electric Power Research Institute, EPRI, (1995), *The Emission Allowance Market and Electric Utility SO₂ Compliance in a Competitive and Uncertain Future*, EPRI TR-105490s, Palo Alto, CA.

Ellerman, A.D. and J.P. Montero (1996), *Why are allowance prices so low? An analysis of the SO₂ emissions trading program*, working paper 96-001, MIT Center for Energy and Environmental Policy Research, February.

Ellerman, A.D., R. Schmalensee, P.L. Joskow, J.P. Montero and E.M. Bailey (1997), *Emissions Trading Under the US Acid Rain Program: Evaluation of Compliance Costs and Allowance Market Performance*, MIT Center for Energy and Environmental Policy Research, October.

Fieldston (1994), *Fieldston's Guide to Phase I and Phase II Units*, Fourth Edition, Fieldston Publications, Inc., Washington, DC.

Hahn, R.W. (1989), 'Economic prescriptions for environmental problems: How the patient followed the doctor's orders', *Journal of Economic Perspectives,* **3**, 95–114.

Hahn, R.W. and G.L. Hester (1989), 'Marketable permits: Lessons for theory and practice', *Ecology Law Quarterly,* **16**, 361–406.

Hausker, K. (1992). 'The politics and economics of auction design in the market for sulphur dioxide', *Journal of Policy Analysis and Management,* **11**, 553–572.

ICF Resources Incorporated, ICF, (1989), *Economic Analysis of Title IV (Acid Rain Provisions) of the Administration's Proposed Clean Air Act Amendments (H.R. 3030/S. 1490)*, Washington, DC, September.

ICF Resources Incorporated, ICF, (1990), *Comparison of the Economics Impacts of the Acid Rain Provisions of the Senate Bill (S.1630) and the House Bill (S.1630)*, Draft Report prepared for the US Environmental Protection Agency, Washington, DC, July.

Joskow, P. and R. Schmalensee (1998), 'The Political Economy of Market-Based Environmental Policy: The U.S. Acid Rain Policy', *Journal of Law and Economics,* **41**, 89–135.

Joskow, P., R. Schmalensee and E.M. Bailey (1997*), The Market for Sulphur Dioxide Emissions*, unpublished manuscript, Department of Economics, MIT, February.

Montero, J.P. (1997a), *Volunteering for market-based environmental regulation: The Substitution Provision of the SO₂ Emissions Trading Program*, working paper 97-001, MIT Center for Energy and Environmental Policy Research, January.

Montero, J.P. (1997b), 'Optimal Design of a Phase-in Emissions Trading Program with Voluntary Compliance Options', Chapter 2 Ph.D. thesis, *Topics on Market-Based Environmental Policy*, MIT, unpublished.

National Economic Research Associates (1994), 'Key issues in the design of NOx emissions trading programs to reduce ground level ozone', EPRI TR-104245, Electric Power Research Institute, July.

Pasha (1993), *1993 Guide to Coal Contracts*, Pasha Publications, Inc., Arlington, VA.

Pasha (1995), *1995 Guide to Coal Contracts*, Pasha Publications, Inc., Arlington, VA.

Pechan (1993), *The National Allowance Data Base Version 2.11: Technical Support Document*, E.H. Pechan Associates Inc., prepared for the US Environmental Protection Agency's Office of Atmospheric Programs-Acid Rain Division, Washington, DC.

Pechan (1995), *The Acid Rain Data Base Version 1 (ARDBV1)*, E.H. Pechan Associates Inc., Contract no. 68-D3-0005, prepared for the US Environmental Protection Agency's Office of Atmospheric Programs-Acid Rain Division, Washington, DC.

Tietenberg, T. (1992), *Environmental and Natural Resource Economics*, Third Edition, Harper Collins Publishers, New York, NY.

U.S. Environmental Protection Agency, EPA, (1996), *1995 Compliance Results: Acid Rain Program*, project # EPA/430-R-96-012, Washington, DC, July.

U.S. Government Accounting Office, GAO, (1994), *Allowance Trading Offers and Opportunity to Reduce Emissions at Less Cost*, GAO/RCED-95-30, Washington, DC, December.

3. Cost savings, market performance and economic benefits of the US Acid Rain Program

Dallas Burtraw

1. INTRODUCTION

Title IV of the 1990 US Clean Air Act Amendments regulates emissions of sulphur dioxide (SO_2) from electric utility facilities and instituted two important innovations in US environmental policy. The more widely acknowledged of these is the SO_2 emissions trading program, which is designed to encourage the electricity industry to minimize the cost of reducing emissions. The industry is allocated a fixed number of total allowances and firms are required to hold one allowance for each ton of sulphur dioxide they emit.[1] Firms are allowed to transfer allowances among facilities or to other firms, or to bank them for use in future years. This approach enables firms operating at high marginal pollution abatement costs to purchase SO_2 emission allowances from firms operating at low marginal abatement costs, thereby lowering the cost of compliance.

The second and less widely acknowledged innovation is the annual cap on average aggregate emissions by electric utilities, set at about one-half of the amount emitted in 1980. The cap accommodates an allowance bank, so that in any one year aggregate industry emissions must be less than the number of allowances allocated for that year plus the surplus that has accrued from previous years. Unlike most previous regulations in the US, including technology standards or emission rate standards, the emissions cap represents a guarantee that emissions will not increase with economic growth.[2]

This paper begins with a summary of recent projections of the *long-run* costs of compliance when the program is fully implemented in the next decade, and estimates of *potential cost savings* stemming from the trading program in the long run. Second, I evaluate how well the allowance trading has worked to date, and what one can expect to happen in the future.

Most attention has been focused on the reduction in 'out-of-pocket' compliance costs that may result from allowance trading. However, compliance costs are not the same thing as economic costs. A third focus of this paper is to explain how hidden economic costs inflate the total cost of the program in an important way, and how recognition of these costs provides an important lesson for the design of future programs. Fourth, I return to the primary purpose of the program, which after all is to reduce acidification of the environment and associated effects on human well-being. An economic assessment of benefits, though extremely uncertain, indicates that benefits are an order of magnitude greater than costs under the program. An important component of this favourable assessment rests with the design of the tradable permit program which has helped to reduce costs substantially.

2. COSTS OF THE SO$_2$ PROGRAM AND COST SAVINGS FROM ALLOWANCE TRADING

To make sense of the wide variety of claims about the costs of the SO$_2$ program one has to put these claims in historic perspective. In the 1980s there were over seventy proposed pieces of legislation that suggested a variety of regulatory approaches aimed at the problem of acidification.

One prominent proposal was the 'Sikorski/Waxman' bill in 1983 that sought to rollback emissions, by about the same amount as eventually required under Title IV, by requiring the installation of scrubbers (flue gas desulphurization equipment) at the fifty dirtiest plants.[3] The estimated levelized cost of this proposal ranged from about $7.9 billion per year according to government studies (OTA, 1983) to $11.5 billion per year according to an industry study (TBS, 1983; 1995 dollars).

Another bill (H.R. 4567) in 1986 was aimed at similar environmental gains but promoted cost reductions by applying a target average emission rate for each utility company. Taking account of changes in fuel and other input prices between 1983 and 1986, an industry study (TBS, 1986) found costs would be $7.5 billion per year compared with estimates of $3.5 to $6.2 billion by ICF in a study for the EPA, and $3.4 to $4.3 billion by the OTA (1995 dollars).[4] Though ultimate regulation did not involve either of these approaches the estimates provide an indication of what the program might have cost under alternative regulatory approaches, and have often been used as a basis for comparison.

One of the earliest studies of the cost under an allowance trading system was Elman et al. (1990) who estimated the marginal cost of compliance and inferred this would be the value of emission allowances. Under a perfect trading market, this study predicted marginal costs (presumed to equal allowance prices under perfect trading) of $742-1032 (1995 dollars) and costs of $1935 for imperfect trading, ranging up to $2580 or $5160 at a number of utilities. However, for evaluation of the program compared to prior expectations, the most useful study is ICF (1990), which was done for the EPA and available prior to enactment of the legislation. This study captured more accurately the ultimate design of the regulation, and projected marginal costs of $579-760 (1995 dollars) for full compliance under the program. This and a number of other studies are summarized in Table 3.1.[5]

An important feature of the studies summarized in Table 3.1 is that, as a group, they have successively estimated a sequence of declining projections of annual and marginal costs of compliance. There are several contributing reasons for this. One is that the trading program ignited a search for ways to reduce emissions at less cost, as theory suggests is likely to occur with this type of regulation, and the fruitful results of this enterprise are measured by later studies (Burtraw, 1996).

It is also the case that advantageous trends in fuel markets contributed to a decline in emission rates, making it easier for utilities to attain the goals of the program thereby reducing program costs (Ellerman and Montero, 1998; Burtraw, 1996). Indeed, the right-hand column in Table 3.1 reporting average cost per ton estimated by the various studies reflects this decline. The differences in average cost estimates are due to differences in annual cost reported in the first column, but also they are due to differences in the estimate of tons reduced under the program compared to various specified baseline projections of emissions that would occur in the absence of the program. To the extent these emission reductions would have occurred even in the absence of the SO_2 program then the program should not be given credit; however, it appears the trading program encouraged utilities to capitalize on these advantageous trends while other regulatory approaches might not have.

A third reason for declining projections of cost is that the market structure for industries offering compliance services to utilities was dramatically changed under the trading program. What were previously independent factor markets supplying services to utilities (coal mining, rail transport, and scrubber manufacturing) were thrown into a competition with each other by the program's flexible implementation. This unleashed competitive pressure to find ways to reduce costs in all these markets.

All of the explanations listed appear to contribute to some degree to the decline in estimates of compliance costs. The Carlson et al. (1998) model can help to sort out these factors because it provides a framework in which we can vary factors one at a time and explore their significance. While most of the studies in Table 3.1 rely on engineering-based models of compliance options and their costs, Carlson et al. use a simulation model based on marginal abatement cost functions derived from an econometrically

Table 3.1 Estimates of long-run (2010) annual and marginal cost

Study	Annual cost (1995 $ billion)	Marginal cost per ton SO$_2$ (1995 $)	Average cost per ton SO$_2$ (1995 $)
Carlson et al. (1998)	1.1	291	174
Burtraw et al. (1998)	0.9		239
White (1997) [EPRI]		436	
ICF (1995) [EPA]	2.3	532	252
White et al. (1995) [EPRI]	1.4–2.9	543	286–334
GAO (1994)	2.2–3.3		230–374
Van Horn Consulting et al. (1993) [EPRI]	2.4–3.3	520	314–405
ICF (1990) [EPA]	2.3–5.9	579–760	348–499

estimated long-run total cost function for electricity generation for a sample of over 800 generating units over the period 1985-1994.[6] From an economist's perspective, this study is superior because it takes into account behavioural responses to changes in relative input prices. These behavioural responses generally take the form of substitution among inputs to reduce jointly the costs of generating electricity and of complying with emission reduction requirements. The econometric approach also affords a method for measuring the role of technological change in reducing the costs of SO$_2$ abatement over time, and to develop forecasts of future compliance costs and gains from trade that implicitly incorporate future behavioural changes including future responses to changes in technology.

Table 3.2 presents several estimates using this model, varying assumptions about fuel prices and technological change. The columns in the table represent the annual cost of a command and control approach (uniform emission rate standard), the annual cost of efficient trading, its associated marginal abatement cost and finally the estimated gains from trade that are available from efficient trading.

The first row in Table 3.2 reports numbers for a benchmark scenario that uses assumptions comparable to those in previous studies, including assumptions that relative fuel prices remain stable at 1995 levels, technology including the utilization rate of scrubbers is characterized at 1995 levels and the historic method for measuring emissions based on sampling of coals and engineering formulas remains in effect. The retirement rates for coal facilities, and replacement with scrubbed coal technology, are taken from projections by the Energy Information Administration (EIA, 1996). The

Table 3.2 The contribution of price and technological change to compliance costs

Scenario	Command and control (1995 $m)	Efficient trading (1995 $m)	MAC (1995 $)	Potential gains from trade (1995 $m)
Benchmark estimate: (1995 prices/1995 technology)	2,230	1,510	436	720
Benchmark with 1989 prices/1989 technology	2,670	1,900	560	770
Preferred estimate	**1,820**	**1,040**	**291**	**780**

estimates assume that no additional retrofit scrubbers are constructed after Phase I.

This benchmark predicts long-run marginal abatement costs will be $436 (1995 dollars). The second row presents an estimate under most benchmark assumptions but with prices held to their 1989 level (implying a higher price for low sulphur coal relative to high sulphur coal than obtained in 1995) and the time trend for technological change (factor productivity) also held at 1989 levels.[7] From this vantage point, marginal abatement costs rise to $560, or 28 per cent greater. One should note that this is not far from that offered by ICF (1990) calculated with comparable information reported in Table 3.1.

The last row in Table 3.2 presents the Carlson et al. (1998) preferred estimate, reproduced for convenience from Table 3.1. Compared to the benchmark, this scenario adopts 1995 prices and 2010 technology. It assumes utilization rates and performance of in-place scrubbers continues to improve. It assumes a slower retirement rate of coal-fired facilities, and half of retired facilities are replaced by gas. Also it assumes that the use of continuous emission monitoring systems in place of the historic measure of emissions will raise emission estimates and necessitate a greater level of control.[8] Explicitly missing from consideration in all of these studies is the influence of other potential regulatory actions, such as further control on particulates or NO_x emissions or actions to meet global warming goals.

Based on this information and model, the savings from allowance trading that are expected from an efficient allowance market are about $780 million annually, or about 42 per cent of the costs under command and control.

Previous studies (Van Horn Consulting et al., 1993; GAO, 1994) suggested an efficient allowance market would result in cost savings of about twice this much in percentage terms. In all these studies, the command and control approach that is modelled is 'enlightened' in that it is a performance standard (emission rate or emission tonnage standard) applied to each facility, calibrated to achieve the same level of total emissions.[9] This approach already encompasses many of the beneficial incentives of the SO_2 trading program compared to a technology forcing approach by providing individual facilities with flexibility in achieving the standard. Other command and control approaches that were seriously considered in the US, such as forced scrubbing at larger facilities, could have cost substantially more. Forced scrubbing is also the approach embodied in the New Source Performance Standards for SO_2 from power plants.[10]

In summary, estimates of both a command and control approach and allowance trading have fallen over time due to a number of factors. Allowance trading is expected to result in cost savings relative to a command and control approach, but the absolute magnitude of these savings is expected to be somewhat less than previously envisioned due to changes in fuel markets. However, a more rigid approach that forced firms to adopt specified technologies would have precluded them from taking advantage of some of these trends in the industry. Compared to this, allowance trading could be argued to constitute a greater savings than we estimate.

Though they are substantial by any accounting, cost savings have been exaggerated in many accounts of the program. Advocates of ambitious climate change policies have suggested that SO_2 allowance prices are 'so low' and that economists and engineers got it 'so wrong' that policy makers should virtually ignore cost projections when developing new regulations such as a carbon permit trading program (or trading of nitrogen oxide (NO_x) permits). These exaggerated comparisons have often used inconsistent estimates of cost, leading to erroneous conclusions.[11] The most obvious of these errors is to compare allowance prices today directly with long-run marginal cost estimates. This is erroneous because long-run marginal cost estimates describe costs that will not be incurred until late in the next decade, when the allowance bank is drawn down and net contributions to the bank are zero. Allowance prices today should be proximate to short-run marginal cost and these are related to long-run marginal costs by the rate of interest. Discounting long-run marginal costs for the year 2010 to the present reduces them by about two-thirds!

A proper comparison of program costs indicates they are expected to be less by almost one-half that indicated in information available to legislators in 1990.

Further, program costs are perhaps half again the cost of an inflexible technology standard. However, they are not reduced by fifteen fold, as some have claimed.[12] Furthermore, as described previously, a significant portion of the actual decline is due to factors exogenous to the program. Nonetheless, after accounting for these factors the remaining decline in costs is impressive, and in general it points toward success for the program.

3. PERFORMANCE OF THE PROGRAM TO DATE

The previous section reported on estimates of the cost of compliance when the program is fully implemented. The second phase of the program begins in the year 2000, when an expanded set of facilities will be brought into the program and the average emission rate for all facilities will reduce to about 1.2 lb per million Btu. In the first phase of the program, which began in 1995, firms have been over-complying in order to save allowances in the bank and to ease the transition into Phase II. In the second phase, utilities will begin to draw down their allowance banks until net contributions to the bank are zero and annual emissions equal annual allocations for an average year. This is projected to occur by the year 2010.

A specific economic relationship is expected to govern use of banked allowances, and the magnitude of the marginal costs in a given year. As previously mentioned, allowance prices in a given year should reflect marginal abatement costs in that year. To appreciate why this is so, imagine instead that allowance prices were less than a firm's marginal costs. Then the firm could decrease its compliance activities and purchase allowances in the market as an alternative means of compliance, earning positive net revenues.

A similar reasoning governs the relationship between marginal costs at different points in time. Marginal costs in any given year should equal the present discounted value of marginal abatement costs in the future. Imagine instead that allowance prices were less than the present discounted value of marginal costs in the future. Then again the firm could purchase allowances in the current year and 'bank them' for use in place of compliance activities in the future, generating net revenues. Of course, the converse would hold as well, if allowance prices were greater than these respective measures of marginal costs. Hence, the banking provision in the allowance market serves an intertemporal arbitrage function that allows firms to identify the least cost means of compliance over time just as allowance trading allows firms to identify the least cost means of compliance over geography.

Using this relationship from economic theory provides one way to check on the performance of the market and the likely accuracy of estimated costs. If cost estimates for the long-run are correct, and using a discount rate of 8 per cent reflecting the opportunity cost of capital for firms in the industry, current allowance prices should be about one-third of projected long-run costs. The present discounted value of long-run marginal costs of $291 in

2010 should be about $95 in 1997. Allowance prices hovered between $100 and $110 for most of 1997, suggesting that the model is roughly consistent with current activities, and that intertemporal arbitrage is working to an important degree. The explicit omission of other potential regulatory actions (NO_x, CO_2) in the models may explain much of the remaining difference.

Another way to measure the performance of the market to date is to look at the allocation of compliance activities among firms in the current period. Economic theory suggests that the marginal cost of compliance activities should be the same at all facilities (except as may be constrained by local ambient air quality restrictions).

To investigate this Carlson et al. (1998) evaluated their estimated marginal abatement cost functions at the level of emissions in the industry in 1995. These results are reported in Table 3.3. The cost of efficient trading is projected to be $552 million, with a marginal cost for fuel switching activities of $101. This compares with a cost under a command and control emission rate standard of $802 million, representing a savings of 30 per cent.[13] Further, the projected marginal cost of $101 is remarkably close to allowance prices in this period (around $90 in 1995), reinforcing the notion that intertemporal arbitrage is working as it should.

However, the second row of the table reports the estimated actual cost of compliance when the estimated abatement cost functions are evaluated using observed emissions at individual facilities. The *actual* cost to the industry in 1995 is estimated to be $832 million, or 50 per cent more expensive than a least cost solution (reported in row 1) according to the model. The only other estimate for 1995 that we are aware of is Ellerman et al. (1997) who found costs in 1995 to be $726 million.

The notion of an industry marginal cost does not apply in this context, since costs presumably differed among firms. However, Carlson et al. calculate the marginal cost at each facility weighted by that facility's portion of total generation, and summed for the industry this results in an estimate of $180. Ellerman et al. do not report marginal cost but they find an average cost from fuel switching activities of $153. Both of these figures compare poorly with observed allowance prices in 1995. We consider the proximity of the Carlson et al. econometric estimates to the Ellerman et al. survey estimates of actual costs, and the distinction between these estimates and the estimated cost of efficient compliance, as evidence that in the first year of the program there were unrealized potential gains from trade suggesting that important imperfections characterized the allowance market in the first year of the program. Moreover, the difference between the observed price of allowances (approximately $90 in 1995) and both Ellerman et al. and Carlson et al. estimates of actual compliance cost provides further evidence that the new program of allowance trading was not yet a mature institution in 1995.

Table 3.3 Cost estimates for compliance in 1995

Study	Annual Cost (1995 $m)	Marginal cost per ton SO$_2$ (fuel switching) (1995 $)	Average cost per ton SO$_2$[a] (1995 $)
Carlson et al. (1997) Efficient trading	552	101	194
Carlson et al. (1997) Actual emissions	832	180 (weighted marginal cost)	291
Ellerman et al. (1997)	726	153 (average cost)	210

Notes:
a Includes scrubbing costs.

What appears to have occurred in 1995 is that different patterns of compliance behaviour co-existed in the industry. Many utilities appear to have taken advantage of the flexibility afforded by the allowance program to find ways to reduce costs of compliance, including taking advantage of allowance trading *per se*. However, many other utilities appear to have pursued a solitary strategy, rationalizing to some degree the cost of emission reductions within the firm, but not taking advantage of the allowance market to rationalize costs with other firms in the industry (Bohi and Burtraw, 1997).

This glance at the first year of performance in the market is disconcerting, but it may be a poor indicator of the rich long-run prospects for the program. One should expect that an industry that has heretofore been subject to cost recovery rules in a regulated setting would take some time in adjusting to a new incentive-based approach to environmental regulation. In fact, one can be relatively confident that the future holds better things in store for the program. One reason is that trading activity is increasing. Trades can be recorded with the EPA at any time prior to the use of an allowance for compliance, and recorded trades are monitored in the EPA's electronic, on-line Allowance Tracking System (ATS). The EPA has developed an algorithm for classifying trades as 'economically significant' if they are transfers between independent firms, and the majority of trades that are recorded have been transfers for accounting convenience or other reasons within firms. However, the number of economically significant trades has virtually doubled each year through 1997.

A second reason for optimism about the efficiency of the market is that the industry-wide level of emissions increased slightly in 1996. An adjustment was necessary because the weighted average costs in 1995 were greater than the present discounted value of marginal costs in the future and greater than allowance prices that reflect the latter measure. Behaviour at the outset of the program appears to have been risk averse, with firms making sure they could achieve compliance through a 'go-it-alone' strategy. Subsequently, there appears to be a growing level of comfort with the use of the market as a way to ensure compliance.

A third reason for optimism has to do with over-arching trends in the electric utility industry in the US. The industry is in a fundamental period of realignment as competition at the wholesale level, and perhaps ultimately at the retail level, is beginning to emerge. This type of competition is placing pressure on the industry to find ways to reduce costs in all segments of its business. One should not expect the industry to absorb $300 million in unnecessary costs in the future when allowance trading provides a fairly simple means of reducing those costs.

4. COMPLIANCE COSTS VERSUS ECONOMIC COSTS

Though widely known, it is not often acknowledged that compliance costs and economic costs are not the same thing. Compliance costs describe the out-of-pocket expenses by a firm or industry to comply with regulations. Economic costs describe the value of goods and services that were lost to the economy due to the regulation. This can include so-called hidden costs or benefits, such as costs incurred but not reported as compliance costs or indirect productivity changes that result from environmental compliance.

One type of important hidden cost stems from the interaction of the program with the pre-existing tax system. Important distortions away from economic efficiency stem from pre-existing taxes. Labour income taxes are particularly important because of their magnitude in the economy. Labour taxes impose a difference between the before-tax wage (or the value of the marginal product of labour to firms) and the after-tax wage (or the opportunity cost of labour from the worker's perspective). This difference causes workers to substitute away from labour to leisure compared to an efficient outcome were these two measures equal.

Any regulation that raises product prices potentially imposes a hidden cost on the economy by lowering the real wage of workers. This can be viewed as a 'virtual tax' magnifying the significance of previous taxes, with losses in productivity as a consequence. If there were no pre-existing distortions in the economy, the impact of regulatory costs would be of little concern. However, the cost of distortions associated with taxes grow more than proportionally with the size of the tax, and hence the hidden cost of regulation can be of great importance when pre-existing taxes are taken into account.

This hidden cost has been termed the tax interaction effect (Parry, 1995) and it tends to erode the usual efficiency benefits identified with setting prices to include external costs. The tax interaction effect is particularly important in the allowance trading system, relative to a command and control approach, because the price of the final product in a competitive market should reflect not only compliance cost for emission reductions but also the opportunity cost (or price) of allowances used for compliance. As the electric utility industry in the US moves toward competition, this effect of allowances on electricity prices is expected to emerge. The trading program is expected to result in significant savings in compliance costs, but commensurably it internalizes additional costs in the way of allowance prices into electricity prices.[14]

Goulder et al. (1997) have investigated the magnitude of the tax interaction effect in the context of the SO_2 program using both analytical and numerical general equilibrium models. They find that this effect will cost the economy about $1.06 billion per year (1995 dollars) in Phase II of the program, adding an additional 70 per cent to their estimated compliance costs for the program.

There are important lessons here for the design of other environmental programs that may refer to the SO_2 program as a model. First Goulder et al. (1997) find that the tax interaction effect is more significant, relative to the magnitude of compliance costs, for programs that are aimed at small emission reductions such as may describe possible policies for CO_2 reductions.[15] Further, since the tax interaction effect is positive even for a small emission reduction, then it is possible for the economic costs of regulation to be greater than the benefits even when compliance costs start at zero.

Second, the cost of the tax interaction effect can be largely (but not entirely) offset by policies that raise revenues for the government, because these revenues can (in principle) be used to offset pre-existing taxes and correct distortions in the labour market resulting from these taxes. The authors find that over half of the economic cost of the tax interaction effect, or $622 million, could be avoided if emission allowances were auctioned rather than grandfathered and the revenue was used to reduce the marginal tax rate on labour income. Unfortunately, the SO_2 program does not raise revenues since allowances are distributed for zero cost. Consequently, the current program design imposes a hidden cost on the economy that could be avoided if allowances were auctioned instead of allocated without charge.

The recommendation that allowances be auctioned comes with significant political liability. The endowment of allowances without charge, so-called 'grandfathering' of allowances, is an important form of compensation to the electric utility industry. The industry's attitude toward the SO_2 program would have been considerably more negative had this compensation not existed. Hence policy makers face a trade-off between efficiency and compensation in the design of the program.

There is an equity aspect to this issue that counter-balances the concerns of industry as well. At the time legislators adopted the SO_2 program in 1990, state public utility commissions were in the business of regulating the industry and setting electricity prices, and they were the safeguard to ensure utilities could not charge customers for something the utilities received for free. Hence, endowing allowances at zero cost was not controversial to the design of the SO_2 program. However, in the near future we expect regulators to exit the business of setting prices, at least with respect to electricity generation, and electricity prices will be set in a competitive market.[16] In the textbook and presumably in the market, SO_2 allowances take on the value of their opportunity cost, and this will be passed on through marginal cost pricing in a competitive electricity market, regardless of how the utility acquired the allowances originally. The value of this endowment, coming out of the hides of electricity consumers and accruing to the industry, is potentially very large.

A potentially important qualification concerns whether coal-fired electric generating facilities which are the source of SO_2 emissions are likely to be the marginal unit – that is, the highest cost unit that is operated to meet electricity demand – and hence will be determining electricity price. For example, at times when a gas-fired unit is the marginal unit, the price of electricity should reflect the marginal costs of that unit and will not reflect allowance costs for coal-fired generation that may be running at costs below the margin. On the other hand, when coal-fired units are the marginal unit then all infra-marginal technologies that operate at less cost than the marginal unit will receive the same price of electricity, which reflects the costs of allowances.

To investigate this issue, we exercised an electricity dispatch model aggregated by season, time block and region, that is maintained at Resources for the Future. The model is intended to characterize the industry under competitive conditions expected to prevail after deregulation. We find that coal-fired facilities can be expected to generate about one-half of all electricity generated in the US, just as they do under current regulatory practice. Further, we find that about one-half of all electricity would be generated when a coal facility is the marginal unit. Hence, on a per kilowatt-hour basis, the effect on electricity prices from emission allowances appears to be about the same as it would be if we were to assume generation from coal-fired units always occurred when these were the only units operating and their marginal costs were to determine electricity prices when they were in operation.

Under the assumption that the program works efficiently and firms value SO_2 allowances at their opportunity cost (the price of an allowance, equal to the marginal abatement cost) then the magnitude of the compensation under the program (the grandfathering of allowances valued at their opportunity cost) far outweighs the compliance cost incurred by firms. I estimate that the present discounted value of this difference is between \$10 and \$20 billion (1995 dollars). This represents a tremendous transfer of wealth from electric utility customers to the industry, and this transfer should be of interest in the design of other programs.

In particular, the design of a CO_2 permit program would involve smaller emission reductions in percentage terms and therefore a much greater transfer of wealth relative to the cost of compliance and also in absolute terms. Both the equity and the efficiency aspects of the tax interaction effect can be largely remedied by a carbon tax or auctioned carbon permits. Recognizing that there may political obstacles to a revenue-raising carbon policy, a hybrid system involving an auction of some portion of the permits and grandfathering the remaining may be a useful compromise.

5. COMPARING BENEFITS AND COSTS

The primary measure of success of the SO_2 program, from the perspective of economics, is the comparison of benefits and costs. Burtraw et al. (1998) describe an integrated assessment of benefits and costs through the year 2030, with benefits quantified for health, visibility and aquatics.[17] The accounting of benefits is incomplete because several environmental pathways could not be modelled completely. The cost estimate and estimate of health benefits are calculated for the entire nation, but visibility and aquatic benefits are calculated only *per affected capita* to illustrate the potential relative magnitude of these benefits; and the estimates do not necessarily apply to the entire nation. Midpoint estimates of the benefits and costs per affected capita for the year 2010 are summarized in Table 3.4.

Table 3.4 Benefits and costs expressed as 'per affected capita' in 2010

Effect	Benefits per affected capita (1995 dollars)
Morbidity	4.09
Mortality	69.25
Aquatic	0.72
Recreational visibility	3.90
Residential visibility	6.79
Costs	6.19

Source: Burtraw et al. (1998)

The study finds that benefits of the SO_2 program are an order of magnitude greater than costs, a result that contrasts sharply with estimates in 1990 that pegged benefits about equal to costs (Portney, 1990). What explains the difference between the earlier and recent estimates?

The lion's share of benefits result from reduced risk of premature mortality, especially through reduced exposure to sulphates, and these expected benefits measure several times the expected costs of the program. Significant benefits are also estimated from improvements in health morbidity, recreational visibility and residential visibility, each of which is approximately equal to costs. These areas, namely human health and visibility, were not the focus of acid rain research in the 1980s, and new information suggests these benefits are greater than were previously anticipated.

In contrast, areas that were the focus of attention in the 1980s including effects to soils, forests and aquatic systems still have not been modelled comprehensively, but evidence suggests benefits in these areas to be relatively small, at least with respect to 'use values' for the environmental assets that are affected.

In the 1980s public attention to air pollution from SO_2 and NO_x emissions largely centred on the problem of acidification ('acid rain'), with particular concern for its affect on water and soil chemistry and ultimately ecological systems. It is surprising to many that relatively low benefits are estimated by economists for effects on aquatics (in Burtraw et al., 1998) or are expected to result from effects on forests and agriculture. One reason is that willingness to pay for environmental improvement depends on the availability of substitute assets. Economists would not expect changes in quality at one site to elicit large benefits if there are many sites available for comparable recreational opportunities. In contrast, individuals do not have the same kind of substitution possibilities with respect to health and visibility, which may help explain the relatively larger benefit estimates for these endpoints. Furthermore, one should note that the low values for aquatics stem from an assessment of *use* values, or *commodity* values in the case of agriculture. Environmental changes may also yield *non-use* values, and estimates for non-use values are not available. Nonetheless, the evidence, based on a small number of relatively narrow studies, suggests these values may be significant.

On the cost side, compliance has cost one-half or less what it was anticipated to cost in 1990. Trends in both directions, that is, increased appreciation of benefits and decreased estimate of costs, have qualified the program as a tremendous success from an economic perspective.

There are huge uncertainties, especially on the benefits side of the ledger, especially in valuation of mortality. Recent economic critiques have argued that the use of the value of a statistical life as the basis for valuing health risks from air pollution, instead of a more appropriate measure of quality adjusted life years lost, could grossly overestimate mortality benefits. In addition, economists have questioned the appropriateness of using labour studies of prime age men to value changes in life expectancy that occur among an older population. On the other hand, we note that because environmental exposures are involuntary, compared with studies of labour market behaviour, the latter may underestimate willingness to pay to avoid environmental exposures. Burtraw et al. (1998) used Monte Carlo analysis and a parametric one-sided sensitivity analysis to investigate some of these sources of uncertainties. Their analysis finds that there is no year in which health benefits alone at the 5 per cent confidence interval are less than the levelized expected costs. These results are illustrated in Figure 3.1, with millions of (1990) dollars on the vertical axis and years of the program on the horizontal axis. As noted, significant benefits are also estimated for improvements in health morbidity, recreational visibility and residential visibility, each of which measures approximately equal to costs. Despite tremendous uncertainties about benefits and costs, the main conclusion that benefits soundly outweigh costs appears to be robust.

6. CONCLUSION

Although tremendous attention has been addressed to the innovative design of the SO_2 emission allowance trading program, an economic approach to policy analysis should perhaps focus first on the comparison of benefits and costs of the program. Evidence to date suggests that benefits are expected to greatly outweigh the costs of the program. Surprises on the benefits side that contribute to this favourable assessment are in benefit categories of human health and visibility that were not the primary focus of research on acid rain in the 1980s. Favourable events on the cost side have to do with the expected successful implementation of the allowance trading program, and with advantageous trends in markets that supply the electric utility sector. Developments in these input markets, which include scrubber manufacturing, coal mining and rail transport of coal, are at least partially related to the SO_2 program. Due to advantageous trends in the industry leading to increased use of low sulphur coal, the quantity of emissions that had to be reduced is less than anticipated. This led to lower costs than many envisioned, and commensurately SO_2 trading could provide a smaller measure of cost savings. However, the SO_2 program deserves considerable credit for providing firms with the flexibility to capitalize on these advantageous trends as they develop their compliance activities.

There is some reason for concern about the ability of the SO_2 market to function efficiently and for firms to capture possible cost savings based on

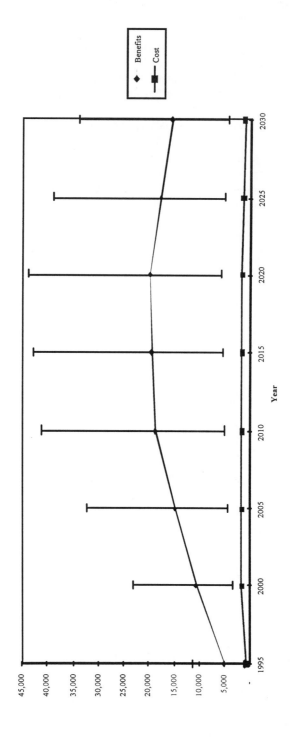

Figure 3.1 Annual 90 per cent confidence intervals for total health benefits compared with expected annualized costs

Source: Burttraw et al., 1998

evidence for 1995, the first year in which the program was binding. However, there are several reasons one can expect the market to become more efficient over time and the long-run prospects for the program are bright.

As scholars and policy analysts attempt to draw lessons from the SO_2 program, one area that should receive significant attention is the manner in which emission allowances are allocated to the industry. Evidence suggests that grandfathering of allowances can impose significant efficiency costs. Furthermore, this approach represents a tremendous transfer of wealth that raises equity issues as well. Rarely in economics do efficiency and equity issues point in the same direction, but in this case they do. The recommendation that follows is that emission allowances should be auctioned or allocated in some means that raises revenue for government that can be used to reduce other distortionary taxes. If the allocation of allowances is to serve as compensation for industry, this function should be weighed carefully against the benefits of raising revenue. A hybrid program in which some portion of allowances are grandfathered and the rest auctioned by the government could offer a compromise that would improve programs of this type in future applications.

NOTES

1   Allowances are allocated to individual facilities in proportion to fuel consumption multiplied by an emission factor during the 1985-1987 period. About 2.8 per cent of the annual allowance allocations are withheld by the EPA and distributed to buyers through an annual auction run by the Chicago Board of Trade. The revenues are returned to the utilities that were the original owners of the allowances.

2   Title IV also used a more traditional approach in setting NO_x emission rate limitations for coal-fired electric utility units, although this approach has been modified to allow emission rate averaging among commonly owned and operated facilities. Hence, there is no cap on NO_x emissions, but Title IV is expected to result in a 27 per cent reduction from 1990 emissions for electric utilities.

3   These plants represented 89 per cent of the nation's pre-New Source Performance Standard coal-fired capacity. Fuel switching to low sulphur fuel and other facility improvements would have been required at other facilities. Scrubbing would have been applied to about half of the affected capacity and accounted for 70 per cent of the SO_2 reduction.

4   It is noteworthy that an industry study (TBS, 1986) suggested the costs would be higher as a result because although 'intra-firm trading' would reduce the need for scrubbing, it would increase reliance on low sulphur coals resulting in an increased premium on low sulphur coal that would raise costs for units already using low sulphur coal. This prediction is contradicted by the turn of events under Title IV, when the cost of lost sulphur coal fell with its expanded use.

5   These estimates describe long-run costs expected to obtain when the allowance bank, which is expected to build up to about 11 million tons by the end of Phase 1 (in the year 2000), is drawn down and net contributions to the bank are zero.

6
    The cost function they estimate treats fuel type (high sulphur and low sulphur coal), labour and generating capital as fully variable inputs. The econometric model consists of the cost function plus two share equations that specify the share of total costs attributed to capital and labour, and an equation for the firm's mean annual emission rate. The study uses a translog form for the cost function, adding dummy variables for each plant in the database to measure fixed effects that vary among the plants. Costs for units with scrubbers are taken directly from reported data. The model does not investigate whether early commitments to build scrubbers were economical, but several studies have suggested that several of these investments were not.

7
    Technological change here captures both exogenous efficiency improvements at the power plant and improvements induced by the program, but it does not capture improvements in scrubber technology and performance.

8
    In 1995 the continuous emission monitors estimated 7 per cent higher emissions than did the historic approach on average, although there was considerable variability among facilities.

9
    In their command and control scenario, Carlson et al. (1998) apply a uniform emission rate standard to all facilities. GAO (1994) and Van Horn Consulting et al. (1993) allow intra-utility trading, but no trading between utilities. GAO (1994) also models a scenario that requires each facility to achieve its SO_2 allowance allocation without trading, and finds cost savings more than double that in the case in which internal trading is allowed in the command and control baseline.

10
    1978 Clean Air Act regulation of sulphur emissions from newly constructed fossil fuel-fired electricity generating facilities imposes a rate-based standard that requires a 90 per cent reduction in a smokestack's SO_2 emissions, or 70 per cent if the facility use low sulphur coal. Although nominally a performance standard, it effectively dictates technological choices and precludes compliance through the use of process changes or demand reduction. The only available technology to achieve such reductions is scrubbing, and the use of low sulphur coal is not a permissible way to avoid the threshold for the strict standard.

11
    Bohi and Burtraw (1997).

12
    For instance, 10 March 1997 EPA Administrator Carol Browner argued: '...During the 1990 debate on the acid rain program, industry initially projected the cost of an emission allowance to be $1500 per ton of sulphur dioxide...Today, those allowances are selling for less than $100.' ('New Initiatives in Environmental Protection', *The Commonwealth* (newsletter), 31 March 1997, Commonwealth Club of California.) See also 'Economists' Cold Forecast; Assumptions: Expect their dire predictions about the impact of the global warming treaty on the United States. Ignore all of them,' by Elaine Karmarck, *Baltimore Sun*, 28 December 1997.

13
    As noted previously, in their command and control scenario, Carlson et al. (1998) apply a uniform emission rate standard to all facilities.

14
    The effect on product prices should occur without regard to how the firm acquired allowances originally, if prices reflect marginal costs and allowances are valued at their opportunity cost.

15
    Small emission reductions require small compliance expenditures, leaving a larger quantity of emissions to be included in a permit trading scheme. Allowance prices would be low, relative to a case with greater emission reductions, but they apply to a larger quantity of emissions. Hence, the portion of costs associated with permit use relative to the portion of costs associated with compliance cost is greater.

16
    This will occur if state or federal policy makers move to retail competition. At the time of this writing, fifteen states have committed to retail competition to be implemented at some future date, and virtually all states are actively considering doing so (Ando and

Palmer, 1998). Even if retail competition is slow to develop, wholesale competition is likely to emerge in the near future.

[17]   The integrated assessment involved nearly thirty researchers at a dozen institutions. The assessment is based on reduced-form models that were calibrated to several larger models of utility emissions and costs, atmospheric transport of pollution, visibility impairment, effects on aquatic systems and human health, and valuation of effects. Economic assessment of costs are calculated with an engineering model constructed for the assessment. Economic valuation of damage to aquatic systems relied on random utility models of recreational use. Health mortality valuation relied on compensating wage and contingent valuation studies and morbidity valuation relied on a number of studies and methods. Valuation of visibility effects at national parks used contingent valuation methods, and valuation of visibility in residential areas used a combination of contingent valuation combined with hedonic property value studies.

REFERENCES

Ando, Amy and Karen Palmer (1998), 'Getting on the Map: The Political Economy of State-Level Electricity Restructuring,' Washington, DC: Resources for the Future Discussion Paper 98-XX.

Bohi, Douglas R. and Dallas Burtraw (1997), 'SO$_2$ Allowance Trading: How Do Expectations and Experience Measure Up?,' *The Electricity Journal*, **10** (7), 67–77.

Burtraw, D. (1996), 'The SO$_2$ emissions trading program: cost savings without allowance trades', *Contemporary Economic Policy*, **14**, 79–94.

Burtraw, Dallas, Alan J. Krupnick, Erin Mansur, David Austin and Deirdre Farrell (1998), 'Costs and Benefits of Air Pollutants Related to Acid Rain,' *Contemporary Economic Policy*, 16 (October), forthcoming.

Carlson, Curtis, Dallas Burtraw, Maureen Cropper and Karen Palmer (1998), 'SO$_2$ Control by Electric Utilities: What are the Gains from Trade?,' Washington, DC: Resources for the Future: Discussion Paper 98-44 (July).

Ellerman, A. Denny and Juan Pablo Montero (1998), 'The Declining Trend in Sulfur dioxide Emissions: Implications for Allowance Prices', *Journal of Environmental Economics and Management*, 36(1), July, 26–45.

Ellerman, A. Denny, Richard Schmalensee, Paul L. Joskow, Juan Pablo Montero, and Elizabeth M. Bailey (1997), *Emissions Trading under the U.S. Acid Rain Program: Evaluation of Compliance Costs and Allowance Market Performance*, Cambridge, MA: MIT Center for Energy and Environmental Policy Research.

Elman, Barry, Bruce Braine and Richard Stuebi (1990), 'Acid Rain Emission Allowances and Future Capacity Growth in the Electric Utility Industry', *Journal of Air and Waste Management Association*, **40** (7), 979–986.

Goulder, Lawrence H., Ian W. H. Parry and Dallas Burtraw (1997), 'Revenue-Raising vs. Other Approaches to Environmental Protection: The Critical Significance of Pre-Existing Tax Distortions,' *RAND Journal of Economics*, **28** (4) (Winter), 708–731.

ICF Resources Incorporated (ICF), (1990), 'Comparison of the Economic Impacts of the Acid Rain Provisions of the Senate Bill (S. 1630) and the House Bill (S.

1630),' prepared for U.S. Environmental Protection Agency, Washington, DC (July).

ICF (1995) 'Economic Analysis of Title IV Requirements of the 1990 Clean Air Act Amendments,' prepared for the U.S. Environmental Protection Agency (September).

Parry, Ian W. H. (1995), 'Pollution Taxes and Revenue Recycling', *Journal of Environmental Economics and Management*, **29** (3) (supplement), S64-S77.

Portney, Paul R (1990), 'Economics and the Clean Air Act,' *Journal of Economic Perspectives*, 4 (4), 173–181.

Temple, Barker and Sloane, Inc. (TBS) (1983) 'Evaluation of H.R. 3400: The 'Sikorski/Waxman' Bill for Acid Rain Abatement', prepared for the Edison Electric Institute (20 September).

Temple, Barker and Sloane, Inc. (1986), 'Evaluation of H.R. 4567: The Acid Deposition Control Act of 1986', prepared for the Edison Electric Institute (14 April).

U.S. Energy Information Administration (EIA) (1996), *Annual Energy Outlook 1997*, DOE/EIA-0383(97), Washington, DC (December).

U.S. Government Accounting Office (GAO) (1994), 'Air Pollution: Allowance Trading Offers an Opportunity to Reduce Emissions at Less Cost,' GAO/RCED-95-30, Washington, DC

U.S. Office of Technology Assessment (OTA) (1983), 'An Analysis of the 'Sikorski/Waxman' Acid Rain Control Proposal: H.R. 3400: The National Acid Deposition Control Act of 1983,' Staff Memorandum (revised 12 July).

Van Horn Consulting, Energy Ventures Analysis, Inc., and Keith D. White (1993), 'Integrated Analysis of Fuel, Technology and Emission Allowance Markets', prepared for the Electric Power Research Institute, EPRI TR-102510 (August).

White, Keith (1997), 'SO_2 Compliance and Allowance Trading: Developments and Outlook,' prepared for the Electric Power Research Institute (EPRI), EPRI TR-107897 (April).

White, Keith, Energy Ventures Analysis, Inc., and Van Horn Consulting (1995), *The Emission Allowance Market and Electric Utility SO_2 Compliance in a Competitive and Uncertain Future,* prepared for the Electric Power Research Institute (EPRI), TR-105490, Palo Alto, CA (Final Report: September).

63 — 99

(USl QV
QL8 H2?

4. Turning theory into practice for emissions trading in the Los Angeles air basin[1]

David Harrison, Jr.

1. INTRODUCTION

Regulators in the Los Angeles air basin have developed an emissions trading program that represents a bold departure from the traditional 'command and control' approach to air quality. The program is called the Regional Clean Air Incentives Market (RECLAIM), an acronym designed to emphasize the objectives of reclaiming both good air quality and a sound economy. The program was approved by the South Coast Air Quality Management District (SCAQMD) in October 1993, after a regulatory development period that lasted almost three years. RECLAIM began operation in January 1994.

The theoretical advantages of the emissions trading approach had been well established long before RECLAIM was developed. Economists have long pointed out that creating a market for emissions can lower the cost of meeting emission reduction targets.[2] Though the theory is simple, there are an enormous number of issues that arise in turning the theory into practice. What is path-breaking about RECLAIM – along with a handful of other emissions trading programs – is that these issues were developed in sufficient detail and with sufficient political credibility for the program to be approved and put in place. Future emissions trading proposals inevitably will have to address many of the same issues.

This chapter begins with background on regulation of air quality in the United States and the Los Angeles air basin along with information on potential cost savings from RECLAIM. The bulk of the chapter consists of discussions of key issues that arose as the theory of emissions trading was turned into a concrete program in RECLAIM. The final section provides some conclusions and implications for future emissions trading proposals.

2. BACKGROUND

The RECLAIM program was developed against the backdrop both of federal air quality control policy and of contemporary developments within the Los Angeles air basin.

2.1. United States air pollution policy context

Air pollution policy in the United States is guided by the federal Clean Air Act (CAA), based largely upon landmark amendments passed in 1970 and supplemented by major amendments in 1977 and 1990. The CAA directs the Administrator of the US Environmental Protection Agency (EPA) to set maximum permissible ambient (outdoor) concentrations for air pollutants. Ambient standards have been set for six air pollutants: lead, sulphur dioxide (SO_2), nitrogen dioxide, carbon monoxide, fine particulate matter, and ozone. (Ozone is formed by oxides of nitrogen (NO_x) and volatile organic compounds (VOCs)[3] in the presence of sunlight.)

States and local air pollution control districts – such as the SCAQMD – are charged with responsibility for developing plans so that the national air quality standards will be met everywhere. The Clean Air Act calls for federal emission standards (i.e., permissible emission rates) for certain sources such as new automobiles and other mobile sources as well as for major *new* industrial facilities. States and local districts take these national emission standards into account in determining the need for state or local controls on existing sources within their jurisdictions. State Implementation Plans (SIPs) are submitted periodically by the states to the EPA for approval.

Federal air pollution policy as of 1990 included several emissions trading programs, including both clear successes and programs whose performance fell far short of their promise.[4] An example of the latter is the set of four Emissions Trading (ET) programs developed by EPA in the late 1970s to increase the flexibility firms had to comply with largely command-and-control regulatory requirements. The most widely known was the bubble policy, in which firms with several sources at the same facility were given the flexibility to achieve an overall emission level equal to the sum of the individual standards. The other three are offsets, netting, and banking. Virtually all commentators give the ET programs a mixed review. Total cost savings almost certainly amount to less than 1 per cent of air pollution control costs, reflecting the small number of actual trades that have taken place. The major problem seems to be that trading is tightly controlled – the regulations take up 47 fine-print pages – and firms have been concerned that any gains they achieve might be confiscated later on through tightened standards or other means.

In contrast, the lead-trading program for gasoline in the 1980s is widely regarded as a success. In 1982, EPA set a more stringent limit on the average amount of lead per gallon – both to reduce lead exposure and avoid problems with catalytic converters on cars – but allowed refiners to meet the requirement by purchasing rights from refineries below the limit. A provision to allow 'banking,' i.e., credits for reducing the average in advance of requirements, was added in 1985. An increasingly vigorous market in lead rights developed, so that by the end of the program in 1987, almost 70 per cent of the lead rights were traded. Trading and banking generated substantial savings and also appeared to speed up the phase-out of lead in gasoline.

The acid rain trading program was signed into law as part of the 1990 Clean Air Act Amendments just as deliberations on what became RECLAIM were beginning in the Los Angeles basin.[5] Electric utility emissions of SO_2 became subject to an overall cap that ratcheted down in two phases, Phase 1 from 1995 to 1999 and Phase 2 in 2000 and beyond. Individual utilities were issued allowances (i.e., the right to emit 1 ton) equal in total to these overall annual caps and were allowed to trade allowances among themselves. This widely-publicized program – with cost savings projected at about 35 per cent of the cost of achieving the same emission reductions with the traditional command-and-control approach – provided a national model for a cap-and-trade program.

2.2. Los Angeles policy context

The Los Angeles region regulated by the SCAQMD consists of a 6,600 square mile area containing the non-desert portions of four Los Angeles area counties with a combined population of approximately 13 million inhabitants in 1990. A combination of emission sources, meteorology, and terrain make this area the most heavily polluted region of the United States as measured by urban ozone.

The SCAQMD has struggled with the task of complying with federal air quality mandates for many years. At the time that efforts began to develop an emissions trading program, air pollution within the basin was governed by the 1989 Air Quality Management Plan (AQMP). The 1989 AQMP is a massive plan – consisting of 130 individual control measures affecting every segment of the region – that was designed to bring the area into compliance with federal air quality standards by 2010. Of the 130 control measures, 116 reduce at least one of the two ozone precursors, NO_x and VOC. Together these 116 control measures were designed to reduce emissions of NO_x and VOCs by about 80 per cent by the year 2010.

The cost of this control strategy would be enormous, estimated to be about $13 billion (1988 dollars) per year or about $2,200 annually for every household in the region (Harrison, 1988). Indeed, interest in emissions trading was due in large part to the need to develop a less expensive means of achieving the stringent air quality targets. Policy makers were concerned that excessive control costs would drive businesses out of the region, exacerbating the recession that gripped California at the time. These conditions – as well as its earlier experience with emissions trading under the federal offset program and a multi-facility bubble program developed for electric utilities – motivated the SCAQMD to sponsor major workshops on emissions trading in October and December of 1990. In February 1991, the Governing Board of the SCAQMD authorized a full-scale feasibility study and the formation of a broad-based Advisory Committee and a smaller Steering Committee to assist in the development of what eventually became RECLAIM. The feasibility study was followed by rule development and final approval of RECLAIM by the SCAQMD Governing Board in October 1993.

2.3. Potential gains from emissions trading in the Los Angeles air basin

It was possible as RECLAIM was being developed to make rough estimates of the potential cost savings from emissions trading in the Los Angeles basin. The SCAQMD had developed data on control costs for source categories that would be covered by RECLAIM. For example, the average cost per ton of VOC for the 50 source categories and control options that are included in these data ranged from $113 per ton to $86,970 per ton.

This wide variation in cost per ton suggests that overall costs could be reduced substantially by emissions trading, which encourages a shift in control effort from source categories with high costs to those with lower costs. Using the source category data to calculate a least-cost supply curve indicated that emissions trading could reduce the cost of meeting the emission targets set by the AQMP by about 40 per cent (Harrison and Nichols, 1992). Similar results were reported by researchers at the SCAQMD, who reported that RECLAIM would reduce costs by about 42 per cent (Johnson and Pekelney, 1996). This figure underestimates the potential savings because it ignores cost variability among individual sources within a source category and does not take into account the possibility of expanding the program to other source categories. On the other hand, these estimates assume that all of the potential gains from trading across source categories would be realized, thus ignoring transaction costs and other obstacles to realizing all the potential gains (Stavins, 1995).

3. KEY ISSUES IN TRANSLATING THEORY INTO PRACTICE

Virtually everyone in the policy debate over RECLAIM agreed that emissions trading had the potential to lower the costs of meeting the ambitious air pollution reduction targets in the Los Angeles basin. Translating those potential gains into a concrete program required dealing with many issues, both design elements of the program and concerns about the impacts of the program on the region. This chapter focuses on the following five issues:[6]

1. Type of trading system. What would be the unit of trade, i.e., would trading be in terms of emission reductions or emissions allowances?
2. Scope. What companies would be included in the program? What sectors? What emissions cut-off would be set?
3. Initial allocation. How would the initial entitlements be allocated among the participating companies?
4. Geographic and seasonal constraints. What constraints, if any, would be imposed on trades in different time periods? In different locations?
5. Administrative considerations. Would trading parties have to obtain pre-approval of trades from the SCAQMD? What requirements would be imposed to monitor and enforce the program?

These and other issues were explored in many meetings of the RECLAIM Advisory Committee and Steering Committee as well as in documents developed by the SCAQMD over the course of the feasibility review and rule development process.[7] The following sections discuss these issues as well as the final decisions embodied in the RECLAIM program that was passed by the SCAQMD Governing Board in October 1993.

3.1. Type of trading program

Two general types of trading programs can be developed depending upon the nature of the commodity that is traded:

1. Emission reduction credit. These programs trade emission reductions, i.e., a reduction from a given baseline level. Examples include EPA's offset program used for new sources and a car scrappage credit program developed in the Los Angeles basin.
2. Emission allowances. These programs trade emissions allowances, i.e., the right to emit one unit (e.g. pound). The acid rain trading program is a prominent example of this type.

The initial trading unit envisioned for RECLAIM was the first option, the emission reduction credit or ERC. Trading ERCs was seen as having several advantages. For one thing, the concept already existed in both in EPA's ET programs as well in SCAQMD rules implementing the ET programs in the Los Angeles basin, particularly the requirement that new sources obtain 'offsets' for their emissions from existing sources. In addition, trading emission reductions would avoid the appearance of creating a 'license to pollute.'

Against these advantages were a host of serious disadvantages due to the lack of firm benchmark for measuring emission reductions. Experience indicates that it is important that buyers and sellers be clear about what is being traded. Should the benchmark for calculating emission reductions be a firm's allowable emissions based upon the regulations in force? Or should emission reductions be measured relative to the firm's actual emissions? Actual emissions are typically substantially below allowable emissions, in part because the variability in control actually achieved by control technologies means that firms must aim to do better than the standard if they are to be in compliance all (or virtually all) of the time. Trading reductions from allowable emissions thus creates the possibility of 'paper trades,' i.e., trades of reductions that would have occurred regardless of the program. But measuring reduction credits from actual emissions creates the possibility of perverse incentives – firms might increase their actual emissions in order to develop the capacity to make 'reductions' in the future. Moreover, experience with EPA's ET programs suggests that attempting to avoid problems of paper credits can result in a highly restrictive and ineffective trading program (Harrison and Nichols, 1990).

The RECLAIM program ultimately chose to base trading primarily on emission allowances, which were called RECLAIM Trading Credits or RTCs. (As noted below, however, emission reduction credits for mobile and area sources were included in the program.) An RTC constituted an allowance to emit one pound of pollutant. Compliance with RECLAIM meant participating companies had to have RTCs equal to the emissions from their facilities that were included in the program. The unit of trade in RECLAIM is thus equivalent to the unit established in the 1990 Clean Air Act Amendments under the acid rain trading program.

3.2. Scope of RECLAIM

Determining the scope of the RECLAIM program involved several related issues:

1. What pollutants should be included?

2. What types of emission sources (e.g. utilities, automobiles, solvents) should be included?
3. What size cut-off for sources should be adopted?

Pollutants
The RECLAIM program was motivated in large part by the need to obtain compliance with the federal ozone standard. The meteorological models developed by the SCAQMD indicated that both NO_x and VOC emissions would need to be reduced by about 80 per cent in order to achieve compliance with the ambient ozone standard. Thus, RECLAIM initially was thought of as a program that would be applied to both NO_x and VOC emissions.

Environmental groups objected to using an emissions trading program for VOCs on two major grounds.

1. Toxic effects. VOC emissions include pollutants that are considered actual or potential toxic pollutants (e.g. carcinogens) under Section 112 of the Clean Air Act. Concerns were expressed that allowing companies to trade VOC emissions may result in increased emissions of toxic pollutants.
2. Monitoring problems. About 40 per cent of VOC emissions in the South Coast came from solvent use (e.g. hair spray, paint) and other small emission sources that were arguably more difficult to monitor than the stationary sources that were more important for NO_x emissions.

The net result was a decision by the Coalition for Clean Air, an environmental group participating actively in the development of RECLAIM, to limit its recommendations to a program for NO_x emissions.

Although the initial emphasis in RECLAIM development was on ozone, the SCAQMD also considered expanding the program to include sulphur dioxide emissions. As noted, the 1990 Clean Air Act Amendments include a program for SO_2 trading among electric utilities. Although SO_2 emissions are relatively low in the Los Angeles air basin – and the area was projected to be in compliance with the ambient standard for SO_2 – there would still be some cost savings from allowing SO_2 sources to trade among themselves.

The final RECLAIM program adopted in October 1993 included NO_x and SO_2 emissions. VOC emissions were not included in the program, although the SCAQMD indicated its intention to develop a RECLAIM program for VOCs as well.[8]

Emission sources and size cut-off
The SCAQMD initially recommended that all permitted stationary sources be included in the program. That criterion would mean about 5,200 NO_x

facilities would be included. The SCAQMD, however, became concerned about the administrative problems of including small stationary sources in the program. Facilities emitting less than four tons per year represented about 4,600 of the 5,200 permitted sources but accounted for only about 5 per cent of the NO_x emissions from these sources. Narrowing RECLAIM to a smaller universe of sources would reduce the administrative and compliance problems.

Both industry and environmental groups supported extending RECLAIM to include mobile and area sources. The Regulatory Flexibility Group, a group of major companies that participated actively in RECLAIM deliberations, recommended that these sources be brought into the program by giving credits to companies that reduced emissions below the levels called for in the AQMP. Environmental groups such as the Coalition for Clean Air supported the creation of a broad-based plan for NO_x, although, as noted above, the group did not support a trading program for VOCs.

The SCAQMD in October 1993 approved a cap-and-trade program for stationary sources as well as a framework for including mobile source credits. The cap-and-trade program was generally limited to stationary sources emitting more than four tons per year. Smaller sources were included if they were in source categories for which the majority of sources were in RECLAIM, in order to avoid the need for a dual regulatory program. These criteria meant that 390 facilities were included in the NO_x market and 41 facilities in the SO_x market. RECLAIM replaced more than 30 adopted rules and 12 future potential rules. The annual rate of reduction for these sources was 6.8 per cent per year for SO_x and 8.3 per cent per year for NO_x.

RECLAIM allowed facilities to meet their cap targets with the use of mobile source emission reduction credits that were created under SCAQMD rules. When RECLAIM was approved, the SCAQMD had a program giving credits for scrapping older cars. The programs have since been extended to other mobile sources and to area sources.[9]

3.3. Initial allocation of allowances

Determining the formula to allocate initial RTCs to sources proved to be contentious and complex but ultimately manageable.[10] Theory indicates that the initial allocation of allowances does *not* affect the overall cost savings from emissions trading; under trading parties have incentives to achieve cost-minimizing controls regardless of the initial distribution of allowances.[11] But the initial allocation does quite clearly affect the distribution of gains from trading among the participants.[12]

The formula initially proposed for RECLAIM was based upon uniform reductions from each facility's 1987 emissions. The allocation in the first year of the program, initially set for 1993, would be equal to a reduction of

30 per cent from 1987 levels, reflecting the average annual decline called for in the AQMP. Under this initial proposal, these allocations would be reduced by a fixed per centage each year at levels necessary to meet the overall RECLAIM/AQMP targets by 2003.

Many concerns were raised about the fairness of this formula for distributing initial allocations.

- Prior controls. Industries and firms that reduced emissions before 1987 argued that it was unfair to ignore their substantial prior investments and reward those who had not made these pollution control investments.
- 1987 unrepresentative. Some companies argued that special circumstances (e.g. plant shutdowns) made emissions from their facilities unduly low in 1987. This issue was particularly important to some industries that had been in recession during 1987. These facilities argued that allocations should be based upon the average or the highest emissions level over some multi-year time period (e.g. 1987-91).
- Offsets. Equipment placed in service after 1976 in the Los Angeles basin was subject to new source regulations, which included a requirement to offset emissions. Owners of facilities that had met these offset requirements argued that allocations should be increased to reflect these emission reductions.
- Recent growth. Using a prior period as the basis for the initial allocation is bound to squeeze facilities that were growing rapidly. There was a concern expressed that no facility should 'start in the hole,' i.e., face a large reduction requirement in the first year or two of RECLAIM.

The SCAQMD considered literally dozens of alternative allocation formulas during its deliberations on RECLAIM. The final allocations were based upon complicated formulas in which each facility received three sets of allocations of tons of NO_x and/or SO_x: a starting allocation for 1994; a mid-point allocation for 2000; and an ending allocation for 2003. The basic ton allocations are based upon multiplying an appropriate emission factor (i.e., pounds per million Btu of energy input) for each of the three years by a single value for historic throughput or usage that is determined by each facility's peak activity over the period from 1989 to 1992. The emission rates for each of the allocation years are based upon adopted rules, as of December 1993, for each facility. The 1994 allocations are supplemented by the offsets facilities had obtained to comply with new source review requirements. In addition, facilities were given non-tradable credits for the first three years of the program if their reported 1987, 1988 or 1993 emissions were greater than their starting allocation. Allocations for each intermediate year for each facility were calculated based upon straight-line interpolation between the 1994, 2000, and 2003 allocations. The allocations were constant for 2003 and thereafter. The final step was to adjust the total allocations to equal the overall targets in 2002 and 2003 set under the AQMP for the source categories covered by RECLAIM.[13]

This complex allocation mechanism takes into account the many equity issues raised during the deliberations.[14] Allowing facilities to use peak activity over a four-year period avoided the use of an unrepresentative year. Basing allocations on emission rates under AQMP rules provided different rates of reduction for different facilities based on their prior controls. Adding offsets to facilities' RECLAIM credits gave credits for previous emission reductions. Providing three years of non-tradable credits if current (1993) emissions were greater than the 1994 allocation avoided facilities 'starting in the hole.'

In sum, the initial allocations that were developed in RECLAIM were designed to accommodate concerns about equity and fairness. Although the allocations were considerably more complex than the simple formula initially proposed, the allocations provided a politically-acceptable – and unambiguous – starting point for trades.

3.4. Geographic and temporal restrictions

The SCAQMD had to determine whether restrictions would be placed on trades in different time periods (e.g. days, seasons) and different geographic areas.

Geographic restrictions
Because ozone formation takes place over several hours, upwind sources located near the coast contribute more to elevated ozone levels in the Los Angeles basin than downwind sources located inland. California legislation requires that the SCAQMD take spatial factors into account in its offset program for new sources. To meet these requirements, the SCAQMD had divided the basin into 38 zones for purposes of developing new source offsets and had developed a complex set of trading restrictions.

Initially, the SCAQMD considered using the same 38 zones for RECLAIM and prohibiting inter-zone trades. Dividing RECLAIM into 38 separate markets could, however, sharply reduce the potential cost savings from trading and also create the potential for some sellers or buyers to exert market power. One alternative would be to create a single market for trading purposes, but to develop different trading ratios depending upon the relative importance of a ton emitted in different zones within the air basin. Such a system would allow all buyers and sellers to participate in the same market, although it would create a much more complicated system and require quantification of the trading ratios.

The final RECLAIM program involved a two-zone system in which the air basin was divided into coastal (upwind) and inland (downwind) zones. Inland sources could obtain and use RTCs from either zone, while coastal sources could only obtain and use RTCs that originated in the coastal zone.[15] These restrictions were intended to avoid increasing the fraction of emissions in upwind sources while avoiding the problems of including many individual zones.

Timing restrictions

The SCAQMD considered whether the time period for RTCs should be daily, monthly, quarterly, yearly, or some other period. It also considered whether facilities should be able to bank emissions, i.e., reduce emissions below the allowable level in one period and use the banked RTCs in a subsequent period. The SCAQMD originally proposed a pounds-per-day system for NO_x and a pounds-per-month system for VOCs. Banking would not be permitted. The daily limit for NO_x was intended to make RECLAIM consistent with the SCAQMD's recently promulgated NO_x multi-facility bubble for electric utilities, which involved a daily cap. The monthly cap for VOCs was based upon a concern that emissions needed to be capped over relatively small time periods in order to avoid high emissions on a given day. Rejection of banking was based upon a concern that emissions from the bank could contribute to overall emissions exceeding the AQMP target in some future year, and thus delaying compliance with the ozone standard.

Several commentators criticized these short time periods both as unnecessary and as potential constraints on cost savings. Industry and others argued that RECLAIM should be based upon annual emissions to provide greater liquidity of allowances and to avoid putting cyclical, seasonal, or highly variable emitters at a disadvantage. Such flexibility was particularly important without any provision for banking. Moreover, with regard to a daily NO_x limit, there appeared little reason to let the utility bubble dominate the design of RECLAIM. The SCAQMD's intermediate response to these concerns was to define the trading unit as pounds per quarter for both NO_x and VOCs.

The final RECLAIM system provided for an annual program, with facilities required to report their emissions to the SCAQMD each quarter. Facilities have a one-month reconciliation period after the first three quarters and a two-month reconciliation period at the end of the year. Although banking is not permitted, facilities are divided into two compliance cycles, one from 1 January to 31 December and the other from 1 July to 30 June. This system provides many of the advantages of banking because transactions can be conducted with facilities in either cycle.

3.5. Administrative considerations

The performance of an emissions trading program depends in large part on how it is administered. The disappointing performances of EPA's ET programs are due in large part to the many administrative restrictions on trades, including the need for pre-approval of trades. If trading is cumbersome and uncertain, trades will not take place.[16] Many administrative issues arose in the design of RECLAIM. Two of the most significant were: (1) SCAQMD oversight and related reporting requirements for trades; and (2) monitoring requirements to demonstrate compliance.

Oversight and reporting requirements

Concerns about SCAQMD oversight and market reporting requirements were linked to concerns about enforcement of the program. Some commentators during the early deliberations – when the SCAQMD was considering trades in emission reductions rather than emissions allowances – argued that SCAQMD should oversee the market and require buyers and sellers to obtain pre-approval of trades. Critics of pre-approval, including the Regulatory Flexibility Group, pointed out that the SCAQMD would not need to review individual trades under an annual allowance-based program because its only concern is whether the source has sufficient allowances in a given year to cover that year's emissions. The Regulatory Flexibility Group did, however, support reporting requirements designed to enable the SCAQMD to maintain proper records and monitor compliance.

The final RECLAIM program did not include pre-approval of trades by the SCAQMD, although the SCAQMD did retain a role in maintaining an RTC list, registering transactions, and otherwise providing information. Brokers, exchanges, and other intermediaries were encouraged to enter the RECLAIM market and facilitate trading of RTCs. RTC futures, options, or other derivative markets were allowed. The SCAQMD consolidated permits for individual units into one facility permit as a means of simplifying market transaction and reporting requirements. The facility permit would keep track of RTC allocations as well as market transactions.

Monitoring and enforcement

RECLAIM requires that the SCAQMD monitor annual emissions at facilities both to ensure that individual facilities comply with RECLAIM and to determine whether RECLAIM sources as a group are meeting the overall targets. As noted, the annual allocations of RTCs are the product of emission rates (e.g. pounds per million Btu of energy input) and throughput or activity levels (e.g. annual Btu's of energy input). Determining compliance thus requires that these two elements be measured, typically separately. Monitoring systems differ greatly in complexity and expense. The least expensive approach is to monitor throughput with a flow meter and use a standardized emission rate. The most expensive option is to monitor emission rates or total emissions using continuous emissions monitors (CEMs). Industry groups recommended that expensive CEMs only be required where they are appropriate and cost-effective, which is generally where they were required under the existing SCAQMD rules. Environmental groups tended to support the more expensive monitoring requirements, which appeared to provide greater accuracy. As noted, environmental groups opposed a RECLAIM market for VOCs in large part because of the difficulties with monitoring VOC emissions from diverse sources within a facility. During the deliberations, the SCAQMD evaluated various protocols that could be used to monitor emissions from different types of facilities.

The final RECLAIM program emphasized the use of CEMs. The RECLAIM rules include sections with details on protocols for measuring both NO_x and SO_x emissions. All major sources are required to install CEMs. As noted, the RECLAIM program passed by the SCAQMD Governing Board in October 1993 did not include VOCs.

4. CONCLUSIONS AND IMPLICATIONS

Translating the theory of emissions trading into a politically-acceptable and workable program in the Los Angeles basin was a major accomplishment. The development of RECLAIM provides several important lessons for future efforts to use emissions trading to achieve air quality objectives.

4.1. A cap-and-trade program can be developed for emitters in diverse sectors and in different size categories

RECLAIM provides an important prototype for including emitters from diverse sources in a single trading program. Other trading programs, such as the lead trading program for gasoline or the acid rain trading program for electric utilities, have included only a single sector. Including many sectors tends to magnify the potential gains from trade, because different sectors are likely to have widely different control costs.

RECLAIM includes facilities that generally emit more than four tons per year. This cut-off is considerably smaller than the size limit in the acid rain trading program. RECLAIM thus shows that large and medium-sized emitters can be included in a trading program.

4.2. Mobile and area sources can be included in a trading program

RECLAIM allows participants to use credits from mobile and area sources to meet emission targets. The prototype for these credit programs was a program to develop emission credits through scrapping older cars that was initially developed by a private company and included in RECLAIM. These credit provisions are also an example of how cap-and-trade programs and credit-based trading programs can be integrated.[17]

4.3. Acceptable caps can be set if they are based upon external criteria

Cap-and-trade programs differ from traditional command-and-control regulations because they limit overall emissions. Typical emission standards are expressed as rates (e.g. emissions per Btu) and thus do not directly cap total emissions. Firms that expect to expand output might be expected to oppose a cap-and-trade program because of the emissions cap.

The emissions cap in RECLAIM was acceptable to the affected industries because it mirrored the overall cap set under the AQMP. The SCAQMD has predicted the emission reductions that would achieved by the emission standards in the AQMP – as well as the resulting overall emissions – when it established the AQMP as a means of achieving compliance with ambient ozone standards. The implication was that emission standards for these sources would be tightened if overall emissions exceeded the targets. As a result, sources were willing to accept the declining emission caps set because they represented a more flexible means of achieving the emission reductions that had already been required under existing and planned regulations.

4.4. Acceptable initial allocations can be worked out

Determining initial allocations is inevitably a complex and 'messy' process. Issues of fairness and equity arise, often seen differently through the prisms of individual circumstances. The RECLAIM example shows that allocation formulas can be worked out that provide acceptable allocations to participants while at the same time providing regulatory agencies with assurance that starting points for trades are clear.

4.5. Simple solutions are often best for the many specific design elements that must be specified

There are an enormous number of design elements that must be specified in order to translate the theory of emissions trading into a specific program. In many cases, there is a trade-off between the 'ideal' and the 'practical.' For example, emissions in different time periods (e.g. seasons) and different locations clearly will have different effects on ambient ozone concentrations and exposure. An 'ideal' trading program would take these differences in account (e.g. by creating different trading ratios for emissions in different sub-regions). Incorporating such differences may, however, create an unwieldy or unworkable system.

RECLAIM tended to resolve these issues in favour of a workable program. For example, rather than setting up many different trading zones or trading ratios, RECLAIM simply differentiates between coastal (upwind) and inland (downwind) sources. Rather than creating separate markets or ratios for different months or seasons, trading is in terms of annual emissions. These and other simplifying features lead to a workable program that avoids collapsing from the weight of program details.

NOTES

[1] This paper builds on the author's experience as a consultant to the South Coast Air Quality Management District (SCAQMD) and to two other groups, the California Council for Environment and Economic Balance (CCEEB) and the Regulatory Flexibility Group (RFG). The author was a member of the Advisory Committee set up by the SCAQMD to assist in the development of RECLAIM and directed two reports on emissions trading in the South Coast air basin. The first report (Harrison and Nichols, 1990) provided background on emissions trading and developed a proposal for a broad-based trading program to deal with ozone precursors; this report was sponsored by CCEEB and presented at a workshop organized by the SCAQMD in December 1990 to initiate the process. The second report (Harrison and Nichols, 1992) analysed the economic impacts of RECLAIM; it was sponsored jointly by CCEEB and RFG and presented to the SCAQMD Governing Board. The author would like to thank (in alphabetical order) Patricia Leyden, Albert Nichols, David Pekelney, Victor Weisser, and Robert Wyman for contributions to previous reports and discussions of RECLAIM. The comments expressed in this paper, however, do not necessarily reflect the opinions of the SCAQMD, CCEEB, RFG, or the above-named individuals. The author alone is responsible for any errors or omissions the paper might contain.

[2] Dales (1968) is usually considered the first complete treatment of the theoretical advantages of the emissions trading approach.

[3] Hydrocarbon compounds that contribute to ozone are variously referred to as hydrocarbons, volatile organic compounds (VOCs), reactive organic gases (ROG), and reactive organic compounds (ROCs). I use the term VOCs in this paper.

[4] See Harrison and Nichols (1990) for additional discussion of the emissions trading programs that preceded RECLAIM.

[5] See Ellerman et al. (1997) for an excellent summary and analysis of the acid rain trading program.

[6] Many other issues arose during the deliberations surrounding RECLAIM. For example, concerns were raised about the economic impacts of RECLAIM on employment in the region and on small businesses in particular. The SCAQMD undertook a major study of the economic impacts of RECLAIM using a state-of-the-art regional economic model (see Johnson and Pekelney, 1996). Harrison and Nichols (1992) and Harrison (1994) discuss

the economic impacts of RECLAIM, including a case study of the economic impacts on small businesses.

[7] The major documents included: five Working Papers produced by SCAQMD staff released during the nine-month long feasibility study and a set of Summary Recommendations published in the Spring of 1992 (SCAQMD 1992); recommendations of the Regulatory Flexibility Group under the overall direction of Robert Wyman (Regulatory Flexibility Group 1991); and recommendations of the Coalition for Clean Air (1992) drafted by Joel Schwartz. As noted, NERA submitted a report sponsored by the RFG and CCEEB in March 1992 (Harrison and Nichols, 1992).

[8] The SCAQMD staff developed a RECLAIM program for VOCs, although it was not adopted by the Governing Board.

[9] These credit programs have been expanded. Mobile source credits can currently be obtained for car scrappage, vehicle repair, lower-emitting on- and off-road vehicles, truck stop electrification, and lower-emitting lawn and garden equipment. In addition, SCAQMD Rule 2506 allows credits for NO_X and SO_X emission reductions from area sources with a 10 per cent discount.

[10] Two other related issues were addressed with regard to the initial allocation: (1) would facilities lose their initial allocations for future years if they shut down? (2) would new facilities receive allocations? After considerable discussion, the SCAQMD decided not to confiscate allowances if facilities shut down and not to provide allocations to new facilities. The same decisions were made in the acid rain trading program.

[11] The cost savings can be affected if the allocation affects the transactions costs. See Stavins (1995).

[12] See Harrison (1996) for conceptual and empirical evaluations of the distributional implications of alternative initial allocations.

[13] This process – which was referred to as the mid-point or end-point 'shave' – involved reducing each facility's allocation by the per centage needed to achieve the overall AQMP target emissions.

[14] See SCAQMD (1993) for an explanation of the details of the RECLAIM allocation.

[15] This restriction on coastal sources applies to new or relocated sources and to existing sources whose allowances would exceed their initial allocation.

[16] See Harrison and Nichols (1990) and the sources cited therein for discussion of the administrative issues associated with EPA's ET programs and their impacts on the programs' usefulness.

[17] It may eventually be desirable to expand the RECLAIM cap-and-trade program to include mobile and area sources. For example, emissions from small combustion sources might be included by tracking fuel market sales.

REFERENCES

Coalition for Clean Air (1992), *Marketable Permits: The NO_x Universe – Recommendations of the Coalition for Clean Air*. Los Angeles, CA: Coalition for Clean Air, February.

Dales, J.H. (1968), *Pollution, Property and Prices*. Toronto, Ontario: University of Toronto Press.

Ellerman et al. (1997), *Emissions Trading Under the US Acid Rain Program: Evaluation of Compliance Costs and Allowance Market Performance*. Cambridge, MA: MIT Center for Energy and Environmental Policy Research.

Harrison, David Jr. (1988), *Economic Impacts of the Draft Air Quality Management Plan Proposed by the South Coast Air Quality Management District,* prepared for the California Council for Environmental and Economic Balance. Cambridge, MA: National Economic Research Associates, Inc., 5 December.

Harrison, David Jr. (1994), *The Distributive Effects of Economic Instruments for Environmental Policy.* Paris: Organisation for Economic Co-operation and Development.

Harrison, David Jr. (1996), *The Distributive Effects of Economic Instruments for Global Warming.* Paris: Organisation for Economic Co-operation and Development.

Harrison, David Jr. and Albert L. Nichols (1990), *Market-Based Approaches to Reduce the Cost of Clean Air in California's South Coast Basin,* prepared for the California Council for Environmental and Economic Balance. Cambridge, MA: National Economic Research Associates, Inc., 28 November.

Harrison, David Jr. and Albert L. Nichols (1992), *An Economic Analysis of the RECLAIM Trading Program for the South Cost Air Basin,* prepared for the Regulatory Flexibility Group and the California Council for Environmental and Economic Balance. Cambridge, MA: National Economic Research Associates, Inc., March.

Johnson, Scott Lee and David M. Pekelney (1996), 'Economic Assessment of the Regional Clean Air Incentives Market: A New Emissions Trading Program for Los Angeles,' *Land Economics* 72(3), 277–297, August.

Regulatory Flexibility Group (1991), *A Marketable Permits Program for the South Coast: Recommendations of the Regulatory Flexibility Group.* Los Angeles, CA: Latham & Watkins, 20 December.

South Coast Air Quality Management District (1992), *RECLAIM: Marketable Permits Program Summary Recommendations.* Los Angeles: South Coast Air Quality Management District, Spring.

South Coast Air Quality Management District (1993), *RECLAIM: Volume 1: Development Report and Proposed Rules*, Revised Draft. Los Angeles, CA: South Coast Air Quality Management District, July.

Stavins, Robert N. (1995), 'Transactions Costs and Tradable Permits', *Journal of Environmental Economics and Management*, **29**, 133–147.

PART II

Introducing Trading in Europe

5. Emissions trading in the European Union: practice and prospects

Ger Klaassen

1. INTRODUCTION

Broadening the range of instruments is one of the key priorities of the EU's environmental policy. The Commission of the European Communities has recently agreed a communication on environmental taxes, charges and levies in the single market (COM (97) 9) and has also adopted a communication on environmental agreements (COM (96) 561 final). It has remained relatively silent, however, on the use of emissions trading. This is remarkable since there is now extensive practical experience in the use of such instruments and growing demands to use emissions trading to tackle the problem of climate change.

The objective of this chapter is to discuss the potential contribution of emissions trading to the environmental policy of the EU. This is done by giving a broad-brush and incomplete overview of the practical experience with emissions trading in the EU, followed by a discussion of the potential for extending the use of the instrument.

This chapter uses a broad definition of emissions trading which encompasses:

- *tradable permits:* where there is up front allocation of emission rights to individual polluters and organized trade;
- *bubbles/netting:* where a group of plants is allocated a maximum level of pollution;
- *offsets:* where individual polluters are allowed to take measures at other polluting sources to meet legally required emission reductions; and
- *joint implementation (JI):* where two or more parties co-operate to jointly achieve a total emissions objective, with flexibility in the relative contribution of different parties.

2. EXISTING USE OF EMISSIONS TRADING IN THE EU

2.1. Introduction

This section describes the design, cost-effectiveness and environmental effectiveness of a number of emissions trading schemes in the EU. The section first discusses international trading schemes and then evaluates a number of national schemes.

2.2. International transfers of ozone depleting substances

Transfers under the Montreal Protocol
In 1987, a number of countries signed the Montreal Protocol to control substances that deplete the ozone layer and agreed that both the production and consumption of CFCs and Halons should be reduced to their 1986 levels. The Protocol was amended in 1990 to include a complete phase-out of the production and use of CFCs by the year 2000, together with the inclusion of three more ozone depleting substances. This was followed by further amendments in 1992 which adjusted the phase-out schedules and extended controls to further substances. The Protocol regulates both the production and consumption of ozone depleting substances, where consumption is defined as production plus imports minus exports (Klaassen, 1996). It allows parties (countries) to transfer production quotas to other parties for the purpose of industrial rationalization aiming at economic efficiency or in response to anticipated shortfalls in supply resulting from plant closures. The production quotas are allocated to the parties on the basis of their 1986 levels of production.

In the original Montreal Protocol, the following rules for the transfer of production quotas applied:

- the total combined levels of production of the parties concerned were not allowed to exceed the agreed overall production limit;
- the transfers were not allowed to increase individual production levels by more than 10 (1992 and later) to 15 per cent (beyond 1998) of the base-year (1986) level; and
- the secretariat had to be notified of transfers no later than the time of the transfer.

With the amendments of 1992, the transfer of production quotas was extended to all pollutants and the 10 to 15 per cent restriction was removed. Parties were allowed to transfer any portion of their calculated level of production of any of the controlled substances, provided that the total level of production did not exceed the overall limit. The secretariat still had to be notified of the transfers, their terms, and the period for which they apply.

Ozone trading in the European Union

The EC has translated the Montreal Protocol commitments in a separate regulation (Council regulation (EEC) No. 594/91 of 4 March 1991). This was amended in 1992 (Council regulation (EC) No. 3952/92) and 1994 (Council Regulation (EC) No. 3093/94) to enable a more rapid phase-out of ozone depleting substances and to incorporate new substances. These regulations limit the import of ozone depleting substances and allocate production and consumption quotas to individual producers (chemical companies). Consumption rights are described as rights to place products on the market either for own use (in products) or by others (such as export), or use in the Community prior to phase-out.

Both production and consumption quotas are allocated to producers on the basis of base year production levels (1986 or 1989, depending on the substance controlled). Table 5.1 gives an overview of the allocation of production rights for CFCs and Halons after the 1991 regulation and with the 1992/1994 regulation.

Table 5.1 Allocation of CFC production rights in the EU[1] (1986 = 100)

Regulation	Pollutant	1992	1993	1994	1995	1998
1991	CFCs	100	50	50	32.5	0
	Halons	100	100	100	50	0
1992	CFCs	100	50	15	0^2	0
	Halons	100	100	0	0^2	0

Notes:
1. Production of CFCs and Halons (Annex I substances).
2. Except for essential uses in case of Halons and with one year delay for CFC's from minor producers.

Source: EC regulation 594/91 and EC regulation 3952/92

The producers are allowed to exceed their allocated production levels either domestically, within the EC, or with any other party to the Protocol, provided that the sum of the calculated production levels does not increase. They can also transfer consumption rights but they cannot use a consumption right without having a production right as well. In this way consumption and production are linked. In the case of international transfers, both the EC and the member states involved have to agree beforehand. In the case of national transfers, only the member state has to agree and the EC has to be notified.

Consumption rights are only transferable to other producers within the EC and the EC has to be notified.

Producers, importers, and exporters have to report data to both the EC and the member states on: production; quantities recycled or destroyed; stocks; imports; exports; and amounts placed on the market. This information is audited by an independent consultant. Enforcement is up to the member state.

Cost savings
Estimates of the cost savings of the transfers are not available (Klaassen, 1996). Table 5.2 shows that from 1991 to 1994, 19 transfers (covering one year periods) involving EU companies took place. Four trades covered transfers for more than one year (totalling eleven annual transfers). The amount transferred was 123460 tonnes of CFCs (Group I), or 13 per cent of the allowable production. The majority of the transfers were between EU companies and were intrafirm rather than interfirm. The number of transfers increased in 1993 and 1994 because allowable production levels were cut back considerably in 1994 and complete phase-out was planned for 1995.

The principal reason for the transfers is the cost savings involved in concentrating the remaining production since the production of CFCs is subject to considerable economies of scale. Transaction costs are low because the number of firms involved is small and pre-approval of the transfers requires little administration. Transfers are usually accepted although delays may occur. The EU refused transfers of CFCs in two cases. In one case the transfer was not approved by the Member State involved and the transfer periods were not in line with the specified control periods. In the other case the transfer involved a country without an agreed production ceiling. Initially transfers faced higher transaction costs since the interpretation of EU rules was disputed. It was unclear whether production rights could be transferred without transferring consumption rights as well and whether transferring consumption rights would infringe EU competition rules. In several cases approval was delayed because approval from individual member states was delayed. The rules were clarified in the course of 1993.

Environmental effectiveness
The trading provisions in the Montreal Protocol have had a significant positive impact on the achievement of the Protocol's environmental goals. The transfers enabled parties to agree upon a rapid phase-out since it enabled the chemical companies to concentrate production and shift rapidly to more profitable substitutes. Problems existed with transfers to article 5 (developing) countries that have no agreed production and consumption limits as the baseline for transfers was unclear. In practice, transfers with

Table 5.2 Transfers of CFCs involving EU companies (Group I)

Year	Allowable production (tonnes)	Amount transferrred (tonnes)	Total No.	Transfers (no.) of which			
				EU-Internal	with non-EU	intra-firm	inter-firm
1991/92[1]	644069	27100	4	4	0	4	0
1993	214690	53645	7	7	0	6	1
1994	64407	42715	8	5	3	7	1
TOTAL	923166	123460	19	16	3	17	2

Notes:
1. This pertains to 1/7/91 – 31/12/92.

Source: Internal EC files on industrial rationalization (until May 1997)

article 5 parties appear to bear the risk of being rejected (Peaple, 1993). Problems existed also with US companies because the baselines under US legislation were either allowed or actual production for US firms, whatever was lower. In this case EU firms wanting to sell to US firms had to meet the stricter US regulation of actual production levels rather than allowed production under EU legislation. Transferability of production quotas has not led to an increase in actual production since approval was rejected in these cases.

2.3. National emissions trading schemes

Offsets in FRG
In Germany the transfer of emission reduction obligations is possible for air pollution. Two rules exist: the plant renewal clause and the compensation rule. The operation of these rules should be seen in light of the two-tier strategy aimed at maintaining air quality standards on the one hand, and minimizing emissions as far as technically possible on the other hand (Schärer, 1994). Similar rules exist in Austria (Glatz et al., 1990, pp. 47–48). The plant renewal clause pertains to the construction of new plants in areas where air quality standards are exceeded. In principle, the Federal Immission Protection Law and the Technical Guidelines for Air Pollution Control rule out construction of such plants, even if these plants meet the state-of-the-art emission standards. The 1974 technical guidelines, however, do allow the construction of a new plant in a non-attainment area if the new plant replaces an existing plant of the same kind. These plants need not be from the same firm, but must be located in the same area. In 1983 these guidelines were extended: not only the closing of an existing plant but also its renovation could be used to offset the additional emissions of a new plant. The offsets, however, would have to lead to a

reduction in the annual average pollutant concentration in the area, and the new plant would have to meet the state-of-the-art emission standards.

The compensation rule was included in the 1986 revision of the technical guidelines. As part of the revision, existing installations had to be modernized to meet the stricter emission standards, usually within five years. The core of the compensation rule is that the clean-up period can be extended to eight years if emission reduction measures taken at existing installations (by the firm or by other firms) would provide more emission reductions than would otherwise result from the application of the technical guidelines for each individual plant. This compensation rule can only be used by installations within the same geographical area of impact and for the same pollutants or for pollutants with comparable impacts.

The cost-effectiveness of the plant renewal clause is limited, because air quality standards are only exceeded in a few areas. The rules of the clause further restrict its cost-effectiveness. The clause can only be used if the additional impact of the plant on ambient concentrations is limited to 1 per cent, if the additional emissions are offset by emission reductions of plants in the same area, and if the new plant starts operating after the improvement of the existing plant becomes effective. Furthermore, the clause does not apply to the location of new plants in attainment areas, even if this would lead to an exceedance of air quality standards.

The contribution of the compensation rule to cost savings is also small. The rule has been used in only 359 out of 21,154 clean-up cases (Bundesregierung, 1996). 43 per cent of these cases took place in the former Eastern Germany and the remainder in Western Germany. The most important reasons for its restricted use are (Schärer, 1994; Sprenger, 1989):

- the short time limit for compiling renewal plans (one year);
- the stringent emission reduction requirements at existing installations;
- the necessity of multiple trades since most new firms emit more than one pollutant; and
- the small size of the areas in which offsets are allowed.

The environmental impact of both the renewal clause and compensation rule is neutral to positive. The renewal clause prevents increases in emissions in non-attainment areas. The compensation rule can only be used if total emissions are reduced further (Sprenger, 1989).

Power plants bubbles in the Netherlands
In 1990, the State of the Netherlands and the 12 provincial governments signed a covenant with the association of electricity producers (SEP) on the reduction of sulphur dioxide (SO_2) and nitrogen oxides (NO_x) emissions (SEP, 1991). The covenant establishes ceilings on the total emissions of both

pollutants from the public power plants, which results in lower emissions than would have resulted from existing legislation in the form of emission and fuel standards. The ceilings offer the electricity producers a means to reduce emissions in a more cost-effective way than requiring similar emission standards for classes of installations. Similar bubble agreements exist in Belgium, Denmark, and the United Kingdom (HMIP, 1996; CEC, 1995).

The objective of the covenant is to reduce SO_2 emissions to 18 ktonnes and NO_x emissions to 30 ktonnes by the year 2000. In 1989, emissions of SO_2 and NO_x from the SEP were 41 ktonnes and 74 ktonnes respectively. Although there are four electricity producers, decisions on the fuel use and the utilization of the power plants are made by the SEP. The costs of production are also settled by the SEP and distributed among the producers. In a sense the bubble implies intrafirm rather than interfirm trading, because the SEP operates as a kind of holding company.

The SEP can implement the bubbles within certain limitations:

- Existing power plants have to meet the existing emission standards.
- Relatively new plants have to meet more stringent emission standards, laid down in the covenant.

Regarding enforcement and monitoring, the SEP has to produce a plan for reducing emissions which must be judged by an expert commission. The SEP has to report to this commission every two years. Individual producers have to report to both the provinces and the SEP. The provinces agree to implement the covenant, but can impose more stringent requirements if necessary in order to meet local air quality standards. Parties can alter the covenant in the case of unexpected environmental changes or if electricity demand or imports depart substantially from what was planned. The parties can also dismiss the covenant if they cannot agree on the emission reduction plans or if the ceilings cannot be met by any reasonable means. This can only be done if consultations have failed.

The electricity producers expect that the covenant will save them half of the additional costs (around 500 million guilders) compared to an alternative policy of setting stricter uniform emission standards to meet the same ceiling. The cost savings are achieved by applying more effective pollution control equipment on those combustion installations that have a longer remaining lifetime, have more operating hours per year, or have to be upgraded anyway (Klaassen, 1996).

Regarding environmental effectiveness, the question is whether the covenant can indeed meet the total emission ceiling. On the one hand, the covenant offers several possibilities to exceed the caps (such as use of CHP, modifications to electricity forecasts and non-operating FGD) and the SEP can eventually back out of the agreement. On the other hand, the government can respond by threatening the more expensive alternative: setting more stringent uniform emission standards in new legislation. The SO_2 target for the year 2000 was, however, already reached in 1994. This implies that the target for 1994 was overachieved. The expected decrease in NO_x emissions is such that the targeted emission levels for both 1994 and 2000 are expected to be met (SEP, 1994).

2.4. Concluding observations on EU experience

To date, experience with emissions trading concepts in the EU has been relatively restricted. Only one international system has been successfully employed and a restricted number of member states have embarked on the use of sector specific bubbles and offset systems. No EU country has implemented full emissions trading so far, although the EU-wide trading of ozone depleting substances goes a long way.

According to experts from the EU member states, the following barriers exist for a more widespread implementation of emissions trading schemes (CEC, 1997a):

- existing national and international legislation and permitting procedures may be incompatible with trading emission rights or may limit their application;
- the geographical dependence of many pollution problems creates difficulties since restrictions on trade will either raise transaction cost or leave the market too thin to really develop;
- existing legislation has already led to significant investments in pollution control equipment which limits the scope for cost savings from trading;
- the initial distribution of permits is thought to be a significant political problem and industry has so far been unenthusiastic about trading; and
- the reliance upon traditional environmental regulations has created a cultural barrier to the introduction of market based solutions.

In spite of these barriers, interest in EU countries is growing and several countries are studying the use of emissions trading to solve particular problems.

3. POTENTIAL SCOPE FOR EMISSIONS TRADING IN THE EU

3.1. Introduction

One could envisage two principal tasks for the EU with regard to the use of emissions trading:

* to develop and implement *international* (among member states, EU-wide and possibly wider) trading schemes.
* to facilitate the use of *national* emissions trading schemes by member states.

A number of criteria can be used to examine the potential scope for emissions trading:

* cost-effectiveness (reaching the environmental objective at lowest costs);
* environmental effectiveness (the extent to which the environmental objectives are met);
* administrative practicability (ease of monitoring and enforcement, information requirements and administrative costs); and
* political acceptability (distribution of costs and benefits and the compatibility with the existing institutional framework).

A number of circumstances influence the success or failure of an emissions trading scheme in practice, including: the type of pollutant; the number of participating sources and their market power; the level of transaction costs and the legal status and certainty of pollution rights (Heister et al., 1990). These will have to be borne in mind when assessing the potential scope for introducing trading. The remainder of this section will first examine the scope for international trading schemes and then look at the facilitation of national trading schemes.

3.2. International emissions trading schemes

Introduction
This section gives a rough indication of the potential scope for international emissions trading schemes. It is based on a restricted literature review and personal contacts with policy makers in the field of climate change and transboundary air pollution. Table 5.3 gives an indicative assessment of the potential scope for the use of international emissions trading schemes for a number of pollutants.

Table 5.3 The potential scope for EU-wide emissions trading schemes

	Potential cost savings (billion ECU/year)	Environmental effectiveness	Practicability	Political acceptability
1. CO_2 - worldwide	43-135[1]	high	medium	medium
2. CO_2 -EU	5-13[2]	high	medium	medium
3. Ozone depleting substances	low	high	high	high
4. SO_2	0. 1 to 6[3]	medium	low	low
5. Ground level ozone	low	low-medium	low	low

Notes:
1. See Bollen et al. (1996). Lowest cost saving is for standstill in 2005 and JI among Annex I countries only. Highest cost saving is for 10% reduction compared to 1990 and JI for all countries.
2. Estimate based on CEC (1997b) for a reduction of 10 to 15% in CO_2 emissions compared to 1990 for the EU in 2010. Coherence (1991) and Barrett (1992) provide earlier estimates.
3. Lower estimate based on scheme that meets deposition targets with legal constraints. Higher estimate based on single zone trading throughout Europe without deposition constraints (Klaassen, 1996).

Trading greenhouse gases

The scope for international carbon dioxide (CO_2) trading schemes is significant. Cost savings may range from around 5 to 13 billion ECU per year for a system that assumes trading of national quotas in the EU for reductions of 10 to 15 per cent compared to 1990 (CEC, 1997b). More substantial cost savings can be envisaged when this system would be implemented in all developed countries or even world wide. This figure should be regarded as indicative: first, a number of cost-effective options were not included in the analysis; and second, the assessments assume that countries actually trade in order to minimize costs and that all sectors are subject to trading schemes. Including small industries, transport and households may lead to excessively high transaction costs (Koutstaal, 1997) although some believe this to be feasible (Heister et al., 1990). Even restricting trading to the electricity sector in the EU, covering 30 per cent of the emissions, could lead to significant cost savings in absolute terms.

The environmental effectiveness of emissions trading is, in principle, relatively high for CO_2 emissions and greenhouse gases since the location of the sources does not matter, and only the absolute volume of emissions counts. As with the Montreal Protocol, problems might occur if countries or firms are allowed to trade with partners in countries that have no agreed national emission ceilings. If emissions trading or joint implementation was applied to countries or companies that have been allocated individual emission rights, the environmental result should be equivalent to that without trading. With sufficient monitoring and enforcement, emissions trading guarantees that the ceilings are met. The environmental effectiveness hinges very much on whether emission rights are allocated up front or determined on a case-by-case basis. If countries without agreed baseline are involved or emission rights are allocated for projects such as deforestation for which allocation of baseline emissions is disputed there will be uncertainty on the extent to which real emission reductions have been achieved.

The administrative practicality of the system is unknown. Emission inventories will have to be drawn for every type of CO_2 policy. If trading is included, extra efforts may be required for negotiating the initial permit distribution, for the registration of permit transfers and possibly for monitoring. If JI with countries without agreed emission ceilings is introduced, the administrative problems will increase. In this case, the determination of the baseline emission allocation may be a controversial and cumbersome procedure, as experience with EPA's emissions trading policy has shown (Klaassen, 1996).

The political acceptability is more difficult to judge. Most EU member states seem to prefer the use of taxes to control CO_2 emissions and some suggest that there is no room for emissions trading as an additional economic instrument. The Community and a number of developing countries are reluctant to embrace joint implementation since they believe that developed countries should reduce emissions at home first. Some EU member states, the USA and other developed countries are actively promoting the introduction of joint implementation and emissions trading in the new Protocol to the Framework Convention on Climate Change (FCCC). The EU itself has already settled for joint implementation implicitly since it is striving to meet its reduction commitment for the EU as a whole. This implicitly allows trading off emission reduction commitments among the EU member states. A political advantage of a system of emissions trading would be that it would fit well with ongoing climate negotiations which aim at differentiated ceilings for signatory countries. The setting of binding quantitative ceilings as a first step (allocation of initial rights) in an emissions trading program may be difficult to negotiate as these ceilings may restrict the growth of individual sectors or countries. Stakeholders might prefer more flexible instruments such as negotiated agreements. Emissions trading of course may ease these difficulties by providing the means to adjust individual ceilings in a cost effective manner. Summarizing, the potential cost savings of CO_2 trading are significant, but the political acceptability of such a system and its compatibility with a system of taxes remains a primary concern.

Ozone depleting substances

Transfers of ozone depleting substances have been shown to work in practice. The analysis in the previous section revealed that the possibility to transfer rights was actively employed. The environmental objectives were met, the administrative requirements were simple and the political acceptability was high. The system of transfer should be extended to new substances and the approval process should be simplified.

Trading sulphur dioxide emissions

The potential costs savings of Europe-wide SO_2 trading can be significant (Klaassen, 1996). Since the environmental objectives consist of meeting air quality or acid deposition standards at specific locations, constraints need to be built into international trading schemes. Effective constraints lead to a significant reduction in the potential cost savings. The achievable cost savings are also constrained by existing national and EU legislation prescribing fuel and emission standards for source categories. Negotiations on the joint implementation of agreed national ceilings for SO_2 under the Second Sulphur Protocol did in principle create a legal opening for international trading among countries. However, the parties to the convention have so far been unable to reach final agreement on the rules and conditions that should guide emissions trading. The prime reason for this is that countries are sceptical that significant cost savings are available and they are afraid that joint implementation would allow acid deposition in their own countries to increase.

Ground level ozone

Two precursor substances (NO_x and VOCs) lead to the formation of ground level ozone. A major problem is that the location of the emitting sources as well as the amount emitted determine the environmental impacts. Again this might imply constraints on a trading scheme that could reduce the potential savings. On the other hand (inter-regional) emissions trading schemes for ozone precursors are actually in place in the USA. Since air quality standards for ozone appear very difficult to attain without significant emission reductions, costs are likely to be high so the potential cost savings of inter-regional trading in parts of the EU may well be significant. However, actual EU legislation such as the VOC Directive on industrial plants will tend to limit cost savings in practice since it requires meeting emission limit values or drawing up national plans to meet the same reductions. The environmental effectiveness and the administrative practicability of such schemes requires further analysis. The political acceptability of the scheme might suffer from the same problems as SO_2 trading.

In conclusion, the scope for international trading seems to be especially constrained by its limited political acceptability. In view of the potential cost savings, and the existing experience with ozone depleting substances, efforts may have to focus on greenhouse gases, while taking into account political sensitivities and the compatibility with other instruments.

3.3. Promoting the use of national emissions trading schemes

The EU could also stimulate the use of national emissions trading schemes by member states in that it:

- promotes the use of national emissions trading schemes by clarifying and/or creating the legal conditions for the use of this instrument; and
- explicitly allows the use of emissions trading in community legislation geared at solving specific environmental problems.

First of all, clarifying the conditions under which member states can use emissions trading schemes could promote the actual use of the instrument. For example, the Commission of the European Communities has finalized a Communication on the use of environmental agreements (COM (96) 561 final) which provides general guidelines for guaranteeing the transparency of negotiated agreements. Similarly, the Commission finalized a Communication on environmental taxes, charges and levies in the Single Market (COM (97) 9) which explains the legal framework for the use of environmental taxes and charges in member states. A similar Communication could be envisaged on emissions trading. This is only meaningful if the existence of uncertainty on EU legislation constitutes a major barrier for implementing national trading schemes. According to environmental economic experts of the EU member states, uncertainty on EU legislation is not a major barrier to the introduction of emissions trading (CEC, 1997a). Others, however, believe that uncertainty, especially on the compatibility of the EU's Integrated Pollution Prevention and Control Directive (CEC, 1996) with emissions trading, is a major concern so this warrants attention.

The objective of the IPPC Directive is to achieve integrated pollution prevention and control for a number of (mainly industrial) activities so as to achieve a high level of protection for the environment as a whole. Installations under IPPC can only operate with a permit. This permit may cover one or more installations on the same site operated by the same operator. The permits have to include limit values which are to be based on BAT (Best Available Techniques), without prescribing a specific technique. Best available techniques means:

- 'Best': most effective in achieving a high level of protection for the environment as a whole;
- 'Available': developed on the appropriate scale, under economically and technically viable conditions, taking into consideration cost and advantages, and reasonably accessible;
- 'Techniques': the technology used as well as its design, maintenance, operation and decommissioning.

The limit values are defined as the mass, concentration or level of an emission which may not be exceeded during one or more periods of time and may be supplemented or replaced by equivalent parameters or technical measures. The limit values shall take account of the technical characteristics, the geographical location and local environmental conditions as well as long distance or transboundary pollution. The Directive requires that member states introduce legislation and administrative procedures for its implementation. The Directive does not have to be transposed word-for-word into member state legislation, but its results have to be achieved both in law and in practice. Is emissions trading compatible with the Directive? Clearly, the Directive explicitly allows netting: a joint permit for installations at the same site operated by the same operator. In addition, member states can always set more stringent measures than required under IPPC and must even do this if it is needed to meet environmental quality standards set out in EU legislation. These additional measures (going beyond BAT defined in IPPC) could take the form of emissions trading. In line with the BAT requirements of the IPPC Directive, such more stringent measures could imply one of the following:

- limitation or modification of economic activities of installations concerned;
- utilization of techniques considered not to be available under economically and technically viable conditions;
- use of techniques for which costs outweigh advantages.

Although the information exchange on BAT prescribed in the Directive helps to clarify the meaning of BAT in practice, there is enough leeway to allow more concrete, but tradable emission rights to play a complementary role to BAT under IPPC. In conclusion, national emissions trading schemes can be combined with the IPPC Directive provided that IPPC requirements are fulfilled.

Secondly, the Commission could more systematically address the use of emissions trading when preparing environmental legislation geared at solving particular environmental problems. A good example of this type is the draft Directive on VOC emissions from solvent using industries (COM

(96) 538). The Directive's main elements are: i) emission limit values for new installations in certain sectors; ii) emission limit values for existing installations to be met by 2007; and iii) the possibility for member states to implement a national plan that would use other means to achieve the same emission reduction as would be achieved by the limit values. The Directive therefore allows member states a certain flexibility to meet the same emission reduction at less cost by implementing economic instruments. Another example is the Directive on Large Combustion Plants of 1988 which prescribes emission standards for new plants and sets a ceiling on the total emissions from existing plants. The latter allows member states to implement more flexible, 'a la carte' solutions, such as the national bubbles for the electricity sector that have been used in various member states such as Belgium, Denmark, the Netherlands and the United Kingdom as means to comply in a more cost-effective way.

3.4. Possible areas for introducing emissions trading in EU legislation

Not all pollutants are equally suited to emissions trading. Table 5.4 gives an indicative overview of the extent to which pollutants qualify for the use of tradable permits (Heister et al., 1990).

Table 5.4 Pollutants that potentially qualify for national emissions trading schemes

Air	Water	Soil
$++ CO_2$	– euthrophying	- household waste
$++$ CFC/Halons	components	- other waste
$+$ nitrogen oxide	-- heavy metals	
$+$ sulphur dioxide		
- carbon monoxide		
$+$ volatile organic		
compounds		
-- particulate matter		
-- noise		

Notes: $++$ appropriate $+$ less appropriate
         - less suitable   -- unsuitable

CO_2 is especially equipped to be the subject of an emissions trading scheme although the technical and administrative requirements are not to be underestimated. The same holds for ozone depleting substances and other greenhouse gases. Nitrogen oxides and sulphur dioxide offer possibilities although the potential cost savings may be limited since technical measures have already been implemented to a large extent. Hot spots might require trading to be restricted to regional markets which will limit the potential cost savings. Similarly, the scope for VOC trading may be limited by the multitude of compounds involved, and the local and peak occurrence of the ozone smog (Heister et al., 1990). Practical experience in California with NO_x trading showed that trading for ozone precursors is not impossible. The potential for carbon monoxide is small since the environmental effects are highly localized. The application for particulate matter is problematic because of the lack of data on the actual sources contributing to the problem. Studies in the US suggest significant cost savings of emissions trading schemes in urban settings (Klaassen, 1996). Finally, noise pollution is unsuited to emissions trading due to its very local character.

For water pollution, emissions trading for euthrophying pollutants is conceivable but would be confined to point source industrial polluters. Agricultural sources would necessarily be excluded. Furthermore, the combination with public waste water treatment facilities and existing charge systems may limit the scope for trading. This is mainly so since pollution control equipment and institutions are already in place. The fact that pollution control equipment is in place means the potential cost savings are smaller since we have sunk costs. The fact that an institutional setting is present implies that political barriers (adjustment costs) are likely to be high. The net benefits of the change towards emissions trading might not outweigh the adjustment costs of making the change. Similarly, heavy metals trading could be envisaged for industrial sources, but not for agriculture and traffic. Local hot spots as well as the use of existing pollution control measures might limit the potential. Household waste is in principal a problem of quantity due to restricted availability of waste depositories and a problem of externalities in the form of gaseous emissions from waste depositories. In this case a price policy seems to be a more appropriate instrument. For dangerous waste, technical measures aimed at reducing the impact that cause the problem appear to be more appropriate.

In conclusion, a number of air pollutants are potentially attractive for the use of national emissions trading schemes, but the scope is more limited for water pollution and solid wastes. Experts from the EU member states (CEC, 1997a) recently identified the following priorities:

- increase the knowledge-base and exchange of information on emissions trading;
- analyse the scope for trading greenhouse gases, especially on a world-wide level; and
- create room in specific EU legislation for measures to implement national emissions trading schemes.

4. CONCLUSIONS AND DISCUSSION

This chapter examined the potential scope for emissions trading in the European Union. Emissions trading (-like) schemes have so far had limited application in the EU. However, where they have been implemented their use has been successful: pollution costs have been reduced, sometimes significantly, and environmental objectives have been met in a more flexible manner. The chapter suggested that policy interventions from the EU could consist of two types of tasks:

- to develop and implement *international* (EU-wide and possibly wider) trading schemes
- to facilitate the use of *national* emissions trading schemes

The analysis suggests that while the scope for international emissions trading schemes is restricted, the trading of greenhouse gas emissions may offer some promise. Here, the potential cost savings are considerable and it appears to be administratively feasible. The political acceptability of such a scheme, however, is currently an issue of concern. The EU could probably reap the highest net benefits if it systematically creates scope for the use of national emissions trading schemes when drafting specific legislation and clarifies EU legislation affecting emissions trading where necessary. The areas which seem to fit best are air pollution problems at a national scale.

ACKNOWLEDGEMENTS

This chapter represents the personal opinion of the author and does not necessarily reflect the views of the European Commission. Comments from David Noble, Michel Racquet, Jan Scherp, Massimo Suardi, Geoff Tierney, Peter Wicks and Steve Sorrell on (parts) of this chapter, as well as discussions with participants at the ENVECO meeting on 25 February 1997 in Brussels, are appreciated.

REFERENCES

Barrett, S. (1992), 'Reaching a CO_2 emission limitation agreement for the Community: implications for equity and cost-effectiveness', in *European Economy*, Special Edition No. 1: the economics of limiting CO_2 emissions', Commission of the European Communities, Brussels, pp. 3–25.
Bollen, J.C., A. Toet and H. de Vries (1996), 'Evaluating cost-effective strategies for meeting regional CO_2 targets', *Global Environmental Change*, chapter 153.

Bundesregierung (1996), 'Sechster Emissionschutzbericht der Bundesregierung', Bonn. Drucksache 13/4825, Deutscher Bundestag 13 Wahlperiode.

Coherence (1991), *Cost-effectiveness Analysis of CO₂ reduction options,* synthesis report and country reports, Commission of the European Communities, Brussels, May.

Commission of the European Commission (1995), *Report from the Commission to the Council on the implementation of the Large Combustion Plants Directive 88/609/EEC,* Brussels.

Commission of the European Communities (1996), Council Directive 96/96/EC of 24 September 1996 concerning integrated pollution prevention and control, *Official Journal of the European Communities,* **39**, 10 October, Brussels.

Commission of the European Communities (1997a), *Minutes of ENVECO meeting of 25–26 February 1997,* DG XI, Brussels.

Commission of the European Communities (1997b), 'Climate change – Analysis of proposed EU emission reduction objectives for Kyoto', Commission Staff Working Paper (unpublished).

Glatz, H., C. Krajasits and E. Pohl (1990), 'Mehr Markt oder mehr Staat in der Umweltpolitik? Umweltzertifikate und kontingente als Instrumente der Umweltpolitik', Österreichischer Arbeiterkammertag, Wien.

Heister, J., P. Michaelis and E. Mohr (1990), *Praktische Einsatzmöglichkeiten für Zertifikate im Rahmen marktwirtschaftlicher Umweltpolitik in der Bundesrepublik Deutschland und in der EG,* Institut für Weltwirtschaft an der Universität, Kiel.

Her Majesty's Inspectorate of Pollution (1996), 'Background Brief on the Electricity Supply Industry', 26 March, London.

Klaassen, G. (1996), *Acid Rain and Environmental Degradation; the Economics of Emissions trading,* Edward Elgar, Cheltenham, UK, and Lyme, US.

Koutstaal, P. (1997), *Economic Policy and Climate Change: Tradable Permits for Reducing Carbon Emissions,* Edward Elgar, Cheltenham, UK, and Lyme, US.

Peaple, N. (1993), Interview. EC DGXI, Brussels, 15 December.

Schärer, B. (1994), 'Economic incentives in air pollution control: the case of Germany', *European Environment,* **4**(3), 3–8.

SEP (1991), *Plan van aanpak ter uitvoering van het convenant over de bestrijding van SO₂ and NOₓ,* Samenwerkende Electriciteits Producenten, Arnhem.

SEP (1994), *2e Voortgangsrapportage betreffende de bestrijding van SO₂- en NOx-emissies van de electriciteitsproduktie bedrijven in de jaren 1992 en 1993 in het kader van het convenant,* Samenwerkende Electriciteits Producenten, Arnhem.

Sprenger, R.-U. (1989), 'Economic incentives in environmental policies: the case of Western Germany', chapter prepared for the Prince Bertil Symposium on economic instruments in national and international environmental protection policies, Hasselby Castle, Stockholm.

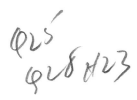

6.   Designing a scheme for SO_2 trading in Norway

Geir Høibye

1. BACKGROUND

In 1989, the Confederation of Norwegian Business and Industry (NHO) together with the other Nordic Industrial Federations engaged the Norwegian Centre for Economic Studies (ECON) to examine the role of emissions trading in the European response to climate change. The study included an examination of the economic benefits of US trading schemes, and made detailed proposals for a cost effective climate change trading scheme in Europe. The study was presented to the Norwegian authorities in 1991. This was the starting point of the Norwegian government's engagement in what later became the concept of joint implementation (JI) in the climate change negotiations. While Norway has led the field in this area, the benefits of this approach are now accepted by the majority of Annex I countries.

In this way, tradable permits and joint implementation form a central part of NHO's present work on climate change. We do not believe, however, that a trading scheme for greenhouse gases (GHGs) within Norway is a workable option. Instead, we believe that the greatest potential lies with international trading and joint implementation. These can be integrated into Norway's existing cabon dioxide (CO_2) taxation and the voluntary agreements between industry and government. Engagement in international projects through either JI or trading could be an attractive and cost effective alternative to fulfilling Norway's commitments in the Kyoto agreement. Should the possibility be provided, it will be up to the government to make it a reality.

Norway first introduced CO_2 taxes in 1992, and they currently are of the order of 18–20$/barrel of oil.[1] The taxes are levied on off-shore gas use, gasoline, diesel and heating oil, and coal used for heating purposes.[2] In total, the CO_2 tax applies to 60 per cent of total emissions. For the sectors covered, most of the cheap options for reducing CO_2 emissions should already have been utilized. Energy intensive industries are exempt from the tax, but are instead subject to long term voluntary agreements to reduce greenhouse gas emissions per unit of output.[3] With a 100 per cent hydroelectric system, there are limited possibilities to reduce emission from utilities.

To reduce CO_2 emissions in other countries by trading and joint implementation would be a cost effective way of meeting Norway's future commitments in a new Protocol. To be effective, this should not be confined to governments but should also involve industry. They must therefore be given appropriate incentives in domestic climate change instruments to do this.

The potential for trading in the area of climate change forms the backdrop for NHO's proposals on sulphur dioxide (SO_2) trading. This is a means to win first hand experience with trading, while helping to solve a priority environmental problem in Norway in an cost-effective way. Experience in domestic emissions trading can be of value for future engagement in international trading, both for Norwegian industry and for the government.

2. THE SULPHUR PROTOCOL

Norway is one of 30 signatories to the 1979 UNECE Convention on Long Range Transboundary Air Pollution (CLRTAP). Two Protocols for the control of sulphur emissions have been agreed under this Convention, with the second being signed in Oslo on 14 June 1994. This Protocol was based on Integrated Assessment Models which estimate how sulphur deposition could be reduced to a specific level at the lowest possible cost for Europe as a whole. Targets for the level of sulphur emissions by each country up to 2010 were based on:

- physical information on the number and location of emission sources;
- scientific modelling of the transport and deposition of acidifying pollutants;
- scientific information on the sensitivity of individual ecosystems;
- engineering-economic modelling of the cost of pollution abatement options; and
- assumptions about the underlying energy scenario.

This methodology of burden sharing and the implications for future Sulphur Protocols based on the same principles made the outcome and the commitments in this Protocol acceptable to Norwegian industry. NHO therefore supports the goals and commitments in this Protocol, and Norway will take its share of abatement costs within this larger European picture. Our work on tradable permits began before the Protocol was signed in Oslo. NHO was testing whether tradable permits were able to meet our commitments with the lowest possible costs for our members and for Norway as a whole.

It is important for Norway to keep its commitments under the Sulphur Protocol, despite the fact that more than 90 per cent of the acid rain that falls over Norway originates in other countries. The main sources of sulphur deposited in Norway are:

United Kingdom:	24%
Germany:	19%
Poland and former Czechoslovakia:	11%
former Soviet Union:	11%

Norway's own emissions form 7 per cent of the total.

The reason for Norway keeping to its commitments is not so much the environmental impact of those emissions, but the moral leadership and leverage it supplies to ensure that other countries keep to their commitments. As a large net importer of sulphur emissions, Norway has a national interest in promoting cost efficient instruments to reduce future emissions. This is because cheaper means of controlling emissions should encourage the negotiation of more stringent emission targets.

3. WHY USE TRADABLE PERMITS?

Under the Sulphur Protocol, total emissions from Norwegian sources are limited to 34 000 tonnes of SO_2 per year from the year 2000. The allowance will probably be lower from 2010, due to new commitments in the next Sulphur Protocol. The vast majority of these emissions derive from combustion of oil products – primarily diesel, heating oil and heavy fuel oil (HFO).

The main goal for NHO was to find a means of fulfilling Norway's present and future commitments at the lowest possible cost for Norwegian business and industry. A trading system was selected as it combines cost effectiveness with a guarantee of meeting the target. The proposed system has a number of innovative features and is the first of its type in Europe. The main elements in the NHO proposal are:

1. A sulphur trading scheme will be established covering 98 per cent of Norwegian emissions. All emissions must be covered by a sulphur permit, where a permit is equal to one tonne of SO_2. The permits are issued annually and are used up when applied against emissions.

2. Permits can be bought, sold, traded or banked for use in future years but are not to be used in advance. Permits can be bought from the authorities or from other companies. Approximately 80 per cent of the permits will be distributed free each year ('grandfathered'), while the remainder will be put up for sale in auctions.

3. The permits will be held by two main groups: large emission sources and oil companies. The first group will need permits to cover their own emissions, while permits held by oil companies will cover emissions from a multitude of small emission sources – including domestic heating, transportation and small industry. The only exemption from the scheme is fuel wood burnt in domestic households.

4. All participants must ensure that they hold sufficient permits at the end of March each year to cover their emissions over the previous year. This three month 'make up period' should be sufficient to acquire additional permits if a shortfall was experienced.

5. Some 55 per cent of the permits will be distributed to large process industries that are regulated by the Norwegian Pollution Control Authority (NPCA). The main elements of the present system of pollution control will be kept unchanged to ensure that local air quality is kept within acceptable norms. NPCA will distribute permits, free of charge, using a distribution rule of 60 per cent of 1989–90 emissions. The per centage is chosen to ensure that emissions stay within Norway's total commitments. These permits are allocated annually for a 10–15 year period.

6. The trading scheme will replace the present SO_2 tax on mineral oil. For emissions from light oil products the oil companies will have to balance SO_2 emissions and permit holdings. Costs will be covered by the sales price of the products. NHO have proposed that oil companies receive permits, free of charge, using a distribution rule of 60 per cent of 1989–90 emissions resulting from the sales of such light products. For oil products with higher sulphur content, the permits will have to be bought by the user. The oil companies are, however, willing to supply permits while selling their products for those customers who require this.

7. The 1.5 per cent of emissions that derive from biofuels and local government garbage incineration will also be included in the trading system. These sources will also receive grandfathered permits based on 60 per cent of 1989–90 emissions.

8. For investments in reducing SO_2 in 2000, 2001 and 2002, NHO has proposed a system of bonus permits. These should reduce the risk for trading partners engaging in long term agreements in the first few years of trading. NHO believes that such bonuses will lower market risk and get investment and trading started even in the early stages of a trading scheme.

9. The Sulphur Protocol includes provisions for joint implementation, although the detailed rules have yet to be agreed. The spatial dependence of sulphur deposition restricts the scope for JI, but NHO would nevertheless like this to be an option in the Norwegian trading scheme. The most likely trading partners would be Denmark or the UK. It is unlikely, however, that JI will be top of the list of companies' abatement options, at least in the short term.

4. PERMIT DISTRIBUTION

The rules NHO have proposed for distribution of permits are as follows (in round figures).

Process industries	19 000 tonnes SO_2 permits
Suppliers of oil products	7000 tonnes SO_2 permits
Other (biofuel, local government)	500 tonnes SO_2 permits
The government for sale	6600 tonnes SO_2 permits
Total	33 100 tonnes SO_2 permits

The total figure is less than the Norwegian target of 34 000 tonnes/year due to the exclusion of some very small sources of SO_2 emissions (e.g. fire wood in households). This means, however, that 97–98 per cent of total emissions will be included in the trading system.

The government's permit holdings will be sold through auctions, which will be held at least twice a year. Since the government holds around 20 per cent of the total number of permits, the auctions will play a significantly more important role than in the US Acid Rain Program, where only 3 per cent of permits were sold in this way. These auctions should give a firm price signal to participants and should form a baseline against which companies may compare the cost of individual abatement action. NHO believes that this will give the system liquidity, and will reduce worries that companies may be unable to obtain permits when required. The compromise mix of grandfathering and auctions aims to capture the advantages of both while minimizing the associated problems.

The government also has an interest in selling permits to cover part of the loss from the removal of the sulphur tax. Sales of permits will not, however, fully compensate for the loss of this tax income. This revenue stream has been sharply reduced anyway, as a result of both reductions in emissions and the use of tax breaks to stimulate sales of light oil products with lower sulphur content.

In 1996, emissions of SO_2 in Norway were around 36 000 tonnes of SO_2.[4] This means that the additional reductions required in the trading scheme will not be large. However, the trading scheme will ensure that emissions stay below 34 000 tonnes/year from the year 2000. To establish a trading scheme without having to reduce emissions too much should help the learning process. This is important, as trading is a new and unfamiliar instrument in Norwegian environmental policy. Generally, the success of such a trading scheme will not be determined by the first few trades, although these may be interesting for economists. Instead, political and public support will be determined by the scheme's ability to meet environmental commitments and by the visibility of investment in sulphur cleaning being financed by the selling of permits in the market.

NHO have had to meet a range of design criteria from the government when developing the trading proposals. The first was to keep emissions below 34 000 tonnes/year from the year 2000. The second was to be able to meet future, more stringent commitments in the next round of Sulphur Protocols. We have agreed that the number of permits will be reduced for all companies and the government by the same per centage as given by a new Protocol.

Thirdly, the Sulphur Protocol does not allow for banking. Emissions kept below the limit of Norway's commitments in one year will not give credits for future years. Therefore, if the domestic trading system is to include banking, some additional constraints are required. The approach adopted is to reduce the total number of permits distributed to a level below the national target in the later years of the trading program. This gives some room for the use of banked permits while reducing the risk that the Norwegian target will be exceeded. In the future, Norway hopes that banking will be allowed in any subsequent Protocols. This will provide significantly greater flexibility for a trading system and will not threaten the environment as damage from acidification is primarily related to cumulative deposition – which will be unchanged.

5. THE EXPECTED PRICE OF PERMITS

Simulations by the NHO suggest that abatement costs and permit prices will be relatively low up to 2005 – in the range 5 to 10 NOK/kg SO_2 (0.6 to 1.25 ECU/kg SO_2). By comparison, the present Norwegian sulphur tax is 2.1 ECU/kg SO_2. The low price is due to low cost abatement opportunities that are currently unexploited, together with the low forecast growth in emissions. Estimates of sulphur abatement costs suggest that one third to one quarter of emissions can be removed at a lower cost than the present tax.[5]

In the first years of a trading scheme, most companies will want to obtain a surplus of permits for reasons of security. The resulting demand may lead to higher prices. When the market has become more established, companies may be happy to operate with a smaller margin of permits over emissions as they will be confident that additional permits may be obtained if required. We know that allowance prices in US Acid Rain Program were two to three times higher for the first sales in 1992 compared to the situation in 1994 to 1996.[6] In this instance, the early prices were strongly influenced by the relatively high forecasts of abatement costs that characterized the initial stages of the program. Nevertheless, it is generally true that companies are risk averse, and this may make prices higher in the beginning of a program than later on, when confidence in the program has grown.

Strict enforcement is a fundamental feature of a successful scheme. The proposed system will fine companies that do not have sufficient permits to match emissions. To be an effective deterrent, this fine should be fixed at a rate that is significantly higher than the market value of the permits.

The price of permits in Norway up to 2010 will depend both on the provisions of any subsequent SO_2 Protocols and the underlying growth in emissions. If new commitments to reduce SO_2 emissions are agreed for Norway and the EU countries in line with the recently proposed EU Acidification Strategy, then the price of permits could go up as high as 2 to 2.5 ECU/kg SO_2.

NHO have accepted that the total number of permits in 2010 will be 10 per cent lower than in 2000, to ensure that emissions stay below 34 000 tonnes/year even with the right to bank permits for future use. This figure will, however, be adjusted in the future (up or down) when the commitments for Norway in a new Protocol for 2010 are finally made clear.

6. INDUSTRIAL INVOLVEMENT IN THE PROCESS

Industrial involvement in the design of the trading scheme has had a number of advantages. The most important of these is that the two most intractable issues in scheme design – the distribution of permits between companies and sectors and the choice of base year – have been solved internally by industry. Similarly, involvement in the design of the scheme has prepared the major participants – notably the oil companies – for its introduction. This is preferable to the more usual procedure of government proposing an instrument and then having to explain it to industry. The motivation for industry to come up with such a scheme was also influenced by its experience with a less favoured alternative – the sulphur tax. The result is a cost effective alternative that satisfies both government and industry.

NHO took responsibility for co-ordinating the research on sulphur trading and working with the various companies who would be affected by such a scheme. These discussions were very important in developing the final proposals. Trade organizations for the process industries and oil suppliers also had an important role to play. ECON made a valuable contribution as a partner in the design of the system and delivered a report that formed part of our proposal to the government. After our proposal was delivered to the government, we also had the pleasure to bring into our discussions in Norway the experience of Mr. John Palmisano from Enron Europe Ltd.

Without active contributions from all these sources and also an openness from the Norwegian Department of the Environment, this proposal could not have been developed in such a short time-frame (one and a half years). The work within the Norwegian Green Tax Commission, which started up shortly after our proposal was made, did create some delay in the government's handling of the trading proposals. However, the proposal by the US government to support international trading of greenhouse gases acted to increase interest in our proposals.

7. TIMETABLE

NHO have proposed that trading begins in 1998, to make contracts possible in time for the year 2000 when the UNECE target first applies. Investment in the process industries will most probably be based on long-term contracts to sell permits. The government's auctions should begin in the same year, and 1999 might be the first year that Norwegian companies have to match SO_2 permits and emissions.

The government will present its conclusions on whether to use SO_2 taxes in all sectors or to go for tradable permits in April 1998. At the same time the government will also present their proposals regarding 'green taxes' based on proposals from the Norwegian Green Tax Commission.

NOTES

[1] This should be compared with the European Union carbon/energy tax proposals which envisaged introducing a tax at $3/barrel, rising to $10/barrel over seven years. These proposals were defeated following opposition from the UK and other member states.

[2] Coal used as a reduction material in metal smelters is exempt.

[3] The agreements involve 450 companies represented by twelve trade associations. These account for some 80 per cent of industrial CO2 emissions.

[4] This is a very small fraction of the European total. For comparison, UK emissions in 1995 were 2,365,000 tonnes, or 65 times the Norwegian figure.

[5] Estimates based on industry figures to the Norwegian Pollution Control Authority, 1992. Only oil users pay the current tax. Many of the low cost abatement opportunities are for process emissions from the metal industry and other sectors.

[6] See Ellerman et al., this book, Chapter 2.

7. Trading emissions and other economic instruments to reduce NO$_x$ in the Netherlands

Chris Dekkers

1. INTRODUCTION

Discussions on alternative systems of emission control have taken place in the Netherlands since the early 1980s, when the first draft of the national legislation on sulphur dioxide (SO$_2$) and nitrogen oxides (NO$_x$) Emission Limit Values (ELVs) was introduced. In 1983, a combined mission of industry and government representatives went to the US to see for themselves what alternative systems were being considered (Heijwegen and Aronds, 1983). A range of more flexible systems of emission control were being developed in the US, including: single site and multi-site bubbles; emission offsets for new plants locating in non-attainment regions; emissions credit banking; and full emissions trading. Of these ideas, only the bubble concept met with sufficient support in the Netherlands. Emissions trading between different sites and emissions banking were not considered relevant to, desirable or applicable in the Netherlands' situation.

The 1987 Decree on emission limits for combustion plants introduced permitting procedures and conventional ELVs for SO$_2$ and NO$_x$.[1] These were supplemented with provisions for a 'plant bubble' for SO$_2$ emissions from oil refineries (VROM, 1993). At the same time an effort was made to investigate whether the bubble concept could be used to sensibly control NO$_x$ emissions. Through an extensive research project it was concluded that the large differences in actual NO$_x$ emissions in similar process situations made it practically impossible to design a coherent and satisfactory NO$_x$ control system that met the criteria. The idea of an NO$_x$ bubble for industrial plants was (temporarily) abandoned.

In 1990, the national government together with local and regional authorities agreed a covenant with the Electricity Board (VROM, 1990) in which the electricity sector committed itself to SO$_2$ and NO$_x$ emission reductions for the year 2000 that went substantially beyond the anticipated reductions from the existing ELVs. In exchange, the sector would be exempt from the tighter ELVs contained in the proposed 1992 amendment to the combustion plant decree. The electricity sector would obtain flexibility and could use its own judgement in the selection of existing installations where NO_x abatement could take place. This should be more cost effective than applying the amended and tighter ELVs to each existing installation individually. The covenant allows a form of cost optimization for existing power plants that has some resemblance to a system of emissions trading. For new power plants, however, the stringent new source ELVs laid down in the 1992 amended Decree have to be applied. The covenant provides for regular progress reports on the emission reductions achieved and for an assessment of the emission limit values applied in each individual power plant (SEP, 1997).

2. ACIDIFICATION ABATEMENT PROGRAMME AND INSTRUMENTS

In 1989 the national Acidification Abatement Programme was published with short and long term emission reduction targets for passenger cars and other mobile sources as well as stationary sources in industry and other sectors. This replaced an earlier acidification programme introduced in 1984. In the new programme, the interim targets for 2000 were based on an assessment of the technical possibilities for emission reduction in the various sectors, with overall reductions of 80 per cent for SO_2 and 50 per cent for NO_x from a 1980 baseline. For 2010, long term targets were defined with reductions of 80–90 per cent required on the basis of long term environmental objectives and on an assessment of ELVs that would become technically feasible. These 2010 emission targets in the acidification abatement programme were an important element in the first National Environmental Policy Plan (NEPP) also published in 1989 (VROM, 1989). The NO_x reduction targets for stationary sources are shown in Table 7.1.

Table 7.1 Dutch NO_x emission reduction targets (1980-2010) (ktonnes)

Sector	1980	1995	2000	2010	Reduction
Power	83	61	30	16	81%
Refineries	24	17	9	3	87.5%
Other industry	85	64	28	7	92%
Other stationery sources	56	59	24	14	75%
Total	248	201	91	40	84%

Major reductions in SO$_2$ and NO$_x$ emissions were expected from fuel switching, that is, increased gas firing at the expense of coal and liquid fuels. Other measures included retrofitting flue gas desulphurization (FGD) equipment to power plants and larger industrial sources. It was further expected that major emission reductions would be achieved by technological change and replacement of existing installations by new installations. For the SO$_2$ emission reductions realized since the early 1980s, these assumptions have proved correct. Electricity sector SO$_2$ emissions decreased from 200 ktonnes in 1980 to 18 ktonnes in 1994, a cut of 91 per cent. Refinery SO$_2$ emissions reduced from 130 ktonnes in 1980 to 60 ktonnes in 1995, a cut of 53 per cent. Similar reductions were achieved in other sectors, primarily through switching to gas. However, for NO$_x$ emissions from both mobile and stationary sources the picture is very different. In the last three years it has become increasingly clear that the assumptions of the acidification abatement programme with respect to NO$_x$ had been overoptimistic. In particular:

- The rate by which existing plants are replaced by new plants appears to be much slower than the 15 years that had been assumed earlier. Rather, in 1994 the average age of industrial combustion plants was 25 years, and increasing. The number of new conventional combustion plant (i.e. boilers and furnaces) installed over the period 1989-1994 was very small.
- The increase in CHP capacity has been much greater than expected. In 1995, some 25 per cent of the total power generated in the Netherlands was produced by industrial CHP, with a total installed capacity of 5 GWe (COGEN Nederland, 1996). With current ELVs, CHP plants have higher specific NO$_x$ emissions than industrial boilers. This, together with the high growth rates, partly explains the smaller reduction in emissions than had been assumed.
- The development of NO$_x$ abatement technology and low NO$_x$ combustion equipment has been much slower than was anticipated in the acidification programme.

These disappointing developments were further exacerbated by the more critical attitude of industry which began to question the NO$_x$ emission reduction targets for 2000 and 2010. The 2010 SO$_2$ targets (overall 90 per cent reduction) were also opposed as being too ambitious, although here the criticism was less vigorous.[2] The regional authorities charged with the enforcement of the 1987 Decree had also begun to question the cost effectiveness of achieving the required emission reductions through uniform ELVs for each individual plant. Suggestions were made to adopt more flexible emission reduction schemes, such as the bubble approach or tradable permits. At the Ministry of the Environment opinions also began to shift towards more cost effective approaches. Moreover, by 1995 it was becoming clear that NO_x abatement at stationary sources would gain by a thorough evaluation and review. The 1996 draft amendment of the Decree on emission limits for combustion plants (State Gazette, 1996) with proposals to tighten the new source ELVs met with strong opposition from industry. It became increasingly clear that both the emission reduction targets and the instruments used so far to achieve those targets needed a thorough evaluation. The improvements looked for were:

- more flexible legislation and the introduction of more cost effective instruments;
- stimulation of pro-active and more environmentally benign company behaviour;
- improved enforcement of environmental performance;
- introduction of 'market forces' in environmental policy;
- realistic 2010 emission reduction targets;
- further development of 'best available technology'; and
- solutions compatible with national and international legislation.

During this reappraisal process, a number of studies were undertaken to assess the possibilities for more cost effective instruments and/or approaches to abate industrial NO_x emissions. Three options were considered: tradable permits, NO_x taxation; and voluntary cost sharing. These are described in turn below.

3. TRADABLE PERMITS

During 1995, representatives of government and regional authorities met regularly and informally with representatives of industry and environmental groups. In a series of sessions they explored possibilities for rectifying the disappointing developments with respect to the long term NO_x and SO_2 emission reduction targets for the industrial sectors. A study on the applicability of tradable permits for SO_2 and NO_x (VROM, 1995) served as guidance document for a workshop held in June 1995 (Centrum voor Energiebesparing, 1995). The workshop and subsequent meetings further clarified the perceptions of the participants with very different backgrounds and responsibilities. In the end, however, it was clear that it had been a debate between 'believers' and 'non-believers' in tradable permits.

The 'believers' pointed to the virtues of flexibility and cost effectiveness, to the value of market prices for environmental pollution and to the need to make industry responsible for its 'acts of pollution'. They argued that this would reduce the legislative and bureaucratic burden on society and would increase the 'universe' of solutions. The 'non-believers', however, stressed the incompatibility of tradable permits with major principles of environmental policy and/or national and international law. They also felt that tradable permits were no solution for the current problems; did not represent a real alternative to the present legislative system, and would in fact constitute a set-back in the decision making process. Moreover, they were opposed to the grandfathering of permits as this amounted to granting free financial credits to the highest polluting companies while penalizing the more pro-active companies. Finally, the 'non-believers' were of the opinion that it would be impossible to resolve the equity issues raised by the initial allocation of emission rights. Despite their differences on such fundamental principles, the two parties did agree on the following:

- a system of tradable permits would require major changes to existing legislation;
- it would take three to four years to implement if it was decided to change the law;
- such an effort would only be worthwhile if the cost reductions were substantial; and
- it would be useful to investigate the potential cost savings that would result from a system of tradable permits.

It was also agreed that a study on the potential cost savings of tradable permits would have to cover the four major polluting industrial sectors: electricity generation; oil refineries; chemicals and iron and steel. The study would separately address the use of tradable permits for NO$_x$ and SO$_2$ emissions. In April 1996, the terms of reference of the study were agreed with the wide range of participants in the debate: the Ministries of Environment and of Economic Affairs; the Inter Provincial Council (IPO);[3] various industrial associations;[4] and representatives of environmental organizations.[5] A combination of four consultants formed a project team to carry out the study. The costs of the consultants were covered by the two ministries and by IPO.

Three alternative systems of trading were considered, namely: a) the 'bubble', with trading or exchanging emission reductions between sources within an individual plant; b) the 'sector ceiling', with trading or exchanging between individual plants within a sector; and c) the 'industry cap', with trading between the various plants of the four sectors considered. Within each alternative trading system, the costs of achieving the national emission objectives for 2010 were compared with the costs that would result with a system of ELVs applied to each installation individually. The abatement costs and the technical information were to be provided by the companies participating in the study, some fifty industrial plants in total. This information would be sent to the consultant team and compared with their in-house technical database. Questions arising from this comparison would be sorted out between the consultants and the individual companies. The following assumptions and constraints had to be observed:

- The starting point of the study was the 2010 emission reduction targets for each sector as laid down in the National Environmental Policy Plan (NEPP).
- The Ministry of Environment defined the ELVs per installation that would bring about the required 2010 emission reduction targets from the NEPP (Table 7.2).
- The base case situation was the emissions in 1995. The abatement costs of the emission reductions achieved prior to 1995 were to be assessed at the level of individual installations in order to estimate the unabated emission level in 1995. This would allow unbiased 'base case' comparisons between different plants and sectors and also allow an unconstrained assessment of the 2010 abatement costs for all plants.
- Investments in new installations, capacity increases and new plants were to be considered only as far as these investments were officially and publicly confirmed. Planned investments or capacity increases that did not meet this criterion would not be taken into account.
- Technical measures for NO_x abatement considered in the study were: low NO_x burners; flue gas cleaning through Selective Catalytic Reduction (SCR) and/or Selective Non-Catalytic Reduction (SNCR); and steam injection for gas turbines. It was further assumed that, in the investment decision tree, low NO_x burners would be installed first and SCR or SNCR would be added if additional abatement was required. For each technique a fixed reduction rate was assumed.
- Technical measures for SO_2 abatement considered in the study were: a) low sulphur coal, fuel cleaning and FGD for the electricity sector; b) energy conservation, fuel switching and fuel cleaning for the industrial sector; and c) fuel switching, fuel cleaning and FGD for the refinery sector.
- Costs related to the introduction of a tradable permit system were not taken into account, nor any other non-technical costs that would be involved when such a system was operational.

These assumptions and constraints served solely the purpose of the study, i.e. to estimate the potential cost reductions that would result from the three alternatives considered to the present system of ELVs per installation.

Table 7.2 Emission limit values (ELVs) used in the study on tradable permits

Sector	Technology	NO$_x$	SO$_2$
Chemicals and Steel	Gas turbines	15 g/GJ	
	Gas fired furnaces & boilers	50 mg/Nm^3	35 mg/Nm^3
	Gas fired furnaces > COT 600·C	80 mg/Nm^3	
	Process installations with emissions >100 tonnes SO$_2$ or NO$_x$ per annum	200 mg/Nm^3	200 mg/Nm^3
Refineries	Gas turbines	15 g/GJ	500 mg/Nm^3
	Gas fired furnaces & boilers	50 mg/Nm^3	500 mg/Nm^3
	Gas fired furnaces & boilers	80 mg/Nm^3	500 mg/Nm^3
	Catalytic cracker	100 mg/Nm^3	500 mg/Nm^3
Electricity	Emission ceiling 2000	30 ktonnes	18 ktonnes
	Emission ceiling 2010	16 ktonnes	18 ktonnes
	ELV gas fired 2010	18 g/GJ	
	ELV coal fired 2010	40 g/GJ	80 g/GJ

3.1. The outcome of the study 'Choosing to Gain'

One of the findings of the 1995 evaluation of the acidification abatement programme was that the majority of future NO$_x$ and SO$_2$ reductions in industry would have to come from existing installations. The study 'Choosing to Gain', published in May 1997, confirmed the earlier perceptions of, first, the large differences in NO$_x$ abatement costs between different types of installation within each sector; and second, substantial cost differences between different sectors (Inter Provincial Council, 1997). In general, the NO$_x$ abatement cost curve follows the shape indicated in Figure 7.1. The curve suggests that by exchanging emission reductions between high cost and low cost investment options, a large reduction in costs can be achieved. This applies both within plants, in the case of the bubble approach, and between companies, in the case of a sector ceiling.

The results of the study are summarized in Table 7.3. A system of regulatory ELVs per installation (Table 7.2) would lead to a total annual abatement cost of approximately 1400 million guilders for achieving the 2010 NO$_x$ emission targets. Cost savings of 28 per cent, 41 per cent and 47 per cent respectively would be possible if the bubble approach, the sector ceiling and the industry cap were implemented.

For individual sectors of industry the cost savings can be quite different. For oil refineries, annual cost savings of 45 million guilders would be achieved through implementing refinery bubbles. A limited additional saving

Figure 7.1 Typical cost curve for NO$_x$ abatement

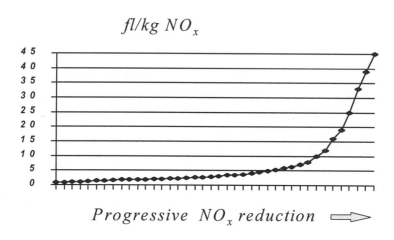

Table 7.3 NO$_x$ annual abatement costs with alternative regulatory approaches (million guilder)

Sector	Uniform ELVs	Plant bubbles	Sector ceiling	Industry cap
Power	710	510	450	450
Refineries	240	195	175	175
Steel	185	135	105	100
Chemicals	210	135	54	25
Total	1339	971	787	710

Notes:
1. Covers capital and operating costs of abatement.
2. Capital costs based on 10% interest rate and depreciation over 10 years for electro-mechanical components and 25 years for construction.

of approximately 20 million guilders would be achieved from a sector ceiling, and no further savings would be possible through inter-sector trade (industry cap). For the chemical industry, significant savings are achievable from each stage: 75 million guilders from plant bubbles; a further 80 million from a sector ceiling, and an additional 30 million from an industry cap. The differences result from the relative shape of the abatement cost curves in each sector.

The results for SO$_2$ abatement costs are shown in Table 7.4. Here the situation is somewhat different. With installation specific ELVs, total annual abatement costs are estimated at 580 million guilders. Cost savings of 5 per cent, 26 per cent and 28 per cent respectively would be possible if the bubble approach, the sector ceiling and the industry cap were implemented. There are two reasons why the annual cost savings for SO$_2$ are so much more modest than the cost savings for NO$_x$. First, the refinery industry in the Netherlands has been allowed to operate plant bubbles for SO$_2$ since the early 1980s. This means the cost savings from SO$_2$ bubbles in the refinery sector have already been realized. However, further cost reductions can be realized with a refinery sector ceiling for SO$_2$ because there remain major differences in abatement costs between refineries. Second, under the 1990 covenant agreed with the Dutch Electricity Generating Board, the electricity industry has been allowed to operate within an SO$_2$ emission ceiling for the whole sector. For these two industries, refineries and electricity, major cost reductions have already been achieved within the present regulatory system. Furthermore, in the electricity sector the costs per tonne of SO$_2$ abated are lower than in the other sectors, while in this sector all major SO$_2$ emission reduction measures had already been taken before 1995. The result is that the possibilities still remaining for further SO$_2$ cost savings with other sectors are rather limited, and certainly less than the cost savings potential in the abatement of NO$_x$ emissions.

Table 7.4 SO$_2$ annual abatement costs with alternative regulatory approaches (million guilder)

Sector	Uniform ELVs	Plant bubbles	Sector ceiling	Industry cap
Power	244	244	244	244
Refineries	154	154	87	86
Steel	128	112	78	64
Chemicals	53	43	21	20
Total	580	550	430	415

3.2. Conclusions and limitations of the tradable permit study

The conclusions of the study can be summarized as follows:

- A system of NO$_x$ trading could achieve annual cost savings of 600 million guilders, or some 40 per cent of the abatement costs of a legislative system based on fixed ELVs.

- Implementing an NO_x bubble for each plant could achieve annual cost savings of 400 million guilders, or some two thirds of the total achievable through an industry cap.
- Major savings can be achieved with a sector ceiling in the chemical industry, while limited additional cost savings can be achieved with such ceilings in the other sectors.
- The potential for abatement cost savings for SO_2 emissions are much smaller than for NO_x. The majority of the cost savings have already been realized as a result of existing provisions in the legislation – namely plant bubbles in the refining industry and a sector ceiling in the electricity industry. Furthermore, in the electricity sector major SO_2 abatement measures had already been taken before 1995.
- Limited additional cost savings are still possible with SO_2 plant bubbles in the steel and the chemical industries.

The limitations and the constraints of the study should not be overlooked:

- The cost data for individual installations were provided by the companies under a confidentiality agreement. This confidentiality allows only a limited assessment of the validity of the various cost assumptions.
- The consultants used fixed reduction percentages for each abatement technology. In practice, the rate of desulphurization or De-NO_x will be variable to a certain degree.
- There were substantial differences in the retrofit costs used by the individual companies that participated in the study. Also, the retrofit costs per sector differed in cases where one would expect similar retrofit situations. This created unbalanced comparisons.
- In the refining industry, the abatement costs for NO_x and SO_2 are strongly influenced by the assumptions for the fuel mix used in the refineries. The assumption of flue gas desulphurization for oil fired furnaces has major cost implications for the NO_x abatement at those furnaces. A switch to gas firing may be a more cost effective solution, but this was not considered in the study.
- Very high retrofit costs were assumed for SO_2 and NO_x abatement in the steel industry.

4. TAXATION OF NO_X EMISSIONS

Although one may have doubts on the individual cost data used in the study and the assumptions made by the consultants, the main conclusion of the study on tradable permits is clear and has been accepted by all parties, namely, that major cost reductions are possible with more flexible systems of legislation. This conclusion was further strengthened in a second study (VROM, 1997) carried out in the Ministry of Environment in which the effects of an NO$_x$ tax were explored. The main conclusion of this feasibility study is that cost effective solutions for NO$_x$ abatement can be achieved by an NO$_x$ tax rising from ƒ 2/kg NO$_x$ in 2000 to ƒ 10/kg NO$_x$ in 2010. Such a tax would force plant owners to carefully consider which cost abatement measures would be cost effective at any given moment of time compared with paying an increasing tax per tonne of NO$_x$ emitted above the threshold Emission Reference Value. The income raised by the tax would be used to subsidize investments in flue gas scrubbing equipment (SCR or SNCR) to reduce NO$_x$ emissions by 60 to 90 per cent.

In this study, the Emission Reference Values used as thresholds above which the tax would have to be paid were the same as the ELVs used in the tradable permit study. On the basis of assumptions of cost minimizing behaviour by industry together with restitution of the tax income via a subsidy programme for NO$_x$ scrubbing equipment, it was estimated that an investment of up to 2 billion guilders would be stimulated by such an NO$_x$ tax. Although there are some clear advantages of an NO$_x$ tax over a system of tradable permits, there are also some disadvantages. A major disadvantage is that an NO$_x$ tax can be seen as a punitive instrument to force the required environmental improvement upon the industry. An uncooperative attitude by the various industrial sectors could then easily become an obstacle to achieving the emission reduction targets.

5. VOLUNTARY COST SHARING

The tradable permit study triggered a debate between the project partners and other interested parties in government and industry on the policy implications of the study and on the steps needed to implement its conclusions. The results of the study on the NO$_x$ tax were also taken into account. In the preparatory discussions for the 3rd National Environmental Policy Plan (NEPP), an evaluation was made of the various environmental objectives. It was clear to everyone that the problems of acidification and ozone would be a top priority during the next four year planning period. This created a need to further reduce NO$_x$ emissions. Early on in these discussions, industry voiced its concerns with respect to the future costs of the NO$_x$ reduction targets and suggested that cost effective reductions could be brought about by a voluntary cost sharing scheme by which industry as a whole would subsidize the investment costs of individual plant owners. By investing in SCR equipment at the larger installations – which are responsible for some 80 per cent of industrial NO$_x$ emissions – cost effective emission reduction could be achieved at a more acceptable annual cost level.

Through mutual participation of companies in the financing of these abatement investments, both the environment and industry as a whole could benefit. These proposals from industry were very much in line with government thinking. Since then, discussions between government and industry have progressed towards a general understanding that such a voluntary cost sharing scheme is technically and economically feasible, and should be set up to achieve the required NO_x emission reductions in a more cost effective way.

The government is convinced of the potential benefits of such a voluntary system and has committed itself to persuade and guide industry into a cost sharing scheme to achieve a 60 per cent reduction in NO_x emissions by 2005 (Table 7.5). Moreover, in the 3rd NEPP, a total of 165 million guilders has been made available as a financial contribution to investment in SCR equipment. In line with the earlier studies on tradable permits and NO_x taxation, the Ministry has estimated the NO_x emission reductions that would be possible with such a voluntary scheme. On the basis of available information, it has been estimated that investment in SCR and other abatement techniques in the larger installations will reduce NO_x emissions by up to 60 per cent at an overall cost of f 3000 to 4000 per tonne (Table 7.6). This would amount to annual abatement costs of 200 to 400 million guilders for the whole industry.

Table 7.5 NO_x emission reductions and the 2005 target (ktonnes)

Sector	1980	1995	2010
Power	83	61	
Refineries	48	26	
Chemicals	9	8	
Steel	24	17	
Other industry	13	17	
Total	177	129	67

The chemical industry is a strong advocate of the benefits and usefulness of such a scheme and is promoting this approach to other sectors of industry that are less committed to such an approach. The Association of the Netherlands' Chemical Industry (VNCI) and the larger chemical companies have agreed to assess, using predetermined costing rules, what the capital and O&M costs are of applying SCR to its 80 major NO_x emitting installations. For some 200 other installations in the chemical industry the costs of emission reductions of less rigorous NO_x abatement measures such as low NO_x burners will be also be evaluated. A working group has been formed to guide these investment studies, while another working group will explore the technical and conceptual aspects of such a scheme.

Table 7.6 NO$_x$ emission reductions against marginal abatement costs in a voluntary cost sharing scheme (ktonnes)

Sector	Marginal abatement costs (Dfl/tonne NO$_x$)					
	f 3000	*f* 4000	*f* 5000	*f* 6000	*f* 7000	*f* 8000
Power	16.21	43.83	43.87	43.87	43.87	43.87
Refineries	10.00	10.93	12.23	12.45	13.03	13.13
Chemicals	11.87	12.32	13.39	13.39	13.47	13.72
Steel	1.46	1.54	6.10	6.80	6.16	6.29
Other industry	9.93	9.93	10.14	10.14	10.21	10.50
Total	49.46	78.56	85.71	86.63	86.73	87.49

The government has indicated that it expects a proposal from industry before the end of 1998 on how to realize the 2005 target. If industry is unable to formulate an acceptable proposal, the government will decide on other means to achieve the required reductions – an NO$_x$ tax being the most likely option. The discussions in 1998 will therefore be crucial in finding new ways to abate NO$_x$ emissions within Dutch industry. At the Ministry, we are confident that by the end of 1998 a solution will be found that is acceptable to the government, to parliament, to the industry as a whole and to other stakeholders, such as environmental organizations.

6. INTERNATIONAL ASPECTS

The system of voluntary cost sharing sought after in the Netherlands could eventually become a solution to similar problems within other EU countries. The proposed EU Acidification Strategy (European Commission, 1997) contains indicative NO$_x$ emission reduction targets for each member state for the year 2010. These vary between 40 and 80 per cent, measured from a 1990 baseline, and are based on a 50 per cent gap closure between current and target levels of exceedance of critical loads for acid deposition. The immediate consequences of such ambitious reduction targets would be that industrial sources in other member states would have to achieve emission reductions similar to those in the Netherlands (see Table 7.7). As the rate of replacement of existing plants by new combustion plants will not be very different from that in the Netherlands, the industrial sectors in other member states would face similar technical and organizational problems to achieve the required reductions.

*Table 7.7 Indicative NO$_x$ emission ceilings from the EU Acidification
Strategy (ktonnes)*

Country	1990	2010 Reference scenario	2010 50% gap closure targets	% reduction
France	1585	895	766	52
Germany	3071	1279	1079	65
Italy	2047	1165	1160	43
Netherlands	575	140	139	76
UK	2702	1244	753	72

A second consideration is that a voluntary cost sharing scheme could also
accommodate cost effective NO$_x$ abatement measures within the
requirements of the EU framework directive on Integrated Pollution
Prevention and Control (IPPC) for industrial installations. According to this
directive, Best Available Techniques for pollution control are to be applied
to existing installations by 2007. We think that a voluntary cost sharing
scheme for NO$_x$ abatement can be designed in such a way that it is
compatible with the IPPC Directive and other elements of community law.
This could then provide an attractive approach for other EU member states to
implement the national requirements resulting from future decisions on the
EU Acidification Strategy.

NOTES

[1] Permits are issued by different authorities depending upon the scale of the installation.
The largest sources are regulated by the provincial authorities and include 60 power
stations, 6 oil refineries and about 400 other industrial firms.

[2] The 90 per cent target represented an additional 56 ktonnes of abatement. While the 80
per cent target for 2000 was considered technically and economically feasible, the 2010
target was considerably more difficult.

[3] The Inter Provincial Council is a consultation body for the 12 Provinces on financial,
social and environmental policy. It has no powers of its own but represents an important
layer of administration between the government and the ministries on one hand and the
municipalities on the other.

[4] The Confederation of Netherlands' Industry and Employers (VNO-NCW); the Federation
of Netherlands' Chemical Industries (VNCI); the Netherlands' Petroleum Association
(OCC); and the Dutch Electricity Generating Board (SEP).

[5] The environmental organizations represented in the discussions were: 'Stichting Natuur
en Milieu' and the 'Zuid-Hollandse Milieufederatie'.

REFERENCES

Centrum voor Energiebesparing (1995), *Workshop verhandelbare emissierechten voor SO$_2$ en NO$_x$ in Nederland* (Proceedings of the workshop on tradable SO$_2$ and NO$_x$ permits in the Netherlands), Delft.

COGEN Nederland (1996), *Cogeneration*, Driebergen, Netherlands.

European Commission (1997), Communication to the Council and to the Parliament on a Community Strategy to Combat Acidification, COM (97)88, Brussels, April.

Heijwegen, C.P and C.A. Aronds (1983*), Emissiewisselbeleid, De toepasbaarheid van het 'bubble concept'* (Emissions trading, the applicability of the bubble concept), Netherlands' Council of Trade and Industry, October.

Inter Provincial Council (1997), *Choosing to Gain: a study of the potential cost advantages of a system of tradable permits*, IPO Publication 105, The Hague, May.

SEP (1997), *3^e Voortgangsrapportage SEP convenant* (3rd Progress Report on the SEP Covenant), The Hague, January.

State Gazette (1996), *Proposal for Amendment to the Decree on Emission Limits for Combustion Plants*, **182**, 16–20.

VROM (1989), *National Environmental Policy Plan: To Choose or Lose*, Ministry of Housing, Spatial Planning and the Environment, SDU, The Hague.

VROM (1990), *Convenant over de bestrijding van SO$_2$ en NO$_x$* (Covenant on the abatement of SO$_2$ and NO$_x$), concluded on 12 June 1990 between the government of the Netherlands, the Provincial governments and the Dutch Electricity Generating Board (SEP).

VROM (1993a), *Decree on Emission Limits for Combustion Plants, as amended by the decree of 5 February 1993*, Ministry of Housing, Spatial Planning an the Environment, VROM 93593/h/1-94 – 1509/033.

VROM (1993b), *Second National Environmental Policy Plan*, Ministry of Housing, Spatial Planning and the Environment, VROM 93561/b/4-94 – 1221/027, December.

VROM (1995), *Verhandelbare emissierechten in het Nederlandse verzuringsbeleid* (Tradable permits in the Netherlands' Acidification Policy), VROM 96302/h/6-95 – 9865/141.

VROM (1997), *NO$_x$ heffing gewogen* (NO$_x$ tax weighted: a scoping study on the effects of an NO$_x$ tax), August.

124-38

H23 P25 Q28 P26

8. Towards tradability of pollution permits in Poland

Tomasz Zylicz

1. BACKGROUND

The year 1989 marked the launch of a comprehensive reform of Poland's environmental policy. From the outset of the reforms, the Economics Department (ED) in the Ministry of the Environment (ME) strongly recommended the use of emissions trading to improve the cost-effectiveness of the new policies. The adequacy of simple forms of emissions trading as an option for former centrally planned economies was widely discussed in political as well as academic fora (Zylicz, 1990). The idea of Tradable Pollution Permits (TPPs) was officially introduced into the National Ecological Policy (ME, 1990), and approved by the Polish Parliament in 1991. Subsequently, TPPs were included in the new Environmental Protection Act drafted in 1991. This Act has yet to be passed, however, as other political priorities have overshadowed environmental concerns since 1991.

The declared preference for TPPs was not an obvious choice since there are few environmental policy instruments considered more controversial. Praised by many, emissions trading is seen by others as an ethically ambiguous solution that, at best, can be contemplated not sooner than the 21st century. The latter was the most frequent message heard by Polish government officials from their Western European counterparts. Nevertheless key environmentalists and some policy makers in Poland took a pragmatic approach. Instead of engaging in theoretical discussions, they carefully studied the implementation record since the 1980s. As a result, soon after the breakthrough in 1989, what once was the subject of academic inquiries became a part of the policy reform package. However, the idea has never been fully accepted by many lawyers, who prefer to minimize departures from the traditional system. As a result, whenever they appeared in draft legal acts, TPPs were introduced as an option without changing the main source- and technology-based approach.

The national policy documents were accompanied by educational publications. In addition to a series of interviews and popular articles, two major reports were translated into Polish and widely distributed in order to enhance understanding of environmental policies in modern market economies. The OECD Economic Instruments for Environmental Protection (OECD, 1989) gave a wide overview of policy experience in the OECD countries, while the US Project 88 report (US Congress, 1988) shed light on 'harnessing market forces' in the United States. The foundations for actual policy initiatives were thereby laid down. What was then required was empirical proof that savings and entrepreneurship can be unleashed if environmental policy is implemented with economic instruments rather than inflexible regulations.

In 1990, ED began the search for a good demonstration site for an emissions trading experiment. Even though the ME was committed to the experiment, the task was not an easy one, since under Polish law it is not the Minister but regional environmental administrators who issue pollution permits. If the administrators were responsible for attaining certain ambient standards, they would have a strong incentive to seek instruments which reduce pollution in a least-cost way. However, they are not and they feel much more comfortable focusing on technology-based requirements. As a rule, they would prefer to continue under non-attainment conditions rather than take the risk of engaging in an emissions trading project whose merits were perceived as controversial and chances of political failure were high in the absence of a satisfactory legal framework.

ED's plans met with interest from a number of environmental policy specialists mainly from the United States. In 1990, the ED reached an agreement with the Environmental Defense Fund (EDF) to jointly develop a pilot project demonstrating the usefulness and viability of TPPs. Dr. Daniel J. Dudek, a senior economist at EDF, together with Mr. Zbigniew Kulczynski, a Ph.D. student at Warsaw School of Economics, started to study possible locations for such a project. Soon it became obvious that the physical and technological characteristics of a site are of less importance than the understanding and willingness to cooperate of a regional environmental administrator. As a result, several potential locations were eliminated.

2. THE CHORZÓW PROJECT

In 1991, upon the request of ED, the Minister of the Environment approved the outline of a pilot project in Chorzów. The ministerial approval was an imperfect substitute for a clear legal provision for emissions trading, and thus it is Dr. Wojciech Beblo, the environmental administrator of the

Katowice region, who has to be credited with the initiative and courage of running the experiment. Once the location was determined, Mr. Kulczynski made a number of trips to Chorzów to: (1) identify potential participants in the experiment; (2) assess benefits from emissions trading; (3) present and discuss the results and recommendations at various public fora in Chorzów; and (4) help the local decision makers to cooperate with each other even in the absence of a fully satisfactory legal framework. All of these tasks were accomplished (Dudek et al., 1992), and turned the experiment into an interesting demonstration project.

It should be noted, however, that no 'emissions trades' have actually taken place in Chorzów, since the Polish law does not recognize 'emission reduction credits'. In 1991, a new Environmental Protection Act was drafted by the government. It included Article 45 which stated that 'the terms of a pollution permit can be transferred (either fully or in part) to another plant subject to the approval of the authority who issued the original permit'. The Act was never approved and thus no 'emission reduction credit' could formally become a commodity. Consequently the whole experiment can be labelled as a tradable permit project in a metaphorical sense only.

In an extensive appraisal of the Chorzów project, Dr. Beblo states that its main outcome was to let its participants (i.e. local polluters and administrators) '..learn how to negotiate in the common interest and recognize values hidden in various assets' (Beblo, 1994). For the first time in implementing environmental policy in Poland a conscious effort was made to optimize the allocation of permits subject to a constraint defined by the desired degree of improvement of ambient quality. In contrast, typical implementation debates elsewhere have focused on technical considerations and – despite rhetoric – treated ambient quality as a residual outcome.

The city of Chorzów used to be one of the worst polluted municipalities in Poland. Two plants located right in the city centre were responsible for a major part of its pollution. These are: the Kosciuszko Steel Mill (hereafter the steel mill) and the Power Plant 'Chorzów' (hereafter the power plant). Table 8.1 characterizes their atmospheric emissions in 1990.

While both plants contributed similar amounts of particulates and sulphur dioxide, the steel mill was a major polluter with respect to carbon monoxide and hydrocarbons. The steel mill had a government-approved restructuring program which envisaged significant emission reductions especially after the year 1995. The cost of achieving pollution reduction through the program was rather low, since most of the planned investment expenditures were to be borne for production purposes. On the other hand, the power plant – an obsolete factory from the 1950s – was expected to be shut down in 5-6 years for technological reasons. Clearly, it would be inefficient to equip it with any modern end-of-pipe installation to reduce the emissions by a significant amount.

Table 8.1 Chorzów project: emissions of selected pollutants in 1990 (tonnes)

Pollutant	Steel mill	Power plant
Particulate matter	4,280	5,067
Carbon monoxide	16,951	200
Sulphur dioxide	3,020	3,071
Nitrogen dioxide	1,716	561
Aliphatic hydrocarbons	492	71
Aromatic hydrocarbons	282	8

Source: Katowice Regional Environmental Authority files

Of the two plants, the former was a typical low-cost one with respect to abatement and the latter was a typical high-cost one. At the same time, the former was in a financial distress, while the latter was relatively better off. It thus seemed obvious that a successful solution to the Chorzów problem would require that:

- the steel mill abates more than the power plant, and
- the power plant participates in the steel mill's abatement costs.

This, however, was easier said than done as Polish law did not recognize the concept of a tradable permit.

Following advice from the ED, the regional administrator used the nearest opportunity to issue new permits for both polluters (whose operations contributed to the violation of ambient standards) to induce a cost-effective allocation of abatement effort. His choice was constrained not only by the absence of the legal notion of an 'emission reduction credit', but also by the fact that the background concentrations of some pollutants should prevent him from issuing any non-zero emission permit. Nevertheless, it did prove possible to reach a consensus between the administrator and polluters to:

- issue permits approximating the cost effective allocation of abatement effort between the steel mill and the power plant;
- make the power plant pay for a more liberal permit than otherwise applicable; and
- assist the steel mill in radically speeding up its restructuring program.

All payments related to the project involved transfers to and from the regional environmental fund. The environmental administrator fully controlled expenditures from the fund, and – to some extent – manipulated its revenues.

Table 8.2 Chorzów project: emissions of selected pollutants in 1992

Pollutant	Steel mill		Power plant	
	tonnes	1992/1990 (%)	tonnes	1992/1990 (%)
Particulate matter	517	12	4,028	80
Carbon monoxide	47	0.3	1,141	570
Sulphur dioxide	972	32	3,226	105
Nitrogen dioxide	769	45	1,782	318
Aliphatic hydrocarbons	0	0	71	100
Aromatic hydrocarbons	0	0	9	112

Source: Katowice Regional Environmental Authority files

Table 8.3 Chorzów project: emissions of selected pollutants from both plants (1990-1992)

Pollutant	1990 (tonnes)	1992 (tonnes)	1992/1990 (%)
Particulate matter	9,347	4,545	49
Carbon monoxide	17,151	1,188	7
Sulphur dioxide	6,091	4,198	69
Nitrogen dioxide	2,277	2,551	112
Aliphatic hydrocarbons	563	71	13
Aromatic hydrocarbons	290	9	3

Source: Katowice Regional Environmental Authority files

The results of the project can be best judged from Tables 8.2 and 8.3. In 1993 the emissions from the steel mill were reduced even further, and close-to-zero emissions were recorded in 1994 (100 kg of particulate matter; 3.4 t of carbon monoxide; 3.6 t of sulphur dioxide, and 51 t of nitrogen dioxide). The emissions from the power plant grew somewhat, but the net ambient effect was unambiguously and remarkably beneficial (Beblo, 1993). Besides, a part of the apparent increase of pollution from the power plant is likely to be a 'paper growth' which resulted from improved monitoring. However, another part of this growth was caused – quite paradoxically – by switching to cleaner fuel of higher calorific value, thereby resulting in a higher combustion temperature (Beblo, 1994).

The 'greening' of the steel mill was predominantly caused by the shutdown of its open hearth furnace, coking plant and all other raw material units. All that would happen sooner or later anyway, but the time factor was critical in this heavily contaminated neighbourhood. It is estimated that the project accelerated the restructuring process of the steel mill by 2.5 years. The compromise it involved was to tolerate high emissions from the power plant. However, regional authorities have had very limited practical control over it, as this is a co-generation plant providing heat not only for Chorzów, but also for several other districts. The most likely conventional scenario would be to tolerate emissions from the power plant (which initiated some abatement activities) for the rest of its life, and to wait and watch how the steel mill struggled with its restructuring program.

On the legal side, the project was made possible by a limited possibility of manipulating the estimated contribution of each plant to ambient pollution concentrations. This allowed the two plants to use different estimates of 'background concentration' levels. Nevertheless, all permit decisions – which included a number of other minor plants not referred to in this chapter – were unconventional[1] and could be considered controversial. In order to avoid confusion and to minimize the risk of having permit decisions challenged by environmental groups, a major education effort was undertaken (Zylicz, 1994). At the national level, the ME published and widely distributed Polish translations of the 1989 OECD report and Project 88, which explained the rationale for using economic instruments in environmental protection. At the local level, efforts were made to let environmental NGOs and the media understand the project and appreciate its benefits. These steps proved to be effective, since no permit decision has been challenged. Instead, many other municipalities approached the regional administrator in Katowice requesting that similar arrangements be applied in their air-sheds. However, because of the lack of a satisfactory legal framework and because of the amount of administrative work (to substitute for the legal framework), the authorities are reluctant to replicate the experiment.

Three conclusions can be drawn from the Chorzów project:

- the value of the TPP approach to address complex restructuring and abatement problems in non-attainment areas was demonstrated;
- a remarkable decrease of emissions was achieved mainly by 'transferring' permits between just two major local polluters; and

- industry and administrators behaved highly cooperatively when assisted by competent external experts.

These observations confirm the viability of simple TPP schemes in an economy in transition, in a heavily polluted region, and without any significant external financial aid.

3. THE OPOLE PROJECT AND BEYOND

In late 1991 there was a change of the government which resulted in slowing down of the pace of policy reform. For a number of years, chaotic political processes adversely affected the development of emissions trading. The draft Environmental Protection Act of 1991 was abandoned. In 1993, an Air Protection Act was drafted as an independent initiative undertaken by the electricity sector. The expectation was that with unclear prospects for a new comprehensive environmental protection law, several sectoral or single-medium legislations had a better chance of being enacted. Power plant operators wished to provide for permit tradability and introduced appropriate clauses (as Articles 25 and 26). Because of the lack of political will, this Act has never been debated in the Parliamentary forum.

A new opportunity arose with a PHARE Programme offer to finance a couple of full scale research projects addressing problems of practical importance for the ME. A study was commissioned to elaborate on the practical steps required to implement tradable permits in a region on a routine basis. In 1994, Atmoterm, a Polish firm which formed a consortium with several other consultants, was granted a contract under the PHARE Programme to prepare an actual implementation in the Opole region in southern Poland (see Atmoterm, 1996, for key elements of the project). Tradable permits also emerged as an important instrument in another PHARE project commissioned by the ME a few months later. This project, whose focus was on methodologies for assessing the costs of meeting international environmental obligations, concluded that the costs largely depend on the policy instruments applied (Peszko, 1996). At the same time, it demonstrated the cost-effectiveness of applying tradable permits in order to let domestic emission sources comply with requirements.

The Opole project was originally conceived as an implementation exercise. Nevertheless, it became apparent that with the political establishment only marginally interested in policy reforms, there would be no chance for an appropriate amendment of the legislation on time. Consequently, the project was redesigned and instead of actual implementation a series of computer simulations served as a test of the legal mechanism developed. The main features of the Opole project are:

- Polluters were subject to both non-tradable source-oriented emission standards, and tradable permits;
- The majority of permits were grandfathered, although there was also a small auction;
- The total amount of permits was derived from a regional attainment plan, and reduced over time;
- The region is divided into six trading zones, with one to one trading within zones and trading based on exchange rates between zones;
- Banking was allowed, but the credits deposited were discounted at a 20 per cent annual rate.

The trading simulations indicated relatively modest cost savings of approximately 20 per cent. This outcome was influenced by the fact that even under the existing Polish system some flexibility is possible. This flexibility means that some of the excessive costs associated with conventional technology-based and source-specific emission standards are avoided. However the political importance of the Opole project is greater than these relatively modest cost savings imply. It represented a serious administrative effort to design a workable trading scheme, and led to a draft chapter for a new Environmental Protection Act that established specific rules for emissions trading.

With the Opole project completed (on paper) in 1996, there seems to be no further need to demonstrate the usefulness of the instrument in the Polish context. The political decision of 1990 was never formally negated, the Chorzów project should have convinced sceptics, the idea is understood by professionals very well, and the media appreciate it. Important design issues were analysed in both practical and theoretical terms (Stavins and Zylicz, 1995). Nevertheless, attempts to implement it proved that there were many specific problems that need to be addressed.

3.1. Tradable permits and non-tradable requirements

One issue that recurs on many occasions in policy debates in Poland is the relation between a tradable permit to pollute and source-specific requirements. The requirements may take the form of:
- an emission standard for a given type of installation (e.g. under the Ordinance of the Polish Minister of the Environment of 1990);
- an emission limit for a given source derived from some ambient quality considerations (a typical solution in Poland); or
- mandating use of a specific technology (e.g. Best Available Technology (BAT), or Best Available Technology Not Entailing Excessive Costs (BATNEEC)).

The primary question is whether purchasing additional permits can free a source from the obligation to comply with such requirements. If it cannot, then why purchase permits in the first place?

While there exist systems where the tradable permit is the only regulatory requirement, as a rule the permit is merely one part of a package of environmental regulations affecting the source. In other words, the permit (whether tradable or not) held by an enterprise may be a necessary condition to operate, but not a sufficient one. For all practical purposes, future tradable permit systems in Poland should be envisaged as coexisting with other regulatory regimes.

Additional concerns result from the recent adoption of the Integrated Pollution Prevention and Control Directive (IPPC) by the European Union. The Directive mandates using BAT as a reference for abatement requirements. Does BAT allow for transferring a permit from one source to another? This question is raised by Polish lawyers. For what is a BAT? It is a technology which can be actually applied and which minimizes emissions per unit of performance in a given sector.[2] If a firm can bring its emissions down to a certain level then, by definition, BAT cannot be less stringent than what the firm has just achieved. Therefore, whenever BAT is required then the least polluting firm sets a standard for everyone else and eliminates the notion of a 'surplus' emission reduction and emissions trading.

Even though theoretically possible, this extreme understanding of BAT can never become a political option. It would eliminate incentives to innovate and doom economies to stagnate. Instead, here BAT will be understood pragmatically as a level of emission per unit of output that eliminates excessive pollution at source. It will not be revised immediately after a technical improvement has occurred, but rather periodically at reasonable time intervals once the new technology builds a successful operating record.

To elucidate the relationship between tradability of permits and emerging European legislative issues, the Polish ME together with Harvard Institute for International Development (HIID) organized a policy workshop in June 1996. The workshop provided an opportunity to assess Polish plans to introduce emissions trading from the point of view of the US practical experience and the European legal framework.

Ger Klaassen, who spoke at the workshop on behalf of the Environment Directorate of the EU, made it clear that the IPPC Directive imposes some extra requirements on pollution sources, but it does not preclude emissions trading (Klaassen, 1996).[3] Nevertheless the latter cannot overrule source and/or site-specific conditions that policy makers in Europe are likely to retain. As an example, Dr. Klaassen quoted the regulatory framework for the power sector in the UK.[4] Power stations in England and Wales are subject to two types of emission limit. The first (type A) are geared to protecting local air quality and to ensuring that critical load effects from individual power stations are addressed. The second (type B) are stricter, and take into account the combined effect of releases from power stations on the environment and, in particular, on critical loads. The site specific B limits may be varied provided that: 1) the sum of the B limits does not exceed a maximum specified portfolio limit for each group of sources; and 2) no station exceeds its A limit. The net effect is that groups of sources have an emissions 'bubble' and can trade emissions between plants. Taken together the limits are designed to incorporate the principles of BATNEEC. Since the UK definition of BATNEEC is broadly equivalent to the IPPC definition of BAT,[5] such a framework may be considered to be consistent with the IPPC Directive.

Polluters are also subject to double requirements in the US Acid Rain Program (McLean, 1996). Each source has to comply with a non-transferable emission limit as set in its individual pollution permit. On top of that, each participating source is allocated an emission allowance – more restrictive than the permit – which can be freely traded. This system very much resembles the British 'type A/type B' scheme. It should be noted that an emission permit in this framework is not identical to an emission allowance. A source may buy a number of tradable allowances but may not be allowed to operate unless it complies with the terms of its non-tradable permit. To formally stress the difference, the legal system uses two distinct concepts – a permit and an allowance. The architects of the program have avoided using the earlier concept of an 'emission reduction credit' – implicitly referring to a permit, which served as the baseline for reductions – in order to emphasize the two requirements: one non-transferable and the other transferable.

In the Opole project, sources are subject to dual constraints too. First, a source may be required to comply with some technological and/or ambient requirement. Second, it is expected to comply with annual (or bi-annual) reduction targets mandated by the regional administrator and resulting from general policy considerations. Additionally, as in the US Acid Rain Program, anyone can buy an emission allowance, but not anyone can emit the corresponding amount of pollution.

From the point of view of a polluter the distinction between a permit and an allowance may seem like nothing but an added complexity. But there are advantages of such a scheme. First of all it frees environmental authorities from estimating the environmental impact of individual transactions, since there are other constraints that prevent excessive pollution from any source. Additionally, as not only prospective polluters can buy emission allowances, governments, environmental groups, and individual citizens may enter the market and thus – by retiring allowances they have just purchased – express their preferences with respect to the amount of pollution. Such activities vitalize the demand side of the market, help to sustain prices and ultimately reward those who contribute to the supply, i.e. those who abate more than required.

3.2. Lessons from the US

Clarification of the constraints that should or could accompany emissions trading and its compatibility with European laws might have been the most important outcome of the workshop. Nevertheless the list of topics covered in discussions was much longer. In particular, it has become clear that the US experience with tradable permits is extremely diversified. The two systems presented at the workshop – Acid Rain and RECLAIM (Leyden, 1996) – exemplify two different scales and two different legal regimes.

The Acid Rain Program creates a country-wide market for allowances. Emission sources can trade without constraints, regardless of the distance between them. There is also an option to bank unused allowances for future use (without discounting). Authorizing unconstrained intercontinental and intertemporal trades was justified by the goal of the program, i.e. to decrease acid deposition over a twenty-year period (1990-2010). As sulphuric emissions migrate over large distances and their depositions accumulate in lakes and soils, neither the exact location of emission nor its timing seemed crucial. This, however, does not mean that the program risks creating pollution 'hot spots' caused by an excessive accumulation of allowances at one particular site. Anybody can buy permits but not everybody can actually use them as a passport to pollute. A source has to comply with the terms of its pollution permit which is both site-specific and non-transferable.

The most important feature of RECLAIM is its local scope. The program is supposed to improve ambient air quality in the South Coast area of California. Its geographical scope is thus quite limited. Because of the severity of the pollution problem in the Los Angeles area, the size of the market is further reduced by a division into two impact zones according to environmental sensitivity and population exposure. These factors, coupled with the large scale of emission reductions required, imply abatement costs five to seven times higher than in other US programs. Another difference of the RECLAIM program is that, given its local focus, the same permit combines short-term local and long-term regional requirements. This rather unusual design was justified by two factors. First, Los Angeles polluters are subject to extremely severe abatement requirements so that none of the sources are likely to earn (and therefore sell) a large volume of emission reduction credits. Second, due to the high level of pollutant concentrations, the exact location of a pollution source is of secondary importance.

A number of the polluters from the Los Angeles basin simultaneously participate in two emissions trading schemes – Acid Rain and RECLAIM.

They can buy Acid Rain allowances, but the RECLAIM requirements make it unlikely that they will ever use them to increase emissions above their initial allocations. This example illustrates three principles. First, firms may participate in more than one permit market operating independently. Second, purchasing a permit or an allowance is not identical with acquiring the right to pollute. Third, for the same emission reduction, a firm may get more than one credit. The latter principle corresponds to the fact that reducing emissions yields multiple benefits (e.g. local and continental) and those who abate should face incentives reflecting all of these benefits.

An important feature of the RECLAIM scheme is a rigorous reduction schedule, with overall emission reduction targets that are translated into annual reduction steps that polluters must comply with (although not individually but rather as a group). This is in sharp contrast with conventional approaches which give industries or municipalities a reasonable amount of time to achieve the target without interim check-points. The usual outcome observed under such regimes is that a significant portion of the sources ignore the regulation and hit the deadline while keeping excessive emissions. The more widespread this pattern becomes, the more difficult it is to conduct an effective enforcement action. As a rule, the government amends the regulation and postpones the deadline. In both Poland and the United States one can find examples of this policy failure. Therefore it is worth noting that the Opole project replicates the good practice of translating an overall long-term goal into annual steps that are much easier to enforce.

The workshop participants had the opportunity to discuss various technical details of permit market design. All the US speakers emphasized one key rule: 'keep it simple!' Vitality of the market, political support, and effective cooperation with businesses depend on the stability, transparency and simplicity of the trading mechanism (Sleszynski, 1996). To illustrate how bureaucracy can be kept to a minimum, the participants were shown the Acid Rain Program permit application. It consists of three pages with just several boxes to be filled out. The US experts stressed that one should often sacrifice theoretical accuracy for the sake of simplicity in order to make the system work and benefit the environment. An example of such a compromise is reducing the number of trading zones or simplifying exchange indices. From this perspective, some participants considered the Opole project with its six trading zones too complicated.

The representatives of the Air Protection Department in the Polish ME raised a number of questions regarding the daily operation of permit markets. One important issue is confidentiality of emission and transaction data. Under the US law, some trading details cannot be disclosed but the total emissions of a given pollutant discharged from the plant is publicly known. Another issue is the inclusion of small sources in the trading system. In general, because of transaction and administrative costs, there are limits to extending the market over such pollution sources. Policy makers and authorities should investigate whether alternative instruments, such as input and pollution taxes, performance standards, fuel specifications, or subsidies for upgrading equipment can achieve the overall goal at a lower cost.

Strict enforcement is also an important aspect of emissions trading. Under the US Clean Air Act, participants of the Acid Rain Program are exposed to three types of sanctions. First, failure to comply with the sulphur allowance requirement results in a fine of $2000 per ton.[6] Second, violating the terms of a site-specific permit triggers a fine of $25000. Third, any excess emissions are automatically deducted from future allocations to the firm. The strict monitoring requirements makes these sanctions almost impossible to evade, and to date no firm has exceeded its allowance allocation.

Another practical issue raised at the workshop was how to win the support of the parliament for a law that – like the US Clean Air Act or a prospective Polish Environmental Protection Act – must be full of technical concepts and details that are incomprehensible to a layperson. While it is true that the law may not be understandable for an average member of parliament, environmentalists need to cooperate with politicians who are likely to be 'champions' of an innovative regulation. Winning the support of the Polish Parliament for tradable permits will require a lot of communication and educational effort.

4. EPILOGUE

A new Environmental Protection Act – commissioned by the ME – was drafted in 1996. As previously, it included a provision for tradability of permits (this time in Article 88) which gave an opportunity for regional administrators to authorize permit transfers subject to some constraints. The new feature was that the Article referred to an ordinance that sets specific rules for emissions trading. Such an ordinance was in fact prepared under the Opole project and it could have been incorporated into the main Act. The drafters, however, retained their original scepticism and apparently preferred to minimize the presence of the instrument they consider controversial.

The 1996 Act devoted an entire chapter to pollution offsets. Economists may be surprised with the attention given to this special case of emissions trading, but it can be explained by the fact that offsets were historically the earliest form of the instrument in the USA. They were also included in the German air protection legislation in the 1970s, where they proved to be of little practical importance as only a dozen or so trades took place under the so-called modernization clause.[7] The Polish chapter on pollution offsets illustrates the fact that it takes time before policy makers get accustomed to new ideas. How many years will it take before a general scheme of tradable permits can be accepted as a routine mechanism?

With the 1996 draft abandoned in 1997 (mainly due to the political dynamics of an election year), it is likely that the introduction of tradable permits will be put aside for many months again. There is not much that can be done within the environmental economics profession to promote the case. Emissions trading has become a permanent item on the policy reform agenda. The most important obstacles come from elsewhere. Amending environmental laws competes in parliamentary fora with other issues seen by politicians as higher priorities. This is compounded by the fact that European Union environmental policies – a natural reference for policy makers in Central and Eastern Europe – largely ignore the tradable permit option.

An optimistic scenario envisages growing pressures towards making Poland's environmental policies more cost-effective. The outcome of this process must be a legal framework that recognizes transferability of permits. A pessimistic scenario extrapolates the political logic of the last few years. It envisages more studies, more drafting committees, more Environmental Protection Acts, and more cost-saving opportunities forgone.

NOTES

1. A conventional permit – developed using conventional procedures – would have required zero emissions since the sources were located in a non attainment area.
2. See the definition in Article 11, European Commission 1996.
3. See also G. Klaassen, this book, Chapter 5.
4. See S. Sorrell, this book, Chapter 11.
5. The definition of 'available' in Article 11 of the Directive includes '.... taking into consideration the costs and advantages'. This is comparable to the UK definition '..not entailing excessive costs'.
6. Compared to a current market price of around $100/ton.
7. See the discussion G. Klaassen, this book, Chapter 5.

REFERENCES

Atmoterm (1996), 'Tradable emission permit system', in Harvard Institute for International Development, *Marketable Permit Workshop: Proceedings*, Jadwisin (Poland), pp.14–17.

Beblo, W. (1993), 'Ochrona powietrza w województwie katowickim', *Rzeczpospolita*, 25 February (Dodatek ekologiczny nr 2) ('Air protection in Katowice region').

Beblo, W. (1994), letters to T. Zylicz, Katowice, 24 March and 30 May.

Dudek, D., Z. Kulczynski., and T. Zylicz (1992), 'Implementing tradable rights in Poland: a case study of Chorzów'. *Proceedings of the Third Annual Conference of the European Association of Environmental and Resource Economists*, Cracow, Vol. 2, pp.58–75.

European Commission (1996), Council Directive 96/61/EC concerning integrated pollution prevention and control, *Official Journal*, Vol. 39, 10 October.

Harvard Institute for International Development and Polish Ministry of Environment (1996), *Marketable Permit Workshop: Proceedings*, Jadwisin (Poland).

Klaassen, G. (1996), 'Emissions trading and the EU IPPC Directive', in Harvard Institute for International Development, *Marketable Permit Workshop: Proceedings*, Jadwisin (Poland), pp.24–26.

Leyden, P. (1996), 'The South Coast Air Quality Management District (California) RECLAIM Program and Related Trading Initiatives – Description, Benefits, Realities, Lessons-Learned', in Harvard Institute for International Development, *Marketable Permit Workshop: Proceedings*, Jadwisin (Poland), pp.34–35.

McLean, B. (1996), 'The US Clean Air Act Title IV Acid Rain Program – Description, Benefits, Realities, Lessons Learned', in Harvard Institute for International Development, *Marketable Permit Workshop: Proceedings*, Jadwisin (Poland), pp.27–33.

Ministry of Environment (1990), *National Ecological Policy*, Warsaw.

OECD (1989), *Economic Instruments for Environmental Protection*, Paris.

Peszko, G. (1996), 'Emissions trading as a potential instrument of compliance with the Second Sulphur Protocol by the power sector in Poland', in Harvard Institute for International Development, *Marketable Permit Workshop: Proceedings*, Jadwisin (Poland) pp.18–23.

Sleszynski, J. (1996), 'Workshop summary', in Harvard Institute for International Development, *Marketable Permit Workshop: Proceedings*, Jadwisin (Poland), pp.46–53.

Stavins, R. and T. Zylicz (1995), 'Environmental policy in a transition economy: designing tradable permits for Poland', *RFF Discussion Paper No. 9*, Resources for the Future, Washington, DC.

US Congress (1988), *Project 88: Harnessing Market Forces To Protect Our Environment*, A Public Study sponsored by Senator T. E. Wirth (Colorado) and Senator J. Heinz (Pennsylvania), Washington, DC.

Zylicz, T. (1990), 'Environmental policies for former centrally planned economies', paper presented at the First Annual Conference of the European Association of Environmental and Resource Economists, Venice.

Zylicz, T. (1994), 'Environmental policy reform in Poland', in T. Sterner (ed), *Economic Policies for Sustainable Development*, Kluwer, Dordrecht, pp.82–112.

PART III

Trading and National Regulatory Traditions

(Germany)
H23 Q2⁵
Q28

9. Tradable emission permits in German clean air policy: considerations on the efficiency of environmental policy instruments

Bernd Schärer

1. INTRODUCTION

Since 1984, Germany has made major efforts to improve air quality and reduce acid deposition. A total of around 30,000 power stations and industrial plants have been required to reduce emissions, and a further 13,000 new plants have been granted approval. In both cases, emissions were limited according to the principle of 'Stand der Technik' or state of the art.

The most important regulations for limiting emissions from plants subject to permitting are the Ordinance on Large Firing Installations (Großfeuerungsanlagen-Verordnung – GFAVO) of 1983, issued on the basis of the Federal Emission Control Act (Bundes-Imissionsschutzgesetz – BImSchG), and the *TA Luft* of 1986. Both of these have been in force in eastern Germany since 1990. The foundations of the clean air policy of the BImSchG relating to stationary plants are summarized in Box 1. The details of this are governed by the *GFAVO* which lays down emission limits for all large combustion installations (>50 MW thermal input) according to the state of the art. These must be put into effect immediately by all new plants and within a transition period of six to eight years by older plants. The *TA Luft* defines emission limits for all remaining plants subject to permitting and prescribes a clean-up transition period for old plants of three to eight years.

Parallel to the development and execution of these regulatory policies an extensive discussion has taken place in Germany on the use of economic instruments, particularly environmental taxes and tradable permits. This discussion has led to numerous proposals for applying economic instruments in addition to, or instead of, traditional regulatory policy. To underline the serious preoccupation of the German environmental policy community with

Box 1 The dual-track strategy of German clean air policy

German clean air policy covers both the various forms in which air pollution can manifest itself and the full range of environmental policy instruments. Of greatest practical significance are environmental quality standards and emission limit values which supplement each other to form a dual-track strategy.

Environmental quality standards, as maximum values for pollutant concentrations in the air and maximum rates of deposition, serve as protection from negative environmental effects. These protection thresholds are derived from scientific information. Comprehensive concepts for environmental quality standards are difficult to establish, however, since this information is often incomplete. Moreover, such concepts cannot be implemented directly, but rather via emission requirements for the sources responsible, on the basis of extensive dispersion modelling.

German clean air policy emphasizes the independent role of emission limit values and product standards which – apart from highly toxic pollutants – are not derived from environmental quality objectives but reflect the technical feasibility of emission abatement at its source. Technological development is thus an independent factor, and in practice is the main driving force behind environment policy decisions and practical implementation measures. The legislative foundation for this is the precautionary principle, established in the Federal Emission Control Act of 1974, which provides for emission reduction requirements for all sources according to the state of the art. It mandates decision-makers to take action based on technical feasibility (state of the art control technology), rather than confining action to defence against concrete, known environmental hazards.

these new kinds of instruments, just a few important initiatives from the state domain are mentioned here:

- The Federal government commissioned an inter-ministerial working group to examine and report on the scope for economic instruments as early as 1983.[1] In 1984, the German Federal Parliament (Deutscher Bundestag) expressly demanded the use of economic instruments for the impending ecological clean-up programs (Bundesumweltministerium, 1988).
- The 1984 report of the Federal Environmental Agency on the 'Possibilities for implementing economic instruments to reduce emissions from stationary sources' both recommends emissions trading and contains concrete proposals for its implementation. Furthermore, a supplementary proposal for the use of emissions trading in the *GFAVO* was provided by the industrial associations as early as 1983.[2]

The discussion of this subject, in which environmental groups and scientists have also participated, is considerably more extensive than would have been expected in view of its limited impact on regulatory practice. The central axis of the discussion was and is the economic efficiency argument. This chapter first discusses a number of considerations related to the economic efficiency of emissions trading, before a more detailed examination of the obstacles to establishing this instrument in Germany. The final section of the chapter discusses the insights gained from this experience and the implications for the supposed efficiency advantages of economic instruments.

2. ON THE EFFICIENCY OF ENVIRONMENTAL POLICY INSTRUMENTS

The design and selection of policy instruments for environmental protection depends on two key criteria: effectiveness in attaining the ecological objectives and economic efficiency. The second of these is best achieved by instruments that require only limited intervention in the internal decision making of companies. In other words the instrument should ensure a high degree of flexibility and favour least cost solutions.

A favourite in the instrument kit of environmental policy to combat air pollution is the trading of pollutant emission rights. The idea behind this instrument is to establish property rights over formerly free environmental goods and thereby subject them to the laws of the market. This approach is claimed to protect the environment effectively and to be more economically efficient than the traditional alternative of uniform emission limits. Free trade with emission property rights (emission permits) should allocate the measures required to achieve a particular emission reduction target such that only the most cost effective measures are applied. Under standard economic assumptions regarding the operation of the permit market, the equilibrium distribution of emissions will be attained when the marginal costs of emission abatement are equal for all sources.

In addition to the theoretical attractions of this model, traditional regulatory instruments have met with considerable criticism because of a variety of assumed failings. They are claimed:

- to be too expensive, since variations in abatement opportunities and control costs between plants are not adequately taken into account;
- to provide no incentive to polluters to reduce emissions below current regulatory requirements, and thus to inhibit innovation and long term ecologically sound development; and

- to be too bureaucratic in their implementation and thus too expensive; particularly as approval procedures take too long and hamper economic progress.

Textbook treatments of economic instruments suggest that they provide a positive alternative in each case. They are economically efficient, provide a continuous incentive for technological innovation and minimize cumbersome and expensive bureaucracy (Wicke, 1991).

3. APPROACHES TO THE USE OF TRADABLE PERMITS IN CLEAN AIR POLICY

The correctness of these claims will now be assessed in the context of the German clean up programs for stationery sources – the *GFAVO* and the *TA Luft*. A pilot emissions trading program for the reduction of VOC emissions is also discussed.

3.1. Cleaning-up large combustion installations

Stringent emission limit values for power stations and industrial combustion installations with a thermal output of more than 50 MW were mandated by the *GFAVO* in 1983. To achieve these standards most plant had to be retrofitted with flue gas desulphurization (FGD) for sulphur dioxide (SO_2) and selective catalytic reduction (SCR) for nitrogen oxides (NO_x). This was implemented in a phased program, ending in 1993. By that time around 170 desulphurization plants and 140 SCR plants had been completed, at a total cost of 21.3 billion D-Marks (14.3 million for FGD; 7 million for SCR). The annual costs, including capital services, amount to around 4 billion D-Marks with abatement costs for SO_2 of about 2300 D-Marks/tonne and NO_x of about 2700 D-Marks/tonne. These measures reduced total emissions by around 90 per cent (Schärer, 1993).[3] In eastern Germany, where the *GFAVO* came into effect in 1990, corresponding clean-up measures are still being carried out at the present time. These should likewise lead to a reduction in emissions of around 90 per cent by 1998.

There have been numerous proposals for economic instruments to either supplement or replace the uniform emission limits used in the *GFAVO*. Proposals for the use of emissions trading for the impending clean-up work came from industry in 1983 (for SO_2) and from the *Umweltbundesamt* in 1984 (for NO_x). These and many other suggestions were not taken up by the regulatory authorities. They failed because of the doubts of policymakers that, first, an ecological effectiveness comparable to the regulatory powers of the *GFAVO* would be possible; and second, that greater economic efficiency could be achieved. The following are the arguments most commonly employed:

- A significantly different allocation of the necessary emission reduction measures was not expected in view of the exacting emission limit standards and because of the relative homogeneity of the regulated sources. As a consequence, economic instruments could not be expected to provide significant cost savings.
- The short implementation periods, oriented towards the minimum times for planning, approval and construction, left hardly any time for the development of economic efficiency through trading. The environmental policy at that time favoured short-term success in emission reduction.
- Environmental taxes were opposed since they would result in a withdrawal of liquidity from firms at precisely the time when finance was required for investments in emission reduction.
- Both environmental taxes and emissions trading created the possibility of regional impairments in air quality (hot spots). This was considered to be unacceptable.

The results of the *GFAVO* demonstrated that the refitting of an entire sector by clear regulatory standards can also have economic advantages. Thus, the 'serial production' of control technology achieved considerable rationalizations and cost reductions in the production of desulphurization and DENOX plants (Schärer, 1993).

The success of the *GFAVO* made a considerable contribution to improvement of air quality in Germany and acid deposition throughout Europe. Its economic efficiency, however, was frequently criticized with reference to a corresponding regulation of power stations in the USA. The Acid Rain Program in the 1990 Clean Air Act Amendments (CAAA) commonly serves as an example for the use of emissions trading in environmental policy (Schärer, 1996). This program covers a similar range of plant to the *GFAVO*, but with the difference that it is not based on uniform emission limit values but rather on tradable permits (allowances) allocated to each plant. One allowance is worth 1 ton of sulphur dioxide, and the number of allowances distributed each year corresponds to the total tonnage of emissions allowed in each year.[4]

A decisive difference between the German and US schemes is the stringency of the emissions target. Whereas a reduction of over 90 per cent of SO_2 emissions is expected during the execution time of the *GFAVO*, the Acid Rain Program only attains emission reductions of 50 per cent, with no expectations of a tightening of the emission target before 2010. The difference in rigour of the two schemes explains the broad scope that is available to US power station operators for finding cost effective solutions.

According to recent work by MIT, the allowance trading program has reduced the cost of controlling SO_2 emissions by one third to one half (Ellerman et al., 1997). Such cost saving potential is not transferable to the German situation however, on account of the considerably stricter emission limits. It must thus be considered, in assessment of these figures, that the trading margin shrinks with increasing rigour of the emission limit requirements, and that hardly any possibilities exist for cost saving if emission reduction targets are oriented towards the state of the art of control technology.

3.2. The compensation model of the *TA Luft*

Another large clean-up program for stationary sources was begun in 1986 with the amendment of the *TA Luft*. Except for the large combustion installations and waste incineration plants (the latter were regulated separately in 1990 by the 17th *BlmSch Ordinance*) the *TA Luft* covers all the remaining plants subject to permitting (over 50,000) and lays down the emission limit requirements for these according to the state of the art. Depending on the hazard potential and amount of emissions, the old plants are granted transition periods of three, five or eight years for the re-equipment. In the old Federal States the re-equipment had to be concluded by 1994 or the plants shut down. In the new Federal States the measures have to be concluded by the middle of 1999.

The effects of this program on emission reduction have not yet been fully assessed for the whole of Germany. However, the data available for the Federal State of North Rhine-Westphalia demonstrate the magnitude of emission reduction that can be achieved by the affected plant:

- around 65 per cent for carcinogenic emissions,
- around 60 per cent for fine-particle inorganic emissions,
- around 42 per cent for gaseous inorganic emissions,
- around 55 per cent for organic emissions.

In 1985, the discussion about tradable permits found its consolidation in a change of the *BlmSchG* with corresponding embodiment in the *TA Luft*. This provides the possibility of deviating from the emission limit values when 'compensation' measures comparable to the US bubble policy are implemented.

The compensation rule of the *TA Luft* is a compromise in the direction of tradable permits. The rule states that a plant's clean up period can be extended if it can be demonstrated that control measures taken at neighbouring plants can provide an equivalent or greater reduction in emissions. The rule can only be used by installations within the same geographical area and for the same pollutants or for pollutants with comparable environmental impact. This regulation can be interpreted as a rudimentary form of tradable permits.

The practical importance of the compensation rule is very limited. Despite considerable support for individual measures by legislative, administrative and scientific bodies, there have only been a very small number of actual compensation transactions. Thus, the sixth *Immissionsschutzbericht* (Air Quality Report) of the Federal government identifies only 350 plants, out of a total of 23,000 plants requiring refitting, which made use of compensation (Bundesumweltministerium, 1996).

The failure of the compensation rule of the *TA Luft* is judged very guardedly in the relevant policy analyses. Frequently, the restrictive legal requirements, entirely subordinate to the plant clean-up target, are given as the reason for the failure (Kalmbach and Troge, 1989). However, from talks with firms and regulators, it is apparent that the stringency of requirement under the *TA Luft* leaves little scope for significant cost reductions. Following this, it would appear that the potential cost advantages of compensations were so slight that they could be readily offset by the legal certainty and transparency of the administrative regulations.

3.3. A pilot project in tradable VOC permits

Following the unsuccessful attempts to establish tradable permits in the *GFAVO* and *TA Luft*, a further area is currently being investigated for the application of this instrument. In a pilot project run by the *Umweltbundesamt*, 'Tradable permits for the reduction of volatile organic compound (VOC) emissions from plants not subject to permitting', a scheme for emissions trading is being developed, with the assistance of the trade associations of the polluters involved (Scheelhaase, 1997). The concept is to be tested in a two to three year pilot phase, beginning in 1998, and after that be introduced into the implementation of a corresponding EU Directive (CEC, 1995). The project is primarily targeted on small vehicle finishing shops, of which there are some 12,000 in Germany. These are currently unregulated, but contribute significantly to VOC emissions, which play an important role as precursor for summer smog (ground level ozone).

The pilot project involves a small number of firms whose participation is voluntary. These may be located anywhere in Germany as 'hot spots' are not seen as a constraint. The permits will be distributed free by a clearing authority and reduced in number in several stages. Monitoring will be through mass balance records of input and output stocks of paints and solvents, backed up by spot audits by the environmental authorities.

In the preliminary work on the VOC emissions trading model it has become apparent that many of the measures to reduce VOC emissions from vehicle refinishing shops are to a large extent economic *per se* (i.e. negative abatement cost). In other words, cost saving measures exist which have not been used up to now. This investment bottle-neck could be due to a lack of information, incorrect pre-investment analyses or neglect due to the small cost savings involved.

4. ON THE EFFICIENCY ARGUMENT

The efficiency of an environmental policy instrument is to be understood as its suitability to induce polluters to attain any predetermined emission objective at the lowest possible cost (Endres, 1985). Economic instruments are argued to offer greater efficiency than could be achieved by regulatory instruments such as uniform emission limit values. The reason for this difference lies in the different marginal abatement costs of the individual emission sources.

The principal way in which environmental taxes and tradable permits achieve an emission reduction target is shown in Figure 9.1, which represents the possibilities and costs of emission reduction for two different emission sources A and B. The following comments can be made about this presentation.

Environmental taxes encourage polluters to apply those abatement measures that are cheaper than paying the tax. In this way, the tax rate controls the rigour of the abatement measures applied by each polluter, and consequently the stock of all the measures applied by the regulated sources. In contrast to tradable permits, environmental taxes give no guarantee of attaining an ecological objective.

In the case of tradable permits, the ecological objective is specified in terms of an allowed quantity of emissions. A fixed number of permits are distributed to participating sources in accordance with this target. Trades within the permit market set a price for the permits which is related to the cost of abatement. Firms which can control pollution more cheaply than buying a permit will control up to the point where control costs equal permit costs. The excess permits the firm holds can then be sold for a profit. Firms which have high abatement costs can cover their obligations by purchasing permits in the market. In the absence of market barriers, trade will continue until all trading opportunities have been fully exploited. At this point, the distribution of control responsibility will be cost effective, with the marginal control costs being equalized across all sources and equal to the permit price.

Both instruments equalize and minimize abatement costs for the participating sources and for society as a whole. In the example chosen (Figure 9.1) the marginal abatement costs for achieving the given environmental objective (reduction of 100 emission units) are 60 D-Marks

Figure 9.1 Effectiveness and efficiency as a result of emission limit value regulation and economic instruments

With increasing homogeneity of the regulated emission sources, i.e. their abatement measures and costs in order to achieve a predetermined emission target, the cost saving potential by the employment of economic instruments is diminished.

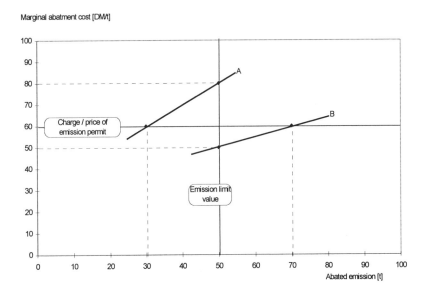

and are thus lower than could have been attained by uniform emission limit values (80 D-Marks for A and 50 D-Marks for B).

At this point the usual reasoning on instrument efficiency ends. However, the experience of the *GFAVO* and the *TA Luft* implies that this reasoning is oversimplified. The following conditions are also relevant and must therefore be taken into account when examining the efficiency debate. Economic instruments can only reduce abatement costs if, first, the regulated sources have a wide range of abatement costs, and second, the cost savings through trade exceed the transaction costs of using the permit market.

The first condition implies that the smaller the difference in abatement costs between plants (the closer the cost curves are in Figure 9.1) the less it becomes worthwhile for a company to consider measures implemented at other plants in its own emission reduction plans. If the cost difference between plants is small, the argument for the higher cost efficiency of economic instruments is undermined. In the extreme case of identical cost curves for the regulated plants, there can be no difference in the cost efficiency of uniform standards and economic instruments. In a similar vein, the second condition implies that, if the savings through trade are small they may easily be swamped by the transaction costs of using the permit market. Trading is only viable if both transaction costs are small and the potential savings through trade are large.

Wide variation in abatement cost is therefore a precondition for the efficiency superiority of economic instruments over uniform emission limits. A further aspect of this is illustrated in Figure 9.2. Economic instruments essentially give preference to economic efficiency advantages over the stringency of the environmental target to be achieved. An environmental policy aimed at fully exploiting the potential for emission reduction, and therefore oriented towards state of the art control technology, is compelled to cut back the decision margin of the plant operators. As a result, the flexibility available and thus the efficiency advantages of the economic instrument is reduced.

In Figure 9.2, it is assumed that emissions have to be cut to 45 per cent of their initial level. However, for the environmental problems targeted by the *GFAVO* and *TA Luft,* emission reductions of up to 90 per cent are achievable, using low emission materials and fuels as well as advanced (state of the art) technologies. This leaves unavoidable residual emissions equal to 10 per cent of the initial level. With these markers, the 'bandwidth' of the activity margins for emission permit trading is staked out. If an operator attains the maximum emission reduction of 90 per cent in this model, then a second operator taking over the permits on offer does not need to implement any emission reduction measures at all. Flexibility and tradability margins thus result from the distance between the technically possible emission reduction and that required by the environmental objective. Clearly, this range of efficiency tends to zero with increasing convergence of the emission objective and the technically possible emission reduction.

One further point is that economic instruments make heavy demands on the operator for economic calculations which contrast the costs of emission reduction measures with the cost of purchasing tradable permits or paying environmental taxes. Consequently, an important precondition for the efficient functioning of economic instruments is that such an evaluation can be made without unreasonable effort by the plant operators involved. If this precondition is not met, tradable permits and environmental taxes will fail to create sufficient incentives and will not set the desired market processes into motion.

Figure 9.2 Efficiency of economic instruments as the result of the stringency of the emission limitation target

With the increasing rigour of the emission limit requirements the potential for efficiency development by the employment of economic instruments is diminished.

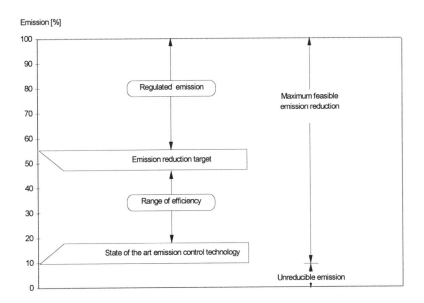

5. CONCLUSIONS

The achievement of economic efficiency through the use of emissions trading assumes three preconditions:

- the sources targeted by the instrument must exhibit a wide range of abatement costs;
- the potential cost savings through trade must be high relative to the transaction costs; and
- the polluters involved must have the resources to engage in the required economic calculations, without incurring unreasonable costs.

The experience of the German clean-up programs for stationary sources suggests that these preconditions are not always met. This may represent a considerable obstacle for the successful application of emissions trading in environmental policy.

NOTES

1. On 14 June 1983, the Federal Government commissioned an inter-ministerial working group to examine the question of whether and if so to what extent economic instruments, and tradable permits in particular, represent suitable and economically viable instruments of clean air policy. Upon completion of its deliberations, the working group presented its results to the Cabinet in the form of two reports (11 April 1984 and 18 December 1985). A request to examine possibilities for the use of economic instruments in connection with matters relating to the rehabilitation of existing plants was also directed to the Federal Government by the German Bundestag, through a decision adopted on 9 February 1984. The Federal Government submitted its opinion on this subject to the German Bundestag by way of a 'Report on the more rapid and extensive reduction of emissions of existing plant' (Bundestag publication no. 10/2965 of 5 March 1985). The trading of pollution permits between existing plants located in close spatial proximity to one another was seen to be a concrete area for possible application. The possibility of using compensatory schemes was incorporated into the Federal Emission Control Act in 1985 as part of the amendment to the Act and in 1986 to the *TA Luft* (subsection 4.2.10).

2. Neither the Federal Environment Agency report or the industrial associations' proposals are formally published. At that time, industrial pollution policy was largely an internal debate between the regulatory authorities and affected industries.

3. A comprehensive assessment of this program, the legal requirements and the measures which took place are provided in Schärer and Haug (1990).

4. This is not strictly true, as the use of allowance banking may lead to emissions in any single year exceeding the number of allowances distributed.

REFERENCES

Bundesumweltministerium (1988), *Vierter Immissionsschutzbericht der Bundesregierung* (Fourth Air Quality Report of the Federal government), BTDrs. 11/2714, pp.41–43.

Bundesumweltministerium (1996), *Sechster Immissionsschutzbericht der Bundesregierung* (Sixth Air Quality Report of the Federal government), BTDrs. 13/4825.

Commission of the European Commission (1995), 'Proposal on the Limitation of the Emissions of Organic Compounds due to the Use of Organic Solvents in Certain Processes in Industrial Installations', Brussels.

Ellerman, A.D., R. Schmalensee, P.L. Joskow, J.P. Montero and E.M. Bailey (1997), *Emissions Trading Under the US Acid Rain Program: Evaluation of Compliance Costs and Allowance Market Performance*, MIT Center for Energy and Environmental Policy Research, October.

Endres, A. (1985), *Umwelt- und Ressourcenökonomie* (Environmental and Resource Economics), Wissenschaftliche Buchgesellschaft Darmstadt, p.51.

Kalmbach, S. and A. Troge (1989), 'TA Luft – Kompensationslösung bewährt?' (Compensation Rule Worthwhile?), *Umweltmagazin,* November, pp.31–35.

Schärer, B. (1993), 'Technologies to clean up power plants – Experience with a DM 21 billion FGD and SCR retrofit program in Germany', *Staub-Reinhaltung der Luft,* **53**, 157–160.

Schärer, B. (1996), 'Neues von der amerikanischen SO_2-Börse' (New developments from the American SO_2 Market), *Gefahrenstoffe-Reinhaltung Luft,* **56**, 3–4.

Schärer, B. and N. Haug (1990), 'Bilanz der Großfeuerungsanlagenverordnung' (Critical Review of the Effects of the Ordinance on Large Firing Installations), *Staub-Reinhaltung Luft,* **50**, 139–144.

Scheelhaase, J. (1997), 'Design and introduction of tradable permits for VOC emissions: a pilot model', Paper presented at an international workshop on *the Institutional aspects of economic instruments for environmental policy,* CESAM, Eigtveds Pakhus, Asiatisk Plads, Copenhagen, 20–21 May.

Wicke, L. (1991), *Umweltökonomie* (Environmental Economics), Verlag Franz Vahlen München.

10. Public policy and institutional trajectories: what about introducing SO$_2$ emissions trading in France?

Christine Cros

1. INTRODUCTION

In the context of economic globalization and the market-oriented transformation of nation-states, long established institutions and systems of public regulation are being undermined. Often, the institutions and practices that are challenged the most are those that symbolize the distinctive cultural characteristics of individual countries. This trend is often perceived as a threat to features considered to be vital for the preservation of national identity. This is presently the case with the French doctrine of 'public service'.[1] A tension exists between the changes brought by a conquering international market ideology and a political will to retain values, concepts and forms of regulation which have been conceived until now as integral parts of the Social Contract. This tension provides the general framework within which the issue of changing environmental regulatory regimes can be discussed.

Two very different perspectives on the process of change of regulatory regimes may be obtained from neo-classical economics and political science. Within economic theory, the choice of a policy instrument is supposed to be guided by the search for economic efficiency. The cost effectiveness of one instrument as compared to another will depend on specific features of the implementation context, including: the number of agents to be regulated, information asymmetries, heterogeneity, the relative slope of damage and abatement cost curves, the abatement options available and the possible impact on technological innovation (Godard and Beaumais, 1994). This view is generally coupled with a denunciation of current administrative and regulatory measures (termed 'command and control') which are claimed to provide inadequate or inappropriate incentives and to generate various sorts of inefficiencies and distortions.

In contrast, the analyses supplied by political science focus on the fact that policy choices are more dependent on specific features of the institutional framework than on the characteristics of the problem to be solved. New policies would therefore be designed not so much around the problem itself but as a reaction to the consequences of previous policies, or to be consistent with national policy styles (Merrien, 1993). Others think public decisions result mainly from rhetorical practices and logic (Majone, 1989), or are derived from specific forms of compromise achieved between several 'justification orders'[2] (industrial, market, civic, tradition, etc.) each with established institutional rules and cultures (Boltanski and Thévenot, 1991). Economic efficiency is then just one element of the current modern rhetoric, but is interpreted and translated in multiple ways according to institutional context.

Can we build a bridge between these two viewpoints? This is attempted here through the concept of 'institutional trajectories', which gives insight into how a regulatory regime could move nearer to economic efficiency through the use of economic instruments.[3] We have chosen to confront what are often conceived as two absolutely incompatible traditions: the 'French way' of environmental public management and emissions trading. The first is a technical, but negotiated regulation of industrial pollution and health risks by engineers belonging to the civil service (Lascoumes, 1994); while the second is a novel economic instrument, introduced first in the US as a means to increase flexibility and reduce costs. The arena in which this is examined is the control of long range air pollution by sulphur dioxide (SO_2), an area in which the US has implemented an ambitious country-wide permit trading system as part of the 1990 Clean Air Act Amendments (Godard, 1994). The main question asked is: are there any absolute obstacles which make it impossible for a permit trading system to be used in France to control SO_2 emissions from stationary sources? What are the assumptions behind this presumed impossibility, which seems so obvious to many people in France?

The conclusion of our investigation is rather simple. There are no major legal or institutional obstacles to the introduction of emissions trading in France. The 'French way' could absorb emissions trading in the forms in which it has evolved; indeed, it has already done so to some limited and rather informal extent. There are several independent lines of evolution, both in the specific field of air pollution regulation and more broadly in forms of French and European public policy, which may converge to facilitate the acceptance of emissions trading. In particular, trading could be seen as an attractive means to recover some of the regulatory flexibility which has been lost during the past few years. Instead, the main obstacles to its introduction are identified as lying elsewhere. Most importantly, the various actors participating in the system of air pollution regulation are broadly satisfied with the present regulatory approach. Current unsolved problems are insufficient to mobilize key actors in favour of a new approach. There is also an important so-called 'moral' obstacle, related to the presumed perception of emissions trading by public opinion. The very concept of a 'right to pollute' is rejected in a legal tradition in which rights have been given a positive content.[4] Environmental organizations are hostile to any change that could be considered as an acknowledgement of such a 'right to pollute'. The idea that industrialists could make money by selling pollution rights is considered illegitimate. Pollution should be treated as a necessary evil, not a business opportunity.

These two obstacles do not exclude all types of instrument included in the category of 'tradable permits'. They may allow, for example, such limited developments as local bubbles or netting. However, they are likely to block the most developed forms of trading, the ones that most closely resemble a fully functioning market. The door to emissions trading may therefore be open in France, but pushing it further may prove very difficult.

2. A VERY SIMPLE THEORETICAL MODEL OF REGULATORY CHANGE

The analysis here is based on a rather simple theoretical model of institutional trajectories for public policies (Godard, 1995). The concept of an institutional trajectory links the scope for regulatory change to the previous, inherited features of the regulatory regime. Since the existing regulatory regime embodies costly investment in institutional forms, it is not an easy endeavour to change the whole regime. This will only happen if it is perceived to be essential or if it provides a means to capture very significant benefits. Without these conditions, innovation will mainly be achieved at the margin of existing rules, making compatibility with this existing framework a critical condition.

More specifically we assume that, for a new instrument to be introduced, several conditions have to be met:

1. There must be an emergent problem;
2. It cannot be solved within the current political framework;
3. A new political instrument may be able to solve it;
4. An interest group thinks so and wants it to be implemented;
5. The profile of the instrument fits the general institutional trajectory of the country.

According to this theoretical framework, the dominant forces for change are the characteristics of the problem to be solved and a rationale of problem-solving, rather than economic efficiency *per se*. These are the key drivers of either the process of change or the active conservation of the existing regulatory regime. This viewpoint suggests that institutional trajectories which could allow the introduction of new cost-effective, economic instruments should primarily be driven by arguments and expectations which are not linked to economic efficiency as such. To some extent, economic efficiency should be considered as an extra bonus, adding to more practical virtues related to the specific concerns of various actors. This is the way we suggest the scope for SO₂ emissions trading in France should be examined.

3. THE FRENCH SYSTEM OF AIR POLLUTION CONTROL

Institutions embody rules which structure beliefs and values. They generate conventions, some of which are not explicit, but structure the behaviour of individuals by providing a framework for action. This section describes the operation of this process in the French system of pollution control. This is followed by a more general analysis of the evolution of public action in France.

The French system of air pollution control is predominantly legalistic and administrative, despite a limited financial mechanism in the form of a financial tax.[5] The regulations had originally aimed at the technological and quantitative control of emissions at source. This approach had to evolve because of the introduction, via European Union Directives, of environmental quality objectives such as pollutant air quality standards and critical loads[6] for acid deposition. The coexistence of these two elements creates tensions and introduces new difficulties.

3.1. An industrial and technological approach

Before the adoption of the new air law in December 1996, air pollution control was considered as one element of the broader regulation of industrial activity and was enabled by the 'installations classées' (IC) legislation.[7] Air pollution has a very subordinate status within the Ministry of the Environment. It is administered by the Bureau of Atmosphere, which is one of seven divisions of the Service of Industrial Environment which in turn is only one part of the Department of Pollution and Risk Prevention. In contrast, water has its own department.

The Direction Régionale de l'Industrie, la Recherche et l'Environnement (DRIRE)[8] which are in charge of IC control at a regional level have been the main actors in the system. Originally they were a decentralized service of the Ministry of Industry, then in charge of the promotion of industrial development. Now the Ministry of the Environment can also intervene, but air quality is still seen as primarily an industrial problem. The DRIRE have always given priority to industrial competitiveness when examining and authorizing industrial plant. National technical standards for emissions were available but the DRIRE could decide whether to use these in individual cases. This meant that DRIRE could exercise a great deal of discretion when establishing standards for individual installations. Since the DRIRE are sensitive to the general aim of supporting and encouraging economic activity, companies have generally preferred to *negotiate* the evolution and implementation of regulatory constraints rather than face general binding measures. The goal has been to obtain improvements without standardized constraints but with negotiated individual measures on a case by case basis. This approach was integrated, which means that it took into account pollution in all media (soil, air, water, wastes). This negotiated policy has achieved significant reductions in industrial air emissions. There is a consensus among public officials, industry, and private organizations[9] on the pragmatism and efficiency of this system.

The DRIRE policy was based on the obligation to implement technical measures that do not entail excessive costs, but not on the attainment of defined environmental objectives. However, the involvement of France in international environmental agreements together with its membership of the EU has led it to modify its regulatory system. Environmental quality standards must now be included.

3.2. A difficult evolution towards environmental quality standards

In 1979, France signed the UNECE Convention on Long Range Transboundary Air Pollution (LRTAP). Following this, it was involved in the negotiation of several protocols for the control of SO_2 and NO_x emissions. Parallel to the UNECE developments, the EU was greatly expanding its involvement in environmental policy, with the Maastricht Treaty of 1993 finally establishing environmental protection as one of the basic objectives of the Union. In 1980, the European Council adopted a Directive (80/779) on air quality standards for SO_2 and particulates and this was later followed by standards for nitrogen oxides and ozone. To combat the problem of acid rain, the EU adopted the 1985 Large Combustion Plant Directive, which gave national targets for the reduction of SO_2 and NO_x emissions from plants of more than 50 MW. In its Fifth Environmental Action Program, the EU fixed an objective that critical loads should not be exceeded in any EMEP[10] grid cell. A strategy for reducing emissions further to move towards this objective is currently under discussion.

French policy is obviously constrained by the UNECE obligations and the relevant EU Directives. However, the French government was very slow to translate the first Directives on ambient air quality into national law because they introduced a system of air pollution control that was very different from its own. They introduced obligations to achieve specific environmental results rather than technical requirements for individual sources. It is very difficult to guarantee the attainment of environmental quality objectives within the traditional French approach. Historically, while a company may have been required to conform to certain technical measures, it could locate a plant without reference to local environmental conditions. Any new company would increase total emissions. The negotiated regulation could only control this situation by requiring subsequent emission reductions from the plant.

Moreover, industrial technology is only a part of the air quality problem. Air pollutant concentrations are partly the result of industrial emissions, but are also derived from transport, tertiary and residential sector emissions. As environmental quality standards become more stringent, it becomes increasingly difficult to guarantee them through controlling only industrial emissions. The French administration did not want to confront the dual logic of 'means' control (industrial emissions) and 'results' control (environmental quality standards) and therefore postponed the second for as long as it was possible. As a consequence, the EU Directives were only translated into French law when the traditional system of regulation had led to air quality that complied with current European standards.

With the signing of the Sulphur Protocols to the UNECE Convention, the French government committed to reduce national SO_2 emissions further. The first Protocol required a 30 per cent reduction in SO_2 emissions by 1993, measured from a 1980 baseline. Again, it is difficult to reconcile such a quantitative goal with a technical approach to controlling individual source emissions. The target was eventually reached, not with the help of particular environmental measures but as an indirect consequence of the French electronuclear program.[11] In this way, the problem of the articulation of different approaches had been avoided, but it could not be so in the future.

The French dilemma emphasizes the tensions between two different approaches to the control of environmental problems: one focuses on the continuous improvement of industrial technical performance, and the other on specific environmental objectives. The first is dependent on technical innovation and the rotation of capital stocks, that is, on economic issues; whereas the second is based on scientific knowledge of the health and environmental impact of pollutants, framed as an external constraint on economic decisions. At the European level, the two approaches coexist, emphasizing the inability of each to guarantee both economic and ecological viability and to satisfy all the parties involved. This two-level approach is contradictory. What are technical improvements for if environmental quality is already controlled? Why do you need environmental quality standards, if the best technological processes not entailing excessive costs are already being implemented? As well as these internal difficulties, the inertia of the French political system creates additional problems. The French authorities introduced environmental quality standards very late, without changing the existing structure of IC regulation to allow them to be articulated. As the objectives become more and more stringent, the tensions in the system become greater, leading inevitably to a locking point.

The nature of this problem gives an indication of a potential way to solve it. The framework which allows a specific environmental objective to be achieved through a regulatory approach that is both cost-effective and technically flexible is a tradable permit scheme. Moreover, tradable permits seem highly suited to current trends within French public institutions.

4. GENERAL TENDENCIES IN THE EVOLUTION OF FRENCH PUBLIC INSTITUTIONS

The recent evolution of French public institutions is characterized by three themes: a constraint: the emergence of environmental concern; a goal: deregulation; and a reality: decentralization (Linotte et al., 1992). What is notable here is that deregulation and decentralization lead in the same general direction as tradable permit schemes.

The aim of deregulation is to reintroduce autonomy in private decision making and to transfer the implementation of public policy to decentralized agents. It does not imply the abandonment of strategic direction by the state, which must still establish the framework of rules and objectives. What it does do is leave the precise management of action to those agents who possess the best information. Regulation can leave space for a range of approaches to achieve the same result. As Chevallier notes: '....incentives are becoming the favourite instruments of state regulation as they are more economic in their use, more flexible in their effects and certainly more efficient in their results' (Chevallier, 1987). Following this trend, economic approaches now take a central role in public policy. With the globalization of markets and the acceleration of technical and economic change, there is an increasing need for rapid adaptation and effective information flows within public administration. What deregulation does is to transfer the development of the rules which guide economic activity to professionals. As a tradable permit scheme makes the distribution of emissions reduction dependent on the private agreements and strategies of decentralized agents, it belongs to the same organizational family. It also preserves the public interest through the use of quantitative constraints on total emissions within a region.

Some market ideologists emphasize the virtues of free markets as if they could work without any state intervention. This is a poor representation of any tradable permit scheme. This instrument shows very clearly how a market is an institutional construct, based on rules and institutions established by the state, and needing important 'investment in forms' to ensure equivalence in trade (Thévenot, 1986). In France, most goods and service markets have been constrained by regulatory measures for a long time. This framework has slowly evolved towards less regulation, but keeping a general level of state control. The corresponding view of markets is the same as for a tradable permit scheme; that is, an articulation of decentralized trades and administrative control. This is why it is interesting to pay special attention to particular organizations which have regulated markets for over two decades: independent administrative authorities.

The emergence of independent administrative authorities is linked to deregulation. Such authorities are established when a government wants to keep a policy area under control but without direct administrative supervision. This can be for scientific or technical reasons, but also when it wants the area to have some independence from direct political control. (Examples include the Competition Council and the Audiovisual National Council.) The independent administrative authority has a double mission: the control of a particular sector to organize the production of, or control the use of, an essential public good; and the preservation of public freedom. It must ensure that a wide range of interests are taken into account and it may have to arbitrate between them. The authority has to organize a continuous system of control for the activities within its responsibility. As Winckler observes, 'control by this type of authority involves the acknowledgement that a non perfect local solution of an economic problem is better than the transparency of a general/totalitarian solution managed by executive power' (Winckler, 1988, p.78). Again we note that this trend has many features in common with tradable permits.

'The idea is to protect citizens, enlighten users and to release socio-economic forces that will generate efficiency, dynamism and competitiveness, free from heavy state control. To protect, to enlighten and to release: a lot of authorities are built into the heart of the laws which go in this way; but to protect, to enlighten and to release without anarchy' (Hubac and Pisier, 1988, p.120).

But 'to be introduced, an independent administrative authority needs a sufficiently open administrative space' (Longobardi, 1995, p.172). This last point can create problems insofar as the French administrative space of air pollution regulation is far from being free. At present, the DRIRE is not an independent administrative authority. It is a regional body of the Ministry of Industry under joint guardianship of the Ministry of the Environment. While historically it has been able to exercise a great deal of discretion, this was primarily due to a lack of specific regulations on air pollution control. As standards become more stringent, the DRIRE may lose its scope for discretion.

We previously emphasized the difficulties the French system had in introducing environmental quality standards. There is a growing need to link standards centred on means to those centred on results. Then, we have shown that a tradable permit scheme is by nature convergent with several evolutionary trends within French public institutions. However, these general conditions are not sufficient to achieve implementation of the instrument. For this to occur, some additional and more particular conditions must also be met.

5. AN ADMINISTRATIVE CONTEXT MORE PERMISSIVE THAN IT FIRST SEEMS

A tradable permit scheme is based on the allocation by an administrative authority of permits to emit a precise quantity of pollution. But an overall limit on the quantity of pollution from a sector is, from an economic point of view, a potential barrier to entry for new firms. There are only two ways to reduce the negative impact of this on competitiveness:

- Allow any industrial unit to emit pollution, taking account of the technical and economic possibilities for emission abatement, but without considering the contribution of that pollution to the overall quota for the sector. This is the current system, but it is unable to guarantee air quality, and can lead to the overall pollution quota being exceeded.
- Constrain total emissions below a strict threshold, but at the same time allow emission quotas to be tradable between economic agents. This is a way to guarantee the attainment of the overall environmental objective but without fixing the quotas available to individual plants.

However, a new and apparently considerable obstacle arises at this point. According to a basic principle of administrative law in France, 'the administrative allowance is by nature not tradable' (Moinard, 1994, p.14). This principle is related to the inalienable nature of public sovereignty. Can this obstacle be overcome? Yes indeed. Several cases show that in the real world, when the legislator needs it, solutions have been found.

We can take the organization of taxi activities as an example. To be able to operate, a taxi driver must obtain an operating licence. The business value of this depends on whether the licence can be sold when the driver ceases operating. Before 1973, case law had established the principle of trading licences, but this was forbidden by a ruling in March 1973 (Moinard, 1994).

Following this, licences were freely allocated but with a ban on selling them. Taxi drivers who obtained licences before this new rule could still sell them, but not the others. This double-rule system proved to be difficult to manage, and the ban on selling licences generated black market trades. Consequently, a new revision of the rule has now been introduced. Today, any driver can legitimately propose a successor and is allowed to transfer his licence through a private transaction. This is justified by the fact that 'it is not the licence which is traded – as an administrative licence cannot, by definition, be traded – but the business, the trade depending on the allocation to the party of the licence by administrative authority' (Moinard, 1994, p.24). Senate debates did not care about this indirect licence transfer; the problem was that the transfer had a monetary component.

This case is not exactly the same as the trading of emissions allowances, but it suggests that a tradable permit scheme could be implemented, provided there is a political will to do it and without requiring a revolution in public law. Moreover, economic and fiscal regulations for other occupations also authorize the trade of administrative licences. This old agreement can be taken as a French habit of national institutions: 'Through professional bodies, administrative acts become a matter of economic calculation, thereby allowing speculation to occur' (Batailler, 1965, p.1055).

Overcoming such apparent obstacles is insufficient however for the effective implementation of the instrument. We also need some agents to actively promote it, and a means to integrate it into the current system of air pollution control.

6. SOME INITIATIVES AND EXPERIMENTS

Interviews with people who are responsible for the management of air pollution at the national level suggest a strong aversion to the idea of emissions trading. In spite of this reaction, it is worth noting that the same people were quite satisfied with some recent experiments which were not identified as tradable permit mechanisms, although they are very close to some US initiatives which are commonly included in the same family. These experiments were taken as a proof that the French system does not need a new instrument, especially a market instrument. On the contrary, we see them as evidence of the pressing need to introduce new ways of increasing the flexibility of the current system. With these experiments, the DRIRE has effectively organized an informal implementation of 'regulation trades'. This allows for two neighbouring plants to negotiate with each other and with the DRIRE to achieve a modification of current regulatory obligations. One plant may emit more pollution, provided that the second plant emits less. This approach effectively places an 'emissions bubble' over the two industrial locations, in a similar manner to the early US emissions trading program.

Similar experiments have occurred at a more local level in the field of water regulation. One concerned two plants owned by two different companies producing saltwort in the same neighbourhood. The production process for saltwort inevitably generates chlorides. These are routed through a decantation tank and then, since 1974, through a modulation tank which allows the discharge rate to adapt to the flow rate of the river. By this means the plants are able to fulfil the permit requirements for 'added concentrations' – i.e. the plant discharges must not increase pollutant concentrations in the river by more than 400 mg/l. There is a stringent institutional constraint in this case as the river is an international one and is therefore covered by the Bonn Convention. This Convention includes binding targets on pollutant concentrations. Traditional regulatory controls on industrial plants are unable to guarantee this. In this case, leakages from the tanks led to the concentration targets for the river being exceeded and the conditions of the permit being broken. To obtain new permits, the plants were required to make three types of improvement:

- a decrease in tank leakages;
- a reduction in pollutant concentrations in the river;
- an increase in the credibility of the system, through making the plants liable for prosecution if they violate permit conditions.

During the two years of examination procedures for the new permits, the directors of the two plants negotiated together. This led to a permit to control their emissions jointly, with the aim of allowing the required standard to be met while optimizing their abatement actions. This enables the plants to jointly fulfil the added concentration goal. This permit is allocated between both plants while providing clear powers of enforcement to the regulatory authorities. If the specified concentration is not exceeded, the regulator will not intervene. If there are excessive quantities of the pollutant in the river, the regulator will punish the plant which has exceeded its initial quota. This means that, provided the overall pollutant concentration stays within the required limits, the two plants can optimize their discharges and abatement costs.

Another example illustrating the use of an emissions 'bubble' can be given from the area of SO_2 itself. Following ratification of the first UNECE Sulphur Protocol, the French administration asked the national electricity generator, Electricité de France[12] (EdF), to reduce SO_2 emissions from its power plants by 30 per cent by 1993. A purely administrative and technical approach would have led to a requirement to reduce emissions uniformly at each plant. This is an inflexible and expensive approach and was not the solution adopted. Instead, the company was given the flexibility to optimize its emission reduction plans. The company sought to achieve the required reductions while minimizing its costs by taking into account various economic parameters such as the age of plant and its residual life time, the effective costs of desulphurization investment and the local air pollution conditions. This was not a market system, since only one company was involved, but it was a national bubble with compensations of emissions between several units.[13]

7. A LACK OF SUBJECTIVE CONDITIONS

In spite of these experiments, subjective conditions in France do not look favourable to the introduction of emissions trading. The agents involved in the management of industrial air pollution are largely satisfied with the current structure of regulation. Some particular points are disputed, but no one is questioning the whole organization of the system. Indeed, the DRIRE is taken as exemplifying an efficient and pragmatic approach to regulation. Implementation of EU Directives and changes in the civil responsibility of State agents have led to a somewhat more rigid approach and several actions by the DRIRE have attracted criticism for the resulting loss of flexibility. Nevertheless there are no problems which would lead agents to seriously promote a significant change to the present regulatory regime.

The use of emissions trading in air pollution regulation is criticized on two main grounds. The first is essentially semantic and is linked with an understanding of allowances as giving a 'right to pollute'. Industries have been allowed to emit pollutants below specified thresholds for a long time, but this is considered as a constraint inherited from an initial state where no regulation was in place. In contrast, a tradable permit scheme is seen as instituting a new positive right of nuisance, and so does not seem justifiable within French legal traditions. A judicious choice of the legal framework and the words to describe it could perhaps overcome this difficulty, provided some agents were convinced of the instrument's value.

The second point is linked to the introduction of financial mechanisms and commercial interests into an environmental management system, dedicated to improving air quality. Pollutant emissions are not considered as a necessary consequence of a productive system, but as a public nuisance or even a moral evil. To be able to earn money by selling the right to hurt people is taken to be absolutely illegitimate. Of course, companies would not be able to sell allowances if they did not first reduce their emissions. Financial gain is therefore linked to a real improvement in environmental quality, but the opponents of emissions trading do not generally perceive this.

A further point is that a tradable permit scheme, as any other type of economic instrument, leads to an internalization of environmental externalities and thereby adds another dimension to economic competition between companies or sectors. But companies do not currently want to compete on environmental performance as well as traditional grounds. The environment is not taken as a factor of production which has to be economically managed, but as a moral goal for which companies agree to co-operate. The introduction of rivalry and competition through emissions trading is based on a radically different perception of the acceptable goals and mechanisms of environmental protection.

It is worth noting that although the agents involved in environmental regulation at a national level are largely opposed to the instrument, this is not necessarily the case for the people involved in local air pollution management. The latter, who have to cope with the practical realities of emission abatement and attainment of air quality standards, are more aware of the opportunities offered by trading. While they share the mistrust of the financial aspects of trade, they are interested in the possibility of having specific local arrangements to increase flexibility and cost-effectiveness. We can illustrate this with the case of air quality in the 'Pond of Berre' – an air quality region surrounding the pond and town of Berre. Due to a high concentration of industry, this is one of the most polluted regions in the country. The medium term pollution standard is enforced, but there are still some shorter periods of poor air quality depending on particular weather conditions. Concentrations of SO_2 can reach 1500 $\mu g/m^3$ during these periods, as compared to the World Health Organization (WHO) standard of 350 $\mu g/m^3$. During such pollution episodes plants have more stringent constraints upon their emissions, but as yet these are insufficient to achieve conformity with the WHO standards and will have to be strengthened. Most people we interviewed in this region thought that the possibility of 'switchable quotas' would be very attractive and a real improvement compared to non tradable emissions limits. With switchable quotas plants do not buy or sell quotas, but *co-operate* to optimize emission reductions during pollution episodes. The emphasis is industrial co-operation, rather than a quota market.

8. CONCLUSION

Institutional frameworks in France and Europe have recently evolved in a direction which should increase the scope for introducing emissions trading within the French system of air pollution regulation. As a result, it is no longer true (if it has ever been) to say that the instrument would be radically opposed to the 'French way'. The only major obstacle which impedes the use of such an instrument is the lack of motivation of the agents concerned. They seem to be only partially aware of the real objective of introducing such mechanisms. This does not signify that there are no difficulties with the present system of regulation. Problems are being encountered in meeting binding environmental quality standards whilst ensuring economic efficiency. This is an area where tradable permits have much to offer. The examples given above are typical situations where environmental conditions have reached saturation point for institutional (the Bonn Convention), or health (WHO standards) reasons.

If the administration developed a tradable permit scheme it would retain a real power of regulation. We can imagine that a particular institutional structure would have to play a mediating role for the development of such practices, avoiding emphasis on the financial aspects of the instrument. The informal spontaneous experiments described above provide good examples of how this may work in practice. In France, it is not the market aspects of emissions trading which could help develop the instrument. Instead, it could be developed under the banner of a new form of co-operation, both between companies and regulators and between companies themselves. The concept of 'switchable quotas' would perhaps be the appropriate term for introducing the instrument in the French context, avoiding the cultural trap of the concept of a 'right to pollute'.

In the field of air pollution control, the administrative role is occupied by the DRIRE, leaving very little room for another authority. Can we imagine the DRIRE being reconstituted as an independent administrative authority? Or could its environmental responsibilities be devolved to such an authority? Such a move would return some flexibility of action to a regulator that was in danger of losing it. At the same time, it would enable the new system to benefit from established regulatory practices and from the detailed knowledge of industrial reality that the DRIRE has. It could also be a way to institutionalize and develop informal practices which currently only exist at a limited level, but may ultimately provide a bridge towards a larger scale system of trading.

NOTES

[1] The French doctrine of public service is based on three fundamental principles: a) equality for each citizen; b) adaptability to the context; and c) continuity through time. While service organizations must comply with each of these principles, economic efficiency remains a secondary consideration. Economic efficiency is therefore a plus, but the three other points are inescapable and may be in conflict with it.

[2] These are value frameworks which provide legitimation for actions.

[3] This chapter presents an outline of the results obtained from a research project conducted by CIRED in 1995-1996, with the financial support of the ADEME (Economics and

Forward Studies Service) and the Ministry of Environment (Research Service) (cf. Cros and Godard, 1996).

4   See the Universal Declaration of Rights established by the French Revolution.

5   The tax is applied to emissions of SO_2, NO_x and volatile organic compounds, but is set at a very low level. For example, the SO2 tax during the 1990-1995 period was 180F per tonne compared to the estimated marginal cost of sulphur removal of 3200F. The tax has little incentive effect and is primarily a device to raise revenue. The resources are distributed among polluters to help technological development.

6   Critical loads are defined as the maximum levels of acid deposition below which, according to current scientific knowledge, no significant damage to sensitive ecosystems can be demonstrated.

7   IC (installations classées) are listed in a nomenclature and defined as industrial sources which are able to generate a danger or a nuisance. The sources discussed in this chapter correspond approximately to those covered by the EU Integrated Pollution Prevention and Control (IPPC) Directive.

8   Regional Department of Industry, Research and the Environment.

9   Including the Interprofessional Technical Centre of Studies on Atmospheric Pollution (CITEPA), the Information and Training Centre on Industrial Environment (CFDE) and the Association for Atmospheric Pollution Prevention (APPA). The organizations have a significant role in the French public scene on atmospheric pollution.

10   EMEP stands for the Cooperative Program for Monitoring and Evaluation of the Long Range Transmission of Air Pollutants in Europe. This is a subsidiary body to the LRTAP and provides the official estimates of pollutant transportation and deposition within Europe.

11   A comparison can be made with the UK where obligations to reduce sulphur emissions were achieved through a switch to gas in electricity generation. This was an unanticipated consequence of electricity privatization, rather than the direct result of environmental measures. See Chapter 11.

12   EdF is an integrated electricity utility, incorporating generation, transmission, distribution and supply. It owns most of the generating capacity in France, the bulk of which is nuclear.

13   Similar provisions were made in the UK for the two main generating companies – National Power and PowerGen. See Chapter 11.

REFERENCES

Batailler, F. (1965),'Les Beati Possidentes du droit administratif (les actes unilatéraux créateurs de privilèges)', *Revue de droit public et de la science politique*, 1051–1096.

Boltanski, L. and Thévenot, L. (1991), *De la justification. Les économies de la grandeur*, Gallimard, NRF Essais, Paris.

Chevallier, J. (1987), 'Les enjeux de la déréglementation', *Revue de droit public et de la science politique*, pp. 281–319.

Cros, C. and Godard, O. (1996), *Trajectoires institutionnelles et choix des instruments de politique publique. Les marchés de droits à polluer aux Etats-Unis et en France. Le cas de la pollution atmosphérique*, Rapport pour le Programme 'Prospective et veille scientifique' du ministère de l'Environnement, CIRED, Paris.

Godard, O. (1994), *L'expérience américaine des permis négociables dans le domaine de la pollution atmosphérique*, Rapport pour le Programme 'Prospective et veille scientifique' du ministère de l'Environnement, décembre, CIRED, Paris.

Godard, O. (1995), 'Trajectoires institutionnelles et choix d'instruments pour les politiques d'environnement dans les économies en transition', *Revue d'études comparatives Est-Ouest*, **26**(2), 39–58.

Godard, O. and Beaumais, O. (1994), 'Economie, croissance et environnement: de nouvelles stratégies pour de nouvelles relations', *Revue Economique, Hors série 'Perspectives et réflexions stratégiques à moyen terme'*, 143–176.

Hahn, R. and Hester, G. (1989), 'Marketable permits: lessons for theory and practice', *Ecology Law Quarterly*, **16**(2), 361–406.

Hubac, S. and Pisier, E. (1988), 'Les autorités face aux pouvoirs', in C.A. Colliard et G.Timsit (eds), *Les autorités administratives indépendantes*, (Coll. Les voies du droit), Paris.

Lascoumes, P. (1994), 'L'écopouvoir', Paris, Ed. La Découverte.

Linotte, D., Mestre, A. and Romi, R. (1992), *Services publics et droit public économique*, Litec, Paris.

Longobardi, N. (1995), 'Autorités administratives indépendantes et position institutionnelle de l'administration publique', *Revue française de droit administratif*, **11**, 171–177.

Majone, G. (1989), *Evidence, Argument and Persuasion in the Policy Process*, Yale University Press, New Haven and London.

Merrien, F.-X. (1993), 'Les politiques publiques entre paradigmes et controverses', in CRESAL (éd.), *Les raisons de l'action publique. Entre expertise et débat*, Ed. l'Harmattan, (Coll. Logiques politiques), Paris.

Moinard, L. (1994), *Rapport fait au nom de la commission des affaires économiques et du plan sur le projet de loi relatif à l'activité de conducteur et à la profession d'exploitant de taxi*, (Rapport no. 48), Sénat, Paris.

Thévenot, L. (1986), 'Les investissements de forme', *Conventions économiques*, Cahiers du Centre d'Etudes de l'Emploi, PUF, Paris.

Winckler, A. (1988), 'Conseil de la concurrence et concurrence des autorités', *Le Débat*, (52), 76–97.

/170-207

925
928 1423

11. Why sulphur trading failed in the UK[1]

Steve Sorrell

1. INTRODUCTION

The use of emissions trading for the control of sulphur[2] emissions was first proposed by the UK government in 1992 as an attractive means to overcome problems with the existing regulatory framework (DoE, 1992). Despite repeated pronouncements in favour of 'sulphur quota switching' (as it was termed) and a strong commitment to economic instruments and deregulation, the idea was eventually dropped in 1996. This chapter explains why this occurred and draws some general lessons for the implementation of emissions trading in Europe. These lessons are particularly relevant to carbon trading after Kyoto.

The chapter begins by describing the various European regulations on sulphur emissions and the way these have been implemented within the UK. This is followed by an account of the radical changes in UK energy markets over the last decade and the impact of these on sulphur emissions. The evolution of the debate on sulphur quota switching is then described, showing how the proposals faced a series of obstacles that ultimately proved insurmountable. Six reasons are proposed for the failure of the scheme, namely:

- independent developments in energy markets;
- a conflict of regulatory principles;
- a conflict of regulatory culture;
- a conflict over quota allocation;
- persistent regulatory uncertainty; and
- inadequate political support.

The wider implications of these lessons are then considered.

2. EUROPEAN REGULATORY CONTEXT

The European framework for regulating sulphur emissions is characterized by complexity, uncertainty and overlapping requirements. The UK has obligations both as a member of the European Union and as a signatory to the UNECE Convention on Long Range Transboundary Air Pollution (CLRTAP). The most important requirements are as follows:

2.1. The Air Framework Directive (AFD)

The first 'framework' Directive on emissions from industrial plant was agreed by the Community in 1984. It does not specify emission limits for any particular class of plant, but lays out the circumstances under which certain types of plant may be authorized to operate and which plants and substances will be subject to controls. The Air Framework Directive (AFD) introduced the concept of *best available technology not entailing excessive costs* (BATNEEC) into EU legislation, a concept which has played a central role in the UK. New plants are required to apply BATNEEC, while existing plants (operating before 1987) must gradually adapt to BATNEEC, taking into account a range of considerations including the length of the plant's remaining life. Excessive costs are defined in relation to 'the economic situation of undertakings belonging to the category in question', and not to the circumstances of an individual plant.

2.2. The Integrated Pollution Prevention and Control Directive (IPPC)

The AFD was superseded in 1996 by the Directive on Integrated Pollution Prevention and Control (IPPC). This is a framework Directive for industrial sources which adopts an integrated approach to pollution in different media. The Directive is closely modelled on the system of Integrated Pollution Control (IPC) established in the UK in 1990, and requires the adoption of Best Available Techniques (BAT) to prevent or minimize pollution of the environment as a whole. The concept of 'not entailing excessive cost' is effectively absorbed into the definition of availability (Skea and Smith, 1997). Qualifying installations require a permit to operate and existing plant (pre 1997) are required to upgrade to BAT standards by October 2007.

2.3. The Large Combustion Plant Directive (LCPD)

The Large Combustion Plant Directive (LCPD) was first proposed by the Commission in 1983 following strict German legislation to tackle the problem of acid rain (Boehmer-Christiansen and Skea, 1991). UK opposition to the Directive was one of the main reasons it took five years to agree. The final Directive established emission limits[3] for NO_x and SO_2 for new combustion plant, together with national emission reduction targets for existing (pre 1987) plant. The UK was required to reduce sulphur emissions from existing plant by 20 per cent by 1993, 40 per cent by 1998 and 60 per cent by 2003, measured from a 1980 baseline. The Directive applies to boiler plant with a thermal input of more than 50 MW. Both the new plant limits and the emission ceilings were due to be revised in 1995, but agreement on this had not been reached at the time of writing.

2.4. The UNECE Second Sulphur Protocol

In June 1994, the UK signed the Second Sulphur Protocol under the UNECE Convention on Long-Range Transboundary Air Pollution (CLRTAP).[4] The aim of the Protocol was to base national emission reduction targets on the contribution of each country to acid deposition on sensitive ecosystems. In practice, the negotiation of targets was highly political and several countries obtained derogations (Castells and Funtowicz, 1997). The Protocol commits the UK to reducing its *total* SO_2 emissions by 50 per cent by the year 2000, 70 per cent by 2005 and 80 per cent by 2010, measured from a 1980 baseline.

While the UK obligations are less stringent than the original UNECE proposals, they nevertheless represent a significant advance upon the LCPD requirements. The key difference is that the UNECE targets cover *all* sulphur sources, including a large number of small plants which are currently unregulated.

2.5. Regulatory overdetermination?

In addition to these requirements, sulphur is regulated through standards on air quality and the sulphur content of liquid fuels. The complexity of the current situation is illustrated by Table 11.1. Many provisions are overlapping and some represent conflicting regulatory philosophies. The most important of these is the tension between upgrading individual plant to BATNEEC standards under the Air Framework and IPPC Directives and the use of national emission ceilings by the LCPD, the UNECE Second Sulphur Protocol and the recently proposed Acidification Strategy. This tension is a central feature of the quota switching story. Notably, it derives from the European regulatory framework rather than UK regulatory practice.

Table 11.1 *Regulatory provisions affecting sulphur emissions in the EU*

Area	Provision	Date	Reference	Key elements
EU framework Directives on industrial pollution control	Air Framework Directive (AFD)	1984	84/360/EEC	Framework Directive for control of air pollution from industrial plant. Introduced BATNEEC.
	Integrated Pollution Prevention and Control Directive (IPPC)	1996	96/61/EC	Framework for cross media pollution control from industrial installations. Supersedes AFD from 1999 onwards.
EU combustion plant	Large Combustion Plant Directive (LCPD)	1988	88/609/EEC	New plant emission limits for SO_2 and NO_x National emission ceilings for existing plant.
	Proposed revisions to the LCPD	Draft 1997		Proposed revisions to both emission limits and national ceilings.
EU fuel quality standards	Directive on the sulphur content of liquid fuels	1993	93/12/EC	Sulphur content of gasoil limited to 0.3%. Road diesel limited to 0.04%.
	Proposed revisions to the liquid fuels Directive	Draft 1997		Proposal to limit sulphur content of heavy fuel oil to 1%.
EU air quality standards	Air quality - smoke and SO_2	1980	80/779/EEC	Limit and guide values for sulphur concentration in ambient air.
	Assessment and management of ambient air quality	1996	96/62/EC	Provides framework for ambient air quality management. To be followed by 'daughter' Directives specifying limit values for individual pollutants.
EU strategy	Draft Strategy to Combat Acidification	Draft 1997		Proposals for integrated approach to control of acidifying pollutants. Includes revisions to LCPD and liquid fuels Directive, together with national emission ceilings and other measures.
UNECE provisions	Second Sulphur Protocol	1994		National targets for sulphur reduction from all sources to 2010. New plant emission limits and fuel specifications based on EU Directives.
International Maritime Organisation (IMO)	International Convention for the Prevention of Pollution from Ships (MARPOL)	1973		EU in discussions with IMO on limiting sulphur content of bunker fuels.

3. NATIONAL REGULATORY CONTEXT

The AFD was implemented in the UK through the system of Integrated Pollution Control while the LCPD was implemented through the National Plan.

3.1. Integrated Pollution Control (IPC)

Framework
UK industrial pollution policy underwent a number of innovative reforms in the late 1980s (Jordan, 1993). One stimulus for these was the need to restore confidence in a regime which had become discredited due to the confidential working relationship between regulator and regulated (Smith, 1997, chapter 4). Administratively, a unitary pollution regulator, Her Majesty's Inspectorate of Pollution (HMIP), was created in 1987 from an amalgamation of pre-existing regulatory bodies; while procedurally, the Environmental Protection Act of 1990 introduced the new system of Integrated Pollution Control (IPC).

IPC is a cross-media approach to regulation, whereby releases to air, water and land are regulated together. It aims to prevent the situation where control of pollution in one medium leads to increased pollution in another. IPC procedures are more formal and transparent than the air regulations which IPC replaced, including a statutory requirement for public information registers. Between 1991 and 1997, all of the relevant industrial sectors were brought into IPC, and in 1997 the cross media approach evolved further with the creation of a new Environment Agency from HMIP, the National Rivers Authority and Waste Regulation Authorities.

Under IPC, no prescribed process can operate without an authorization. Authorizations contain legally binding conditions to:

- ensure that BATNEEC is used to prevent the release of prescribed substances or, where that is not practicable, to reduce releases to a minimum;
- consider what is the best practicable environmental option (BPEO) to cause the least harm to the environment as a whole; and
- ensure compliance with obligations under EU Directives and international law (DoE, 1997).

To obtain authorization the operator must submit an application, including technical information about the process, measurement of emissions and a timetable for upgrading to BATNEEC standards. Authorizations contain release limits, monitoring requirements and a timetabled improvement program. The last is a central feature of IPC and may include either emission limits to be achieved by a target date in the future, or a requirement for feasibility studies.

Evolution and practice

With IPC, HMIP aspired to a new, 'arms' length' relationship with industry which would be tougher, more transparent and accountable (HMIP, 1991a, p.6).[5] This aspiration was reflected in the first set of 'guidance notes' on combustion plant regulation, which suggested that all plant should upgrade to the LCPD new plant standards by 2001 (HMIP, 1991b).

In practice, this 'top down' approach proved impossible to implement. HMIP was dependent upon industry for technical and economic information, but the latter frequently lacked even the most basic monitoring data (Skea et al., 1995; Allott, 1994). This made it difficult to establish whether the recommended emission limits constituted excessive cost. Lacking an alternative source of information, the regulator was forced to return to the co-operative and confidential relationship with industry that characterized the previous regulatory regime[6] (Allott, 1994; Smith, 1997). The first round of authorizations were largely a holding exercise, bringing plants into the system and setting limits at current emission levels. The improvement program became primarily a vehicle for establishing adequate monitoring regimes and environmental management practices, postponing emission reduction to a later stage. Timetabled requirements to achieve standards were replaced with feasibility studies to generate the required information. The revised combustion plant guidance notes retreated from prescriptiveness, emphasizing the importance of inspector judgement at the site level (HMIP, 1995a, p. 1).[7]

Interpreting BATNEEC

The effectiveness of IPC hinges on the interpretation of BATNEEC. It is the inspectors' job to interpret BATNEEC in the context of general guidance published by the Department of the Environment[8] (DoE) and the process specific guidance notes issued by HMIP. The latter may include emission limits, but these have no statutory force (DoE, 1997).

Formal interpretation of BATNEEC in the UK has been strongly influenced by the wording of the AFD. The DoE recommends a three stage process, involving assessment of whether:

1. BAT involves excessive costs in relation to the value of the environment;
2. BAT is affordable given the general viability and financial position of processes within the sector; and
3. the costs or environmental impacts at a site differ sufficiently from the norm to justify different standards (DoE, 1994b).

This guidance emphasizes that '....the question of affordability cannot be revisited on the basis of the financial health of the plant or company' (DoE, 1994b). This prescription bears little relation to implementation practice. Effective implementation of these guidelines would require the regulator to have a comprehensive database of the performance and costs of best available technologies, together with data on the economic performance of individual sectors and monetized assessments of environmental impacts (Pearce and Brisson, 1993). This data is only available in a limited and imperfect form and the primary source is industry itself. As a result, the practical interpretation of BATNEEC has departed significantly from these guidelines. Despite the DoE's continuing insistence on sectoral affordability (DETR, 1997a, pp. 14-16), an implicit criterion of 'firm affordability' has dictated the negotiation of site level standards (Dair et al., 1997).

3.2. National Plan for large combustion plant

Under the LCPD, the UK was required to submit a national programme of emissions reduction to the European Commission. The programme incorporated a National Plan, which was a requirement solely under UK legislation. The Plan incorporated targets for large combustion plant (LCP) in the electricity supply (ESI), oil refining and other industry sectors, with separate targets for England and Wales, Scotland and Northern Ireland. The England and Wales ESI was further subdivided into the two main non-nuclear generating companies – National Power and PowerGen. Quotas of SO_2 emissions were allocated to each sector for each year up to 2003. Thus, whereas the LCPD required only that total UK emissions were less than the targets in the years 1993, 1998 and 2003, the National Plan required that the individual sector targets were met each year. The Plan also required that 8 GW of coal fired plant be retrofitted with flue gas desulphurization (FGD), although only 6 GW of this was ultimately completed.

Two important points about the quota allocation methodology are as follows:

- Initial (baseline) quota allocations for 1991 were based upon estimated emissions for that year and were often crude due to inadequate data.
- Subsequent quota allocations declined at different rates in each sector following a variety of considerations of 'practicality, equity and economics' (DoE, 1989).

Table 11.2 summarizes the quota allocations for key years of the Plan.

Table 11.2 National Plan quota allocations (ktonnes of SO₂)

Sector	1980	1991	1994	1998	2000	2003
ESI:						
National Power		1595	1373	982	857	660
PowerGen		1085	969	669	583	450
England & Wales	2776	2680	2342	1651	1440	1110
Scotland	142	109	102	99	77	57
Northern Ireland	88	92	75	53	46	35
Total ESI	3006	2881	2519	1803	1563	1202
Refineries:						
England & Wales	218	86	85	82	80	78
Scotland	50	14	14	13	13	12
Total Refineries	268	100	99	95	93	90
Other Industry						
England & Wales	543	273	233	201	177	140
Scotland	78	39	34	29	25	20
Total Industry	621	312	267	230	202	160
TOTAL	**3895**	**3293**	**2005**	**2128**	**1858**	**1452**

Source: DoE, 1990

The Plan required that each sector should contribute an emission reduction that was at least equivalent to a pro-rata translation of the LCPD target (DoE, 1989). Secondary considerations included:

- no sector should be able to achieve its obligations through business as usual;
- credit should be given for historical reductions in emissions;[9]
- allowance should be made for the anticipated high cost of future reductions in emissions;[10]
- the age structure and composition of plant should be allowed for, particularly the 'lumpy' nature of investment on a small electricity system;[11] and
- explicit recognition of planned and likely investment projects should be given.[12]

These considerations created a precedent which informed the debate on allocating quotas under the proposed quota switching scheme.

Implementing the Plan

Until its removal in 1997, the Plan was implemented by the relevant pollution inspectorates in each country under central direction from the DoE. Annual emission limits (quotas) were included in each combustion plant authorization, and the sum of these within a sector had to remain within the sector total. In principle, these quotas were distinct from the so-called 'BATNEEC limit', which was an annual emission limit imposed on the plant by the local inspector. This 'two level' approach was implemented differently in the England and Wales ESI than in the other National Plan sectors.

In the former, each power station was assigned a fixed BATNEEC limit and a separate quota allocation. The BATNEEC limit was designed to protect local air quality and to ensure that critical load[13] effects from individual power stations were addressed. The individual plant quotas were generally lower than the BATNEEC limits and their sum was equal to the company total under the National Plan. Importantly, each company was given the flexibility to swap quotas between power stations provided that neither the company total or the individual plant BATNEEC limits were exceeded. In effect, the companies were allowed to operate a constrained emissions bubble.[14] The rationale for this was that it allowed cost effective operation of plant within an integrated electricity system.

In the other sectors, no distinction was made between BATNEEC limits and quota allocations. Instead, each plant was given a single, fixed annual limit which acted as both. This limit typically reflected the existing level of emissions, although the requirement to keep within the Plan led to some plants being restricted. Since the limits were fixed they did not reflect the decline required by the National Plan. Furthermore, since no plant was allowed to exceed its annual limit, this approach prevented multi site companies from operating an emissions bubble.[15]

No plants were allocated quotas up to 2003, which was the final year of the LCPD. Instead, compliance in future years was subject to the negotiation of the individual plant improvement programs. The focus of these was upgrading individual plant to BATNEEC standards by 2001, a requirement which was distinct from, and potentially more stringent than, the National Plan.

From the beginning, therefore, the implementation of the Plan was:

- *partial* – as quotas were only allocated for the first few years;
- *inconsistent* – between different sectors and types of plant; and
- *in conflict* – with the basis of the IPC system which was upgrading individual plant to BATNEEC standards.

It was on this confused pattern of implementation that quota switching was proposed to be introduced.

Before discussing the quota switching story it is necessary to outline the fundamental changes that were taking place within the UK energy market, as these were to have major implications for environmental policy.

4. THE TRANSFORMATION OF THE UK ENERGY MARKET

The UK pioneered the privatization and liberalization of the electricity and gas industries, a process which is becoming established world-wide. In the space of eight years this process has transformed the UK energy market and led to a major reduction in sulphur emissions.

4.1. Gas markets

The UK has an integrated gas transmission and distribution system supplying indigenous North Sea gas to nearly all parts of the country. British Gas, the monopoly supplier which developed this network, was privatized in 1986 with its structure intact. It retained a monopoly of the tariff market (<733 GWh/year), subject to price controls, while the contract market was opened up to competition. From 1988 onwards, the gas market was subject to a series of interventions with the aim of encouraging new entrants. These interventions enabled new entrants to capture a significant fraction of the emerging market in gas for electricity generation and to 'cherry pick' the best sites in the industrial and commercial sectors (Parker and Surrey, 1994). By March 1994, British Gas had lost 45 per cent of the contract market and competition was becoming self sustaining (Stern, 1997).

British Gas misjudged the pace of increasing competition and locked itself into long term take or pay contracts for a greater volume of gas than it could sell. The resulting supply surplus led to major price reductions and the company suffered serious financial penalties. In 1996, British Gas was demerged into separate transportation and trading businesses, in preparation for the final stage of competition in 1998 when all customers are able to choose their gas supplier.

Gas prices have fallen continuously since privatization, due to lower production costs, stringent price regulation, increasing competition and the recent supply surplus. Since 1989, gas has been the fuel of choice in the domestic, public, commercial and industrial markets and has penetrated the new market of electricity generation with extraordinary speed. Total UK gas consumption grew by 62 per cent between 1989 and 1996, with electricity

Table 11.3 Trends in UK natural gas consumption (TWh)

Sector	1989	1990	1992	1994	1996	% change
Electricity generation	6.1	6.4	17.9	114.6	190.7	+3022.0
Other fuel industries	43.7	44.9	63.1	168.7	255.5	+484.6
Industry	159.1	164.1	146.8	164.3	186.5	+17.2
Domestic	290.6	300.4	330.1	329.7	375.8	+29.4
Public administration	34.8	35.4	43.8	41.1	52.0	+49.3
Commercial & misc.	49.9	49.9	56.1	60.1	68.1	+36.6
Total	578.0	594.6	639.9	763.9	938.0	+62.3
Gas as % of UK primary demand	22.9	23.6	25.1	29.7	35.6	

Source: Department of Trade and Industry, 1997

generation accounting for half of the increase. Table 11.3 summarizes recent trends.

4.2. Electricity markets

The England and Wales ESI was restructured in 1989 and, with the exception of the nuclear power stations, transferred to private ownership in 1991.[16] Ownership of the fossil fuel power stations was divided initially between two new private companies, National Power and PowerGen. The new system was de-integrated vertically (by function) and horizontally (by region) and incorporated competition in both generation and supply.[17] Generation competition was introduced immediately, while supply competition is being phased in over a nine year period. As with gas, from 1998 all consumers are able to choose their electricity supplier.

The introduction of competition has had a dramatic impact on generation. Since 1990, National Power and PowerGen have closed over 16 GW of coal fired plant – almost 30 per cent of their starting capacity. Gas fired Combined Cycle Gas Turbine (CCGT) capacity has grown from zero in 1989 to 13 GW in March 1997, and now accounts for around 30 per cent of UK electricity generation (Watson, 1998). Completion of all the planned CCGT stations would bring total capacity to over 19 GW, of which some 9 GW would be owned by independent producers.[18] The change in market share is summarized in Tables 11.4 and 11.5.

The rush to construct CCGT capacity was aided by low capital costs, short lead times, minimal siting difficulties and low gas prices. New independent power producers (IPPs) bought gas on 15 year 'take or pay' contracts, backed up by 15 year electricity supply contracts to the regional electricity

Table 11.4 Changes in UK generation plant mix (1989-2000) (MWe)

Technology	1989	Dec. 1996	2000[2]
Conventional Steam	54397	41686	33500
Nuclear	8308	12916[1]	12916
CCGT	-	12303	19000
Gas turbines/Oil engines	3313	1637	1637
Hydro	4182	4245	4245
Other Renewables	148	474	1000
Total	70348	73261	72982

Notes:
1. The difference between this figure and that for 1989 is misleading since only one new nuclear power station (Sizewell B, 1200 MW) was added to the system in the early 1990s. The rest of the difference may be attributed to improvements in the performance of existing nuclear plants.
2. Estimates from Watson (1998). Assumes that capacity of hydro, nuclear and gas turbines/oil engines remain at December 1996 levels. CGGT figures taken from the SPRU CCGT database.

Source: Department of Trade and Industry, 1997; Watson, 1998

Table 11.5 Thermal input to electricity generation (1989-96) (% of total)

Fuel	1989	1990	1992	1994	1996
Coal	64.6	65.3	61.3	50.3	43.0
Oil	9.4	11.0	10.5	5.5	4.6
Gas	0.7	0.7	2.0	13.4	21.5
Nuclear	23.6	21.3	24.1	28.8	28.9
Hydro	0.5	0.6	0.6	0.6	0.4
Other	1.2	1.1	1.4	1.4	1.7
Total	100.0	100.0	100.0	100.0	100.0

Source: Department of Trade and Industry, 1997

companies (RECs).[19] In response, National Power and PowerGen built their own CCGTs without requiring such long term contract cover. The result was a 'dash for gas' which both significantly increased UK gas demand, and drastically reduced the market for UK coal. This dash shows no sign of abating, despite the higher risk of plant investment in a liberalized market.[20]

At the time of privatization, coal supplied 65 per cent of UK electricity and the 80 Mtonnes taken by the ESI accounted for 75 per cent of the UK coal market. UK deep mined coal prices were significantly higher than world prices, so to protect the industry the government brokered contracts between the generators and British Coal for a transitional period until 1998. Under these contracts, the volume of coal supplied to the ESI has fallen steadily to 30 Mtonnes in 1997, with prices now close to international levels. The contracts are currently being renegotiated, but with full liberalization of the electricity market there is little possibility of giving further protection to domestic coal. Despite major productivity gains, the closure of most of the remaining deep mined capacity looks inevitable (Parker, 1997).

4.3. Impact on sulphur emissions

These radical changes have led to a rapid decline in UK sulphur emissions. Total emissions fell by 37 per cent between 1990 and 1995, with power station emissions falling by 42 per cent. Large combustion plant accounted for 74 per cent of the total in 1995, compared to 85 per cent in 1990. The pace of decline is accelerating: power station emissions are forecast to fall to 500 ktonnes by 2001, less than one fifth of their 1990 level (Environment Agency, 1998). Table 11.6 summarizes these trends.

Table 11.6 Trends in UK SO_2 emissions (1980-95) (ktonnes)

Source category	1980	1990	1991	1993	1995	% change since 1990	% of total
Power stations	3007	2722	2534	2096	1588	-41.7	67.1
Domestic	226	108	115	112	68	-37.0	2.9
Commercial/public	197	84	80	87	55	-34.5	2.3
Refineries	281.0	181.0	189.0	234.0	196.0	8.3	8.3
Iron & steel	128.0	88.0	86.0	77.0	62.0	-29.5	2.6
Other industry	876	414	424	424	252	-39.1	10.7
Transport	115.0	113.0	112.0	114.0	107.0	-5.3	4.5
Other	83.0	46.0	45.0	41.0	37.0	-19.6	1.6
Total	4913	3756	3585	3185	2365	-37.0	100.0
LCP	3880	3200	2747	2329	1756	-45.0	74.0

Source: Department of the Environment, Transport and the Regions, 1997b

Three points should be noted about these trends. First, they occurred almost entirely independently of environmental regulation. With the exception of the FGD retrofits, most investment was driven by economic considerations, with reduced sulphur emissions as a useful by-product. Throughout this period the UK was well within its international obligations on sulphur and the IPC improvement programs for individual plant had yet to bite. While National Power and PowerGen could portray CCGT investment as a strategic response to future sulphur limits, it is likely that much of this investment would have occurred anyway. Since the FGD plant would have reduced emissions by, at most, 400ktonnes, at least 62 per cent of this reduction was largely zero cost abatement.[21]

Second, by far the greatest reduction in emissions occurred in the England and Wales ESI, which was the dominant source of UK sulphur emissions in 1990 and received the largest allocation of quotas under the National Plan. Since these developments were unforeseen when the National Plan was drawn up, the England and Wales ESI was left with a huge quota surplus. For this sector, the National Plan targets became irrelevant.

Finally, the failure to anticipate these trends has twice led the UK to negotiate relatively lenient sulphur reduction targets. The first was the concessions obtained from the EU during the LCPD negotiations, while the second was the extended 2010 deadline obtained under the UNECE Second Sulphur Protocol. In both cases, compliance has proved significantly easier than was originally anticipated.

5. THE QUOTA SWITCHING STORY

5.1. Origins

The use of emissions trading for the control of sulphur emissions was first suggested by the DoE in 1992 (DoE, 1992). From the beginning, the idea was referred to as 'sulphur quota switching', reflecting both the use of the term quotas in the National Plan and, perhaps, a reluctance to identify too closely with trading mechanisms.

The government had signalled its interest in market based instruments on several occasions, culminating in a 'presumption in favour of economic instruments rather than regulation' in the Second Year Report on the Environment White Paper (DoE, 1992). The idea gained support from a deregulation drive launched in February 1993, as economic instruments could be portrayed as lowering the burden on industry (DTI, 1994). The US Acid Rain Program was becoming established at that time, and early reports suggested that it would be a success (Sorrell, 1994a). The adoption of a similar scheme for the UK looked attractive as it could help resolve a series of problems with the National Plan, while providing assurance that international commitments would be met.

The problem with the National Plan was that the rigid sectoral and regional targets were increasingly inappropriate in a rapidly changing energy market. Table 11.7 summarizes LCP emissions and quota allocations in 1993, showing the percentage 'surplus' in each sector.

Table 11.7 UK LCP sulphur dioxide emissions and quota allocations – 1993

Sector	Capacity (GWth)	Emissions (ktonnes)	Quota (ktonnes)	Surplus (ktonnes)	Surplus (%)
ESI					
National Power	166.3	1116.4	1497	380.6	25.4
PowerGen	44.2	841.8	1019	177.2	17.4
England & Wales	210.5	1958.2	2516	557.8	22.2
Scotland	13.8	52.8	104	51.2	49.3
N Ireland	6.4	78.0	80	2.0	2.5
Total	230.7	2089.0	2700	609.4	22.6
Industry					
England & Wales	n/a	154.1	241	86.9	36.1
Scotland	n/a	5.9	35	29.1	83.0
Total	15.6	160.1	276	115.9	42.0
Refineries					
England & Wales	7.8	67.7	86	18.3	21.3
Scotland	1.7	11.8	14	2.2	15.9
Total	9.5	79.5	100	20.5	20.5
Total	**255.7**	**2328.5**	**3076**	**747.5**	**24.3**

Source: Sorrell, 1995

Total LCP emissions were 24 per cent below the National Plan target in 1993. The ESI was responsible for 88 per cent of this surplus, of which 82 per cent was in the hands of National Power and PowerGen. These companies had a quota surplus of 558 ktonnes (22 per cent of their allocation) which exceeded the sum of the quotas in the refinery and industrial sectors combined.

While the UK as a whole was well within its target, some sectors were being constrained. To keep within its quota, Northern Ireland Electricity (NIE) had to direct generators to use low sulphur fuel oil at a premium price.[22] Industrial emissions in England and Wales were below the quota, but a combination of factors created a risk that demand for quotas would exceed supply over the next few years (HMIP, 1995b). Companies that could burn both gas and heavy fuel oil (HFO) were appealing against authorizations which required them to burn gas preferentially.[23] Similarly, multi site companies such as British Sugar aspired to the flexibility that the generators enjoyed and had submitted appeals requesting an emissions bubble.

The Scottish ESI was not constrained by its current allocation but was expecting to be hit hard within the next few years. Approximately half its current quota surplus derived from the burning of gas at its Peterhead plant, displacing high sulphur HFO. Gas supplies were expected to terminate in 1998, at the same time as the Scottish quota allocation began to fall. Both electricity output and emissions were expected to rise following the upgrading of the England and Wales interconnector and the construction of an interconnector to Northern Ireland. To keep within its quota, Scottish Power would have to retrofit its Longannet plant with FGD. This would be an inefficient solution as the Longannet plant uses locally mined coal with the lowest sulphur content in the UK.[24]

The picture was therefore one of quota surpluses in some areas, deficits in others and demands for greater flexibility. A system of quota switching seemed the natural way of resolving these problems, while at the same time fulfilling public commitments to economic instruments and deregulation.

5.2. Quota switching chronology

In March 1994, the DoE responded to the mounting problems with the National Plan by organizing an exploratory seminar on quota switching (DoE, 1994a). The stated aim was to develop a more flexible approach to sulphur policy that still guaranteed attainment of national targets. The importance of certainty, practicality and simplicity were emphasized, together with the necessity of working within the existing regulatory framework. Views were sought on the scope of the scheme, options for quota allocation, treatment of plant sales[25] and methods for incorporating geographical constraints. The response was somewhat guarded, with a diversity of views on the equity of quota allocation and an absence of strong support for the idea.

The problems that would beset the proposals were already apparent at this stage. While trying to resolve difficulties with the National Plan, the UK was in the process of moving the goal posts through negotiations for the Second UNECE Sulphur Protocol. These were concluded in June 1994, with more stringent targets for the UK. At the same time, HMIP was beginning negotiations with National Power and PowerGen over the content of their upgrading programmes. These would take over two years to resolve and were conducted independently of the quota switching debate and without the involvement of the DoE.

In May 1994, the DoE began development of a quota switching strategy.[26] Initial indications were that this would include:

- quota switching to be introduced for all plants within the National Plan;
- the existing pattern of quota allocation to be used to facilitate the rapid introduction of the scheme;
- quota switching to be allowed between sectors and across all of the UK;

- authorizations to contain an annual quota allocation to 2003, together with a separate BATNEEC annual limit which would act as a fixed emission ceiling; and
- banking not to be permitted as this could endanger attainment of the LCPD targets.

It was soon recognized that a scheme in this form would be unworkable for three reasons. First, if quota switching was to involve all parties to 2003, it would be necessary to reduce the total *number* of quotas in circulation. The National Plan allocated a total of 1888 ktonnes to LCP in 2003, but the new targets under the UNECE Protocol allocated only 1470 ktonnes to *all* sulphur sources in 2005. Since LCP only accounted for some three quarters of UK emissions, the National Plan targets were inconsistent with the new UNECE Protocol. The quotas could not be made tradable if they may later have to be confiscated.

Second, it was recognized that a *reallocation* of quotas would be unavoidable. The current surplus was so large that, in a free market, the price of a quota would be zero. However, the market would not be free but would be dominated by the generators in England and Wales. Legitimating this degree of market power would be politically impossible, particularly as all other parties believed the original National Plan allocation to be inequitable. These parties wanted access to the surplus quotas, but wanted this through a 'fair' initial allocation rather than purchasing in a market. The equity of the allocation to the Scottish ESI was particularly sensitive.

Finally, the fundamental problem of the relationship between BATNEEC upgrading and the National Plan was left unaddressed. This had to be clarified if there was to be any confidence in the scheme.

By July the DoE was investigating alternative options to overcome these problems, but the solutions proposed introduced more difficulties.[27] It was recognized that quota switching between sectors could not take place without a reallocation. This would be a contentious and time consuming process, but a scheme was required to be introduced before January 1995 in order to accommodate the outstanding appeals. A proposed solution was for quota switching to be allowed within each National Plan sector but not between them. The existing sectoral allocations could be left unchanged, but quotas could be reallocated to plants within the other industry sector on the basis of fuel use. The proposal was that such a scheme could operate until 2003, but could be subject to a review after three years and could be capable of expansion in the context of a wider strategy for the UNECE Protocol. Other elements of the scheme could remain unchanged, including the use of existing BATNEEC limits as an emission ceiling.

This proposal had several flaws. First, the ambiguity over the stability of the scheme neither gave confidence in the long term value of the quotas, nor resolved the problem of consistency with the UNECE targets. Second, the proposal left the ESI in Northern Ireland and Scotland still subject to the market dominance of the generators in England and Wales, while being unable to purchase quotas from other sectors. Third, the retention of the existing BATNEEC limits in the other industry sector would restrict flexibility to the point where quota switching would be largely redundant. Finally, the proposed reallocation on the basis of fuel use would be hugely controversial.

The last two points were of central importance. It was the need to resolve the problems in the other industry sector that was driving the quota switching timetable. HMIP had initially proposed a reallocation to deal with the problem (HMIP, 1994), but this had been shelved while quota switching was discussed. HMIP was drawn reluctantly into the quota switching debate, but remained wedded to the primacy of BATNEEC limits and upgrading programmes under IPC.

By August, the DoE had retreated further. The proposal now was for a strictly limited scheme, confined solely to the other industry sector and operating for only three years.[28] This could address the outstanding appeals and allow experience to be gained with a trading instrument. This experience could be used during the development of a larger strategy for compliance with the UNECE Protocol, which could be developed over the next two years and would address such fundamental issues as quota reallocation and clarification of BATNEEC. An additional consideration was that it was difficult to abandon quota switching at this stage as the DoE was publicly committed to it.

Despite its limited scope, even this proposal was destined to fail. As indicated above, the problem hinged on the relationship between quotas and the BATNEEC annual limit. HMIP were insistent that the latter should remain at the current level, which was largely based on the fuel mix at the plant at the time of IPC application. Quotas could be allocated according to the same criteria, but made separate and tradable. With this system:

- plants using coal or oil had all the quotas they needed and did not need to trade;
- dual fired sites, using either gas or HFO, could not purchase quotas to allow them to increase their HFO use as they were still restricted by their BATNEEC limit; and
- multi site companies such as British Sugar could not implement company bubbles as this would result in exceedances of the BATNEEC limits.

Hence, under these conditions the introduction of quota switching served no purpose. To make room for trading while leaving the BATNEEC limits unchanged, HMIP proposed reallocating quotas on the basis of historical fuel use, regardless of fuel type (Sorrell, 1994b).[29] This was simple and consistent and was justified under the polluter pays principle as rewarding 'clean plant'. The effect would be to *force* trading to occur. Oil and coal users would need to purchase permits, gas users would have a surplus to sell, and dual fired sites would also have a surplus as their BATNEEC limits would prevent them from using all they were allocated.

This rule was consistent but it was not grandfathering. It represented a major departure from the existing distribution of allowed emissions and hence a major redistribution of wealth. Gas fired sites would receive windfall profits while others would be forced to purchase quotas. The justification for this was questionable since historical decisions on fuel use were guided by economics and fuel availability and only rarely by environmental considerations.[30] Gas users argued that they had to pay a premium price for their fuel (HMIP, 1995b, p.4), but the historical data does not bear this out.[31] The proposed reallocation would inevitably attract strenuous opposition from a large number of the affected plants, leading to further appeals and delays in introducing the scheme. With this proposal, HMIP gave priority to encouraging trade, while neglecting both political feasibility and the primary aim of minimizing the cost of pollution abatement.

The obvious way forward in this debacle would have been to relax the BATNEEC annual limits. These could be retained as an emissions ceiling, but (as in the ESI) placed some way above the quota allocation to allow room for trade. This would have provided a framework for cost saving and for resolving outstanding appeals, while avoiding a major redistribution of wealth. But the problem here was the rationale for the BATNEEC ceiling. Since this would be some way above current emissions, it did not represent the 'best' that was currently achievable. Giving priority to National Plan quotas rather than BATNEEC was difficult to justify under IPC legislation and represented a reversal of current practice within HMIP. While there was precedent for such a scheme with the ESI, HMIP took the view that the requirements of the other industry sector were different and therefore justified a different approach. Quota switching therefore foundered on a fundamental point of principle.

5.3. Subsequent developments

While still formally committed to quota switching, there was no further word from the DoE until May 1995. HMIP then announced a revised allocation for the other industry sector for the period 1995-98 (HMIP, 1995b). This did not include quota switching, but relaxed constraints by allocating the 20 per cent of the sector total that had previously been held in reserve. Multi site bubbles were still not permitted, but some other difficulties were overcome. Shortly after, the interim problems of the Northern Ireland ESI were resolved in an informal manner through National Power transferring a small portion of its quota surplus to NIE at zero cost (Utility Week, 1995). NIE's problems were expected to decrease from 1997, as the Ballyumford power station was converting from coal to gas.[32]

In March 1996, HMIP published its long awaited review of the generators' upgrading programmes (HMIP, 1996). The stringency of the agreed targets surprised many observers, but reflected the accelerating pace of the 'dash to gas'. National Power and PowerGen agreed to cut SO_2 emissions from the 23 remaining coal and oil fired stations by 79 per cent from the 1991 level in 2001 and by 85 per cent in 2005.[33] The revised limits allowed continuing use of company bubbles.

The agreed reductions in the ESI, together with the continued expansion of gas use in other sectors, made the development of the UNECE strategy relatively straightforward (Sorrell, 1996a). The main points of the consultation paper published in June 1996 were:

- emission projections indicated that the 2000 and 2005 targets would be met without the need for additional measures;
- compliance with the 2010 target was not assured, but the projected overshoot was small and within the margin for error;
- on this basis there was no need to take any new measures;
- while the overall framework of the National Plan should be retained, the sectoral and geographical constraints could be relaxed;
- quotas should be allocated to individual plant on the basis of BATNEEC; and
- no purpose would be served by a general quota switching scheme.

The final UNECE strategy was published relatively unchanged in December (DoE, 1996). In brief, the dash to gas had allowed the UK to meet its obligations with little extra effort. Quota switching had become redundant.

5.4. Assessment

The above account suggests one straightforward answer to our initial question. *Quota switching failed in the UK because independent developments in energy markets meant it was no longer needed.* The large reduction in emissions achieved through the 'dash to gas' allowed the UK to meet its targets without further measures being required.

This is insufficient however. The account also suggests that quota switching faced fundamental problems quite independent of the developments in energy markets. It is argued here that these problems would have prevented a scheme from going ahead, even if sulphur reduction had proved expensive and improvements in economic efficiency were desired. These problems are of central importance as they apply in widely different contexts throughout the EU and may be equally relevant for carbon trading after Kyoto. The following sections discuss these problems in more detail.

6. A CONFLICT OF REGULATORY PRINCIPLES

IPC and emissions trading have different origins, objectives, philosophies and procedures. At heart they are fundamentally incompatible. Table 11.8 summarizes the key differences.

Sulphur quota switching was an attempt to graft a trading scheme onto the back of IPC. This created the problem of which system should take priority.

Trading schemes require an aggregate target, specified in terms of environmental quality objectives or the total volume of emissions. The relative contribution of different plant to this target is decided through trading in the permit market. In contrast, the focus of IPC is the environmental performance of an individual process at a single site. This must be brought to BATNEEC standards without reference to an aggregate target.

With quota switching, the aggregate targets were represented by the sector and plant quotas, while the process specific requirements were represented by the BATNEEC limits and upgrading programmes. Trading would require the former to take priority, while the latter acted as a 'backstop' protection for local air quality and critical loads.[34] Both the BATNEEC limits and the goals of the upgrading programme would need to be sufficiently lax to allow room for trade. But if room is made in this way, how can the BATNEEC standard represent the 'best' that is available? If a plant can operate with a quota that is below its BATNEEC limit then it is clearly using a technology that is both better and affordable. In that case, the legislation requires the BATNEEC limit to be reduced to reflect this.

Does the operation of company bubbles in the ESI imply that a loose interpretation of BATNEEC can be allowed? Perhaps, but only for a transitional period. Trading requires that the environmental target remain stable for a sufficient period of time to provide confidence in the value of the permits. In contrast, under IPC the regulator is required to continuously monitor developments in BAT and to incorporate these into authorizations. In the ESI, the flexibility provided by the emissions bubble was radically reduced by the stringent requirements of the upgrading program. This went further than was required under the UNECE Protocol, and may achieve emission reductions at a greater marginal cost than available in other sectors (Sorrell, 1996b). Furthermore, the Environment Agency has continued to monitor developments in energy markets. When these indicated that further

Table 11.8 Comparing IPC and emissions trading

Trading	IPC
US origins: Offset policy first introduced in 1976	**European origins:** Technology based principles date from the last century
Economics based: Pollution arises from an absence of well defined property rights. Technology based 'command and control' regulations are costly and inefficient.	**Engineering based:** 'Abating air pollution is a technological problem – a matter for scientists and engineers, operating in an atmosphere of cooperative officialdom....' (Alkali Inspectorate, 1969)
Target based: Overall pollution target, with no specification of individual technologies or emissions standards.	**Technology based:** No overall pollution target, beyond the requirement to minimize pollution using BATNEEC
Hands off: Technology decisions are the responsibility of individual firms.	**Hands on:** Regulator is involved in individual technological decisions.
Wide system boundary: The system under the aggregate emission target can be as wide as a sector, an economy or a geographic region.	**Narrow system boundary:** BATNEEC limits are set for an individual process at a single site.
Single substance/media: Controls a single polluting substance in a single media.	**Multi substance/media:** Controls releases of a wide range of substances to all three media in an integrated manner.
Flexibility via the market: Installation operators can seek flexibility and reduced costs through trading in the permit market.	**Flexibility via negotiations:** Installation operators can seek flexibility and reduced costs through negotiations with the site inspector.

emission reductions could be achieved from the ESI, the Agency brought forward the deadline for the 84 per cent target from 2005 to 2001 (Environment Agency, 1998). This demonstrates that BATNEEC is an evolving target, thereby undermining the stability required for a trading scheme.

The problems faced in the UK under IPC are identical to those faced throughout the EU following the introduction of the new IPPC Directive. In an attempt to reconcile the two, Ger Klaassen from DG XI of the European Commission has recently proposed that trading could be used to 'go beyond' the BAT standards in IPPC (Klaassen, 1998). This could occur where:

- techniques are used that are considered not to be available under economically and technically viable conditions; or
- techniques are used for which costs outweigh advantages.

This would appear to confine trading to marginal adjustments for meeting a very stringent emission target. But in practice, the most relevant target is the commitments agreed at Kyoto on greenhouse gases, which are not stringent. In the above scheme, if a large number of plants become sellers of permits, it is difficult to see how the technologies employed could be claimed to 'go beyond' BAT. But if BAT is adjusted to reflect these developments, the margin for trade is lost.

It is important to note that principles such as BATNEEC may be highly appropriate for complex regulatory situations where a large number of chemical compounds are emitted from many different release points. These represent the most common situations encountered under IPC and would be impossible to handle with emissions taxes or tradable permits. But for point source emissions of a single pollutant into a single medium, market based instruments can have significant advantages. If IPC or IPPC is to be made compatible with trading, it is necessary to ask whether BATNEEC requirements can be relaxed in these special circumstances. UK experience suggests that this is legally and procedurally very difficult to do.

7. A CONFLICT OF REGULATORY CULTURE

Emissions trading is a regulatory innovation that has proved difficult to export beyond the United States. Its origins lie in attempts to introduce flexibility into the rigid and legalistic regulatory framework which prevailed in the US in the 1970s (Sorrell, 1994a, pp. 46–52). The development of the Emissions Trading Program (ETP) can be interpreted as a series of incremental attempts to widen the scope for flexibility (Liroff, 1986).

The economics literature frequently characterizes traditional regulations as 'command and control', a pejorative term which is more representative of US regulatory traditions than those that prevail in the UK. Uniform emission standards can be used as a 'straw man' to exaggerate the potential cost savings of market based schemes. But in a different national context, uniform emission standards may not be the most likely alternative, and flexibility may be introduced in different ways.

It has long been recognized that British and US regulatory styles differ in quite fundamental respects, as summarized in Table 11.9.

Table 11.9 is based on Vogel's comprehensive study which was completed in 1986 (Vogel, 1986). Much has changed in the UK since then, including the increasing dominance of the EU in environmental policy, and the overhaul of the UK system of industrial pollution control through IPC. While these changes have posed challenges to the UK regulatory style, it has survived relatively unchanged (Smith, 1997). IPC has introduced greater transparency into industrial pollution control, improved the quality of pollution monitoring, introduced legally binding emission standards and placed a greater responsibility on operators to account for their plant's performance. Beyond this, however, the traditional cooperative and consensual working relationship between operators and site inspectors remains as firmly established as ever.

Table 11.9 Comparison of US and UK regulatory styles

United States	United Kingdom
Regulations are complex and rigid	Regulations are flexible and informal
Extensive use of uniform standards	Preference for individually negotiated, site specific standards
Suspicion of industry self regulation	Encouragement of industry self regulation
Courts used extensively	Courts used rarely
Minimal administrative discretion	Maximum administrative discretion
Relations between industry and regulator characterized by conflict	Relations between industry and regulator characterized by cooperation
Freedom of information	Confidentiality
High administrative costs	Low administrative costs
Regulation is focus of political conflict	Regulation has low political profile

Source: adapted from Vogel, 1986

Smith (1997) has used the concept of policy networks (Rhodes, 1997, chapter 2) to explain this continuity in regulatory style. This framework may also be used to explain why emissions trading failed.

The key insight behind policy network analysis is that governments cannot achieve policy objectives without the *resources* of other actors. Resources may be informational, organizational, legal, financial or political. Policy is implemented through the interaction of a range of organizations (a policy network) which depend on each other for the resources required to meet the task. For example, the Environment Agency relies on industry for the technical and financial information necessary to determine BATNEEC, while industry relies on the regulator for technical advice on pollution control techniques and the legal authority to continue operation.

Marsh and Rhodes (1992) have characterized policy networks by their membership, the distribution of resources between members, the nature and quality of interactions between members and the degree of consensus on core beliefs. With this, policy networks can be represented by a continuum between an exclusive, tightly knit *policy community* and a much looser *issue network*. This typology is summarized in Table 11.10.

Table 11.10 Types of policy network

Dimension	Policy community	Issue network
Membership	Very limited with some groups excluded	Large and fluctuating
Interactions	Frequent and high quality interactions between all members on all matters related to the policy issue	Contacts fluctuate in frequency and intensity
Continuity	Continuity in values, membership and outcomes over time	Access fluctuates significantly
Consensus	Consensus on values and broad policy preferences	Ever present conflict
Resources	All participants have resources and basic relationship is one of exchange	Many participants have limited resources and basic relationship is one of consultation

Source: Adapted from Marsh and Rhodes, 1992

Smith's argument is that industrial pollution control in the UK is a paradigmatic example of a closed policy community. Operators and site inspectors have a close relationship based on frequent interactions, consensus seeking and trust. Both sides share the core belief that regulation is a technical issue, standards should be negotiated at the site level, and formal enforcement should only be used as a last resort. Crucially, environmental groups, the public and the DoE are *excluded* from this policy community. The DoE sets the overall framework for IPC and has a role in the resolution of appeals, but plays no part in implementation. This exclusion is reflected in the attitudes of industrial operators. While relations with the local inspector are generally good, there is deep suspicion of both the DoE and the central staff of HMIP: '....the (DoE) doesn't understand and doesn't care. I get the impression that they are just a gang of lawyers'.[35]

A primary reason this policy community survived the introduction of IPC unchanged was that HMIP was dependent upon industry for technical, economic and environmental information (Smith, 1997, chapter 6). This is an example of the information asymmetry that market based instruments are designed to circumvent. But in the UK, such instruments are alien to the belief system and rules of the game of the dominant policy community. Quota switching was an imposition from outside the community by the DoE. While the DoE had a legal resource – in that it could introduce primary legislation to modify IPC and require quota switching – this was not one it was prepared to use. Instead, it had to rely on persuasion and the cooperation of a regulator which was fundamentally opposed to the idea. HMIP stood to lose the discretion which was such a central feature of the UK style, while individual inspectors stood to lose control of the environmental performance of 'their' plant. As a consequence, HMIP had no incentive to come up with a politically acceptable quota allocation scheme.

This opposition was shared by most of the industrial operators who, in principle, stood to gain by quota switching. Flexibility was certainly a dominant concern. But they wanted to gain this flexibility through negotiations with the individual site inspectors or through a fair quota allocation. Emissions trading was seen as a complicated and unnecessary device that had no place in the UK.

8. A CONFLICT OVER QUOTA ALLOCATION

Debates over the equity issue of quota allocation played a central role in the quota switching story. First, the original National Plan allocation was considered by most participants to be unfair; second, the recognition that a quota reallocation would take years to negotiate was a primary reason for not proceeding with the original quota switching scheme; and third, HMIP's proposals for reallocating in the other industry sector proved too controversial to be viable.

These problems are not new. The initial allocation of quotas has long been recognized as one of the most intractable problems in establishing a trading scheme (Tietenberg, 1985, pp. 103-113; Grubb and Sebenius, 1992).[36] The allocation must be perceived to be fair but perceptions of equity will differ. Auctions could achieve an efficient allocation, but the scale of wealth transfers involved does not make this politically realistic. To gain acceptance from existing polluters it has generally been necessary to grandfather quotas, i.e. to allocate them according to a formula based on historic emissions or existing regulatory requirements. But this simple prescription is only the starting point of debate. Allocations based on actual emissions may be challenged as rewarding the biggest polluters. Similarly, allocations based on allowed emissions may be challenged if the current distribution is seen as unfair. Since quotas represent valuable property rights, the allocation process will be seized on as an opportunity to maximize individual wealth. But once the allocation rule departs from historic emissions, the equity arguments multiply.

Box 1 summarizes some of the key issues in any allocation debate and illustrates how complex the process may become.

These difficulties may be illustrated by taking the example of the UK ESI – a more homogeneous sector than that covered by the full National Plan. Suppose we wished to devise an equitable initial allocation rule for sulphur quotas, based on historic data for individual sources. Each of the following could provide the basis for an allocation formula:

- thermal input capacity;
- thermal input capacity weighted by average load factor;
- fuel consumption;
- electrical output capacity;
- electricity generation; and
- SO_2 emissions.

In addition, the first five may be modified to allow for the sulphur content of the fuel used. The options are to: a) ignore fuel sulphur content; b) modify by the historic fuel sulphur content at the plant; or c) modify by the UK average sulphur content for the fuel used. Taken together, the proposed measures represent different weightings of plant capacity, thermal efficiency, load factor, fuel characteristics and pollution control technology. Each measure may be justified on equity grounds, but their relative impact will vary. For example, allocating on the basis of fuel consumption allows for plant operating patterns but rewards inefficient sources.

The above measures were applied to baseline data for UK power stations over the period 1992-94 (Sorrell, 1995).[37] The baseline excludes plants that were retired during this period. Table 11.11 summarizes the proportional allocation to the Scottish ESI using these different measures.

Box 1 Issues in quota allocation

Principles: The starting point for debate may be basic principles of equity. A broad distinction can be made between responsibility based principles, such as 'polluter pays', and burden based principles, such as equal percentage cuts (Grubb and Sebenius, 1992). Both are open to a range of interpretations and no single principle is likely to command consensus.

Formulae: An allocation formula could be devised at the level of individual sources, companies or sectors. Source based measures such as thermal input or fuel consumption could be modified by more strategic considerations appropriate to the higher level. A simple formula is transparent but will be challenged as penalizing particular interests. The scale of the problem depends upon the diversity of plants involved.

Negotiations: An alternative to a standardized formula is negotiation between the regulator and the company/sector. Negotiations are more flexible than formulae, but lack transparency, are time consuming and run the risk of capture. A balance between the two is likely, though this will depend on the national regulatory style.

Lead times: With a short interval between proposing a scheme and its entry into force, there is much less scope to propose a major redistribution of quotas – the initial allocation must accommodate current emissions. With longer lead times, redistribution can be more ambitious.

Initial versus subsequent allocations: One approach is to devise an initial allocation which subsequently declines in a pro-rata fashion, linked to the overall emission target. An alternative approach allows subsequent allocations to decrease at a rate that varies between sources, companies or sectors. The choice between the two is linked to the lead time available. If this is short, the second approach may be more realistic.

Historic data versus forecasts: Historic data has generally been used as the basis for quota allocation because it accurately reflects the emission performance and market position of the participating companies. This may be challenged if a company/sector is undergoing rapid change and if future emission levels are expected to be much higher than historic levels. But forecasts are open to manipulation for strategic advantage.

Pollution for Sale

Table 11.11 Proportional allocation of quotas to Scottish ESI under different measures (%)

Measure	Ignore fuel sulphur content	Historic fuel sulphur content	Standard fuel sulphur content
Thermal input capacity	11.76	3.88	8.24
Electrical output capacity	11.47	3.75	7.87
Fuel consumption	10.0	4.01	6.93
Electricity generation	9.72	3.90	6.66
SO_2 emissions	3.61	3.61	3.61
National Plan	**4.05**	**4.05**	**4.05**

Source: Sorrell, 1995

The results dramatically illustrate the equity implications of different formulae. Under the National Plan, the Scottish ESI received 4 per cent of the total quotas allocated to the electricity sector. If historic emissions had been used as a basis, it would have received only 3.6 per cent. But under virtually every other allocation rule, it would have received a significantly larger proportion of the total – in some cases as much as three times more.

The discrepancy is largely due to the historically low sulphur content of the fuels used in Scottish power stations. If we extended the analysis beyond the ESI, both the disparity of plant and the scope for equity disputes would increase.

Allocation problems are not confined to trading schemes, and from one perspective the scope for flexibility should lessen their intensity. But in practice, the reverse is likely to be the case. By making permits tradable, their status as valuable property rights is made more explicit. Unlike credit schemes, allowance based schemes require all allocation disputes to be resolved in full at the inception of the scheme and to remain in force for its full duration (Palmisano, 1997). As the geographical and sectoral scope of the scheme is widened, and as its duration is extended, the intensity of allocation disputes will increase. This may ultimately make the introduction of such a scheme impossible.

9. PERSISTENT REGULATORY UNCERTAINTY

For participants to have confidence in trading, it is essential that quotas have a firm status and that the scheme remains stable for a sufficient period of time. The US Acid Rain Program sets an exemplary precedent in this respect, as there is confidence that the framework of the program will remain unchanged until at least 2010. Such a happy state of affairs seems unlikely in the European context.

In the UK, sulphur regulations have been beset by uncertainty, including:

- the negotiation of targets for the UNECE Second Sulphur Protocol;
- the two years of negotiations over the generators' upgrading programs; and
- the content of the upgrading programs for other combustion plant.

When the UK finally settled on a strategy for compliance with the UNECE Protocol, it was undermined within two months by the proposed Acidification Strategy from the European Commission (European Commission, 1997). This proposed significantly more stringent emission ceilings for the UK, together with revisions to the LCPD and limits on the sulphur content of HFO. Similarly, less than two years after agreeing an upgrading program to 2005 with the England and Wales ESI, the Environment Agency decided to bring forward the target date, without consulting the affected companies (Environment Agency, 1998).

These continual changes are of great benefit to the European environment which continues to suffer from acid deposition in excess of critical loads. However, they make the introduction of a sulphur trading scheme practically impossible.

10. INADEQUATE POLITICAL SUPPORT

Experience in the US suggests that the successful introduction of a trading scheme requires:

- a broad based coalition of political support;
- vigorous lobbying from a small number of 'product champions';[38] and
- accumulation of experience from more limited trading mechanisms (Sorrell, 1994a).

All three were absent in the UK. The primary advocates of a scheme were the DoE, who wished to overcome problems with the National Plan while fulfilling public commitments on market based instruments and deregulation. In contrast, support was largely absent in the closed policy community of regulators and industrial operators. Those sections of industry who could be expected to be sympathetic were primarily concerned with resolving their own particular difficulties rather than supporting a broadly based trading scheme. A few multi-site companies wanted an emissions bubble but had no interest in trading outside the bubble. Parties who had come off badly under the National Plan wanted to resolve their problems through a revised quota allocation. Regional sensitivities were central here as any debate on reallocation would need to involve the DoE, the Scottish Office, the Northern Ireland Department of the Environment, the three corresponding sets of regulators and all the affected companies – a daunting proposition. The DoE also seemed isolated within government, as neither the Treasury nor the Department of Trade and Industry were supportive of the idea.[39]

The final missing ingredient was the lack of support from the public and NGOs. These were outside the policy community and played little role in a debate that was largely confined to government, regulators and individual companies. To the extent that environmentalists were involved, they were opposed to trading on the grounds of its impact on sensitive UK ecosystems (Farmer and Bareham, 1993; Joint Nature Conservation Committee, 1996). A group of government funded nature conservation bodies commissioned research which demonstrated how sulphur trading could damage sensitive areas in the Welsh and Scottish highlands (Brown et al., 1996).[40] While this work had only a marginal impact on the decision to abandon sulphur trading, it did highlight another potential area of conflict: between the UK's espousal of an effects based approach to acidification and the necessity of neglecting spatial considerations in any viable trading scheme.

Trading therefore lacked a winning coalition of political support. This problem was further compounded by the ambitiousness of the early proposals and the paucity of experience with trading mechanisms. The US Acid Rain Program was informed by 15 years of experience with credit based schemes. This was not available in the UK.

11. SUMMARY AND LESSONS

At one level, sulphur trading failed in the UK because it was no longer needed. The UK has been able to meet its international obligations on sulphur emissions without introducing new measures. As with carbon dioxide emissions, the 'dash to gas' has led to significant environmental improvement with little regulatory effort.

On another level, however, sulphur trading was doomed to failure even if the changes in energy markets had not occurred. The quota switching proposals encountered:

- a conflict of regulatory principles between trading and IPC;
- a conflict between trading and the dominant regulatory culture;
- difficulties in resolving the equity issue of quota allocation;
- persistent regulatory uncertainty; and

- inadequate political support.

Any one of these would have presented severe difficulties for a trading scheme. Together they made failure inevitable.

This story has important lessons for both the theory and practice of emissions trading. First, it demonstrates that economic efficiency is an insufficient criterion for instrument choice. Issues of regulatory culture, regulatory interaction and equity must be given equal consideration. As Majone has argued: '...the significant choice is not among abstractly considered policy instruments but among institutionally determined ways of operating them' (Majone, 1976). Environmental economics tends to abstract from institutional issues and focuses on equilibrium analyses that frequently have little relevance for policy. But the more successful advocacy of economic approaches demands that such issues be addressed. The UK story suggests that both understanding and policy relevance could be enhanced by empirical studies of implementation informed by ideas from political science.[41] Of particular interest are the bargaining processes between 'resource interdependent policy actors' and the determining influence that implementing agencies can have on the final policy outcome.

A second valuable lesson relates to the scope for carbon trading after Kyoto. European countries are beginning to consider this at the same time as introducing the IPPC Directive. IPPC includes the novel requirement that installations use energy efficiently and its coverage includes installations that would be natural participants in a carbon trading scheme (European Commission, 1997). The UK Advisory Committee on Business and the Environment (ACBE) has recently suggested that the Directive is implemented in a way which allows for carbon trading (ACBE, 1998). But this raises the possibility of the same conflict of regulatory principles that undermined sulphur quota switching. It is far from clear that the two can coexist. If not, the major opportunities offered by carbon trading may be lost.

NOTES

[1] This account draws on personal interviews and unpublished documentary evidence obtained during consultancy work for the UK government. The author would like to thank Richard Mills of the NSCA and colleagues in the SPRU Environment Programme for their helpful comments.

[2] Sulphur will be used as a shorthand for sulphur dioxide throughout this chapter.

[3] Specified as concentration of the pollutant in the flue gas (mg/Nm3).

[4] The UK was not a signatory to the first Sulphur Protocol, agreed in 1985, which required a 30 per cent reduction on 1980 emissions by 1993. Despite not signing, the UK met the target.

[5] This aspiration derived from a number of sources including European influence, the dominance of the former Radiochemical Inspectorate in HMIP, and a perceived need to restore credibility. See Smith (1997), pp.116–119.

[6] This retreat took place during the early stages of IPC implementation. HMIP's Head of Policy, Douglas Bryce, announced the official abandonment of the arm's length approach on the 24th May, 1993 (ENDS, 1993, p.30). This statement merely confirmed unofficial practice (Smith, 1997, p.157).

[7] For example, '...The achievable release levels in this Note do not take into account site specific considerations and they should not be used as uniform release standards' (HMIP,1995a, p.1).

[8] The Department of the Environment (DoE) was merged with the Department of Transport in 1997, and given the new title of the Department of the Environment, Transport and the Regions (DETR).

[9] Emissions from the Scottish ESI had declined faster than in other sectors in the 1980s due to increased output from hydro and nuclear stations. As a consequence, a pro-rata reduction of 20 per cent to meet the 1993 target had already been achieved. Similarly, refinery emissions in 1991 were only 37 per cent of those in 1980, as a consequence of rationalization, investment in upgrading facilities and increased use of low sulphur crudes from the North Sea.

[10] The oil industry claimed that further investment would be required simply to keep emissions at current levels as low sulphur crude production from the North Sea would be gradually run down.

[11] The allocations for the Scottish ESI did not decline linearly. This is because, with only a small number of plants on the system, investment decisions are inevitably 'lumpy' in their effect.

[12] Compliance in the England and Wales ESI was originally anticipated to rely heavily on FGD retrofits and the 1993 allocation was generous as a consequence to allow for construction lead times. Quota allocations for the Scottish ESI were relatively flat up to 1998 and then dropped steeply under the assumption that some major new investment took place, such as FGD on the Longannet plant.

[13] Critical loads are defined as the maximum levels of acid deposition below which, according to current scientific knowledge, no significant damage to sensitive ecosystems can be demonstrated. The UK has supported extensive research in this area and has strongly advocated the use of critical loads in developing acidification policy. However, it has been reluctant to accept the national emission targets that have been proposed as an outcome of these scientific assessments.

[14] In practice, the BATNEEC limits provided very little restriction on flexibility. The only constrained plants were the oil fired stations along the Thames valley which were rarely used.

[15] Some authorizations supplemented the annual limit with additional restrictions, including fuel quality standards and concentration limits. A concentration limit is more appropriate for protecting local air quality, while an annual tonnage limit is more appropriate for addressing the cumulative problem of acid deposition. SO_2 and NO_x are problematic as they affect both.

[16] The Scottish industry is still vertically integrated while Northern Ireland operates a two tier system. This discussion is confined to developments within England and Wales.

[17] The monopoly areas of high voltage transmission and low voltage distribution are subject to price control by the Office of Electricity Regulation (OFFER).

18   It is likely that the eventual capacity will exceed 19 GW. National Power has already been given the go-ahead for a 1500 MW plant at Staythorpe, due to be completed in 2003. In addition, there are nine projects with a combined capacity of 4500 MW which have planning consent under Section 36 of the Electricity Act.

19   The RECs were part owners of many of these plant and wanted to to develop sources of power independent of the 'duopoly' of National Power and PowerGen. The existence of a captive franchise market until 1998 gave the contracts some security, even when generating costs exceeded the avoidable costs of existing coal fired power stations (Smith, 1994).

20   The build up of new power station orders has grown so large that the government announced a moratorium on new plant construction in December 1997.

21   The actual figure is greater than this as the FGD plants have not run on baseload. The additional cost of FGD equipment has reduced their competitiveness against CCGTs and other coal fired stations. Following legal advice, HMIP concluded that they did not have the power to require FGD equipped plant to be dispatched ahead of unabated plant (HMIP, personal communication).

22   NIE is responsible for the transmission, distribution and supply of electricity in Northern Ireland. It purchases electricity on long term contracts from four independently owned power stations. Legal responsibility for the National Plan was given to NIE.

23   Dual fired boilers purchase gas on 'interruptible' contracts, which allow the supply to be cut off during periods of peak demand during the winter. The gas is diverted to supply the domestic market. Interruptible contracts provide a load balancing function for the gas industry and allow industrial users to obtain supplies at a discount. Heavy fuel oil (HFO) is commonly used as the back up fuel, and the price of HFO and interruptible gas are linked. Gas supplies are rarely interrupted for more than a few days each year, but the dual firing capability allows the user to switch between gas and HFO on the basis of price. Quota allocations prevented companies from burning HFO for more than a few days each year, thus restricting their fuel flexibility. HMIP argued, quite reasonably, that this could be justified as BATNEEC.

24   Longannet coal has a sulphur content of around 0.3 per cent. In contrast, most UK deep mined coal has a sulphur content of 1.4 per cent, which is approximately twice the average of internationally traded coal.

25   This was a pressing consideration as in February 1994 the electricity regulator had obtained an undertaking from National Power and PowerGen on the voluntary sale of 6 GW of coal fired plant. This was part of a settlement to reduce the market power of the two companies, while avoiding a reference to the Monopolies and Mergers Commission. All of this plant was eventually purchased by Eastern Group, a REC.

26   Department of the Environment, personal communication.

27   Department of the Environment, personal communication.

28   Department of the Environment, personal communication.

29   HMIP, Pollution Policy Division, personal communication.

30   In only a couple of cases would industry gain through prior investment in pollution abatement or the use of low sulphur coal or oil on environmental grounds. Generally, minimal attention was paid to environmental issues prior to IPC (Smith, 1997, chapter 3).

31   This argument hinges on the relevant price of interruptible gas and HFO, which is subject to short term fluctuations. In the last few years, the majority of dual fired sites have used HFO for much shorter periods than allowed for in their authorizations. This suggests that interruptible gas has generally been cheaper, particularly following the introduction of gas competition.

[32] The gas will be supplied through a newly constructed interconnecter with Scotland.

[33] These reductions were '...equivalent to fitting FGD at black fossil fuel power stations in operation in 1991' (HMIP, 1996), Assuming that FGD is confined to the Drax and Ratcliffe power stations and that UK coal has an average sulphur content of 1.4 per cent, the 2005 limit would allow a maximum of 25 Mtonnes of UK coal to be used, of which 15 Mtonnes would be at the FGD stations. In practice, neither FGD station is likely to run on baseload; cheap, low sulphur coal imports may substitute for UK supplies and further CCGT construction may reduce the market to below 25 Mtonnes.

[34] This is a feature of other trading programs. For example, power stations participating in the US Acid Rain Program are also subject to State regulations on local air quality (Sorrell, 1994a, p.117). However, in most cases this has provided little restriction on their flexibility to trade sulphur allowances.

[35] Interview with the environment manager of a UK chemical company, July 1994.

[36] Economists are typically sceptical about permit allocation since, in theoretical models, a cost effective distribution of abatement will be achieved regardless of the initial allocation (Montgomery, 1972). The assumptions that must hold for this to occur include low or zero transaction costs and all firms being price takers. This result is consistent with the Coase theorem (Coase, 1960), but has little relevance for practical implementation. Aside from political feasibility, Stavins has shown how with positive transaction costs the initial allocation may reduce cost effectiveness (Stavins, 1995).

[37] Baseline data was derived from company and plant environmental performance reviews, DoE news releases, IPC public registers and contacts with individual power stations. A full discussion of methodological issues is contained in Sorrell, 1995.

[38] For example, introduction of the US Acid Rain Program was helped by a number of influential environmental lobbyists, including Joe Goffman of the Environmental Defense Fund (Sorrell, 1994a, pp. 71–76).

[39] Department of the Environment, personal communication.

[40] This work partly undermined Scottish Power's claims that FGD on the Longannet plant would be inefficient. Despite using very low sulphur coal, it makes a large contribution to critical loads exceedances due to its proximity to the Scottish highlands.

[41] For examples see Hanf (1982) and Anderson (1994).

REFERENCES

Advisory Committee on Business and the Environment (1998), *Climate change: a strategic issue for business*, Department of the Environment, Transport and the Regions, DETR, London.

Alkali Inspectorate (1969), *Annual report of the Alkali Inspectorate for 1969*, HMSO, London.

Allott, K. (1994), *Integrated Pollution Control: The First Three Years*, Environmental Data Services, London.

Anderson, M.S. (1994), *Governance by green taxes: making pollution prevention pay*, Manchester University Press, Manchester and New York.

Boehmer-Christiansen, S. and J. Skea (1991), *Acid Politics: Environmental and Energy Policies in Britain and Germany*, Belhaven Press, London.

Brown, M., S.M. Wright, R.A. Wadsworth, K.R. Bull, A.M. Farmer, S. Bareham, S.E. Metcalfe and D. Whyatt (1996), 'The relative impact of different sulphur emission point sources to acidification on SSSIs in Britain', *JNCC Report,* No. 260, JNCC, Peterborough.

Castells, N. and S. Funtowicz (1997), 'Use of scientific inputs for environmental policy-making: the RAINS model and the sulphur protocols', *International Journal of Environment and Pollution,* 7(4), 512–525.

Coase, R. H. (1960), 'The problem of social cost', *Journal of Law and Economics,* 3(1), 1–44.

Dair, C., J. Skea, A. Smith, S. Sorrell and A. Stirling (1997), 'UK implementation of EC Directive 96/61 on Integrated Pollution Prevention and Control: a response to the Department of Environment, Transport and the Region's (DETR) consultation paper', Science Policy Research Unit, Brighton (unpublished).

Department of the Environment (1989), 'Implementation of the Large Combustion Plant Directive: a consultation paper', DoE, London.

Department of the Environment (1990), *The United Kingdom's Programme and National Plan for reducing emissions of sulphur dioxide and oxides of nitrogen from existing large combustion plants,* HMSO, London.

Department of the Environment (1992), *This Common Inheritance: the Second Year Report,* HMSO, London.

Department of the Environment (1994a), 'Seminar on quota switching for sulphur emissions', Queen Elizabeth II Conference Centre, 14 March.

Department of the Environment (1994b), 'Determining BATNEEC', Air Quality Division memo (unpublished).

Department of the Environment (1996)*, Reducing national emissions of sulphur dioxide: a strategy for the United Kingdom,* HMSO, London.

Department of the Environment (1997), *Integrated Pollution Control: a practical guide,* HMSO, London.

Department of the Environment, Transport and the Regions (1997a), 'UK implementation of EC Directive 96/61 on Integrated Pollution Prevention and Control: Consultation Paper', DoE, London.

Department of the Environment, Transport and the Regions (1997b), *Digest of Environmental Statistics: No. 19 1997,* HMSO, London.

Department of Trade and Industry (1994), *Deregulation: cutting red tape,* Business Deregulation Unit of the DTI, London.

Department of Trade and Industry (1997), *Digest of United Kingdom Energy Statistics 1997,* HMSO, London.

Environment Agency (1998), 'Agency consults on early pollution cuts at power stations', Press Release No. 001/98, January.

Environmental Data Services (1993), 'IPC Guides for Organic Chemicals', *ENDS Report,* No. 220, May.

European Commission (1997), *Communication to the Council and to the Parliament on a Community Strategy to Combat Acidification,* COM (97)88, Brussels.

Farmer, A.M. and S. Bareham (1993), 'The environmental implications of UK sulphur emissions: policy options for England and Wales', *JNCC Report,* No. 176, JNCC, Peterborough.

Grubb, M. and J.K Sebenius (1992), 'Participation, allocation and accountability in international tradable emission permit systems for greenhouse gas control', in *Climate Change: Designing a Tradable Permit System,* OECD, Paris.

Hanf, K. (1982), 'Regulatory structures: enforcement as implementation', *European Journal of Political Research*, **10**, 159–172.

Her Majesty's Inspectorate of Pollution (1991a), *Third Annual Report 1989-90*, HMSO, London.

Her Majesty's Inspectorate of Pollution (1991b), *Chief Inspector's Guidance Note – 1.01 Combustion Processes: Large Boilers and Furnaces 50MWth and over*, HMSO, London.

Her Majesty's Inspectorate of Pollution (1994), 'The National Plan for reducing SO_2 and NO_x emissions: Other Industry Allocation Scheme: Consultation Paper', Pollution Policy Division, HMIP, London.

Her Majesty's Inspectorate of Pollution (1995a), *Chief Inspector's Guidance Note – S2 1.01 – Combustion Processes: Large Boilers and Furnaces 50MWth and over*, HMSO, London.

Her Majesty's Inspectorate of Pollution (1995b), 'The National Plan for reducing SO_2 and NO_x emissions: Other Industry Allocation Scheme: Consultation Paper', Pollution Policy Division, HMIP, London.

Her Majesty's Inspectorate of Pollution (1996), 'ESI review by HMIP: background brief'', Press Release, 26 March.

Joint Nature Conservation Committee (1996), 'Reducing national emissions of sulphur dioxide: comments – a joint response to the Department of the Environment consultation paper', Countryside Commission for Wales, English Nature, Scottish Natural Heritage and the Joint Nature Conservation Committee, Peterborough.

Jordan, A. (1993), 'IPC and the evolving style and structure of environmental regulation in the UK', *Environmental Politics*, **2**(3), 405–427.

Klaassen, G. (1998), 'Emissions trading in the European Union: practice and prospects', Chapter 5, this volume.

Liroff, R.A. (1986), *Reforming Air Pollution Regulation: The Toil and Trouble of EPA's Bubble*, The Conservation Foundation, Washington D.C.

Majone, G. (1976), 'Choice among policy instruments for pollution control', *Policy Analysis*, **2**, 589–613.

Marsh, D. and R.A.W. Rhodes (1992), *Policy Networks in British Government*, Clarendon Press, Oxford.

Montgomery, W.D. (1972), 'Markets in Licenses and Efficient Pollution Control Programs', *Journal of Economic Theory*, **5**(4) December, 395–418.

Palmisano, J. (1997), 'Air permit trading paradigms for greenhouse gases: why allowances won't work and credits will', Available from http://www.erols.com/enviro/erc-all.html.

Parker, M. (1997), *Privatised coal: facing the end of the contracts*, Oxford Economic Research Associates Ltd., Briefing Paper 5/97, Oxford.

Parker, M. and J. Surrey (1994), *UK gas policy: regulated monopoly or managed competition?*, STEEP Special Report No. 2, Science Policy Research Unit, University of Sussex, Brighton.

Pearce, D and I. Brisson (1993), 'BATNEEC: the economics of technology based environmental standards – with a UK case illustration', CSERGE Working Paper WM 93-03, University of East Anglia, Norwich.

Rhodes, R.A.W. (1997), *Understanding Governance: policy networks, governance, reflexivity and accountability*, Open University Press, Buckingham.

Skea, J. and A. Smith (1997), 'The IPPC BAT definition and UK regulatory philosophy', Paper presented at the CBI/NSCA conference *IPPC Directive: Opportunity or Threat?*, CBI, Centre Point, London, 15 July.

Skea, J., A. Smith, S. Sorrell, and P. van Zwanenberg (1995), 'The availability of data necessary to evaluate integrated pollution control', report to the Department of Environment, Science Policy Research Unit, University of Sussex, Brighton (unpublished).

Smith, A. (1997), *Integrated Pollution Control: change and continuity in the UK industrial pollution policy network*, Avebury Studies in Green Research, Aldershot.

Smith, M. (1994), 'Generator re-ignites row over coal policy', *Financial Times*, 14 January.

Sorrell, S. (1994a), *Pollution on the market: the US experience with emissions trading for the control of air pollution*, Science Policy Research Unit, University of Sussex, Brighton.

Sorrell, S. (1994b), 'Sulphur permit quota switching: baseline allocation within other industry', report to the Department of the Environment, Science Policy Research Unit, University of Sussex, Brighton (unpublished).

Sorrell, S. (1995), 'Initial allocation of sulphur quotas: methods of implementing the UNECE Protocol', report to Scottish Power PLC, Science Policy Research Unit, University of Sussex, Brighton (unpublished).

Sorrell, S. (1996a), 'Study of policy instruments for achieving compliance with national targets under the Second UNECE Sulphur Protocol: working papers 1-5', report to the Department of the Environment, Science Policy Research Unit, University of Sussex, Brighton (unpublished).

Sorrell, S. (1996b), 'Cost effective sulphur abatement for the Second UNECE Protocol', report to the Department of the Environment, Science Policy Research Unit, University of Sussex, Brighton (unpublished).

Stavins, R.N. (1995), 'Transaction costs and tradable permits', *Journal of Environmental Economics and Management*, **29**, 133–148.

Stern, J.P. (1997), 'The British gas market 10 years after privatisation: a model or a warning for the rest of Europe?', *Energy Policy*, **25**(4), 387–392.

Tietenberg, T.H. (1985), *Emissions trading: an exercise in reforming pollution policy*, Resources for the Future, Washington D.C.

Utility Week (1995), 'Pollution deal agreed', 22 September, p.9.

Vogel, D. (1986), *National Styles of Regulation*, Cornell University Press, Ithaca and London.

Watson, J. (1998), 'Advanced fossil fuel technologies for the UK power industry', submission to the governments' review of power station fuels, Science Policy Research Unit, University of Sussex, Brighton.

PART IV

Scoping Studies: Water and Waste

12. Least-cost pollution allocations for probabilistic water quality targets to protect salmon on the Forth Estuary

James S. Shortle, Robin Faichney, Nick Hanley and Alistair Munro

1. INTRODUCTION

A fundamental result in environmental economics is that efficiency in pollution control requires allocating pollution abatement among sources so as to equalize marginal abatement costs. The welfare-theoretic foundation of this rule, modified appropriately when abatement by one source is not a perfect substitute for abatement by another due to locational differences, is well established for situations in which ambient concentrations are non-stochastic (Baumol and Oates, 1988). In situations where ambient concentrations are stochastic, pollution control properly defined involves improving the distribution of ambient concentrations rather than reducing a scalar value (Mäler, 1974). Nevertheless, most studies of allocative efficiency in water pollution control side-step formal consideration of the stochastic element. Pollution control is measured on the basis of estimated changes in long-term average or expected flows, and control costs are defined over these flows.

In this chapter, we explore the impact of reductions in biological oxygen demand (BOD) discharges on ambient dissolved oxygen (DO) concentrations in the Forth Estuary, Scotland. We focus on the implications of uncertainty over the impact of these discharges on the least-cost allocation of abatement between pollution sources, the costs of pollution control, and the use of market mechanisms (in particular, tradable permits). The most serious effect of pollution in the Forth Estuary is a low level of dissolved oxygen (DO) in the summer months caused by high levels of biological oxygen demand (BOD). Low DO levels inhibit salmon migration upstream at critical times. A minimum DO level, specified as an Environmental Quality Standard (EQS), is set for the Estuary at 4.5 mg/l. This is considered the minimum level that will permit salmon migration. The Scottish Environmental Protection Agency (SEPA) negotiates BOD discharge limits (consents) with point sources, with a main objective of maintaining levels above the EQS. However, the EQS has not been satisfied on a consistent basis. The standard is regularly breached in the upper reaches of the Estuary during the summer months. The work reported here builds on earlier results obtained for the Estuary by Hanley and Moffatt (1993).

Uncertainty about the impact of BOD reductions on DO concentrations has at least two sources.[1] One is uncertainty about the physical processes governing the relationship between discharges and ambient concentrations. Hydrological models can reduce but do not completely eliminate this type of uncertainty. The second source is the inherent variability of natural processes, such as stream flow and temperature. With uncertainty about physical processes and natural variability, pollution control measures cannot be designed to achieve water quality targets exactly and continuously. Holding emissions constant, there may be times at which the targets are violated, and other times at which water quality exceeds the targets by a wide margin. Reducing the frequency or probability of violations would require tighter emission controls and higher control costs. One issue we examine is the trade-off between the probability of meeting standards and the costs of control. A second issue is the impact of the probability of meeting standards on the allocation of control across sources. Without uncertainty, least cost control requires that emissions reductions be allocated among sources to equalize the marginal costs of improving ambient concentrations. However, with uncertainty about the impact of emissions on ambient concentrations, the allocation of emissions reductions among sources should take into account the relative risk associated with different sources. For instance, a source with low abatement costs may not be preferred to sources with higher costs if the uncertainty about the impact of emissions reductions on ambient quality associated with the low cost source is greater than the uncertainty associated with higher cost sources (Shortle, 1990).

Our study combines data from a simulation model of water quality in the estuary with abatement cost data gathered from major pollution sources. We begin with an overview of the pollution problem on the estuary and then proceed to describe the simulation model, cost data, and their use to study efficient allocations.

2. WATER QUALITY IN THE FORTH ESTUARY

The Forth Estuary, located in central Scotland, runs from its tidal limit at Stirling to its sea-ward limit at the Forth Road Bridge, near Edinburgh, where it becomes the Firth of Forth. It is a multi-use resource, providing water supply for industrial uses, recreational facilities, habitat for many types of bird, and a receptacle for effluent disposal for both industry and municipal sewage works. The principal industries located along the estuary are petrochemical plants (concentrated around Grangemouth), distilling and brewing, yeast manufacture, fine chemicals and paper mills. The principal rivers draining into the estuary are the Forth, Teith, Allan, Avon, Devon, Carron and Black Devon. Water quality is currently regulated by the SEPA, which sets performance standards known as 'consents' for every discharger. These specify limits on the quantity and quality of discharges, and are enforced by a combination of continuous monitoring and spot-checks.

The most significant water quality problem in the Forth Estuary is the seasonal sag in dissolved oxygen (DO) that tends to occur in the upper estuary (Figure 12.1). The timing corresponds to low freshwater flow and high temperature conditions in the summer months. Figure 12.2 shows the dissolved oxygen longitudinal profile from February and June 1992 surveys. The EQS (Environmental Quality Standard), at 4.5 mg/l (95th percentile), regarded as the lowest acceptable level, is set to minimize detrimental effects on migrating fish such as salmon.

The immediate cause of low DO is biological oxygen demand (BOD). BOD is primarily due to the decay of organic material, and is commonly measured and thought of as a unitary component, in terms of the amount of oxygen that would be consumed under certain conditions. Thirteen point source discharges of BOD are present on the Estuary, eight from private industry and five from local authorities, with daily BOD loadings ranging from 4 to 14,068 kg/day.

3. MODEL OF POLLUTION CONTROL WITH UNCERTAIN TRANSFER COEFFICIENTS

For this analysis, a model of pollution abatement on the Forth Estuary with uncertain transfer coefficients is developed. Let a_i be abatement by source i ($i = 1,2,..., m$) and $c_i(a_i)$ be the corresponding abatement cost function. Aggregate abatement costs are then

$$c = \sum_{i=1}^{m} c_i(a_i) \tag{1}$$

Figure 12.1 Major discharge points along the Forth Estuary

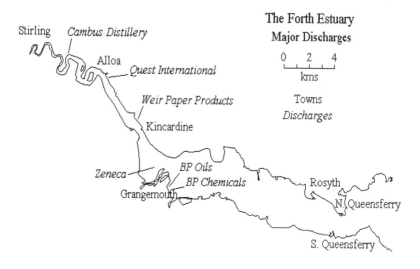

Figure 12.2 Longitudinal profile of dissolved oxygen in the Forth Estuary

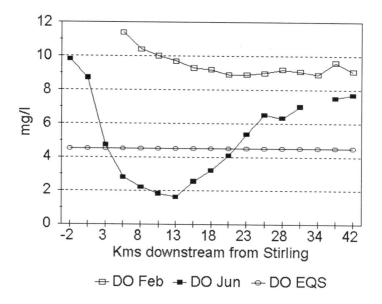

In this analysis we consider the costs of three types of pollution control allocations: (1) uniform abatement standards, (2) least cost allocations for a lower bound on the expected or 'average' DO concentration and (3) least cost allocations for a lower bound on the probability that the DO concentration exceeds a target. The lower bound for the second type of allocation is referred to as a 'deterministic' constraint and corresponds to the type of constraint used in traditional cost-effectiveness analysis. Assuming a linear relationship between emissions and ambient concentrations, the constraint for any one point in the estuary can be expressed as

$$E\left(\sum_i t_i a_i\right) \geq TR \tag{2}$$

or equivalently, as

$$\sum_i \mu_i a_i \geq TR \tag{3}$$

where t_i is the transfer coefficient for source i (measuring the impact of source i's emissions on water quality at a defined point in the estuary), $\mu_i = E(t_i)$, and TR is the difference between the target DO level and the baseline average. Thus, TR is the desired increase in the DO level from the baseline average, measured at some critical point in the estuary.[2]

The lower bound for the third type of allocation is referred to as a 'probabilistic' constraint. It takes the general form

$$\text{Prob}\left(\sum_i t_i a_i \geq TR\right) \geq \rho \tag{4}$$

where $0 \leq \rho \leq 1$ is the minimum probability of achieving the target. This probability is a policy choice variable. The probabilistic constraint provides the planner with a greater degree of control than the deterministic constraint. The former only requires the target to be satisfied on the average. In principle, frequent violations could occur. The latter explicitly controls the frequency of violations.

The exact mathematical form of (4) will depend on the probability density functions of the diffusion coefficients. Because these are unknown (and would probably be too cumbersome to work with in any but the simplest cases), we follow standard practice and replace (4) by a certainty equivalent (Vajda, 1972). If the number of sources is large, the ambient impacts of the individual sources are independent, and no single source's ambient impact is dominant in the variance, then, by the Central Limit Theorem, the diffusion coefficients would be normally distributed. In this case, (4) could easily be replaced by an equivalent constraint of the form (Beavis and Walker, 1983)

$$\sum \mu_i a_i - k_\rho \left(\sum_i \sum_s a_i a_s \sigma_{is} \right)^{1/2} \geq TR \qquad (5)$$

where k_ρ is the value of a standard normal variable (z) such that Prob ($z \geq k_\rho$) $\geq \rho$ and

$$\sigma_{is} = E\left[(t_i - \mu_i)(t_s - \mu_s) \right]$$

However, these assumptions are not reasonable for the Forth Estuary, since there are a small number of point sources and ambient impacts are not independent. Accordingly, a normal distribution cannot be claimed by appeal to the Central Limit Theorem.

An alternative form of the probabilistic constraint which can be used without knowledge of the underlying density functions is based on Chebyshev's Inequality. In particular, Chebyshev's Inequality states that for any positive constant k

$$\text{Prob} \left(| \sum_i (t_i - \mu_i) a_i) | < k (\sum_i \sum_s a_i a_s \sigma_{is})^{1/2} \right) \geq 1 - \frac{1}{k^2}$$

Given this result, it must also be true that

$$\text{Prob} \left(\sum_i t_i a_i > \sum \mu_i a_i - k (\sum_i \sum_s a_i a_s \sigma_{is})^{1/2} \right) \geq 1 - \frac{1}{k^2}$$

From this it follows that Prob $\left(\sum_i t_i a_i \geq TR \right)$ will be at least ρ if abatement levels are constrained to satisfy the inequality

$$\sum_i \mu_i a_i - k \left(\sum_i \sum_s a_i a_s \sigma_{is} \right)^{1/2} \geq TR \qquad (6)$$

provided

$$k = \left(\frac{1}{1-\rho}\right)^{1/2}$$

The inequality constraint defined by (6) is by construction more restrictive than the certainty equivalent that would be implied by the underlying (but unknown) density function for the diffusion coefficients.

Assuming that $c_i(a_i)$ is continuous, the Kuhn-Tucker conditions can be used to characterize the least-cost solutions for each type of constraint. In the case of the deterministic constraint, the Lagrangian function for minimizing (1) subject to (3) is

$$L_d = \sum_{i=1}^{m} c_i(a_i) + \lambda_d \left[TR - \sum_{i=1}^{m} \mu_i a_i \right] \tag{7}$$

where λ_d is the Lagrange multiplier. The first order conditions include

$$\frac{\partial L_d}{\partial a_i} = c_i' - \lambda_d \mu_i \geq 0$$

$$\left(\frac{\partial L_d}{\partial a_i}\right) a_i = 0 \tag{8}$$

$$a_i \geq 0 \ i=1,2..., m.$$

Rearranging (8), we have the familiar property that

$$\frac{c_i'}{u_i} = \lambda_d \tag{9}$$

for all sources with positive abatement levels. This result implies the conventional equality of marginal clean-up costs.

Now consider Chebyshev's Inequality. The Lagrange function for minimizing (1) subject to (6) is

$$L_p = \sum_{i=1}^{m} c_i(a_i) + \lambda_p \left[TR - \sum \mu_i a_i - \left(\frac{1}{1-\rho} \right)^{1/2} \left(\sum_i \sum_s a_i a_s \sigma_{is} \right)^{1/2} \right] \quad (10)$$

where λ_p is the Lagrange multiplier. First order conditions include

$$\frac{\partial L_p}{\partial a_i} = c_i' - \lambda_p \left[\mu_i - \left(\frac{1}{2} \right) \left(\frac{1}{1-\rho} \right)^{1/2} \left(\sum_i \sum_s a_i a_s \alpha_{is} \right)^{-1/2} \sum_s 2 a_s \sigma_{is} \right] \geq 0 \quad (11)$$

$$\left(\frac{\partial L_p}{\partial a_i} \right) a_i = 0, \ a_i \geq 0, \ i = 1, 2, ..., m$$

Rearranging terms we have

$$\frac{c_i'}{\left[\mu_i - (1/2) \left(\frac{1}{1-\rho} \right)^{1/2} \left(\sum_i \sum_s a_i a_s \sigma_{is} \right)^{-1/2} \sum_s 2 a_s \sigma_{is} \right]} = \lambda_p \quad (12)$$

It is apparent from this result that the optimal relationship between marginal costs will depend on variances and covariances as well as on the mean effects of abatement. Allocations that equalize marginal clean up costs are no longer least-cost.

4. DATA

The data required for this study are emissions reduction costs and the impacts of emissions on the distribution of ambient concentrations by pollution sources in the Estuary. The major anthropogenic sources of pollution on the Estuary were identified using data from the SEPA. Pollution control costs from each source were obtained from a questionnaire and follow-up interviews. The BOD content of effluent is one of the most important items specified by SEPA discharge consents. The questionnaire was designed to elicit the cost of reducing BOD discharges.

The questionnaire posed a number of hypothetical situations, asking by what means, and at what cost, each firm's discharge of BOD could be reduced by given amounts over given timescales. Reductions of 10 per cent, 25 per cent, and 50 per cent over one year and five years were specified.

Meetings with participating firms were used to discuss the objectives of the questionnaire and to help clarify any uncertainties. Most of the firms were very co-operative. In almost all cases, a cut within one year was not considered possible. We therefore focus on the longer time span. Even then, in some cases, not all levels of reduction were considered feasible. In two cases, levels other than those suggested in the questionnaire were given as the consequences of pollution control strategies either already being implemented, or most likely.[3] Despite the willingness of some of the municipal authorities to cooperate, all of the sewage treatment works had to be omitted from the economic model due to insufficient economic information (these works were in any case smaller sources of BOD than the industrial sources).

Based on the survey of BOD sources in the estuary, marginal abatement costs for each step on the abatement cost function ('abatement capacity') for source are assumed to be constant, with the unit cost depending on the abatement capacity. Marginal costs and the abatement capacities they apply to are reported in Table 12.1. Because of data limitations, only five of the eight sources are included. Total abatement costs in the actual simulation model are given by:

$$c = \sum_i \sum_j c_{ij} d_{ij} a_i \qquad (13)$$

where:

$c_{ij} \equiv$ marginal abatement cost for source i with abatement capacity j
     (£/100 kg/day)

$d_{ij} \equiv \begin{cases} 1 \text{ if capacity is type } j \\ 0 \text{ otherwise} \end{cases}$

$a_i \equiv$ total abatement by source i (100 kg/day)

$j = \begin{cases} 1 \text{ if } 10\% \\ 2 \text{ if } 25\% \\ 3 \text{ if } 50\% \end{cases}$

The impacts of changes in emissions on ambient concentrations were simulated using MIKE 11 (Wallis and Brockie, 1997). MIKE 11 is a modelling system for rivers and channels produced by the Danish Hydraulic Institute. It has been successfully used to model estuaries and is also widely used for purposes ranging from flood prediction and control to waste water plant design. It consists of a number of modules, of which this project utilized the Hydrological (HD) and Water Quality (WQ) modules. The HD module was run first, to determine water movement, and then the WQ module, to determine the fates of the various dissolved and suspended substances. The model was calibrated using 1992 data.

MIKE 11 is a one-dimensional (cross-sectionally averaged) dynamic model, and as such was deemed suitable for this project largely because the Estuary varies from being partially to well mixed, as opposed to stratified, thus one (longitudinal) dimension was likely to be sufficient. Tidal features were deemed likely to have a significant effect on water quality, requiring a dynamic as opposed to a steady-state model.

Developing the model involved the selection and testing of key parameters such as bed resistivity, diffusion coefficients and typical solar radiation, in order to calibrate it such that predicted values provided a good match to observations. Unfortunately, the limitations of the data available to us at that time meant that the model could not be as detailed or accurate as, for instance, that of Wallis and Brockie (1997). The model does, however, predict the double low and high tides characteristic of the Estuary.

Due to problems encountered with MIKE 11, estimated DO levels had to be post-processed using regression analysis to factor in the effect of sediment resuspension by tidal flow on DO. Given generally long computation times, and the fact that estuarial DO only drops significantly during the first two thirds of the summer, we chose a period of about 3 weeks during July 1992 to run the model under a 'worst case' scenario. By cutting BOD inputs for each major point source, and holding all other inputs constant, it was possible to calculate the marginal effect of each source's impact on water quality at defined points along the Estuary (since MIKE 11 predicts water quality at a range of levels of spatial disaggregation).

In fact, these values vary to some extent over time, and we show here (Table 12.1) the mean of the daily values for each discharger at Reach 4 over the three week period.[4] We present and use data for Reach 4 in this analysis since this reach is where the oxygen sag condition is critical for salmon migration. The values represent mg/l increase in DO per 100 kg/day reduction in BOD. The variance-covariance matrix of the transfer coefficients is presented in Table 12.2.

5. RESULTS

Pollution control allocations that minimize costs subject to the deterministic constraint and the probabilistic constraint were computed. We consider in each case targets (TR) that would correspond to increases in the DO level of at least 10 per cent, 20 per cent, 40 per cent, and 49 per cent of the feasible increase in Reach 4 for the three week period given the baseline emissions of

Table 12.1 Model parameters

Source (Capacity 100 kg/day)	Marginal abatement cost (MC_i) (£/100 kg/day)	Expected diffusion coefficient ($E(t_i)$) $\left(\dfrac{\text{mg}}{1} / \dfrac{100\text{kg}}{\text{day}}\right)$	$MC_i/E(t_i)$	Coefficient of variation ($cv(t_i)$)
Firm A				
(1) $0 \leq a_A \leq 18.19$	288800	0.0000707	4.08×10^9	2.36679
Firm B				
(1) $0 \leq a_B \leq 1.34$	15200	0.011775	1290870	0.17180
(2) $1.34 < a_B \leq 6.68$	60800	0.011775	5163482	0.17180
Firm C				
(1) $0 \leq a_C \leq 35.17$	7800	0.012326	632808	0.16573
(2) $35.17 < a_C \leq 70.34$	6900	0.012326	559792	0.16573
Firm D				
(1) $0 \leq a_D \leq 2.60$	1800	0.005659	318077	0.27850
(2) $2.60 < a_D \leq 5.20$	7800	0.005659	1378335	0.27850
Firm E				
(1) $0 \leq a_E \leq 6.85$	200	0.000419	477,324	0.93658
(2) $6.85 < a_E \leq 17.12$	52000	0.000419	1.24×10^8	0.93658
(3) $17.12 < a_E \leq 34.24$	140700	0.000419	3.36×10^8	0.93658

Table 12.2   Variance-covariance matrix for diffusion coefficients in reach 4
            ($*10^{-8}$)

	Firm A	Firm B	Firm C	Firm D	Firm E
Firm A	2.8	-23.0	-9.3	8.1	5.4
Firm B	-23.0	409.3	-11.0	-190.0	-64.0
Firm C	-9.3	-11.0	417.3	239.0	10.3
Firm D	8.1	-190.0	239.0	248.4	45.2
Firm E	5.4	-64.0	10.3	45.2	15.4

the polluters included in the model. The maximum feasible increase in the DO level, which we denote as DOmax, is simply the difference between the average DO level with baseline emissions and the average DO level with no emissions by this set of polluters. In addition to these least-cost allocations, we consider equivalent-effect uniform percentage cuts in emissions by each pollution source in the model, to mimic a command-and-control uniform regulation outcome. For the deterministic constraint and the uniform emissions reductions, the targets imply corresponding percentage gains in the average DO level relative to DOmax. By construction, satisfying the probabilistic constraints will require an increase in the average DO level in excess of the target. For the probabilistic constraints, we consider minimum probabilities of success of 50 per cent, 75 per cent, 90 per cent, 95 per cent, and 99 per cent.

Model parameters are presented in Tables 12.1 and 12.2. The MINOS solver in the General Algebraic Modelling System[5] was used to obtain the solutions to the cost minimization problems. In implementing this standard procedure, equation (13) was converted into a piecewise continuous function in a set of artificial variables in order to have a continuous model. Abatement costs for the least-cost simulations and uniform emissions cuts are given in Table 12.3. These costs are given in index form relative to the least-cost solution for a 10 per cent increase in the expected DO level relative to DOmax. Changes in the mean and variance of the DO level are given in Table 12.4.

Least cost abatement levels for individual firms under both the deterministic and probabilistic constraints are given in Tables 12.5 to 12.9. For each DO target, there is one solution for the deterministic model but five solutions for the probabilistic model corresponding to the different minimum probabilities of achieving the target. The differences in the allocation of abatement between sources between the two types of constraints reflects the different treatment of risk. With the deterministic constraint, abatement is allocated among sources according to the relative cost per unit of increase in expected DO levels, beginning with the cheapest and moving to more expensive sources until the target is satisfied. The relative cost of increasing

Table 12.3 Relative total abatement costs

Target[a] (%)	Uniform regulation TC	Deterministic TC	Probabilistic ρ (%)[b]	Probabilistic TC
10	7.35	1.0	50	1.07
			75	1.08
			90	1.10
			95	1.18
			99	1.21
20	18.23	2.04	50	2.11
			75	2.11
			90	2.13
			95	2.15
			99	2.23
30	31.46	3.00	50	3.04
			75	3.05
			90	3.06
			95	3.08
			99	3.14
40	47.26	3.92	50	3.96
			75	3.97
			90	3.98
			95	3.99
			99	4.04
45	55.17	4.42	50	4.95
			75	4.99
			90	5.09
			95	5.19
			99	5.63
49	61.49	7.07	50	7.35
			75	7.36
			90	7.38
			95	8.08
			99	29.56

Notes:
a. Costs are expressed relative to the cost of the least-cost allocation for 10 per cent increase in the expected DO. The cost for this case is £120,256.2.
b. Increase in the three week daily average DO level relative to the maximum feasible increase.

Pollution for Sale

Table 12.4 Percentage reduction in mean and variance of DO level (%)

Target	Uniform		Deterministic			Probabilistic	
	Mean	Variance	Mean	Variance	ρ	Mean	Variance
10	10	19	10	20.943	50	10.229	20.926
					75	10.323	21.107
					90	10.509	21.465
					95	10.718	21.866
					99	11.588	23.521
20	20	36	20	39.032	50	20.200	38.946
					75	20.282	39.086
					90	20.445	39.360
					95	20.628	39.668
					99	21.389	40.939
30	30	51	30	54.759	50	30.171	54.619
					75	30.242	54.721
					90	30.381	54.924
					95	30.538	55.150
					99	31.190	56.087
40	40	64	40	68.124	50	40.143	67.943
					75	40.201	68.014
					90	40.318	68.156
					95	40.448	68.314
					99	40.991	68.968
45	45	69.75	45	73.53	50	45.132	72.075
					75	45.186	72.068
					90	45.295	72.055
					95	45.417	72.040
					99	45.931	71.972
49	49	73.99	49	74.35	50	49.129	73.896
					75	49.183	73.979
					90	49.289	74.156
					95	49.408	74.359
					99	49.912	74.098

the expected DO level for a source is the ratio of the marginal cost of abatement to the expected diffusion coefficient. These ratios are given in Table 12.10. Accordingly, Firms C, D, and E, which have the lowest initial cost per unit of DO increase, are used in all solutions for the deterministic constraint (note the marginal costs increase substantially for firm E after this initial step). Other firms, which are much higher cost, are only included when the low cost capacity of Firms C, D, and E is fully utilized.

With the probabilistic constraints, the cost per unit of expected increase in DO does not provide sufficient information to determine the allocation of abatement to minimize the costs of achieving the probabilistic goal. This is

Table 12.5 Least cost allocations: target: 10 per cent improvement in DO

Source	Deterministic	Probability (α)				
		50%	75%	90%	95%	99%
Firm A	0	0	0	0	0	0
Firm B	0	0	0	0	0	0
Firm C	10.41%	11.68	11.79	12.00	12.24	13.24
Firm D	25.00%	0	0	0	0	0
Firm E	10.00%	0	0	0	0	0
Total	10.00%	10.23	10.32	10.51	10.72	11.59

Table 12.6 Least cost allocations: target: 20 per cent improvement in DO

Source	Deterministic	Probability (α)				
		50%	75%	90%	95%	99%
Firm A	0	0	0	0	0	0
Firm B	0	0	0	0	0	0
Firm C	21.83%	23.07	23.17	23.35	23.56	24.43
Firm D	25.00%	0	0	0	0	0
Firm E	10.00%	0	0	0	0	0
Total	20.00%	20.20	20.28	20.45	20.63	21.39

Table 12.7 Least cost allocations: target: 30 per cent improvement in DO

Source	Deterministic	Probability (α)				
		50%	75%	90%	95%	99%
Firm A	0	0	0	0	0	0
Firm B	0	0	0	0	0	0
Firm C	33.25%	34.46	34.54	34.70	34.88	35.63
Firm D	25.00%	0	0	0	0	0
Firm E	10.00%	0	0	0	0	0
Total	30.00%	30.17	30.24	30.38	30.54	31.19

Table 12.8 Least cost allocations: target: 40 per cent improvement in DO

Source	Deterministic	Probability (α)				
		50%	75%	90%	95%	99%
Firm A	0	0	0	0	0	0
Firm B	0	0	0	0	0	0
Firm C	44.68%	45.85	45.92	46.05	46.20	46.82
Firm D	25.00%	0	0	0	0	0
Firm E	10.00%	0	0	0	0	0
Total	40.00%	40.14	40.20	40.32	40.45	40.99

Table 12.9 Least cost allocations: target: 50 per cent improvement in DO

Source	Deterministic	Probability (α)				
		50%	75%	90%	95%	99%
Firm A	0	0	0	0	0	0
Firm B	4.26%	17.11	17.80	19.16	20.70	27.18
Firm C	50.00%	50.00	50.00	50.00	50.00	50.00
Firm D	25.00%	0	0	0	0	0
Firm E	10.00%	0	0	0	0	0
Total	45.00%	45.13	45.19	45.30	45.41	45.93

Table 12.10 Least cost allocations: target: 60 per cent improvement in DO

Source	Deterministic	Probability (α)				
		50%	75%	90%	95%	99%
Firm A	0	0	0	0	0	0
Firm B	45.29%	50.00	50.00	50.00	50.00	50.00
Firm C	50.00%	50.00	50.00	50.00	50.00	50.00
Firm D	50.00%	46.63	48.43	50.00	50.00	50.00
Firm E	10.00%	0	0	4.09	12.34	47.14
Total	49.00%	49.13	49.18	49.29	48.41	49.91

because the probabilistic constraints include the impact of emissions reductions by different sources on the variability of emissions as well as the impact on the expected DO level. Some insight about the relative effects on the risk of violating the target can be gained from the coefficients of variation of the diffusion coefficients for the different sources in Table 12.1. For instance, note that while Firms D and E are the lowest cost sources for increasing the average DO level, they have high coefficients of variation relative to Firm C. This would suggest that while a given level of emissions abatement by Firms D and E can produce an increase in the expected DO level at a low cost, the risk of violation of the target will be higher than for other sources.

The covariances between the transfer coefficients are also important. If the covariances between two sources are positive, then, other things being equal, the variation in the DO level will be higher than if they are independent or if the covariances are negative. The importance of this risk effect is evident in the extensive use of Firm B, which is relatively costly per unit of expected DO increase but which also has a relatively low coefficient of variation. Note also that Firm B has a negative covariance with other sources, which provides an additional advantage to use of this source. The negative covariance effect can also be seen in the 49 per cent target scenario, when firm D enters the solution in preference to the lower cost first step for E, since D has a negative covariance with the two other sources that are already part of the solution, whereas E does not.

However, the differences between the solutions with the deterministic and probabilistic constraints are the most interesting feature. There are several points deserving note. First, for any DO target, the expected increase in DO with the probabilistic constraint is higher than with the deterministic constraint (see Table 12.4). The difference in percentage terms is greater the greater the minimum required probability of success. That this will be the case follows logically from the form of the constraints. On the other hand, the emissions levels are not necessarily lower with the probabilistic constraints than with the deterministic constraint. This is because the allocation of abatement between sources, each with a different expected transfer coefficient, is different. The reasons for the difference in the allocation of abatement was discussed above. The costs of the probabilistic standards are substantially greater than the costs of the deterministic standards, with the difference increasing with the required minimum probability of success and decreasing with the DO target (see Table 12.3).

6. IMPLICATIONS FOR MARKET MECHANISMS

Amongst the class of market mechanisms for the control of water pollution, tradable permit markets have attracted much attention, as a potentially-efficient means of pollution controls which can avoid the financial transfers of pollution taxes. Tradable permit markets for pollution control involve trading in either emissions or expected contributions to ambient concentrations. Trading in expected contributions to ambient concentrations would in principle produce results analogous to those for the deterministic constraint. If the goal is to achieve a water quality target defined in terms of average DO concentrations, then trading would, in equilibrium, be cost effective. However, it is apparent that the allocations produced by trading in expected contributions would not provide a high degree of protection against violations of the target unless the target is very stringent. This suggests that trading in expected contributions to ambient concentrations (or emissions) may not be desirable if a high probability of satisfying the standard is considered necessary.

Extended trading schemes that provide a greater degree of risk protection can be developed in principle. For instance, Beavis and Walker propose trading in expected emissions levels and also in variances in emissions levels when emissions are stochastic. However, this approach would be cumbersome and would fail to account for the effects of trades on covariances and possibly other important aspects of the distribution of emissions.

These comments should not be taken to imply that emissions trading is undesirable under stochastic conditions. Whilst trading under such conditions may be unlikely to replicate the least-cost solution, trading may still generate cost-savings relative to command and control. As can be seen from Table 12.3, the size of these potential cost savings are very large so even a very inefficient permit market could still save society a substantial amount (there are of course many reasons why permit markets may not achieve the least-cost solution: see Munro et al. (1995) for a review).

Comparing command-and-control outcomes with least cost outcomes we also note that, in this empirical case, the latter are less risky than the former (as measured by the variance reduction in Table 12.4). However, it is not possible to generalize this result to other empirical settings, since it depends on the variance-covariance matrix and relative marginal abatement costs. It does have an important policy implication, however: namely that the regulator and/or researchers interested in modelling pollution control strategies should gather information on both the variability and cost of emission reductions, rather than on the cost alone.

In conclusion, this chapter has introduced an explicit treatment of uncertainty into the modelling of water quality improvements. This was shown to produce a change in the nature of the efficient, least-cost outcomes. That these changes were relatively small in this case does not imply they would be small in other cases. Finally, we noted that such uncertainty reduces the likelihood of permit markets achieving the least-cost outcome. How to design permit markets to better cope with this source of uncertainty in a practical fashion is clearly an important policy challenge.

NOTES

1. A third source of uncertainty is stochastic discharges. Discharges are often partly stochastic. Although stochastic emissions have received some attention in the literature (e.g., Beavis and Walker, 1983; Brännlund and Löfgren, 1996), we do not address this issue here.

2. In this model, we work with a single monitoring point in the estuary only. This may be thought of as the most water-quality sensitive point on the estuary. Adding further monitoring points complicates notation without changing fundamental results.

3. The levels were 70 per cent and 80 per cent.

4. A reach is a longitudinal section of the estuary in the model, with the size defined by the user.

5. The General Algebraic Modelling System (GAMS) is a widely used interface for constructing and solving mathematical programming models (Brooke et al., 1988). MINOS is a particular solution routine developed by Murtagh and Saunders (Murtagh and Saunders, 1987).

REFERENCES

Baumol, W. and W. Oates (1988), *The Theory of Environmental Policy*, Cambridge: Cambridge University Press.

Beavis, B., and M. Walker (1983), 'Achieving Environmental Standards with Stochastic Discharges' *Journal of Environmental Economics and Management*, 10:103–111.

Brännlund, R. and K. Löfgren (1996), 'Emissions Standards and Stochastic Wasteland', *Land Economics, 72*, 218–230.

Brooke, A., D. Kendrick and A. Meeraus (1988), *GAMS: A Users Guide*, Scientific Press.

Hanley, N. and I. Moffatt (1993), 'Efficiency and Distributional Aspects of Market Mechanisms for the Control of Pollution', *Scottish Journal of Political Economy*, **40** (1), 69–87.

Mäler, K. (1974), *Environmental Economics: A Theoretical Inquiry*, Baltimore, MD: Johns Hopkins University Press for Resources for the Future, Inc.

Munro, A., N. Hanley, R. Faichney, and J. Shortle (1995), *Impediments to Trade in Tradable Permit Markets*, University of Stirling discussion papers in Ecological Economics 95/1.

Murtagh, B. and M. Saunders (1987), *MINOS 5.1 Users Guide*, Report SOL 83-20R,
    Stanford University, January.
Shortle, J. (1990), 'The Allocating Efficiency Implications of Water Pollution
    Control', *Water Resources Research*, **26**, 792–797.
Vajda. (1972), *Probabilistic Programming*, New York: Academic Press.
Wallis, S.G. and N.J. Brockie (1997), 'Modelling the Forth Estuary with MIKE 11',
    Coastal Zone Topics, forthcoming.

928 H23 Q20

13. Designing a scheme for trading non-returnable beverage containers in Germany

Rolf-Ulrich Sprenger

1. INTRODUCTION

1.1. The policy context

The Federal Republic of Germany has initiated the world's most ambitious national solid waste policy, one that has already had international repercussions. The Ordinance on the Avoidance of Packaging Waste (Verpackungsverordnung), passed in 1991, makes industry responsible for its packages to the end of their life, including the costs of collecting, sorting, and recycling packages after consumers discard them. The ordinance thus shifts the cost of managing packaging waste from the public sector to private industry. Similar legislation proposed in Germany would extend industry's life-cycle responsibility to include its products as well as packages, starting with automobiles, electric and electronic equipment, newspapers, and batteries. Germany has, in effect, redefined the bottom line, giving companies an incentive to consider waste management costs when they design and select materials for packages and products. According to German Environment Minister Klaus Töpfer, the Packaging Ordinance 'marks the final abandonment of the throwaway society.'

In Germany, the philosophy of making those who produce packages and products responsible for recycling and disposal is called the 'polluter pays' principle. By shifting the financial responsibility for this waste from local governments to industry, Germany aims to provide industry with an incentive to make less wasteful packages and products. This new responsibility gives industry a powerful stimulus to incorporate waste management considerations into the design and materials selection processes. Although the shift effectively 'internalizes' waste management costs – building them into consumer prices – it does not turn consumer product companies into garbage collectors. German waste management firms and municipalities continue to collect, sort, and dispose of garbage (see Box 1).

Box 1 The Packaging Ordinance at a glance

> **Underlying Principles**
> *Goals:* Reduce packaging waste requiring disposal; and Develop sound materials use practices
> *Concept:* Make industry pay for managing the waste generated by its packages
> *Strategy:* Industry must take back, reuse, and/or recycle packaging materials independent of the public waste management system
> **Implementation**
> Government-mandated recycling rates
> Government-mandated refilling rates for beverages
> Materials industries responsible for recycling
> Industry-imposed fees on packaging materials
> Convenient collection from consumers
> Retailers provide bins so customers can leave outer packaging in stores
> Preservation of existing waste management system

The Packaging Ordinance requires that industry, not the public waste management system, take back, reuse, and/or recycle one-way packaging on the German market. It divides packaging into three categories:

1. Transport – packaging used to ship goods to retailers (e.g. crates, pallets, corrugated containers).
2. Secondary – additional packaging designed to facilitate self-service sales, to prevent theft, or to advertise and market the product (e.g. outer boxes, foils, blister packs).
3. Primary – the basic package that contains the product (e.g. soup can, jam jar, soap-powder box, beverage container).

Transport packaging accounts for about one-third of Germany's packaging waste stream, primary packaging for about two-thirds, and secondary packaging for less than 1 per cent.

The Packaging Ordinance required manufacturers and distributors to take back transport packaging beginning in December 1991, and called for retailers to install bins so that customers could leave secondary packaging in the stores starting in April 1992. The ordinance also stated that, as of January 1993, customers could return primary packages to retailers, and mandatory deposits would be imposed on certain non-refillable containers for beverages, washing and cleaning agents, and water based paints.

The ordinance provided an exemption to the primary packaging regulations if industry would implement an alternative, privately financed plan that could meet specified goals for collecting and sorting packaging materials and for refilling beverage containers. The exemption was granted for an industry plan known as the 'Dual System,' run by the private company Duales System Deutschland GmbH (DSD).

In order to keep its exemption, DSD must ensure that the goals for recycling glass, tinplate (steel), aluminium, paper/paperboard, plastics and composites are met. The ordinance specifies collection and sorting quotas for these materials and states that all sorted materials should be delivered to recyclers (see Table 13.1).

Table 13.1 German Packaging Ordinance recycling quotas, proposed changes ( ), and recycling rates achieved (%)

Material	Actual recycling rates	Recycling Quotas			
	1993	January 1993	July 1995	January 1996	January 1998
Glass	62	42	72	72	72
			(40)	(70)	(70)
Tinplate	35	26	72	72	72
			(30)	(70)	(70)
Aluminium	7	18	72	72	72
			(20)	(70)	(70)
Plastic	29	9	64	64	64
			(10)	(50)	(60)
Paper/Paperboard	55	18	64	64	64
			(20)	(50)	(60)
Composite	N/A	6	64	64	64
			(10)	(50)	(60)

Note: Recycling defined to exclude incineration and include chemical processes such as hydrogenation.

Source: INFORM (1994)

The Dual System operates in conjunction with the existing municipal solid waste management structure in Germany. Consumer product manufacturers pay fees to DSD to place its trademark 'green dot' on their packages. This symbol is intended to represent a recycling guarantee, for DSD then collects and sorts the packages consumers have discarded and directs them to recycles. As long as the ordinance's collecting, sorting, and refilling quotas are met, retailers do not have to 'take back' primary packages and consumers do not have to pay high mandated deposits on non-refillable containers. Packaging waste is collected from kerb-side DSD bins, or from municipal bins for glass and paper.

Although the Packaging Ordinance was not fully implemented until January, 1993, some early indications of its impact have become evident.

- Development of Reusable Shipping Containers: The transport packaging regulations in the Packaging Ordinance have led to the development of new reusable shipping container systems for various products. One such system is based on modular pieces, leased to manufacturers, that are expected to last ten years. After that they can be recycled four or five times into new reusable containers.
- Secondary Packaging Dropped: The ordinance's requirement that stores provide bins for discarding secondary packaging prompted retailers to pressure suppliers to reduce these materials. Changes made by manufacturers include eliminating out boxes, blister packs, and wrappings. DSD claims that secondary packaging has been reduced by 80 per cent.
- Reusing and Reducing Primary Packaging: The ordinance has prompted consumer product manufacturers to modify their primary packages. Changes include reducing the size for boxes, selling liquid and powdered products in concentrated form, using refillable bags or bottles for cleaning products, and replacing packaging made of mixed materials with single material packaging that is easier to recycle.

New green dot fees based on material and weight, introduced in October 1993, are expected to accelerate packaging changes by providing stronger financial incentives for companies to reduce package weight and to use materials that are more cheaply and easily recycled.

However, due to the trend in the use of non-refillable beverage containers, the beverage industry is close to non-compliance with the existing refilling quotas of 72 per cent (see Table 13.2). In case of non-compliance, a mandatory take-back and deposit-refund scheme will be imposed for all beverage containers.

Table 13.2 Use of refillable beverage containers as percentage of all
       beverage containers

Beverage	1990	1991	1992	1993	1994	1995
Mineral water	91.35	91.33	90.25	90.89	89.53	89.03
Soft drinks (non-carbonated)	35.60	34.56	38.98	39.57	38.76	38.21
Soft drinks (carbonated)	74.51	73.72	76.54	76.67	76.66	75.29
Beer	84.39	82.16	82.37	82.25	81.03	78.74
Wine	33.19	28.63	26.37	28.90	28.54	30.82
Total	73.61	71.9	73.54	73.55	72.87	72.16

Note: Target quota for refillable beverage containers is 72.0 per cent.

1.2. Options for policy-makers

Though the present ordinance implies the implementation of take-back obligations and a mandatory deposit-refund scheme if the refilling quota of 72 per cent is not met, it makes sense for policy-makers to investigate other instruments to handle the problem. The options include:

1. Ban on non-refillable bottles and cans
2. Moral persuasion by indication of refilling quotas
3. Take-back and recycling obligations
4. Mandatory deposit-refund schemes for all beverage containers
5. Packaging charges or taxes on non-refillable beverage containers
6. Voluntary self-commitments or negotiated agreements
7. Tradable permits for the use of non-refillable beverage containers

One of the options for stabilizing refilling quotas is a system of tradable permits for non-refillable beverage containers. It is the purpose of this chapter to help assess the expected advantages and disadvantages of a tradable permit system relative to the existing regulations of the Packaging Ordinance. The chapter takes as an example the use of a permit scheme for disposable *beer* containers.

2. TRADABLE PERMITS TO MEET REFILLING QUOTAS FOR BEVERAGE CONTAINERS

2.1. Introduction

In contrast to price based instruments such as taxes, or control based instruments such as bans, tradable permits are a quantity based instrument of environmental policy. Solutions of this kind operate on the basis of a target for the total quantity of environmental utilization. Without such a target, it is impossible to establish a permit system. However, this global target for admissible environmental use serves as more than a guideline; it is also implemented in the form of a regulation. Whether or not an environmentally relevant activity is admissible is decided on the basis of the purchase of permits which correspond to the total environmental impact of the activity.

There has been some experience in Germany with permit solutions in connection with allocations, quotas and concessions, especially in agricultural, transport and energy policy (Huckestein, 1993). In environmental policy, however, quantity solutions are more often the subject of scientific debates or studies of foreign experience in the area of emission-related clean air policy (Krois, 1995). Discussions are intensifying, however, on the possible use of permit solutions for application to conventional goods. Wicke (1978), and Feess-Dörr and Steger (1988) made early contributions in this area, discussing the possible use of bottling permits to control disposable packaging on the beverage market.

2.2. Conceptual issues

The use of permits to promote ecologically sensible packaging on the beverage market leaves considerable scope for policy makers to lay the groundwork. This means that more basic parameters must be set as compared with other instrument options. The following issues must be decided when determining the exact form a permit model is to take:

1. Setting goals in the form of clear quantity targets
2. Definition of the market
3. Licensees and market participants
4. Contents of permits
5. Procedure for allocating permits
6. Market organization
7. Monitoring and sanctions[1]

2.3. Setting goals

A prerequisite for the use of permit solutions is the establishment of concrete quantity targets. These targets must be divisible into clear permit quantities which can be assigned to individual licensees and/or market participants. This prerequisite can be considered fulfilled in the case of permit models which set target quotas for certain kinds of packaging, stipulating a proportion of packaging which must be reusable.

Permit models can be adapted relatively simply to changing market conditions and/or changes in environmental policy goals by changing the total allocation, i.e. by resetting the total admissible licensed quantity.

2.4. Market definition

The market can be defined *geographically* or in terms of *sectors*. The areas for which permits can be issued and within which they can be traded correspond to the areas for which environmental policy goals can be formulated. In the case under consideration this could be implemented on the EU level, national level or state level. A permit solution on the state level seems inadvisable, since the sales structures within the beverage market would probably mean that permit exploitation would have effects outside the states in which licensees are located. An EU-wide solution as proposed by the Federal Ministry for the Economy (1996) does not appear to be feasible at present for political reasons and due to the differing targets within the EU. Therefore, the only remaining option is a national solution within Germany.

The definition in terms of *sectors* of the permit market asks the question of how sensible or practical it is to include all beverage market sectors or market participants responsible for meeting the political quotas for returnable packaging. Due to policy goals regarding the ecological benefits of reusable packaging in certain segments of the beverage market, a sector-based definition of the permit market – based in this case on disposable beer packaging – may be appropriate.

The licensing authority can also reserve certain permit quantities for individual sub-groups. This could be necessary for reasons related to competition policy (to protect the chances of new suppliers of disposable packaging) or European law (to protect the chances of foreign suppliers).

Definition in terms of market sectors would in any case determine the size of the permit market. A large market with many purchasers and suppliers improves both the ability of the permit market to function and the economic efficiency of the transactions, but may also increase the administrative demands in connection with monitoring and inspection of permit utilization.

2.5. Licensees and market participants

Another important decision before introducing a permit model concerns the definition of market participants and/or those who require permits. The state has considerable scope when defining market participants. The permit market could be established at any given level of the beverage packaging or beer market with no risk of causing pricing errors in connection with the target quantity.[2] Participants which could be considered are:

- the packaging industry
- breweries and bottling plants
- importers of beer
- the wholesale sector
- the retail sector.

The decision as to who will require a permit can thus be made on the pragmatic basis of minimizing transaction costs, including the costs incurred through market organization and administrative monitoring.

When beverage packages are sold, the packaging industry is usually not aware of the final use intended for them. Moreover, the various stages of trade are all but impossible to monitor because of the large number of economic units. For these reasons, the transaction costs will be lowest for breweries, bottling plants and importers in this sector.

The restriction of permit obligations to breweries, bottling plants and importers should not necessarily be identical with the definition of market participants. The permit market should be open in principle and not be restricted to those participants who are required to obtain permits. This would then permit economic entities from other levels of the beverage packaging market and other interest groups within society to participate in the market. This may benefit the smooth functioning of the permit market.

2.6. Content of permits

Licensing concepts in environmental policy have always been linked to ecologically undesirable by-products (usually emissions), which are un-marketable. In contrast to this situation, efforts by environmental policy makers to promote economically sensible reusable packaging on the beer market results in a marketable good, i.e. disposable packaging for beer, being made subject to quantity controls.

The large practical benefit of this approach on the level of marketable goods is that permits become a *de facto* prerequisite for the sale of disposable beer packaging (the 'permit act'). In reality, these are no longer emission permits, but rather marketing permits. This link also facilitates the administrative task, because the 'permit acts' are the basis of existing economic activities and require no new definition of emission rights with corresponding measurement and monitoring techniques.

The further specification of the content of permits concerns their temporal validity:

- At first, permits could be issued to companies who already offer disposable packaging. This would mean issuing free permits initially, although the possibility of a calculable devaluation of the permit rights could be provided for.
- To protect companies which have invested in bottling plants for disposable containers, permits could be issued for at least the technical or economic life of facilities currently in operation. This would also imply allocating free permits but for a specified period of time.
- In addition, permits for shorter periods are conceivable. Here, for the most part, the tendency would be towards selling permits by auction or at a fixed price.
- Finally, it is conceivable that permits could be issued with deferred validity periods. In this case, sale by auction would seem to be the appropriate approach.

Permits with varying periods of validity could be traded on the permit market. This is practised under the Acid Rain Program in the USA. Although policy makers have almost total freedom to design a permit solution, the variety of forms available during the introductory phase should be limited. The less the market is fragmented through permits with different periods of validity, the more easily appropriate permit forms can develop spontaneously on the market (Maier-Rigaud, 1990, p.52).

Permits should allocate the right to sell beer in disposable packaging on the German market during the reference period. The permits should be freely tradable and completely transferable, and should not be linked to specific forms of disposable packaging or types of beer. They should be issued in minimum denominations of 1,000 litres per year.

2.7. Procedure for allocating permits

Considerations on how to define the permit market, the companies subject to licensing, the market participants and the contents of permits have made it clear that there is considerable room for manoeuvre when setting up a tradable permit system to promote the use of reusable containers on the beer market. This also applies to the procedure for allocating permits initially.

In principle, several basic models for allocating permits are conceivable:

1. Allocating free permits to suppliers already selling beer in disposable packaging on the basis of past market share ('grandfathering').
2. Allocating free permits as under (1), with the difference that a reserve of permits for newcomers or importers can be established either through devaluation of the current total admissible permit quantity or growth in consumption on the beer market ('modified grandfathering').
3. Auctions.
4. Sale of permits at fixed prices. Subsequently, permits are fully transferable.

The advantages of grandfathering rights on the basis of market share is that those subject to licensing are likely to offer less political resistance to the system and could become accustomed to the new quantity management gradually. In this way, real or imaginary concerns would be reduced. This would also present few problems for distribution and competition policy, since at the beginning the entire supply of permits would be very close to where disposable beer packaging has been used up to the present. The demand for additional permits with scarcity-induced prices and the resulting windfall profits for the present suppliers of disposable packaging would thus remain negligible (Maier-Rigaud, 1994, p.53). The reasons for allocating initial permits under the grandfathering principle are thus mainly political, psychological and pragmatic.

The modified version of grandfathering attempts to combine the benefits of free permits to existing suppliers with the just competitive interests of future suppliers. A reserve of permits for future suppliers of disposable packaging can be fed either by slightly devaluing the permits allocated free to existing suppliers or through the additional permit quantity required due to expectations of consumption growth and an unchanged quota of reusable packaging.

Under the third model, sale by auction, the various permit forms and quantities are auctioned to the highest bidder. The auction is open to all market participants. Permits for an indefinite period, limited permits or deferred permits can be auctioned. Due to the initial uncertainty on future market supply, there is likely to be demand especially for unlimited permits or long-term permits during the introductory phase. After a learning period, short-term permits will probably be in demand as a means of balancing fluctuations. Since the procedure will mean additional costs for present suppliers for the continuation of their disposable packaging activities, this model will meet with the greatest resistance against the introduction of a permit system.

The fourth variant, namely sales at fixed prices, is modelled on the Acid Rain Program and is conceived more as a complementary measure in addition to grandfathering rights and auctioning, intended for those who fail to obtain permits on the market despite intensive efforts. In the end, fixed price sales resemble the tax solution with all its policy problems in determining the right fixed price for achieving the global quantity target.

2.8. Market organization

Policy makers also have considerable room to manoeuvre in the area of market organization (Huckestein, 1993). The legal basis for the institution responsible is rather immaterial as long as it is given clear environmental policy targets, and its freedom to intervene by such means as an open market policy is restricted to such an extent that it cannot undermine the politically determined quantity target. It could be set up with close ties to the environmental administration (Federal Ministry of the Environment, Federal Environment Bureau), as an independent agency or as an organization within the private economy. Whatever form it takes, it is important that it is independent of political directives. This ensures a clear division of responsibility between political decision-making on the total extent of permits and their progressive reduction on the one hand, and the more technical management of the permit market on the other.

A further point which must be institutionally established concerns the transparency of the market and the responsible organization. Within the limits defined by privacy rights it must be ensured that information is published continually on the proportion of permits held by market participants and plans to issue new permits. In addition, the price of permits sold through auctions or fixed price sales must be made known at all times.

There is no need to discuss further details here, since these depend on the concrete form the permit solution takes. For most unresolved issues, there are practical examples from other areas which can assist in decision-making – including quota schemes for agricultural goods, taxis and freight transport. Finally, it is clear that care must be taken to ensure close involvement of the economic sectors which are directly concerned and, above all, the potential participants in the permit market in the decision-making process.

2.9. Monitoring and sanctions

Monitoring and the threat of sanctions, which are also necessary in connection with other instruments, are just as important as market organization for ensuring a functional permit market. One important aspect here is the legal/organizational monitoring measures to ensure that market participants do not exceed the quantities of beer in disposable packaging for which they are licensed. Sanctions are required for such exceedances. These could take the form of a significant punitive fine in addition to the current permit price.

Box 2 provides a summary of the main possibilities for a tradable permit system.

Box 2 Elements and alternatives for the design of a tradable permit scheme for the use of non-refillable beer containers

Total permit quantity	Based on target quota for reusable packaging ('moving target')
Permit denomination	Volume units per year
Permit validity	Indefinite; limited according to technical/economic lifetime of bottling plants; annual or other
Permit allocation authority	EU, Federal government or States
Permit holder and market participants	Packaging producers; breweries/ bottling plants; retail sale/importers; other (NGOs)
Permit allocation procedure	Grandfathering; grandfathering with reserve; auction; fixed price sales
Market organization	State or private
Market control	Devaluation or expansion of permit quantity; open market policy

2.10. Intended mode of operation

In a permit model for controlling the quantity of beer sold in disposable beverage packaging, the subject of the instrumental intervention is not an ecologically undesirable by-product (waste). Instead, a tradable good (disposable packaging) is subjected to quantity control. Environmental policy makers determine an upper limit for the admissible quantity of disposable beer packaging per unit time, i.e. the maximum allowable permit quantity. In principle, permits can be allocated free of charge on the basis of the quantity of disposable packaging used in the past, or through fixed price sales or auctions. Auctioning all available permits represents an attempt to allow the market to make an autonomous decision on the distribution of a good, whose scarcity has been created through the establishment of state quotas for reusable containers. Allowing the permits to be freely transferred ensures a cost effective distribution. In contrast, in the case of grandfathered permits or the initial issue of permits at fixed prices, a market price is established only during a second phase following necessary adjustments and/or substitution measures on the part of those requiring permits. The latter can then enter the market as buyers or sellers. In the case of permit solutions, the adjustment signal for a shift to reusable packaging is also the (permit) price. In the long run it will not be set politically or administratively as in the case of fee or taxation solutions, but rather will arise through the mechanism of supply and demand.

This has the theoretical benefit that state environmental policy will be freed from all forms of direct intervention and any other regulations concerning reusable packaging systems for beer. In addition it will be left up to the economy how to react technically, organizationally and economically to the scarcity of permits for disposable beer packaging.

As environmental policy targets change, the total permit quantity can be raised or lowered so that quantity restrictions are predictable for potential market participants. At the same time the tradability of permits contributes to a flexible and economically efficient distribution of usage rights, oriented towards market needs.

3. ASSESSMENT OF THE VARIOUS TRADING SCHEMES

3.1. Criteria for the assessment

Any environmental quality problem can be managed by a variety of alternative strategies, but it appears that no single strategy is best for all situations (Huckestein, 1993; Ewringmann et al., 1989). Only through a systematic evaluation of the many alternative strategies available for any given problem and a explicit trade-off of the many conflicting effects of any chosen strategy is the desired environmental goal likely to be achieved in an effective, efficient, and equitable manner.

Before any judgements can be made about the merits or drawbacks of a tradable permit system it is necessary to establish some criteria on which to base our evaluation. Such criteria should be useful to the extent that they help assess the actual or expected advantages and disadvantages of a new instrument relative to the existing approach. Although many criteria are possible, the following list seems to encompass the most pertinent considerations for the evaluation of the new approach:

- Environmental effectiveness
- Economic efficiency
- Distributive effect
- Administrative feasibility
- Political acceptance.

In addition, it is important to note that the legal feasibility in terms of conformity with EU legislation is a *conditio sine qua non*.

3.2. Achievement of environmental policy goals

If environmental policy succeeds in setting ecological quantity targets for the desired quotas of reusable beer packaging, then permit models ensure by definition that the quantity targets for the sale of disposable beer packaging are achieved. As with all other instruments for the promotion of ecologically sensible packaging, monitoring measures are needed to ensure that licensees adhere to the usage rights allocated by permits.

By linking permit models to economic goods (disposable packaging for beer) instead of environmentally undesirable emissions or by-products, several ecological risks which can arise in connection with contaminant-related permit models are eliminated. Notably, problems with the material, spatial and temporal equivalence of permits and the related dangers of differing environmental impacts, hot spots, or temporal impact peaks are avoided almost entirely. However, depending on the regional distribution of companies requiring permits and their sales structures, there may be regional concentrations of disposable container use which in turn may mean higher amounts of disposable containers to be disposed of or recycled. This situation can also arise in connection with other instruments, however.

From the point of view of environmental policy, permit models permit a rapid adjustment to changes in the prevailing ecological conditions. Subsequent changes in the quantity target for disposable beverage packaging can be implemented relatively quickly and precisely by increasing the permit quantity or devaluation of permits in circulation. However, appropriate legal precautions must be taken when determining the content of the permits, so that permits are sold or auctioned either for a limited period or with no time limit but with the proviso of calculable depreciation.

An effect which is undesirable from the point of view of competition policy but environmentally quite welcome is the possibility that permits may not be used at all. This could happen if permits were hoarded, for example.

Another potential area of concern is the possibility that suppliers of disposable packaging will divert their production to other beverage markets. In practice, the danger of such counterproductive reactions increases with the specific success of the price and quantity control instruments applied. Since quantity control by means of permits is considered a precise instrument of environmental policy and thus the most promising of those under consideration (assuming effective implementation), it can also be expected to carry the highest risk of such moves to other beverage markets, insofar as they are technically feasible.

3.3. Economic efficiency

Permit solutions seem to be best suited for achieving quantity targets for disposable packaging with the lowest costs to the economy as a whole (static efficiency). The quantity target of environmental policy – the limitation of disposable packaging for beer – is guaranteed through the definition of the total permit quantity and under the assumption that the solution is effectively implemented. Since no supplier can market beer in disposal packages without corresponding permits, adherence to the maximum quantity is guaranteed without further (price-related) control requirements. Under tax solutions, it is only possible to achieve this goal through a process of trial and error.

After permits are introduced, they will become scarce as compared with the initial availability. Since they are tradable, they will command a positive price on the permit market. Individual licensees can then – *ceteris paribus* – weigh the alternative of purchasing more permits against the possibility of converting to reusable packaging or at least increasing the proportion thereof. On the whole, under the permit model the market tends to minimize the total economic costs of achieving the goal (Huckestein, 1993; Maier-Rigaud, 1990; Maier-Rigaud, 1994).[3] Suppliers with low substitution costs (i.e. marginal avoidance costs) will invest more in the shift to reusable packaging, while suppliers with higher conversion costs will tend to buy more permits for disposable packaging.

The permit model is also superior to the instruments discussed above in terms of *dynamic efficiency*. Efforts of individuals within the market to convert to reusable systems are rewarded by low permit requirements and the possibility of selling permits. Since the permit model is a form of quantity control which ensures by definition that the highest allowable quantity of disposable packaging is adhered to at all times, no fine tuning is necessary to guarantee a lasting incentive effect as in the case of tax/fee solutions.

This assumes a long-term scarcity of permits, however, which either arises through demand or is achieved politically through gradual devaluation of available permit quantities. If the state does not reduce the total quantity available, changes in the quantity of permits actually used are not to be expected. The result is more likely to be cost optimization through substitution of reusable for disposable packaging.

Critics argue that permit solutions are economically inefficient because of the danger of distortions to competition. The feared distortions relate to:

1. possible effects on competition of the procedure chosen for allocating permits; and/or
2. the competitive conditions in the permit market.

Economic inefficiencies can appear in the first case if permits are allocated free of charge to the previous suppliers of beer in disposable packaging in the absence of measures to open the market to new domestic and foreign suppliers. If such suppliers can enter the market only by incurring costs for the purchase of disposable packaging permits, then competition will be distorted at the expense of the newcomers.

Such effects can be prevented by auctioning permits or selling them at a fixed price, or, if existing suppliers receive free permits, by establishing a reserve of permits which new suppliers receive free of charge or on special terms.

Licensing models can also prove to be inefficient when the permit market fails to operate properly due to lack of competition. Differences between permit holders in terms of market power, size and financial strength can easily lead to distortions in competition if the permit market is 'thin' with few participants. Under these circumstances, the strategic behaviour of certain market participants can prevent an economically efficient distribution of permits among permit takers (Tietenberg, 1985, chapter 6).

Without doubt, the theoretical possibility exists that auctions or fixed price sales may result in large, market-dominating companies acquiring the permits, thus forcing smaller competitors out of the disposable market segment or even out of the market entirely (Ewringmann et al., 1989). However, if competition functions properly, no company is likely to be able to hoard permits, since hoarding more permits than needed creates opportunity costs which would benefit a company only after the sale of free permits or purchased permits which remain unused. Under functioning competition this danger does not exist in principle, and even in the case of anti-competitive collusion the sale of hoarded permits would, because of the monopolization effect, offer greater benefits to a company which left the cartel.

To combat such dangers and realize the full economic efficiency of permits, it must be ensured that the permit market is operational in the sense that there is sufficient competition and free market access. However, this is less a problem of environmental policy than of competition policy. In the view of legal experts, the provisions of the Restrictive Trade Practices Act banning cartels (Article 1) and guaranteeing that abuses are monitored (Article 22) provide sanction mechanisms which are fully adequate as competition policy instruments (Becker-Neetz, 1988).

3.4. Distribution effects

The procedure for allocating permits for marketing disposable packaging is crucial for the distribution effects of permit models. As outlined above, the possible alternatives are free permits ('grandfathering'), fixed priced permits or auctions.

In contrast to the other two models, free permits do not generate revenues for the state. The transfer of a (later) shrinking supply of utilization rights to producers of beverages in disposable packages results initially in a transfer of wealth which is not measurable in monetary terms. The permit, which is valuable due to its scarcity, represents a capital good, which the economic entities favoured by this 'gift' could sell in order to realize monetary gains. The redistribution towards the owners of the factor capital results from the fact that it is not the state but rather the licensees who can achieve revenues through later sales of permits.

In contrast, with fixed price sales or auctions the government authorities who allocate permits experience real gains in income, which also brings about a change in the distribution of wealth.

Otherwise the effects of permit solutions on distribution do not differ in principle from those of other control instruments listed above. The future scarcity price for permits, the price elasticity of demand and the potential for reflecting permit expenses in product prices are the factors which will determine the subsequent price and demand effects and the corresponding income and distribution effects.

3.5. Administrative feasibility

German environmental policy-makers have no experience with the operability and administrative demands of pure licensing models. In various areas of agricultural, transport and energy policy, quantity solutions in the form of total quantities, quotas or concessions have been practised for some time. However, it remains questionable whether experience with implementation and enforcement in these areas can be applied to the present problem.

The permit solutions presented here create technical, administrative and information demands on both the potential market participants and the environmental authorities.

For licensees and market participants, the primary concern is information and transaction costs. Information costs can come about when determining current and future permit needs and in connection with ensuring market transparency. Depending on the market organization, this may mean disproportionately high information costs for small market participants. In addition, negotiating and other transaction costs are incurred during the purchase or sale of permits. Finally, additional administrative costs may be incurred if the permit market is organized by the industry or if adherence to the utilization rights granted by permits is subject to voluntary self-control.

For the environmental authorities, the main administrative costs are the following, which depend on the details of the model chosen for the permit system:

- determining the total admissible permit quantity;
- division of the permit quantity into individual permits;
- determining the validity periods and, where applicable, the dates for devaluation along with the percentages;
- determining the procedure for allocating permits;
- establishment of the permit market;
- market intervention; and
- monitoring and control of permit utilization.

The first requirement for the establishment of a permit system is the mandatory goal set by environmental policy for the total allocation quantity. Although operational targets should be a matter of course when weighing up the means/end relationship and the successes of environmental policy instruments, price-related and regulatory instruments usually manage with rather 'soft' targets. Permit solutions, on the other hand, require operational, quantitative targets which can be converted to determine a maximum admissible permit quantity and a corresponding division into individual permits. For this reason, permit solutions can be expected to incur higher information costs than other instruments, at least when considered superficially. However, the administrative costs saved when setting targets for alternative instruments are offset to some extent by the loss in precision in environmental policy terms.

Depending on the time frame for the admissible total permit quantity, administrative costs arise in connection with the redistribution and/or the required devaluation.

The central administrative task consists of the selection and implementation of the permit allocation procedure. Especially when free permits are allocated, this entails the development of a suitable and fair calculation procedure for determining the 'baseline'. The distribution of market share which comes about when the first permits are allocated can limit the proper functioning of the permit market, depending on the market constellation and strategic behaviour of market participants. For this reason, authorities need information in advance on the possible behaviour of market participants in order to set up the permit market.

The authorities also have the task of overcoming information problems which could limit the proper function of the permit market. This could necessitate the establishment of a clearing centre, which would serve as an information broker, recording and harmonizing supply and demand on the permit market. To preserve equal opportunities between large and small licensees or market participants and to avoid undesired tendencies towards concentration, the authorities should initiate or implement suitable measures such as supplying corresponding information or providing consultation for smaller licensees or market participants.

Technological rigidities in connection with the substitution of reusable for disposable systems and short-term fluctuations in the capacity utilization rate can lead to abrupt fluctuations in the demand of individual market participants for permits. This can in turn create temporary market bottlenecks and sudden changes in the market price. Frequent fluctuations in the market price prevent an adjustment in the marginal avoidance costs, since it is usually impossible for the licensees to adjust their avoidance costs to a constantly fluctuating permit price. For this reason, environmental policy targets are not reached in a cost-minimizing way where strong and frequent fluctuations in the permit price occur or seem imminent. To prevent such fluctuations, the responsible authority must be in a position to take suitable measures to exert a stabilizing influence on the market. This is presumably less urgent in large markets with many participants, since strong price fluctuations due to the arrival of new consumers, the departure of old ones or temporary unavailability of supplies are less likely. By contrast, 'thin markets' with homogeneous market participants influenced by similar economic conditions are more susceptible to price fluctuations. Such fluctuations cannot always be neutralized through intervention by the licensing authority This is more likely to be the case for suppliers of beer in disposable packaging.

These tasks impose stringent information demands regarding the present and future permit market situation. In addition, legal problems can arise through the authority's obligation to maintain neutrality and confidentiality. For this reason, it may be advisable to devolve certain tasks of permit market management from the state to the licensees and/or market participants. This could simplify permit trade, for instance. To perform these tasks, the permit holders could have recourse to their own institutions (chambers, associations, or newly created self-help organizations). A legal basis is needed before tasks and responsibilities, some of which are sovereign rights, can be transferred to institutions under private law. Such a legal basis must ensure binding enforcement of appropriate ground rules towards all permit market participants, rule out strategic or abusive behaviour on their part, and guarantee the function of competition on the permit market.

Finally there is the task of *monitoring* and *supervision* of the utilization rights granted by the permits, as in the case of other instrumental options to promote ecologically sensible beverage packaging. This requires both an overview of the actual permit distribution by recording all market transactions and the comparison of the actual disposable packaging utilization against the maximum allowable permit quantity.

At first glance there is no apparent reason why the supervision of the permissible permit utilization should result in heavier administrative demands than in the case of tax solutions, for instance. What is more, the monitoring work of the authorities could be significantly reduced through declarations made by permit holders and certified by auditors. However, the authorities will face additional work if the permit revenues through fixed price sales or permit auctions have to be administered.

All in all, it may be assumed that the novelty of permit solutions may result in slightly higher initial administrative costs for performing the pertinent public tasks than in the case of the instrumental alternatives. However, this does not apply to the subsequent period in which the market price is established after permits are allocated.

3.6. Political acceptance

During environmental policy discussions, industry representatives have displayed a preference in principle for economic instruments over regulatory measures and, within the realm of market-oriented instrumental solutions, have frequently favoured tradable permits over taxes/charges. However, this enthusiasm wanes rapidly as soon as concrete applications are examined. Surveys of associations and companies have shown that licensing models are consistently associated in their minds with planned economy measures and individual rationing as practised, for instance, during the Second World War or in the planned economies of the former Eastern bloc. This attitude fails to see that a permit solution does not distribute the quantity to be allocated through administrative assignment of individual rations to the various suppliers and/or licensees. Instead, the market decides autonomously on the distribution of the quantities of goods, which have merely been made scarce through the target quantity (reusable packaging quota) set by the state. A functioning permit market and the free transferability of permits then guarantee an economically efficient distribution.

The present suppliers of beer in disposable packaging strongly resist the idea of permit distribution through fixed price sales or auctions, since this could mean higher costs for these market participants, depending on the price. For this reason, free permits would probably be accepted as the lesser evil.

4. SUMMARY

The discussion on permit models to promote ecologically sensible reusable packaging should have shown that a permit solution offers considerable advantage over other instruments (compare Table 13.3). By controlling quantities, it ensures – *ceteris paribus* – that environmental policy goals are adhered to and also has significant advantages over the other instruments in terms of static and dynamic efficiency conditions.

Table 13.3 Assessment of tradable permits

Criteria	Grand-fathering	Grand-fathering with reserve	Auction	Fixed price sales
Achievement of environmental policy goals				
- Promotion of reusable packaging	+++	+++	+++	+++
- Ecological side effects ('Littering')	+/-	+/-	+/-	+/-
Economic efficiency				
- static/dynamic	++	++	++	++
- economic side effects	-	+	+/-	+/-
Distribution effects	+/-	+/-	+/-	+/-
Administrative feasibility	+	+	+	+
Political acceptance	+/-	+/-	--	--
Conformity to law	?	?	?	?

Legend:
+++ highly positive expectation/effect
++   positive expectation/effect
+   expectation/effect more likely positive
---   highly negative expectation/effect
--   negative expectation/effect
-     expectation/effect more likely negative
+/-   both positive and negative effects; dependent on form chosen
?   effects/evaluation unknown or not estimable.

The danger of competition distortions can be reduced through the choice of the procedure for allocating permits and through monitoring abuses in case licensees exploit dominant market positions. Since permit solutions in the form described here have never been implemented in the environmental area, there is a lack of data on transaction costs. The comparatively high administrative costs, especially during the initial phase, are hardly a decisive argument for rejecting a permit solution, since the price will be established subsequently by the permit market, which will be supported institutionally by existing industry bodies.

It should also be possible to overcome political resistance to quantity allocation through permits, since it is based on a false association with administratively regulated rationing of goods under former planned economies as opposed to distribution through a permit market. However, a modified procedure for distributing permits free of charge which would respect the needs of both present and future licensees should go far towards reducing the undeniable political resistance of the industrial sectors concerned.

NOTES

[1]   On the following discussion compare Huckestein (1993), p. 3 ff; Maier-Rigaud (1990); and Maier-Rigaud (1994), p. 75 ff.

[2]   Unlike taxes where prices may have to be repeatedly adjusted to achieve the required target.

[3]   During adjustment, the fixed cost will rise in jumps, thereby reducing economic efficiency. However, adjustment processes of this type also arise in connection with the other instruments examined here.

REFERENCES

Becker-Neetz, G. (1988*), Rechtliche Probleme der Umweltzertifikatemodelle in der Luftreinhaltepolitik*, Frankfurt/M.

Ewringmann, D. et al. (1989), 'Wirkungsanalysen energiepolitischer Instrumente', study commissioned by the Enquete-Kommission 'Vorsorge zum Schutz der Erdatmosphäre', Cologne.

Federal Ministry for the Economy (1996), 'Konzeption eines Europäischen Linzenzsystems für Einweggetränkeverpackung', Bonn (unpublished).

Feess-Dörr, E. and U. Steger (1988), 'Strategien zur Stabilisierung und Ausweitung der Mehrwegsysteme in der Getränkedistribution – eine ökonomische und ökologische Effizienzanalyse', Kurzfassung, Oestrich-Winkel.

Huckestein, J. (1993), 'Umweltlizenzen: Anwendungsbedingungen einer ökonomisch effizienten Umweltpolitik durch Mengensteuerung', *Zeitschrift für Umweltpolitik und Umweltrecht*, **16**.

Krois, B. (1995), 'Bibliography on environmental policy with certificates', Ifo Institute, Munich (unpublished).

Maier-Rigaud, G. (1990), *Kohlendioxyd-Politik mit Handelbaren Emissionsrechten*, Bonn.

Maier-Rigaud, G. (1994), *Umweltpolitik mit Mengen und Märkten*, Marburg.

Tietenberg, T.H. (1985), *Emissions trading: an exercise in reforming pollution policy*, Resources for the Future, Washington D.C.

Wicke, L. (1978), 'Abfüllizenzen für Einwegflaschen', *Umwelt*, **6**, 412–413.

PART V

International Sulphur Trading

14. Joint implementation for controlling sulphur in Europe and possible lessons for carbon dioxide[1]

Peter Bailey and Tim Jackson

1. INTRODUCTION

The concept of joint implementation (JI) – or activities implemented jointly – now appears either implicitly or explicitly within the language or within the policy frameworks of a number of international conventions. These include the Framework Convention on Climate Change (FCCC), the Biodiversity Convention, the Montreal Protocol (for controlling the release of chlorofluorocarbons) and the Convention on Long-Range Transboundary Air Pollution (CLRTAP).

The general intention under each of these initiatives is to devise mechanisms which allow two or more Parties to meet their obligations to the conventions through activities implemented jointly. So, for instance, it has been envisaged that one Party to the FCCC (the 'donor') might invest in greenhouse gas emission abatement technologies within the geographical borders of a second Party (the 'host'). Ultimately, it has been suggested, appropriate institutional arrangements might be put in place to allow the donor to seek full or partial credit towards its own obligations under the convention for emission reductions resulting from these investments in the host country. The main argument for such a procedure has been from economic efficiency: the costs of greenhouse gas abatement might be lowered by seeking out the least cost options first, irrespective of geographical boundaries.

In spite of general agreement that joint implementation offers potential benefits in meeting international environmental targets, it should be pointed out that some political opposition to the concept has been evident. This opposition has arisen largely from a perception that joint implementation might turn out to be a way in which developed countries (as donors) could avoid taking action at home by intervening in developing countries (as hosts) in ways disadvantageous (in the longer term) to the latter. Whether or not such fears turn out to be justified will depend crucially on the particular institutional and economic frameworks under which joint implementation arrangements are implemented. As yet, these frameworks have not been specified under any of the conventions; and it is prudent to recognize that there are a number of methodological difficulties involved in devising such frameworks (Jackson, 1995).

This chapter takes a brief look at some of the issues which contribute to those difficulties. We look in particular at attempts to devise joint implementation arrangements in the context of sulphur[2] emissions, and discuss the relevance of these issues for the case of greenhouse gas emissions. The work described in this chapter is based on a project supported by DGXII under the Framework IV programme. That project is summarized briefly in the following section.

2. ACCOUNTING AND ACCREDITATION OF ACTIVITIES IMPLEMENTED JOINTLY

Amongst the difficulties associated with using joint implementation as an international policy measure are those associated with accounting for emission reductions, accounting for the costs of those reductions, and devising a mechanism for appropriately assigning credit for the reductions between donor and host countries. These issues are the subject of a major international study involving six separate European institutions.[3] The overall objective of that project is:

- to examine the concept of joint implementation as an institutional instrument relevant to the efficient and fair abatement of greenhouse gas and sulphur emissions.

Specific objectives are:

- to gather information and data relating to 'pilot phase' joint implementation projects set up between Northern and Eastern European countries in the context of the FCCC;
- to gather information and data relevant to the operation of joint implementation arrangements between Northern and Eastern European countries under the Oslo Protocol of the CLRTAP;
- to carry out a broad-based analysis of the data collected from these pilot projects under the following criteria: in technical terms, in economic terms, in terms of environmental effectiveness and in terms of distributional and institutional consequences;

- to examine the methodological basis on which it might be appropriate to *account for* emission reductions from joint implementation projects;
- to examine the methodological basis on which it might be appropriate to *assign credit* to donor nations for joint implementation projects carried out in host nations;
- to explore the use and relevance of integrated assessment models in evaluating joint implementation projects;
- to report on these examinations with a view to informing European Union policy and national policies within the European Union in relation to joint implementation arrangements under the FCCC and the CLRTAP.

The project commenced in June 1996 and will report to the Commission before the end of 1998.

3. SULPHUR EMISSIONS AND THE OSLO PROTOCOL

The 1994 Oslo Protocol is one of several Protocols to the 1979 Convention on Long-Range Transboundary Air Pollution (CLRTAP) organized by the United Nations Economic Commission for Europe (UNECE) in Geneva. It is the follow-up to the first Sulphur Protocol, the 1985 Helsinki Protocol. Thus the Oslo Protocol is sometimes called the Second Sulphur Protocol (SSP).

Sulphur emissions have a wide range of environmental impacts at different spatial scales. However the Oslo Protocol is primarily concerned with acid deposition. It was implicitly assumed that building damage or human health effects were either local, i.e. not transboundary issues, or would be improved anyway as a result of the emission reductions contained in the Protocol. The Oslo Protocol incorporated the 'critical load' concept which is a measure of the natural environment's sensitivity to acid deposition and varies by location. Broadly speaking, the critical load refers to the amount of acid deposition which can fall on a given area before harmful environmental impacts occur.

The relationships between emissions and depositions are calculated by the EMEP[4] programme as part of the CLRTAP. Emissions are estimated within national geographical boundaries. Deposition d_j is mapped onto each 150 by 150 kilometre square according to the formula:

$$d_j = b_j + \sum_i e_i.t_i(1) \tag{1}$$

where b_j is the background deposition on the jth square, e_i is the emission from the ith country and t_{ij} is the 'transfer coefficient' from the ith country to the jth square. The division of the UNECE region into 150 by 150 km squares is shown in Figure 14.1.

For the most part, actual deposition levels in Europe considerably exceed critical loads. The primary environmental objective of the Oslo Protocol was therefore to reduce sulphur deposition below critical loads,[5] and the substance of the Protocol was to set national emission ceilings – i.e. limits to e_i for each country i – with the declared aim of reducing the gap (the 'exceedance') between existing deposition levels and agreed critical loads.[6] So, for example, these deliberations resulted in emission ceilings for the UK which require 50 per cent reduction in sulphur emissions by the year 2000, 70 per cent by the year 2005 and 80 per cent by the year 2010, relative to 1980 emission levels.

4. SULPHUR EMISSIONS TRADING

European regulators have predominately relied on non-market policy instruments to reduce the levels of sulphur dioxide emissions into the atmosphere. The most common regulatory instruments implemented in Europe are emission standards for large point sources, fuel quality standards such as maximum sulphur contents in oil products and national emission ceilings such as those set down by the Oslo Protocol. However, in recent years, market instruments for sulphur emission control have been assessed both by economists and regulators who are keen to implement reduction strategies in more cost-effective ways. The most favoured instrument in Europe has been emission charges (or taxes); several Scandinavian countries and a number of Central and Eastern European countries have introduced charges upon the emissions of a number of air pollutants including sulphur dioxide.

Trading in sulphur emission permits or emission reduction credits has not occurred in Europe so far, although some 'bubble' limits have been set up that give a degree of flexibility on how sources can meet an overall bubble limit.[7] This is in contrast to the situation in the United States of America where emissions trading has been under way for many years and is one of the main policy instruments used to reduce emissions of sulphur dioxide in the Clean Air Act Amendments of 1990.

The principal difficulty faced in designing sulphur emissions trading schemes is the spatial nature of the pollution. Emissions of sulphur from one country are not equivalent to emissions from another country because they will be deposited in different geographical areas with potentially diverse tolerances for acid deposition. In mathematical language, the transfer coefficients t_{ij} are not identical for all countries i, for all squares j. Thus a unit of sulphur emission abatement in one country cannot be equivalent to a

Figure 14.1 Division of UNECE region into EMEP squares

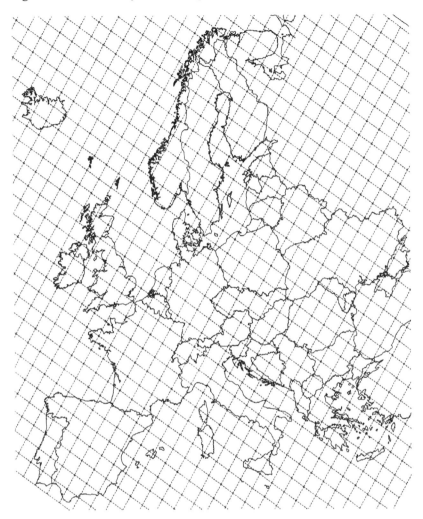

unit of sulphur abatement in another country, and one-to-one trading of emissions is generally invalid.

It is worth remarking here that the sulphur trading system introduced in the US Clean Air Act Amendments *does* have a one-for-one trading system. Effectively, the US system simply ignores the spatial characteristics of sulphur pollution. Or more correctly, we should say that the compromise of allowing one-to-one trading was felt to be worth the gains in simplicity. In practice, there are a range of safeguards in the US system such as State level restrictions on ambient air quality, and simulation modelling of likely future trades have given some confidence that a 'bad' spatial pattern of emissions is unlikely to occur. In Europe, these compromises have proved both politically and scientifically more problematic.

5. JOINT IMPLEMENTATION UNDER THE OSLO PROTOCOL

During preparatory work for the 1994 Oslo Protocol, European systems of sulphur emissions trading were examined by the Task Force on Economic Aspects of Abatement Strategies and by the Working Group on Strategies – the main negotiating body of the CLRTAP. The Protocol itself contains 'enabling' language, designed to allow and perhaps further the development of joint implementation within the Convention. Article 2, paragraph 7 (UNECE, 1994) states:

'The Parties to this Protocol may, at a session of the Executive Body, in accordance with rules and conditions which the Executive Body shall elaborate and adopt, decide whether two or more Parties may jointly implement the obligations set out in annex II. These rules and conditions shall ensure the fulfilment of the obligations set out in paragraph 2 above and promote the achievement of the environmental objectives set out in paragraph 1 above.'

At this time the rules for joint implementation of sulphur emission reductions are the subject of on-going negotiation. It is likely that a certain number of institutional conditions would be imposed; for example, the following institutional conditions have been suggested:

- only Parties to the Protocol may enter into a joint implementation agreement;
- the proposal shall specify the part of its emission reduction obligation one Party will implement through reductions by another Party;
- the proposal shall specify the emission reduction the other Party will undertake in addition to its obligation in accordance with the Protocol;
- the proposal shall contain an assessment of the deposition impact; and
- the proposal shall indicate the level of expected cost savings and the means of compensation chosen.

For reasons already discussed, difficulty has arisen on how to design a system of joint implementation that helps Parties to the Protocol meet their emissions reduction targets (the obligations in annex II and paragraph 2) in a cost-effective manner that is also consistent with the critical load concept (the environmental objectives of paragraph 1). There is general agreement on how emissions cause a change in deposition (see equation (1) above) and why sulphur emissions cannot be traded on a simple one-to-one basis in Europe.

It has been argued that it is possible to convert sulphur emissions into a quantity that *can* be traded by using a sulphur emission 'exchange rate' r defined according to a formula of the following kind:

$$r_{HD} = -\Delta e_H / \Delta e_D \qquad (2)$$

i.e. the allowable increase in emissions (Δe_D) in the donor country D is r_{HD} times smaller than the decrease in emissions (Δe_H) achieved in the host country H. The exchange rate r is supposed to capture the spatial differences which characterize deposition as a result of emissions from the donor country as compared with emissions from the host country.

A little reflection reveals that exchange rates, at least as characterized by equation (2), offer an over-simplification of a potentially very complex situation. In reality, although it is certainly possible to calculate an effective exchange rate r from each transaction, these rates are far from simple, uniform parameters which can be determined on a once for all basis. In general, the value of the exchange rate will depend crucially on a number of other potential constraints which might be imposed upon the situation (Klaassen, 1996; Førsund, 1993; Bailey et al., 1996). For instance, it is likely that little or no increase in deposition will be allowed as a result of a joint implementation agreement in areas where exceedance already occurs. In general, each potential transaction is likely to require some form of environmental impact assessment to check that the resulting deposition levels do not contravene a specified set of rules and conditions. Present discussions suggest that these might include (at least) the following set of constraints:

- a joint implementation agreement shall not lead to an increase in European exceedance of critical loads;
- a joint implementation agreement shall not increase deposition in any EMEP square by more than a specified per cent; and
- a joint implementation agreement shall not increase deposition in third party regions by more than a specified per cent.

From these rules alone it is possible to conclude that a sulphur exchange rate (as defined by equation (2)) is quite likely to be greater than 1, and that we cannot expect to find simple transitive or inverse relations between exchange rates.[8] More importantly, as the following section reveals, we cannot assume that the exchange rate remains constant between two countries throughout all transactions.

6. SULPHUR EXCHANGE RATES – A SIMULATION

We present here the results of modelling hypothetical sulphur trading relationships between Sweden and Estonia and between Austria and the Czech Republic. These examples have been chosen only for illustrative purposes – and in spite of the fact that Estonia is not at present a Party to the Oslo Protocol.[9] Let us assume that Estonia does become a Party to the Protocol and that Sweden wishes to reduce its requirements under the Protocol for emission abatement in 2010 by investing in emission abatement in Estonia. Austria similarly is assumed to want to reduce its emission abatement by investing in the Czech Republic. Let us assume further the following conditions:

1. any transaction must reduce, or maintain at the same level, the total exceedance of critical loads in Europe; and
2. any transaction must not increase deposition in any EMEP grid square by more than a pre-specified percentage.

The critical question we address in this simulation is the following: by how much would it be allowable for the donor country to increase its sulphur emissions (above 2010 target levels) for each kilotonne (kt) of additional emission abatement in the host country, assuming the two rules above apply?

This question was examined using the SEI CASM acidification model (Gough et al., 1994; Bailey et al., 1996) for a range of host country emission abatements from 10 to 100 kt. Using as a reference point the emissions in 2010 that would have resulted from the implementation of the Oslo Protocol, we have calculated the maximum allowable emission increases in the donor country for varying grid level constraints – from no allowable increase in grid level deposition (0 per cent), through to a 5 per cent grid level deposition increase, up to the case where the grid level constraint is removed entirely and only the total European exceedance constraint (rule 1) applies. The mathematical basis for the simulation is presented in Appendix A. The results of the exercise are illustrated in Figures 14.2 and 14.3. The associated sulphur exchange rates are shown in Table 14.1 and Table 14.2.

*Figure 14.2 Maximum allowable donor country emission increases for the
Sweden–Estonia transaction*

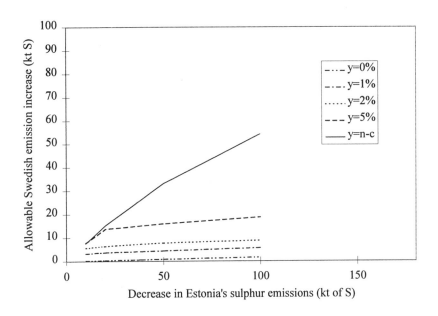

*Figure 14.3 Maximum allowable donor country emission increases for the
Austria–Czech Republic transaction*

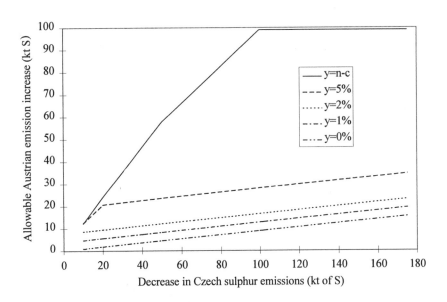

Table 14.1 Simulated joint implementation of sulphur emission transactions between Sweden and Estonia for different deposition constraints

Change in Estonian emissions (kt of S)	Allowable change in grid level dispositions (y %)	Maximum allowable change in Swedish emissions (kt of S)	Sulphur emission exchange rate
-10	0	0.16	62.5
-20	0	0.32	62.5
-50	0	0.8	62.5
-100	0	1.6	62.5
-10	1	3.2	3.1
-20	1	3.7	5.4
-50	1	4.4	11.4
-100	1	5.6	17.9
-10	2	5.6	1.8
-20	2	6.4	3.1
-50	2	7.7	6.5
-100	2	8.8	11.4
-10	5	7.6	1.3
-20	5	13.7	1.5
-50	5	15.9	3.1
-100	5	18.7	5.3
-10	Not constrained	7.6	1.3
-20	Not constrained	15.1	1.3
-50	Not constrained	33.1	1.5
-100	Not constrained	54.3	1.8

Several points are worth making in relation to Figures 14.2 and 14.3 and Tables 14.1 and 14.2. Firstly, it is very clear from this analysis that sulphur exchange rates are highly dependent on the actual rules and constraints under which joint implementation takes place. Differing grid level constraints impose differing exchange rates. Secondly, it is to be noted that the allowable increase in sulphur emissions in the donor country is typically less than the emission reduction in the host country. Even with no constraint imposed at the grid level, the rule of no increase in exceedance (rule 1 above) still prevents donor country emission increases from matching the host country decreases in emissions for the Sweden-Estonia example. For cases where constraints are imposed at the grid level, allowable donor country increases are often considerably lower than the host country decreases in emissions.

Table 14.2 Simulated joint implementation of sulphur emission transactions between Austria and the Czech Republic for different deposition constraints

Change in Czech Republic's emissions (kt of S)	Allowable change in grid level dispositions (y %)	Maximum allowable change in Austrian emissions (kt of S)	Sulphur emission exchange rate
-10	0	0.9	11.2
-20	0	1.8	11.2
-50	0	4.5	11.2
-100	0	8.9	11.2
-175	0	15.5	11.3
-10	1	4.7	2.1
-20	1	5.6	3.6
-50	1	8.3	6.0
-100	1	12.8	7.8
-175	1	19.4	9.0
-10	2	8.6	1.2
-20	2	9.5	2.1
-50	2	12.2	4.1
-100	2	16.6	6.0
-175	2	23.3	7.5
-10	5	12.3	0.8
-20	5	20.7	1.0
-50	5	23.7	2.1
-100	5	28.2	3.5
-175	5	34.8	5.0
-10	Not constrained	12.3	0.8
-20	Not constrained	24.1	0.8
-50	Not constrained	57.9	0.9
-100	Not constrained	99.0	1.0
-175	Not constrained	99.0	1.8

Next, the allowable donor country emission increases show a diminishing return to scale. As host country emissions are reduced, the allowable increases in donor country emissions tend to become smaller. This effect is echoed in diminishing sulphur exchange rates: the more abatement takes place in the host country, the lower the exchange rate for subsequent abatement. The only place where this effect is absent is in the case where no increase in grid level deposition is allowed. But in this case, the allowable increase in donor country emissions is very low – the associated exchange rate is 62.5 for Sweden-Estonia and 11.2 for Austria-Czech Republic transactions.

There are a number of consequences of these effects. The motivation for joint implementation, it should be remembered, is to reduce sulphur emissions in the most cost-effective manner. So, for example, a donor country might invest preferentially in emission reduction in a host country because it is cheaper to reduce emissions abroad than to do so at home. But the reality of greater than unity (and increasing) exchange rates means that emission abatement abroad is considerably less attractive than might be expected from simple cost comparisons. Furthermore, since exchange rates increase with the level of abatement, joint implementation becomes less attractive as time goes on. Effectively, an exchange rate of (say) two means that the marginal cost of abating emissions abroad must be less than half the marginal cost of abating emissions at home, before the donor country will be tempted to invest in emissions reduction preferentially in a host country.

7. COMPARISON WITH GREENHOUSE GAS ABATEMENT

What lessons can be learned from these considerations for the case of joint implementation under the FCCC? Clearly there are some quite considerable differences between the two situations (Table 14.3). In the first place, the problem of sulphur dioxide abatement retains essentially spatial aspects which directly inform the relationships between donor and host in joint implementation arrangements. In the case of greenhouse gas abatement, the assumption of uniform mixing of pollutants in the atmosphere means that the spatial configuration of sources can be considered to be irrelevant to the level of abatement carried out. Although the concept of exchange rates of less than one has been mooted for joint implementation under the FCCC, these exchange rates will not show the same spatial complexity as witnessed under the Oslo Protocol.

Another difference relates to the use of national emission ceilings. These are agreed for all Parties under the Oslo Protocol, but only for Annex I (developed) countries under the FCCC. National emission ceilings allow for the 'closure' of a joint implementation system. If Parties have designated emission ceilings, trading takes place in the context of overall constraints on emission levels and environmental targets (for the Oslo Protocol, the targets are deposition levels at the grid square level in the region as a whole). If emission ceilings are absent, joint implementation arrangements cannot be defined in terms of overall environmental targets. The first Protocol to the

Table 14.3 Differences with respect to issues associated with the JI of sulphur emissions and the JI of greenhouse gases

Issue	Sulphur emissions	Greenhouse gases
Status of science	Acidification science mature although many uncertainties remain	Climate change science developing and major uncertainties remain
Environmental pathway	Usually treated as a non-uniformly mixed pollutant i.e. spatial considerations	Usually treated as uniformly mixed pollutants
Environmental impacts	Direct effects on human health and buildings and indirect effects through acidification of soils	Predominately indirect effects through climate change processes
Mitigation	Source control only	Source control and sequestration
Legislation	Many decades of regulatory experience	Recent regulation only
Emissions trading	Experience of sulphur emissions trading in the United States	No large scale carbon emissions trading systems implemented
Importance of JI	JI is a relatively minor policy instrument within the context of the CLRTAP and the Oslo Protocol at present	JI is set to become a major policy instrument under the Kyoto Protocol to the FCCC

FCCC, agreed at Kyoto in December 1997, provides both for trading arrangements between Annex I countries and for project level joint implementation involving non-Annex I countries without an agreed emission ceiling (the Clean Development Mechanism). The first guarantees closure but the second does not. The design of the second may prove highly problematic, particularly with respect to ensuring that the environmental objectives of the Climate Convention are met.

In spite of these differences between the two situations, there are also some clear similarities (Table 14.4). In particular, both sets of pollutants are now the subject of major international reduction efforts, and both involve transboundary pollution issues. Perhaps more importantly, from the perspective of this chapter, many of the sources of sulphur pollution are also

Table 14.4 Similarities in the issues associated with the JI of sulphur emissions and the JI of greenhouse gases

Issue	Sulphur emissions	Greenhouse gases
Multiple pollutants	SO_2, NO_x and NH_3 all contribute to acidification	CO_2, CH_4 and other gases contribute to climate change
Transboundary pollutant	Efficient control strategies require internationally co-ordinated responses (at the regional/continental level)	Efficient control strategies require internationally co-ordinated responses (at the global level)
UN Conventions	1979 Convention on Long-Range Transboundary Air Pollution	1992 Framework Convention on Climate Change
Economic activities and sectors	Combustion of fossil fuels dominant emission source and power/heat generation very significant	Combustion of fossil fuels dominant emission source and power/heat generation very significant
Clean technology and energy efficiency	Cleaner technologies and energy efficiency can reduce sulphur emissions	Cleaner technologies and energy efficiency can reduce carbon emissions
European countries with economies in transition	Sulphur emissions have been reduced as a result of structural changes in economic/energy system	Carbon emissions have been reduced as a result of structural changes in economic/energy system
Northern European countries	Few energy supply-side sulphur abatement options remaining	Upward pressures on carbon emissions upon the energy supply sector
Application of economic instruments	Experience of emission taxes in Europe	Experience of emission taxes in Europe
Bilateral agreements in Europe	Experience of bilateral assistance to help reduce sulphur emission in countries with economies in transition	Experience of bilateral assistance to help reduce carbon emission in countries with economies in transition
Rules for JI	Rules and conditions for JI of sulphur emission reductions still being developed as part of the CLRTAP	Rules and conditions for JI of greenhouse gases still being developed as part of the FCCC

sources of greenhouse gas emissions; and some at least of the technical avenues for sulphur abatement are also potentially avenues for greenhouse gas abatement.[10] This situation means that there are potentially double dividends in projects which simultaneously reduce both sulphur emissions and greenhouse gas emissions. At the moment, the institutional arrangements for joint implementation are uncertain in both the CLRTAP and the FCCC. Consequently, it is presently unlikely that these potential synergies can be exploited.[11] However, there is clearly an incentive to remedy this situation, particularly when the incentives for investment in joint implementation arrangements for sulphur show diminishing returns to scale.

8. CONCLUSIONS

This chapter has outlined some prospective procedures for joint implementation under the Oslo Protocol to the CLRTAP. By comparison with the Clean Development Mechanism of the Kyoto Protocol, the existence of clear environmental targets under the Oslo Protocol means that it is possible to define joint implementation arrangements without jeopardizing environmental objectives for reducing sulphur deposition exceedance levels. However, the spatial characteristics of acid pollution introduce a level of complexity not encountered in the FCCC. This complexity militates against establishing simple exchange rate arrangements between donor and host countries. Ultimately, an appropriately designed system would be likely to offer diminishing returns to scale, making international sulphur trading less and less attractive to potential donors. On the other hand, the existence of technical synergies between acid emission abatement and greenhouse gas abatement suggests that the institutional arrangements for the two kinds of joint implementation would be well advised to proceed, at least in cognizance of, and perhaps in harmony with, each other.

APPENDIX A MATHEMATICAL REPRESENTATION OF EXCHANGE RATE SIMULATION

The formulation of the simulation problem discussed in this chapter is shown in the equations below:

minimize: a_{donor}
subject to:
$$e_i \quad = \quad E_i - a_i \qquad\qquad i = 1,...,n$$

$$a_i = A_i \qquad\qquad i = 1,...,n \text{ except the donor and host country}$$

$$a_{host} = A_i + A_{project} \qquad \text{Host only}$$

$$a_{donor} \leq A_i \qquad\qquad\quad \text{Donor only}$$

$$d_k = b_k + \Sigma_i t_{ik} e_i \qquad k = 1,...,K$$

$$d_k = u_k + x_k \qquad\qquad k = 1,...,K$$

$$d_k \leq D_k(1 + y) \qquad\quad k = 1,...,K$$

$$\Sigma_k x_k \leq X_{Europe}$$

$$u_k \leq U_k \qquad\qquad\qquad k = 1,...,K$$

where the subscripts are: i = index for sources (source regions are typically countries); j = index for steps of abatement cost curves (stepped marginal cost curves) and is not used here; k = index for receptors (EMEP squares) and the variables (non-negative), constants and coefficients are:

e_i =   emissions after abatement from source i;

a_i =   abatement variable of source i;

E_i =   base emissions from source i (before abatement, year 2010);

A_i =   abatement at Oslo Protocol (year 2010) level for source i;

$A_{project}$ =   additional abatement resulting from Estonian JI project;

t_{ik} =   transfer coefficient from source i to receptor k;

U_k =   critical load in receptor k;

d_k =   total deposition in receptor k;

b_k =   background deposition in receptor k;

u_k =   total deposition up to critical load in receptor k;

x_k =   deposition in excess of critical load in receptor k,

D =   reference deposition in receptor k as a result of the Oslo Protocol (year 2010) emissions,

$1 + y$ =   allowable increase in deposition (by $y\%$) in receptor k relative to the Oslo Protocol level (year 2010),

X_{Europe} =   total European exceedance as a result of the Oslo Protocol (year 2010) emissions.

NOTES

[1]   This work was funded as part of an ongoing project supported by DGXII under the Framework IV programme. We acknowledge the help and advice of all our project partners, in particular, Katie Begg and Stuart Parkinson at the Centre for Environmental

Strategy, University of Surrey. We also wish to thank Steve Cinderby of the Stockholm Environmental Institute at York for help with the GIS mapping.

[2] Sulphur will be used as a shorthand for sulphur dioxide throughout this chapter.

[3] University of Surrey, University of York, Stockholm Environment Institute, Risø National Laboratory, Nutek (Sweden), and EVA (Austria).

[4] EMEP stands for the Cooperative Program for Monitoring and Evaluation of the Long Range Transmission of Air Pollutants in Europe. This is a subsidiary body to the CLRTAP and provides the official estimates of pollutant transportation and deposition within Europe.

[5] More correctly the critical sulphur deposition levels shown on the map in Annex I of the Protocol.

[6] These national emission ceilings were negotiated on the basis of the so-called 'gap 60' scenario in which exceedance of critical loads was to be reduced by 60 per cent.

[7] See Chapter 5.

[8] For example, it is likely to be incorrect to assume the simple inverse relation $r_{HD} = 1/r_{DH}$ which equation (2) seems to imply.

[9] On the other hand, it is informed by a continuing Swedish interest in bilateral investment in emission abatement in the Baltic States.

[10] This is not true of all potential solutions. For example, the use of fluidized bed combustion to reduce sulphur emissions can also increase carbon dioxide emissions.

[11] In fact, the separation of greenhouse related environmental benefits from total environmental benefits implied by the GEF's existing concept of net incremental cost militates against such a synergy.

REFERENCES

Bailey, P.D., G.A. Gough, K. Millock and M.J. Chadwick (1996), 'Prospects for the joint implementation of sulphur emission reductions in Europe', *Energy Policy,* **24**(6) 507–516.

Førsund, F.R. (1993), *Sulphur Emissions trading,* Working Paper, Department of Economics, University of Oslo, Oslo.

Gough, G.A., P.D Bailey, B. Biewald, J.C.I Kuylenstierna, and M.J. Chadwick (1994), 'Environmentally targeted objectives for reducing acidification in Europe', *Energy Policy,* **22**(12), 1055–1066.

Jackson, T. (1995), 'Joint Implementation and cost-effectiveness under the Framework Convention on Climate Change' *Energy Policy,* **23**(2), 117–138.

Klaassen, G. (1996), *Acid Rain and Environmental Degradation; the Economics of Emissions trading,* Edward Elgar, Cheltenham, UK, and Lyme, US.

UNECE (1994), *Protocol to the 1979 Convention on Long-Range Transboundary Air Pollution on Further Reduction of Sulphur Emissions,* United Nations Economic Commission for Europe, Geneva.

272-95

H23 Q2⁵
Q28

15. Economic instruments and institutional constraints: possible schemes for SO$_2$ emissions trading in the EU[1]

Olivier Godard

1. INTRODUCTION

Following the 1979 Geneva Convention on Long Range Transboundary Air Pollution (CLRTAP), two protocols on sulphur dioxide (SO$_2$) emissions have been adopted. The 1985 Helsinki Protocol established a uniform abatement target of 30 per cent for all Parties, on the basis of 1980 emissions, while the 1994 Oslo Protocol defined new national targets for SO$_2$ abatement, which for the first time are differentiated across countries. The Oslo Protocol also fixed emission standards for new sources, and agreed on the specifications of the best available technologies to be used by operators. The agreed long term objective is to reduce SO$_2$ emissions so as to respect critical loads[2] for acid deposition everywhere in Europe.[3] However, the regulatory requirements agreed upon within the Protocol are insufficient to achieve this long-term objective. To reduce the gap, it will be necessary to introduce new policy instruments or significantly tighten existing ones.

The purpose of this chapter is to develop possible organizational schemes for SO$_2$ emissions trading within the EU[4] as a means of achieving a cost-effective trajectory to reach the long run objective. Under good conditions of information and organization, a tradable permit system may enforce an overall environmental constraint while minimizing the total abatement cost. This is why this instrument can at the same time be viewed as bringing an environmental and an economic improvement, when compared to administrative regulatory approaches focused on emission rates (Klaassen, 1996). To be viable, any proposed scheme must prove politically acceptable (distributive palatability), achieve a predictable improvement in environmental quality (environmental effectiveness), and most importantly

272

be consistent with pre-existing basic rules and requirements (institutional acceptability) (Godard, 1995). The latter condition is the central issue addressed in this chapter.

The Oslo Protocol imposes one main constraint on SO_2 emissions: a set of individual national targets to be achieved at three dates in the future: 2000, 2005 and 2010. This choice has been guided by European-wide model optimization exercises aiming at achieving an intermediate objective of a 60 per cent reduction in the gap between current levels of acid deposition and the 5-percentile critical loads for each 150 km by 150 km 'grid cell' within Europe. The Protocol also includes a provision that two parties could be authorized to join their abatement efforts. The detailed rules for this joint implementation concept have still to be determined by the executive body of the Convention. It seems that any such proposal would only be accepted if the parties can demonstrate that it will positively contribute to the long term environmental objective, i.e. improving environmental quality in the whole territory covered by the Convention. In the context of this chapter, I have interpreted this requirement as an implicit second constraint, one submitting any SO_2 allowance trading scheme to the obligation of meeting a percentage abatement target regarding the gap between current levels of deposition and critical loads. The final 2010 target should be a 60 per cent reduction in this gap. However, to avoid a disequilibrium between deposition and emission constraints, the deposition target may evolve with the same target years as the national emission ceilings. For example, we could assume abatement objectives of 55 per cent in 2000, 57 per cent in 2005 and 60 per cent in 2010.

For the design of a trading scheme, this amounts to having two constraints to satisfy: overall national targets related to emissions; and the percentage abatement target as regards deposition in excess of critical loads. For areas where deposition is below critical loads, the second constraint is interpreted as ensuring critical loads are not exceeded. Beyond 2010, more stringent objectives (say 75 per cent or 90 per cent reduction in exceedance levels) could be adopted in a multi-phased approach.

Whatever the level chosen, there is no reason why these two types of constraints should automatically coincide. A key feature of this chapter is to address this specific issue of satisfying two types of constraints when developing an allowance trading scheme. The joint implementation of the first constraint provides a global European cap on emissions, leading to allowances that can be directly expressed in quantities of emissions. The second constraint leads to allowances expressed in quantities of deposition by *unit zone* (see Box 1).

Box 1 Terminology for zones

The chapter uses several definitions of geographical zones:
- *Deposition zone* is a general term for an area receiving acid deposition.
- *Unit zones* are the smallest zones for which critical loads have been determined. Under the UNECE protocols, these correspond to 150 km by 150 km squares.
- *Macro zones* are a grouping of several unit zones on the basis of some rule.
- *Trading zones* are areas within which trading is freely authorized with a one to one exchange rate. Between trading zones, trading may be forbidden or may be allowed with a specific exchange rate (for example 1:1.5). Trading zones may correspond to individual unit zones or a larger grouping of unit zones (a macro zone).

Two families of solutions are then considered:

- A system of two types of tradable allowances working in parallel. Firms have to gather the same amount of the two different types of allowances to obtain a permit to emit a corresponding amount of SO_2.
- An integrated system in which a single allowance type embodies both emission and deposition constraints. Two variants of an integrated system are considered which put different emphasis on the incentive mechanisms imposed on firms and national governments.

Such solutions may be judged rather complex to operate, more complex than those implemented by the Acid Rain Program in the US, for example. Nevertheless, the source of complication is to be found, not in allowance trading as such, but in the existing framework of the CLRTAP and subsequent Protocols. To achieve any further progress towards the long-term goal it will be necessary to address the complication of the transition, whatever the policy instrument chosen. To offer the required level of guarantee, a 'command and control' approach would have to become either excessively stringent or cumbersome. I contend that by lowering the total cost of abatement, allowance trading may help facilitate an overall progression towards the abatement of acid deposition, even if progress cannot be guaranteed at the same pace for each unit zone of the European territorial grid. One major contribution of SO_2 allowance trading could be in the flexibility of timing given to the participating companies. With tradable allowances, firms are given the opportunity to optimize the timing of their investment decisions. This saves capital costs and encourages the efficient and timely adoption of technical innovations.

Approximately 65 per cent of total SO_2 emissions in the EU originate from the generation of electricity. It therefore seems quite natural to begin to implement trading schemes within this sector so as to gain practical experience of the tool within the EU. An opposite view would stress the low level of competition in the power generation sector, since oligopolies or monopolies are common structures in many EU countries. However, recent EU initiatives regarding the introduction of competition in this sector will increase the sensitivity to price signals and market opportunities. Positive synergies may then exist between electricity market liberalization and allowance trading. Further extension of the trading scheme could be advantageously envisaged to oil refineries and to all industrial combustion plant above a certain size (e.g. 25 MW).

The remainder of the chapter is structured as follows. Section 2 provides an overview of some key variables for the design of a trading scheme, while Section 3 discusses the issue of defining trading zones. Section 4 presents a system of two simultaneous, coupled allowance trading mechanisms. Section 5 is devoted to an integrated scheme including an auctioned market for 'unusable allowances', while Section 6 describes an alternative integrated system incorporating compensations for member states. The main conclusions are summarized in Section 7.

2. AN OVERVIEW OF SOME KEY DESIGN VARIABLES FOR TRADING SCHEMES

The success of a trading scheme depends crucially on the details of its design. Here, the following variables are selected for particular attention:

- Basic agents: which parties receive allowances and participate in trade.
- Level of initial allocation: whether this should be carried out at a European or member state level.
- Permitting procedure: how trades should be authorized to ensure that deposition constraints are not exceeded.
- Exchange rate: how emissions from widely separated sources may be compared to achieve approximate equivalence in environmental impact through trading.
- Periodicity: whether parties should be allowed to trade continuously or at periodic intervals.

Figure 15.1 summarizes the choices made for these key variables, while subsequent sections explain these choices in more detail.

Figure 15.1 Key design variables for an EU scheme of SO₂ trading

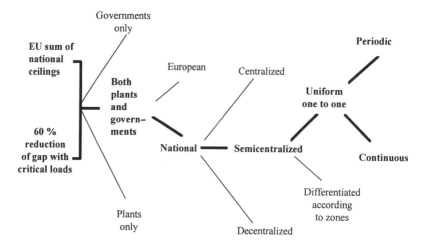

2.1. Who trades?

Two types of actors could legitimately participate in a trading scheme: governments and electricity generators responsible for SO₂ emissions. An international trading mechanism that only operates between governments would leave significant opportunities for cost saving untapped. Because they directly control emissions and have the best access to technical and economic information, firms should be able to engage directly in a trading scheme. However a trading scheme organized solely at the firm level would correspond to a level of political integration which has yet to be achieved by the EU. It is EU member states which have taken on legally binding quantitative obligations under the Oslo Protocol and any trading arrangement must respect these obligations.

In this regard, the Oslo Protocol can be seen as a compromise between an agreement among independent States and a more integrated approach that could be developed if all States chose to behave as the members of a single political community. The EU context of negotiation and decision-making looks intermediate: a network of regular co-operative links has been created and some acceptance of sectoral asymmetries in obligations and burden-sharing has been institutionalized.

The political balance of this compromise is reflected in the basic constraints embodied in the Oslo Protocol. Establishing emission ceilings on a country basis is a response to the first component of the compromise. So, even for an EU-wide allowance trading scheme, the initial allocation of allowances at the plant level should be the responsibility of the individual member states. But the preliminary drafts of the Protocol were conceived with reference to the second component, with the idea of an integrated optimal plan for acid deposition for the whole European territory concerned, a plan sensitive to the location of deposition. This would require trading by individual sources.

These considerations lead to the choice of a *two-level* system, in which there is trading at both the government level and the plant level. Governments retain responsibility for the initial allocation of allowances to plants, together with the legal obligation to meet national emission ceilings. The allocation should provide a predictable framework in which individual plants can engage in trade to improve economic efficiency. Deposition constraints are enforced by the authorization procedures for plant-to-plant trades, which are administered by the central authorities. These are described more fully below.

This choice is consistent with the concern for economic efficiency expressed by the EU as well as the Oslo Protocol. From the viewpoint of the economics of information, the potential for cost-effectiveness can only be exploited by giving appropriate incentives to decentralized management units; that is, to those actors who can most easily obtain the appropriate information concerning the available abatement opportunities, technologies and costs. This is what allowance trading is intended to achieve. If governments were to be considered as the only agents of the system, they would be unable to obtain some of the necessary information to minimize the social cost of abatement.

2.2. Which permitting procedure?

Permitting refers to the authorization procedure for individual plant-to-plant trades. This must ensure that the deposition constraints are not exceeded. There are three broad options:

- A decentralized approach with free trade, i.e. without a specific authorization procedure but according to agreed rules. Typically, trading may only be allowed within the same deposition zone, or between various zones on the basis of a fixed set of exchange rates.

- A semi-centralized approach, based on physical modelling of the net impact of each proposed trade on acid deposition in each zone.
- A centralized or planned approach, in which physical and economic models are used to identify all possible beneficial trades compatible with the current target.[5] In order to be authorized, a projected trade should fit the pre-existing list of advantageous trades. Modelling is not used to authorize each proposal, but is used once, at the beginning of the period, to identify transactions that would be attractive and compatible.

Here, I suggest that a semi-centralized permitting system is the best option. The integrated assessment models used during negotiation of the Oslo Protocol combine physical modelling of the emission, transportation and deposition of pollutants with economic modelling of abatement technologies and costs. However, since the cost functions used in the models are based on national aggregate values, the economic information is insufficient to identify the best opportunities for minimizing abatement costs. This undermines the case for centralized permitting procedures. Instead, it is suggested that the economic part of the modelling exercise is put aside, leaving only the physical models of emission, transportation and deposition of pollutants together with the link between deposition and critical loads. The economic dimension of the allocation will be left to the decentralized calculations of individual sources. Sources will have to compute their own strategy and look for cost effective opportunities to trade.

In this case, the process is as follows:

- the Secretariat enters the distribution of all the allowances resulting from the national implementation of emission ceilings and technological standards into the physical assessment models;
- after a search period, two sources interested in trading find each other and agree on a trade proposal; they submit it to the Secretariat;
- the projected change in the location of emissions is entered in the agreed models which are run to provide forecasts about the environmental impacts for each deposition zone;
- if the project violates the second condition related to the progress towards critical loads, it is not permitted; otherwise it is accepted.

Apart from the administrative burden, this procedure based on bilateral trades may also not lead to a cost-effective allocation. The sequential order of trades would be very important indeed.[6] Whether a transaction is allowed or not may depend on whether or not it is proposed before some other transaction. However, trading can be seen as inducing Pareto improvements, provided third parties are not significantly affected. On the whole the initial allocation will be improved, if not made wholly cost-effective.

2.3. The exchange rate

The environmental impact of SO_2 emissions depends on the location of source and receptor. Hence, 'one unit increase from one source cannot be offset by one unit decrease from another source. The exchange rate, also termed the offset rate, may be greater or smaller than one' (Førsund and Nævdal, 1994). The design of a trading scheme must respect this if it is to be compatible with deposition constraints. Two options are possible:

- to accept trading between trading zones on the basis of exchange rates fixed for the whole period.
- to refuse trading between trading zones, but to define trading zones as covering a large geographical area so as to offer wider trading opportunities and limit transaction and administrative costs.

In the first case, exchange rates should reflect the relative intensity of the marginal damage generated by one unit of emissions. However, it is difficult to find a workable rule that is able to reflect this requirement. First, marginal damage functions are not known and some proxy has to be used. Second, while a practical rule should keep its value through time, the conditions for optimality require a revision of exchange rates after each trade. Since emissions are concentrated in a limited number of sources, individual trades will generally have a non-negligible impact on the distribution of acid deposition. But continual adjustment of exchange rates would make trading unpredictable for agents, significantly complicate investment decisions and be administratively impractical.

The second solution sticks to a one to one exchange rate within trading zones considered to be homogeneous. This simple and robust approach may be viewed as more accessible, and easy to implement, being less dependent on central modelling and revision of information. However, it is not totally satisfying since the supposed homogeneity of each zone is an artificial construct to some extent.

The choice between these depends on both political judgement about the level of environmental guarantees offered and administrative practicality. Most proposals have explored exchange rates,[7] without giving too much attention to guarantees of environmental improvement. Here we explore the second option as it may provide a higher level of guarantee. The key issue then becomes the size of the trading zone and the trade off this implies between environmental effectiveness and economic efficiency. This is discussed further in Section 3.

2.4. Which periodicity?

The issue here is whether agents should be allowed to trade continuously or whether trades should take place periodically through an organized mechanism. This is relevant at two levels: government-to-government trading and plant-to-plant trading. The best solution will depend upon the level.

With a two-level system of allowance trading, governments will trade on the basis of their national caps; once national caps have been decentralized to plants, the latter will trade together at the EU level. The intergovernmental market controlling the level of national caps should be made highly predictable for plants, in order to ensure the security of the allowances they receive from public authorities, and to allow them to engage in rational investment strategies. A clear means of providing this predictability would be to organize a discrete, periodic intergovernmental market (every four years, for instance), with advance transactions, i.e. transactions having effect some years later (say three years). This would mean that plants can move in a predictable institutional environment, with a secure horizon in the range of three to seven years. For plant level trading the period could be much shorter – every six months or a year for example.

An alternative approach would be for governments to regulate the total quotas given to plants on a continuous base, as active operators on national markets. However, this approach could introduce instability and unpredictability into the market, or raise the fear that governments will behave in an arbitrary manner. These factors may turn out to be an obstacle to technological innovation, when the weight and sunk costs of industrial investments in desulphurization equipment are taken into account.

3. ABOUT ZONING AND SCALING

The issue of zoning is a key one for the practicability of the trading schemes considered in this chapter. The first problem to be addressed concerns the scale of trading zones, while the second concerns the criteria by which zones are defined.

At one extreme, we have grid-cells, i.e. relatively small territorial units of 150 km by 150 km. At the other extreme, we face one unique zone, the European territory covered by the CLRTAP Convention. If trading is confined to specific zones, then larger scales provide more opportunities for improving economic efficiency, but this is achieved at the expense of lower levels of environmental security. Smaller scales offer greater environmental security but with fewer opportunities for profitable trade. Maintaining practical viability with sufficient potential for economic efficiency gains should be the relevant criteria for selecting the 'best' scale, not just having a complete guarantee about the environmental protection of every small part of the European territory. In the latter case, too much would be paid for environmental certainty. But how can we proceed in this direction? If the existing grid of 150 km by 150 km is to be used for trading, then allowing trade between all zones using a matrix of exchange rates is inescapable if sufficient flexibility is to be achieved. But this solution would not avoid hot spots and, if the exchange rates remain fixed, it would not provide the expected environmental guarantees. From this, it may seem preferable to stick to a one to one rate of exchange within homogeneous zones. This alternative requires the definition of a limited number of *macro zones* to give sources a sufficient margin of flexibility.

There are two main possibilities for defining such macro zones. The first consists in establishing a number of categories of exceedance of critical loads and in mapping the European territory according to these categories. In this case, two territorial units belonging to the same categories may not be adjacent. Allowing a one to one exchange rate within each equivalence class is appealing, since emissions will have a broadly similar effect on the environment. However, the risk of having hot-spots with an unduly large concentration of pollutants in some places cannot be excluded. Therefore it may be useful and prudent to introduce some additional restriction.

This may be provided by an alternative way of designing zoning – identifying homogeneous geographical zones; that is, zones having a geographical unity in terms of contiguity and at the same time the same broad level of excess deposition over critical loads. Several adjacent cells with similar sensitivity to deposition could be joined in a single macro zone. Such a grouping extends the trading possibilities between deposition allowances. Trades would only be allowed between sources having emissions falling in the same macro zone.

Such a grouping can be made revisable. Since the ultimate target is formulated in terms of respecting critical loads for each basic unit zone, progress in that direction may be supported by a transitional approach to the scaling of trading zones. The initial step would be organized on the basis of a limited number of macro zones. Such macro zones would not constrain sources enough to ensure everywhere compliance with critical loads targets. At later stages, these zones could be scaled-down.

One critical point for the dynamics of scaling from an incentive viewpoint is that the future evolution of the grid should be communicated to participants well in advance so that they can develop strategic compliance plans incorporating early adaptation. Otherwise the outcome could be very inefficient. For instance, mistakes in capital investment might be induced. The authorities might therefore announce that the existing zones would be narrowed five years later, and then again ten years later. Such

announcements of changes in the scale of trading zones will limit the
problem of hot spots from the start, because for every decision having a
medium or long term time horizon, specifically for planning investments
(desulphurization equipment, etc.), plant operators will have to take into
account the announced changes. By the end of the process the long run
targets fixed by the Oslo Protocol, i.e. respecting critical loads at the level of
the grid-cell, will have to be met and this will give much less scope for
trading.

With respect to practical matters, what type of zoning may reasonably be
considered for an initial step? It seems that defining five trading macro zones
in which critical loads are exceeded may make sense on both economic and
ecological grounds. A recommendation proposed by Bailey, Gough and
Millock (1994) considers such a grouping of unit zones having adjacent
sensitivity. Five classes of acid sensitivity are used by them to classify each
grid cell and achieve groupings accordingly.

Such a 'sensitivity' classification is not completely satisfying. Two areas
being classified in the same sensitivity class may suffer unequal damage due
to different levels of deposition: marginal damage not only depends on
sensitivity levels but also on basic deposition received by zones in excess of
critical loads. This is the reason why I suggest consideration of another type
of zoning based on excess deposition over critical loads. With five classes of
excess deposition, five critical macro-zones can be distinguished; they are
surrounded by large areas where critical loads are not exceeded (see Figures
15.2 and 15.3).

This mapping convincingly shows that drawing macro zones is not an
entirely arbitrary exercise. By accepting some kind of 'sacrifice'[8] for a few
cells, it is possible to identify homogeneous zones of a large scale.
Meanwhile, significant areas of the European territory are relatively
unaffected by acid deposition. The latter have depositions that do not exceed
critical loads. The 60 per cent abatement constraint will not be binding for
them. Countries like Spain, Greece and Portugal are broadly in this category.

4. IMPLEMENTING A SYSTEM OF TWO SIMULTANEOUS, COUPLED ALLOWANCE TRADING MECHANISMS

The trading system has to take into account two basic heterogeneous
constraints: national emission caps and deposition limits in unit zones. Given
this, a first possibility is to conceive of two different systems of trading, one
for each constraint, which are coupled together to allow sources to emit a
given amount of SO_2. To obtain the right to emit one tonne of SO_2, a source

*Figure 15.2 Aggregate zoning on the basis of equivalent ecological
sensitivity*

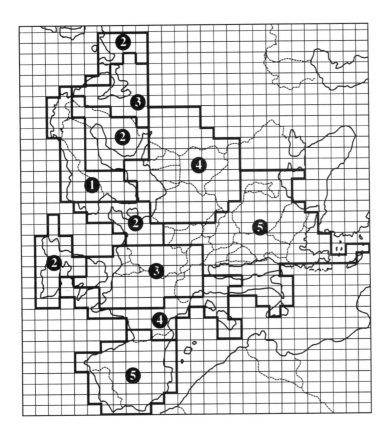

❶ x ≤ 20
❷ 20 < x ≤ 40
❸ 40 < x ≤ 80
❹ 80 < x ≤ 160
❺ 160 < x

*Figure 15.3 Aggregate zoning on the basis of excess acid deposits over
critical loads (1990 data)*

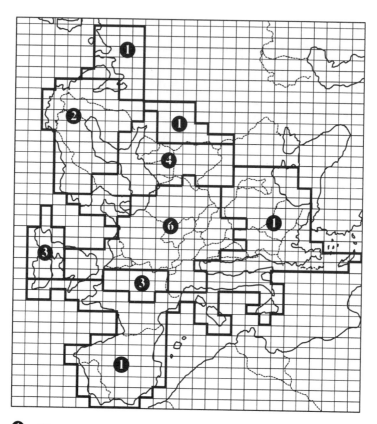

❶ y ≤ 0
❷ 0 < y ≤ 20
❸ 20 < y ≤ 40
❹ 40 < y ≤ 80
❺ 80 < y ≤ 160
❻ 160 < y

having been involved in emissions trading should possess one allowance of each type.[9]

With such a system, each source would then operate in two types of allowance market – one for *emissions allowances*, working at the EU level and based on initial allocations distributed by national governments, and one for *deposition allowances*, focused on the specific constraints for each deposition zone in Europe (including non EU regions) and based on initial allocations distributed by the central authorities (the UNECE Secretariat for example). This system would take account of emissions from sources which belong to the territory of the EU, but generate acid deposition outside the EU. In the framework of the Oslo Protocol, the same basic constraints operate whatever the territory involved.

For the market in deposition allowances, I have chosen to explore only one option, the one in which transactions are only authorized between sources generating deposition within the same deposition zones.[10] In that case, there will be as many markets of the second type as there are deposition zones. If there exist n unit zones in Europe, a source would have to operate on (at most) $n + 1$ markets (the n deposition zone markets and the EU-wide market of nationally allocated emissions allowances).

In order to couple the two types of allowances, a pollutant transportation model (such as EMEP[11]) has to be used for translating emissions into deposition or deposition into emissions. The basic framework for a system of this type is summarized in Table 15.1 and Figure 15.4.

Table 15.1 A double system of allowances

	Emissions allowances	**Deposition allowances**
Units	tonnes	tonnes of deposition in zone i
Number of markets	1	Up to n – the number of unit zones
Trading	unconstrained	only between sources generating deposition in the same zones
Allocation	national governments (political)	central authorities (using EMEP)

This double system of allowance trading may be more practical than it seems at first sight. In the deposition markets, potential trading partners are more limited in number. They may be well-known to each potential participant. Thus, the problem of finding potential partners would be rather

Figure 15.4 A double system of allowances

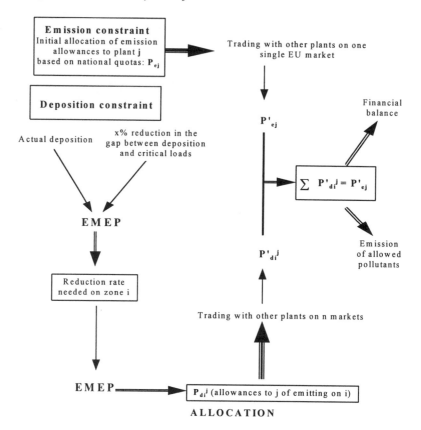

easy to overcome. At the same time, the market could be too thin, making it difficult to find partners ready for an exchange. The possibility of strategic interference amongst competitors (market power) cannot be avoided either. The importance of these difficulties may be expected to be proportional to the number of zones. Similarly the administrative practicality of the scheme is inversely proportional to the number of zones. These considerations strengthen the argument in favour of a small number of zones of large geographical area.

When potential traders know their trading opportunities on the deposition markets, they can adjust their strategy on the market for emissions. The emissions allowance market provides flexibility regarding the way the initial allocation has been dealt with politically by governments, although grandfathering is the most probable choice for political reasons, and provides large opportunities for exchange for suppliers and buyers. No specific additional constraints are necessary on this market since the deposition constraints are tackled by the deposition market.

This heterogeneous combination of two types of allowance can be seen as an incentive to trade. Participants need sufficient allowances of both types (emission and deposition) to be able to continue operating. If they have insufficient allowances of one type they must either buy more or reduce emissions. If they have more allowances of one type than they can use they have an incentive to sell. In each case, it is more rewarding to engage in trade than to stay in their present position.

While this scheme is significantly more complicated than, for example, the US Acid Rain Program, it may still be viable. The complications arise not from the scheme itself but from the dual constraint embodied in the existing UNECE regime.[12] Since these constraints are unlikely to be abandoned, it is necessary to devise a scheme that fully incorporates them. To minimize transaction costs and expand trading opportunities it will be necessary to define trading zones that are larger than the EMEP unit zones – even if this solution does not provide an absolute guarantee of environmental improvement for each unit zone.

The following sections described two variants of an integrated allowance trading scheme. As in the previous scheme, physical modelling of pollutant transportation and deposition plays a central role, in both the allocation of allowances and the authorization of trades. Proposed trades are tested with physical models for ascertaining their impacts on deposition for each unit zone. The variants differ as regards the rules for the initial allocation of allowances and the type of incentive mechanism incorporated to make reaching critical loads targets more attractive to plants (variant 1) and governments (variant 2).

5. AN INTEGRATED TRADING SYSTEM, WITH AN AUCTIONED MARKET FOR 'UNUSABLE ALLOWANCES'

Here, the initial allocation is organized in two steps. First, a potential allocation of 'emission' allowances to individual sources (plants) by national governments is calculated on the basis of national ceilings and allocation criteria chosen by those governments. The subsequent deposition from each source for each deposition zone is then assessed with the help of the EMEP model. In the meantime, the deposition target is used as the basis for a calculation of an overall deposition cap for each deposition zone. These zone deposition caps are then distributed proportionately to the sources responsible for the deposition, also using EMEP. This gives the potential 'deposition' allowances. The two allocations are translated in comparable terms (units of emissions) for each source by using the vector that describes how emissions from a source translate into deposition in the different deposition zones (say 10 per cent on R_1, 30 per cent on R_3, 25 per cent on R_{11}, and so on). Each source will have a different dispersion vector according to its location. At this moment, for each source, two different amounts of potential allowances are considered, the 'emission' one and the one derived from 'deposition'. The lower value of acceptable emissions is then selected, in order to satisfy the more binding constraint. On this basis an *actual* quota of allowances is allocated to the sources. These may be termed *usable and tradable allowances*. They can either be used directly, to cover actual emissions of the source, or traded, if sources take measures to abate their emissions under this quota. Each allowance of one ton of SO_2 is then defined as a vector of deposition in *n* zones.

At the same time, individual sources (plants) are given an extra amount of potential allowances responding to the difference between the less binding constraint (the emission or deposition, it depends on the source location) and the more binding one. This extra amount cannot be used directly but may be used for trading. These can be termed *unusable, tradable allowances*. This extra allocation will supplement the basic entitlement and give an additional incentive to sources to enter into allowance trading, since they can benefit from trading opportunities which remain compatible with both constraints of the regime. The operation of the mechanism could be as follows:

- Just like 'usable and tradable allowances', unusable ones are defined as a deposition vector for one ton of SO_2. Two cases can be considered.

  - Whenever 'unusable and tradable allowances derive from a more binding emission constraint they can be sold freely but they can only be used by the buyer for a use touching the same deposition zones in Europe as the ones that would have been affected if the seller had used them directly. This means that such transactions have to be checked as regards the deposition zones affected. For instance, if 100 tonnes of unusable allowances are sold by a source to another, what is really sold is a deposition right reflecting the structure of deposition of the seller, say 20 tonnes in Z_1, 30 tonnes in Z_2, 50 tonnes in Z_3. So the entitlement obtained through the purchase of 100 'unusable deposition allowances' is a vector $D_{1,2,3}$ (20, 30, 50). It is possible that the buyer cannot use the whole spectrum of what it buys, due to its different location and different structure of deposition from its emissions.

  - Whenever unusable allowances are related to a non binding emission constraint, the deposition vector for one ton of SO_2 will be zero, limiting the possible usage of such allowances to the cases when users need to complement quotas limited by an emission constraint and not a deposition one.

- So, the amount of 'unusable, tradable allowances' may evolve with time, following the various transactions. At any moment, the net amount of 'usable allowances' is defined by the level of the most binding constraint (emission or deposition), and the amount of 'unusable allowances' can be calculated as the difference between the two potential allowances (emission and deposition).
- A financial mechanism could be set up to facilitate the valuation of 'unusable allowances' on a market. They may feed an auction market organized by the authorities on behalf of sources. The revenue raised by the auctions could be refunded to the source entitled to it.[13] This 'last resort market' would be open to any source, but the buyers will be subject to the same constraints of usage that were previously described for all sources.

This system may seem complicated, but once an algorithm has been defined for making calculations plants should be able to deal with the system. The structure of the system is summarized in Figure 15.5.

With such a system, an auction market for allowances is generated in addition to bilateral trades. This has the following advantages:

- It gives additional flexibility and safety to sources and avoids the strategic retention of allowances. The mechanism would be similar to auctions organized by EPA in the US; any source looking for allowances and not finding them through bilateral trade could enter this recourse market.
- It facilitates the emergence of a public reference price for SO_2 allowances, and allows comparisons to be made between the various national markets. This compares with bilateral trades which are normally private, with no release of price information.

In providing a means to make economic use of 'unusable allowances' this integrated system creates an incentive for most countries and individual sources to accept the constraint of the percentage critical loads target, since going further than national ceilings would be compensated for in this way. This may enhance the political acceptability of the regime and accelerate progress towards the target of respecting critical loads. In contrast, if no opportunity to benefit from unusable allowances was given, the political and logical coherence of this integrated solution would be open to question. This is because it would give a strong weight to the critical loads goal without providing the incentives necessary to achieve this goal.

Figure 15.5 An integrated system with an auctioned secondary market

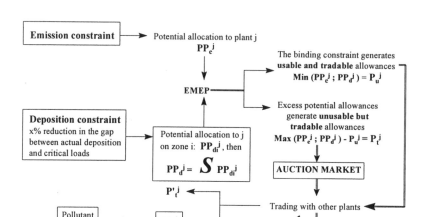

6. AN INTEGRATED SYSTEM INCORPORATING COMPENSATIONS FOR STATES

This procedure for the initial allocation reverses the previous solution. One begins by considering current emissions from sources and simulates, using EMEP, the subsequent deposition in each basic deposition zone. Two cases are then possible. If the critical loads are not exceeded, the source is credited with a 'deposition allowance' corresponding to its current emissions. If the critical loads are exceeded, the current target of a percentage closure of the gap between deposition and critical loads is used to calculate a deposition cap for the deposition zone; this cap is allocated proportionately to each source having deposition in the zone. This defines the *first* formula for determining the potential SO_2 deposition allowances to be received by each individual source. Consider this example: one source S_1 has 3 tonnes of deposition on a deposition zone Z_1, for which the cap is not exceeded, and 8 tonnes of deposition on Z_2 where the cap is exceeded. Then S_1 will first receive 3 P_{d1}. If Z_2 is receiving a total amount of excess deposition of 20 tonnes and the responsibility of S_1 for this is 5 per cent, then (assuming a deposition target of 60 per cent) it will also receive:

$$\{8 - [(20 \times 60\ \%) \times 5\ \%]\} = 7.4\ P_{d_2}$$

So the first potential deposition allocation of S_1 is:

$$P^1_D = 3\ P^1_{d_1} + 7.4\ P^1_{d_2}$$

Then the total amount, E_D, of such SO_2 allowances given to EU sources is calculated to test the compatibility of this allocation with the Oslo Protocol, as regards abatement commitments expressed in national ceilings:

$$E_D = \sum_{i,j} P^i_{d_j} \text{ for each source } i \text{ and zone } j$$

An EU cap on emissions, E_T, is also calculated as the sum of SO_2 emissions compatible with agreed national ceilings. If $E_D \leq E_T$, the first allocation is actually implemented for sources, since it satisfies at the same time the total EU cap and the critical loads target for each European zone. If on the contrary $E_D > E_T$, some additional restriction is needed. It can be argued that a proportional reduction on the *first* formula of allocation of allowances will be the appropriate solution for every individual source. For instance, if $E_D = 1.2 \times E_T$, the actual initial allocation of S_1 will be:

$$P^1_T = (3/1.2\ P_{d_1};\ 7.4/1.2\ P_{d_2}) = (2.5\ P_{d_1};\ 6.15\ P_{d_2})$$

Such a procedure fits an integrated EU political context, since member countries are required to transfer their national quotas to the EU, so as to obtain a global EU-wide cap. The prominent role given to the critical loads targets also fits this context. But under what conditions will this solution be acceptable to governments? Some countries will certainly see their actual quota reduced when compared to the agreed national ceilings in the Oslo Protocol or to the first variant considered above. It seems quite natural to envisage some mechanism of financial compensation. Governments, not sources, are proposed to be compensated, since governments have to be convinced to accept additional restrictions.

What basis can be imagined for this compensation? Since the breakthrough of the Oslo Protocol was only possible because the parties accepted some integrated assessment as a basis for elaborating an optimal international plan, parties could agree to calculate compensation using the same tool. The compensations table could then be calculated as the difference in national costs resulting from two allocations: the agreed

Figure 15.6 An integrated system with compensations for States

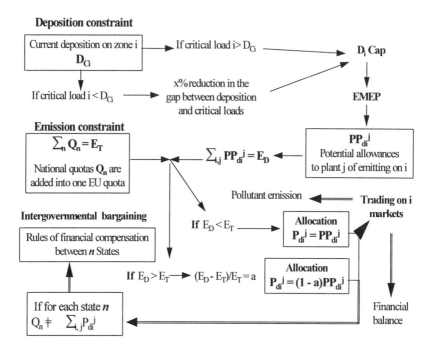

national ceilings of the Protocol and the allocation resulting from the procedure that has been just described.

7. CONCLUSION

The three proposals examined here were specifically conceived to address the two major constraints by which the institutional context of the EU and UNECE SO_2 requirements have been interpreted: national emission ceilings and deposition constraints for geographical zones. What can be the future of such proposals, if they are to become reality? Can we imagine an evolution towards a system of tradable allowances structured by a single constraint, i.e. deposition allowances?

To achieve an evolution towards a deposition allowance trading scheme, two conditions need to be met:

- all countries of the EU must abandon their national quotas to a common EU sovereign body, for redistribution according to some agreed rule (the political condition);

- constraints related to deposition allowances should be more binding, in every area, than the ones related to the emissions allowances (the technical condition).

If, for the sake of discussion, we take the first political condition as met, achievement of the second one looks rather doubtful. Deposition markets would frequently be the more binding ones, but this will not always be the case, since all EU countries have caps on their emissions, but critical loads are not exceeded in significant parts of the EU territory. A double system takes into account different rationales for allocation, which is an attractive property for achieving socio-political acceptability for the trading regime. Moreover the two types of allowances do not cover the same territory: emissions allowances, according to the proposed schemes, would be limited to the EU territory, while deposition allowances will be of concern for all Europe, including non EU deposition zones which are affected by EU emissions.

Evolution towards a one-constraint scheme would required a distribution of power in the EU which is rather different from that at present, where nation states have preserved significant political autonomy. The political equilibrium reached with the Oslo Protocol may be redefined in the future. In the meantime, the type of mechanism that has been presented in this chapter does fit well in this framework. Either a double market system or an integrated one provides the sort of equilibrium needed and may operate for a long time as an intermediate tool between national approaches, as reflected in national ceilings, and the pure co-operative European approach reflected in the critical loads reference.

NOTES

[1] This chapter benefits from the results of a 1996 study conducted by the author and Christine Cros, research assistant at CIRED, for the DGII 'Economic and Financial Affairs' of the European Commission. See Cros and Godard (1998). Financial support from the French ADEME and Ministry of the Environment is also gratefully acknowledged.

[2] Critical loads are defined as the maximum levels of acid deposition below which, according to current scientific knowledge, no significant damage to sensitive ecosystems can be demonstrated. Critical deposition for one zone is the maximum deposition compatible with the critical loads of specific ecosystems and land use within the zone. The 5-percentile critical loads correspond to deposition levels generating no significant damage for at least 95 per cent of the ecosystems within the area.

[3] In the context of this chapter, each time a territorial dimension is implied, 'Europe' or 'European' should be understood as the whole European territory covered by the Oslo

4   Protocol of the Geneva Convention, i.e. including countries outside the EU. Quite evidently, then, EU refers to the territory of the present member countries of the EU.

5   The acronym EU is also intended to cover the European Economic Community for years before the establishment of the EU.

6   This approach has been advocated by van Ierland et al. (1994).

Linear programming models of least cost solutions implicitly assume that trading takes place in a multilateral simultaneous manner. In the real world, trading involves individual transactions occurring sequentially. The models may assume patterns of trade that may be impossible in reality. For example, a bilateral trade between two sources may result in target deposition being exceeded at a particular location, but this in turn may be offset by an additional trade with another source. Such a trading pattern would be allowed in the model but disallowed in reality as pollution targets are (temporarily) exceeded. The models may therefore overestimate the potential gains from trade. For a fuller discussion of this issue see Atkinson and Tietenberg (1991).

7   For an allowance trading scheme based on exchange rates, see Amann et al. (1994).

8   Macro-zoning does not exclude the risk that, in some areas, deposition may increase or may not decrease, though a significant decrease will be achieved in another part of the same macro-zone. Anyway, the target of a 60 per cent abatement rate of excess over critical loads does not directly refer to damage. In places where critical loads may be slightly exceeded, the target is the same as in places where the excess is of a greater magnitude.

9   Plants not involved in emissions trading will just be submitted to the requirements of the emission allowances they receive from their governments. Additional deposition constraints become actual only when plants begin to trade. This reflects the view that trading will be politically accepted only if it provides both an economic improvement (cost abatement) and an environmental improvement.

10   For example, if plant A has deposition in zones a, b, c, and plant B has deposition in zones b, c, d, then A and B can trade their respective depositions in zones b and c. But for this trading to be profitable, A will also have to trade with plant C or D having deposition in zone a, so as to meet all the constraints related to the zones on which emissions are deposited.

11   EMEP stands for the Co-operative Program for Monitoring and Evaluation of the Long Range Transmission of Air Pollutants in Europe. This is a subsidiary body to the CLRTAP and provides the official estimates of pollutant transportation and deposition within Europe.

12   It may be noted here that there are also dual constraints in the US system, but from different origins. Power stations must comply with both the federal Acid Rain Program and state regulations on local air quality. In this case, local regulations, for instance in the Mid-West, frequently commanded investments in scrubbers, leaving important amounts of unused allowances available for sale. Symmetrically, after engaging in such investments, those utilities were uninterested in purchasing allowances.

13   This is termed a zero revenue auction.

REFERENCES

Amann, M., F. Førsund and G. Klaassen (1994), 'Emissions trading in Europe with an Exchange Rate', *Environmental and Resource Economics*, **4**, 305–330.

Atkinson, S. and T.Tietenberg (1991), 'Market failure in incentive-based regulation: the case of emissions trading', *Journal of Environmental Economics and Management,* **21**, 17–31.

Bailey, P., C.Gough and K.Millock (1994), 'Sulphur emission exchange rates', in F.Førsund and G. Klaassen (eds), *Economic Instruments for Air Pollution Control,* Kluwer Academic Publishers.

Cros, C. and O. Godard (1998), 'The economic design of a potential tradable permit system for SO_2 emissions in the European Union', *European Economy,* 'Getting Environmental Policy Right. The Rational Design of European Environmental Policy from an Economic Perspective', Report and Studies (Vol. 1), forthcoming Spring.

Førsund, F. and E. Nævdal (1994), 'Trading sulphur emissions in Europe', in F.Førsund and G. Klaassen (eds), *Economic Instruments for Air Pollution Control,* Dordrecht/Laxenburg, Kluwer Academic Publishers/International Institute for Applied Systems Analysis, pp231–48.

Godard, O. (1995), 'Trajectoires institutionnelles et choix d'instruments pour les politiques d'environnement dans les économies en transition', *Revue d'études comparatives Est-Ouest,* **26** (2), CNRS, juin, 39–58.

van Ierland, E.C., Kruitwagen,S. and Hendrix, E.M.T. (1994), 'Tradable Discharge Permits for Acidifying Emissions in Europe: 'guided' bilateral trade', in F.Førsund and G. Klaassen (eds), *Economic Instruments for Air Pollution Control,* Dordrecht/Laxenburg, Kluwer Academic Publishers/International Institute for Applied Systems Analysis.

Klaassen, G. (1996), *Acid Rain and Environmental Degradation. The Economics of Emissions trading,* Aldershot, UK and Brookfield, US: Edward Elgar.

PART VI

International Carbon Trading

H23 Q25
Q28

16. An emission quota trade experiment among four Nordic countries[1]

Peter Bohm

[handwritten margin note: Denmark, Finland, Norway, Sweden]

1. BACKGROUND

Joint implementation, as it was advanced in the 1992 United Nations Framework Convention on Climate Change (FCCC), reflects the Convention's concern for cost effectiveness in international undertakings to reduce emissions of carbon dioxide (CO_2) and other so-called greenhouse gases (GHG). The general idea behind the concept is that signatories, when engaged in such undertakings, should jointly implement their emission reductions and take advantage of the fact that marginal abatement costs may be lower in certain countries. Thus, emission abatement in such countries could be sold to other countries whose costs are higher, hence enabling both parties to gain from 'emission reduction trade'.

So far discussions and pilot testing of Joint Implementation (JI) have focused on the case where a *developed* country with an assumed stringent emission limit – e.g. to stay below its 1990 emission level by the year 2000, as indicated in the FCCC – buys emission reductions from a *developing* country that does not have any such target.[2] The motivation for this is that developing countries, which have yet to take any action to reduce emissions, may be able to offer attractive low cost emission reduction projects. Some JI projects of this type may also have the advantage of bringing about a technology transfer to the developing country. This type of JI would have to be conducted on a project-by-project basis and not at the level of the two countries' joint national emissions, since the developing country is not committed to a national emission target. However, this type of emissions trade would encounter two major problems with emission monitoring.

The first results from the fact that the nation-wide emissions in the absence of a particular project – the so-called project baseline – cannot be observed and therefore have to be assumed. This means the estimated size of the emission reductions from carrying out the project can only be hypothetical. The second problem is that incentives are created for the contract parties to exaggerate estimates of their emission reductions, the size of which can only be guessed by other parties. In a world where such claims would simply not be taken for granted, monitoring problems make it less likely that this type of JI would deliver any significant amount of cost-reducing services (IPCC, 1996).

An alternative form of JI is between two developed countries both committed to stringent GHG emission limits (IPCC, 1996; Ad Hoc Group, 1995). The reason why this form of JI has attracted less attention seems to be that the marginal abatement costs of all such countries may well be quite high, thereby making emission reduction trade between a pair of them less profitable than trade involving an uncommitted developing country.

However, JI between committed countries has an advantage not shared by the first type of JI, namely with respect to the monitoring of emission reductions. Since the FCCC takes for granted that a country's future carbon emissions (e.g. in the year 2000) can be compared with its emissions at a historical date (e.g. in 1990), presumably by using an estimate of the carbon content of its fossil-fuel use (use = production + imports – exports), the *joint* emissions of two (or more) such countries can be estimated equally well.

Another advantage of the alternative form of JI is the following. While JI involving a non-committed country must concern (large) individual projects, JI between committed countries can, by being monitored at the national level, incorporate all changes in emissions (e.g. all those that result from, say, an increase or introduction of a carbon tax in the seller country). Thus, a 'project' which amounts to reducing the use of a car and, other things equal, materializes as a reduction in fossil-fuel use and hence in carbon emissions, can be covered by this type of JI but, due to the large relative transaction costs, not by JI involving non-committed countries.

The question then is: how significant are the cost savings that can be attained from JI between two or more developed countries committed to stringent emission targets? If significant, it seems that the emphasis on the first-mentioned type of JI has been misplaced and that the form of JI where monitoring does not constitute a serious problem should be considered as an option, perhaps the primary one, capable of reducing the costs of limiting international emissions. This form of JI is in principle the same as a system of tradable emission quotas, or after Kyoto, December 1997, simply 'emissions trading' according to Article 17 of the Kyoto Protocol. It excludes developing countries only as long as they have not accepted to commit themselves to a binding emission target.

2. PURPOSE

The purpose of the experiment reported here is to test the order of magnitude of the efficiency gains which can be achieved by the, hitherto little observed, form of JI between two fresh (or more) developed countries, committed to binding emission targets. Since, at the time of writing, only a few countries seem to be firmly committed to such targets (e.g. of stabilizing GHG emissions by the year 2000 at 1990 levels), and even fewer countries appear interested in a pioneering JI operation of this type, there remains the second-best option of testing the achievements of hypothetical JI negotiations under as realistic conditions as possible.

Denmark, Finland, Norway and Sweden have kept a high profile in the context of international climate change policy. They may also be said to have indicated support for stringent emission targets, especially if some minimum number of other developed countries would do the same.[3] Since 1990, all four countries have undertaken some rather stringent unilateral measures to cut back carbon emissions, primarily by introducing CO_2 taxes. For a number of years, the countries have also co-operated in investigating various policy options, in particular of a JI nature. These options have mainly been discussed by the Nordic Council of Ministers' Ad Hoc Group on Energy Related Climate Issues, whose members are appointed by the governments of the Nordic countries.

In early 1996, the Ad Hoc Group decided to launch an experimental study to examine the abatement cost savings that could be obtained from JI among these four Nordic countries. In the experiment, the countries were represented by negotiating teams that were appointed by the countries' energy ministries or agencies.[4] The teams thus included people whose rank and competence are representative of team members who would participate in real-world negotiations. Prior to the experiment, the teams agreed to *assume* that their respective countries' governments had accepted:

- to stay (at least) within their 1990 emission levels by the year 2000;
- to interpret the FCCC as saying that an individual country could exceed this target level if another country had formally committed itself to a corresponding additional reduction of its emissions; and
- to try and jointly implement their emission reductions among themselves by the year 2000.

Experiments where decision making is hypothetical cannot in general be expected to provide information about the same type of real-world decision making. In particular, the incentives may be altogether different. In this experiment, as explained below, special care was taken to mimic the incentives likely to confront decision makers in actual negotiations.

3. EXPERIMENTAL DESIGN

All four participating countries had some version of a CO_2 tax system in effect in the fall of 1996, when the experiment was carried out. Moreover, these tax systems could be expected to remain in place in the year 2000. Thus, changes in the (weighted average of the) CO_2 tax(es) could be expected to be used to reach the specific emissions levels for that year. More specifically, according to the scenario for the JI experiment, current exemptions, specific rules or regulations for the CO_2 tax systems in each country were taken as given also for the year 2000, and the required emission reductions would be attained simply by adjusting the CO_2 tax rate or weighted average of CO_2 tax rates when these differed between sectors.

JI negotiations, if they had been real, would probably be guided by each country's attempts to minimize the net costs of meeting its international CO_2 emissions commitments. The international agreements reached by a country's negotiators would be subjected to the scrutiny of their government peers, who might be expected to pass judgement on the negotiators' degree of success.

In the case of hypothetical trade negotiations, as here, a feasible incentive mechanism has to be instituted which mimics this driving force as much as possible. As the incentive mechanism chosen for this test, the countries agreed to hand over to a neutral party, prior to the start of the negotiations, their estimated *social* emission reduction cost functions, that is, the relationship that would guide the negotiating strategy of each country, to be released to an international evaluation team after the negotiations were completed. The evaluation team would then assess the JI agreements reached against this background and publish (as is done here) its findings on the relative success of the participating countries in their trade negotiations.[5]

Since the four countries had each published abatement cost studies for their own economy and had kept their Nordic neighbours informed about the implications of potential reductions of their carbon emissions in other ways (e.g. within the Ad Hoc Group), general knowledge of each country's *technical* cost relationships was widespread among all of them.[6] This was a fortunate circumstance because a realistic test of JI in a 'steady state', i.e., after all parties had adjusted to the existence of this co-operative option, would have created strong incentives for each party to investigate not only their own cost abatement relationships but also those of their counterparts prior to making extensive JI commitments.

This type of technical abatement cost information leaves out political considerations concerning the employment and income distributive effects, etc. of emission reductions, which may not be easy to estimate outside an individual country. Although the cost information, common to all the four countries, thus constitutes only part of the information relevant for decision making about JI, it most likely implied that each country would have a pretty good idea about which countries would want to buy and which countries would want to sell emission reductions.

A general view seems to have been – and was also admitted *ex post facto* by the national representatives in the Ad Hoc Group – that the countries all believed that Denmark would be at net seller and Norway and Sweden would be net buyers. The situation for Finland was less clear due to a higher degree of uncertainty about its future emission levels and abatement costs. Thus, the expected 'market structure' was either a monopoly and three buyers or two sellers and two buyers.

Negotiations of the type at issue here can be organized in more than one fashion. They could be multilateral, with each country negotiating simultaneously with all the others using, for example, a stock-exchange-like registration of aggregate demand and supply at announced prices. Alternatively, negotiations could be bilateral. Given that the number of countries was small and that the countries were quite familiar with each other, it was deemed likely that, in a case of real JI negotiations, they would prefer to negotiate bilaterally. Hence, this was the design selected for the experiment.

The JI, or emissions trade, negotiation experiment was carried out during 18–24 September 1996. The instructions to the negotiators included:

- a statement of the year 2000 emission targets and estimated baseline or business-as-usual (BAU) emission levels, according to the information given to the secretariat by each of the four countries' negotiating teams (see Table 16.1 in Appendix 2);
- instructions for estimating marginal social emission reduction costs (in US dollars) for the year 2000, to be handed over to a neutral party prior to the negotiations (the Icelandic delegate of the Ad Hoc Group); each country was asked to provide estimates that covered the emission levels it deemed relevant for the upcoming negotiations;[7]
- the times for the bilateral trade negotiations (by fax): a first round of three days (*de facto* one day and a half), when preliminary or binding agreements might be reached, and a second round, which might end after one day unless there was a demand from at least two parties that negotiations continue for another half day, up to a maximum of four half days (there was no such demand);
- information on the bid, ask and acceptance messages that could be sent bilaterally as well as messages for binding a preliminary contract or annulling a binding contract (which could be done at a cost of 15 per cent of the contract value up to the second day of the second round, 30 per cent thereafter);

- information that preliminary contracts which had not been annulled at the end of negotiations would be binding.

This experimental design, specified in the Instructions to the participants,[8] was determined against the background of the results of a set of pilot tests (as reported in Bohm and Carlén, 1997).

As explained above, the experiment was designed to mimic what real-world JI negotiations among these four countries could be expected to look like in several important respects. It should be pointed out that the hypothetical negotiations could not resemble their real counterparts on all points. Thus, preparations for the negotiations in the real-world case would most likely have been more extensive, especially with respect to estimating the social marginal abatement costs and the year 2000 BAU emission levels. Furthermore, the form of the negotiations may have been different, involving more meetings in person for example, and the duration of the negotiation process may have been much longer. There is no way of finding out the significance of such differences between the experiment and the real world, however trivial they may seem.

One point needs to be stressed: The fact that the cost curves and the BAU estimates may not be a replica of what they would have been if the negotiations were real, and that the deviations in this respect may have differed among the participating countries, does not imply that results in terms of percentage of cost savings achieved must become irrelevant. The primary reason is that the performance of the negotiation teams was assessed against the background of the BAU estimates they made public and the cost curves they deposited for the evaluation group, prior to the negotiations. The incentives provided by this procedure exist regardless of the degree of realism in these data.

4. THE NEGOTIATIONS

Communication between the teams was brisk right from the start of the negotiations. The chronology of the 25 bids and 15 offers made by the parties after negotiations restarted on day 2 are shown in Figure 16.4.

Negotiations slowed down during the third day. The teams could opt for a continuation of the negotiations for another half-day, but no one did. Before the formal conclusion of the negotiations, the secretariat acted as a middleman by suggesting deals midway between the highest outstanding bid and the lowest outstanding ask, but no additional agreement could be reached. The likely reason is shown below – most of the potential gains had already been harvested.

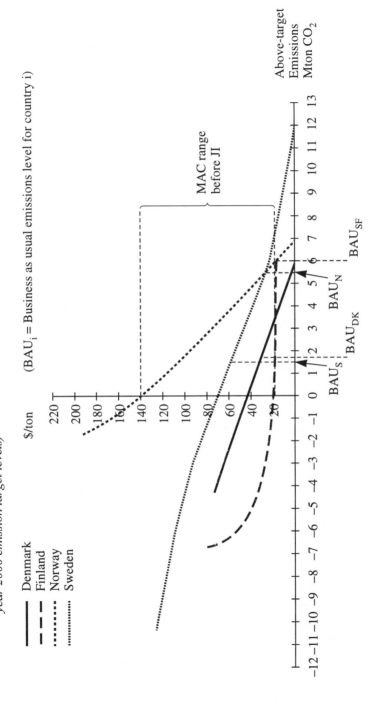

Figure 16.1 Marginal social abatement costs before JI (centred around the year 2000 emission target levels)

(BAU$_i$ = Business as usual emissions level for country i)

Figure 16.2 Marginal social abatement costs after JI (centred around the year 2000 emission target levels)

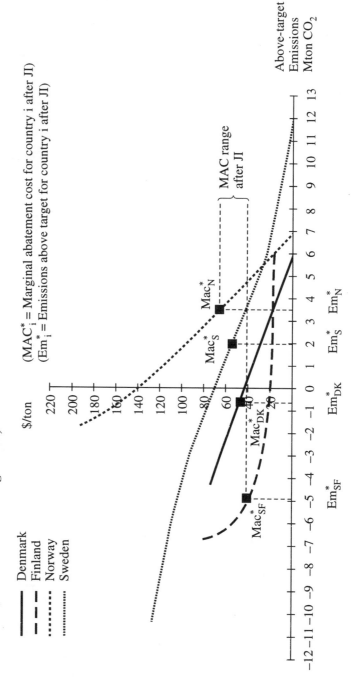

—— Denmark
– – – Finland
········· Norway
············ Sweden

(MAC_i^* = Marginal abatement cost for country i after JI)
(Em_i^* = Emissions above target for country i after JI)

Figure 16.3 Non realized JI gains

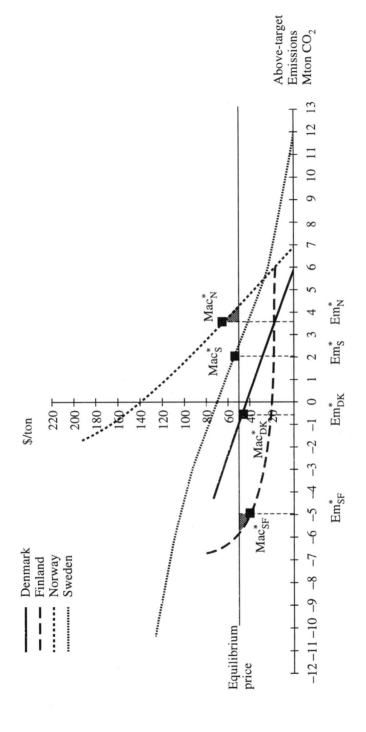

307

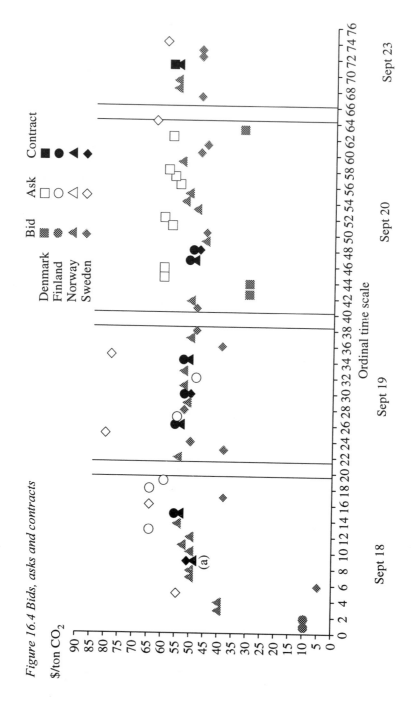

Figure 16.4 Bids, asks and contracts

Note (a): Annulled

308

5. RESULTS

The results of the experiment are summarized here and reported in more detail in Appendix 2.

The marginal social abatement costs reported as relevant for the negotiators' decisions and according to which their JI agreements would be evaluated by the evaluation team are presented in Figure 16.1 (see also the underlying data in Figure 16.5 in Appendix 2). The cost curves, which are centred around the year 2000 emission targets for the four countries, show that the countries, although similar in a number of other respects, emerge as quite different with respect to these costs. As shown in Figure 16.1, the highest marginal social abatement cost (MAC), measured at the emission levels where the countries would end up if each of them had attained their emission targets unilaterally, is about seven times the lowest MAC.

These differences in MAC reveal that there were significant potential gains from JI among the four countries. As expected, Norway and Sweden emerged as buyers. In Figure 16.2, a buyer country is shown by the fact that its emissions in the year 2000 are allowed to exceed its target level. The presumed roles of Denmark and Finland were interchanged in that Finland instead of Denmark became the dominating seller and Denmark was close to being a non-trader (see Figure 16.3).

A total of seven contracts were established, six with Finland and one with Denmark as sellers, and five with Norway and two with Sweden as buyers (see Table 16.4 in Appendix 2). Total trade amounted to 5.5 Mtonnes, almost one third of the total emission reduction required. JI implied that Finland reduced emissions by 5 Mtonnes and Denmark by 0.5 Mtonnes more, and Norway by 3.5 Mtonnes and Sweden by 2 Mtonnes less than their 1990 emission levels

As shown in Figure 16.2, JI significantly reduced the differences in MAC among the countries, but did not eliminate them. A fully efficient emission reduction trade, which would equalize the MACs, would not increase the JI gains to any large extent. This is shown by the shaded grey triangles marked in Figure 16.3. The JI gains actually attained are given by the areas above the sellers', and under the buyers', MAC curves from actual emission levels up to the target level (the origin in the diagram). These gains imply that 96.6 per cent of the maximum potential gains were attained. The gains were achieved by seven contracts only; see Figure 16.4 which shows the sequence of these contracts amid the bids and asks made during the negotiations.[9]

Figure 16.3 also indicates that the achievements by the four countries' negotiation teams were quite similar, in that the attained percentages of potential cost saving, defined by the perfectly competitive benchmark case, were quite similar. (For details see the last column, Table 16.5, Appendix 2.)

Finally, it should be noted that the aggregate abatement costs for the countries to achieve their emission targets for the year 2000 were \$713 million, if attained unilaterally, and \$345 million, or 48 per cent less, after JI as it was arranged here. It should be recalled that this gain concerns one year only, the year 2000. If the countries were committed to targets to reduce carbon emissions for that year, this commitment would most likely be the result of a decision that emissions in the long run must be held down. If so, the JI outcome for the year 2000 would be representative or even directly applicable as well for the year 2001 and so on by similar applications of JI, until such procedures might be replaced by more comprehensive international agreements.

6. CONCLUSION

The primary observations and results from the study were:

- Marginal abatement costs estimated at the assumed carbon emission target level for the year 2000 vary a great deal among the four countries in spite of their general similarities (see Figure 16.1).
- Given estimates of the costs of each country unilaterally meeting its year 2000 emission target, JI in the form of emission quota trade among the four countries succeeded in reducing these costs by around 50 per cent (see Tables 16.5 and 16.6 in Appendix 2, and Figure 16.2).
- The JI operations realized 97 per cent of the potential maximum cost savings (those which would have been attained by a market under perfect competition, see Figure 16.3).
- The performance of the four negotiating teams was quite similar in that their attained percentages of potential cost savings, defined by the perfectly competitive benchmark case, were similar.

Given that this was a one-shot test, where the results may have been influenced by chance events, it may be noted that the test was preceded by eleven pilot tests (using Ph.D. students and monetary rewards), which gave quite similar results.

In conclusion, the results imply that Joint Implementation as emission quota trade among committed developed countries, whereby monitoring problems are avoided, may offer significant cost savings.

APPENDIX 1: EVALUATION REPORT

November 11, 1996
Scott Barrett (London Business School),
Jean-Charles Hourcade (CIRED, Paris) and
Robert Stavins (Harvard University)

Evaluation objective

The objective of the evaluation is to determine how well the negotiating teams performed in their transactions, both collectively and individually. Our primary concern is thus with the outcome of the experiment. However, toward the end of this report we also comment briefly on the design and implementation of the experiment.

Evaluating potential aggregate JI gains

The potential gains from trade can be defined as the difference between the cost of meeting the emission targets unilaterally and the minimum cost of meeting the same collective target. For the former case, marginal abatement costs will typically differ among the countries. For the latter case they will be equalized. The allocation of abatement which minimizes the aggregate cost of meeting the collective target will be identical to that in the perfectly competitive equilibrium. At this equilibrium, all potential gains from trade are exhausted, and all transactions take place at the same price – a price which is equal to the marginal cost of abatement for every country.

Using the cost information supplied by the negotiators, we have calculated the costs of meeting their national emission targets unilaterally as well as the perfectly competitive abatement levels and associated costs. For details, see Appendix 2.

The potential gains from trade amount to $357 million (Appendix 2, Table 16.2). In other words, efficient abatement lowers the cost of achieving the collective emission target by about half (the cost of meeting the targets unilaterally is $713 million while the minimum cost of meeting the collective target is $356 million). This indicates that marginal abatement costs differ substantially between the countries, evaluated at the level of abatement needed to meet the abatement targets unilaterally.

Evaluating the aggregate gains from JI actually achieved

The JI experiment achieved the same collective abatement target at a total cost of $368 million, representing a net gain of $345 million as compared with the outcome where the national emission targets are met unilaterally.

Our calculations indicate that 96.6 per cent of the potential gains from trade were actually realized by the JI experiment. This is a striking result. Actual trading in the United States has resulted in gains from trade on the order of about 50 per cent – and this in the more successful emissions trading programs (Hahn and Stavins, 1991).

We cannot explain why this result occurred. To understand this would require that the experiment be replicated under varying circumstances. However, we suspect that among the factors that have led to this high realization in the gains from trade are that the technical costs of abatement were to a certain extent common knowledge, transactions costs were zero, and the abatement levels for the 'business-as-usual' scenarios were taken as given by the countries.

A related observation is that the prices at which the JI trades took place were very close to the competitive price. The experimental trades took place at prices within 15 per cent of the perfectly competitive price.

It is interesting to note that marginal abatement costs vary substantially even after trading (from $39 to $69 per tonne), despite the fact that trading realized almost all of the potential gains from trade. The reason for this is that the cost curves were fairly steep at the post-trading abatement levels.

We should also note that there are other benchmark outcomes with which we could compare the experimental results. For example, we have calculated the trading that would result were Denmark and Finland able to co-operate as a monopolist in the abatement market (Appendix 2, Table 16.3). This scenario results in a somewhat smaller gain from trade, resulting from the inefficiency of a monopoly market. However, we note that if the monopolist were able to practise first degree price discrimination, then the total gains from trade would be equal to that associated with the perfectly competitive solution; all that would change would be the distribution of the gains from trade and not the aggregate level. In our view, the perfectly competitive solution is the obvious one to use for purposes of comparison.

Evaluating individual country gains from JI trading

The first and perhaps most important observation is that all countries gain from JI trading. Of course, some countries gain more than others. However, care must be taken in interpreting these individual country gains. We have calculated the gains from trade for each of the countries associated with the perfectly competitive solution, and these are very similar to the actual gains from trade realized by each of the countries. This indicates that the differences in the gains realized by the countries mainly reflect differences in the marginal abatement cost functions and levels, not the negotiating skills of the individual countries. Each of the countries realizes at least 91 per cent of its potential gains from trade as defined by the perfectly competitive solution. Nevertheless, there is substantial variation among countries in their percentage cost savings, which range from about 11 per cent in the case of Denmark to 145 per cent in the case of Finland (the latter indicating that engaging in the JI program not only saved on costs for Finland, but was actually profitable).

Comments on the design and implementation of the experiment

Though we are not experts in experimental economics, we believe that the results may depend on the context of the negotiation experiment. As noted earlier, the parties to the bargaining were broadly knowledgeable about each nation's abatement costs, especially their technical abatement costs. We believe that it was commonly known that the marginal abatement costs for Sweden and Norway were 'high', and that these costs for Finland and Denmark were 'low'. Furthermore, there was some indication about the magnitudes of these costs. The fact that the countries involved interact repeatedly over a large range of issues implies that they may share a certain degree of 'trust'. Individual members of the country teams may also have known each other personally. To be sure, this is not a failure of design. To the contrary, the above circumstances may reflect the situation that may arise if trading were actually to be carried out.

APPENDIX 2: RESULTS

Peter Bohm and Björn Carlén

The countries participating in the experiment were taken to be committed to the emission reductions stated in Table 16.1. The countries' social marginal abatement costs are shown in the diagrams at the end of the Appendix.

Table 16.1 Business-as-usual scenarios (BAUs), targets for the year 2000 and the resulting emission reduction commitments (Mtonnes of CO_2)

Country	BAU	Target	Emission reduction
Denmark	53.8	52.1	1.7
Finland	60.0	54.0	6.0
Norway	41.0	35.6	5.4
Sweden	62.9	61.3	1.6
Total	**217.7**	**203.0**	**14.7**

Tables 16.2 and 16.3 present two benchmarks for evaluating the JI outcome in the experiment. Table 16.2 describes the case where JI would take the form of activities on a perfectly competitive market, while Table 16.3 portrays a particular monopoly solution. The tables are organized as follows. Column:

2 – repeats the emission reductions to which the countries are committed;
3 – shows the costs the countries would face if they chose to meet their commitment unilaterally;
4 – shows the net emission reduction trade, i.e., how much each country exceeds (+) or falls short of (-) its emission reduction commitments as a result of perfect JI (Table 16.2) or JI when two countries act as a joint monopoly (Table 16.3);
5 – states emission reductions after JI for each country;
6 – states emission reduction costs after JI for each country;
7 – presents the countries' gains from a case of fully efficient JI; an emission reduction exporting country's gains are calculated as export revenues *minus* the additional abatement costs; an emission reduction importing country's gains equal abatement cost savings *minus* expenditure on imported emission reductions.

Table 16.2 Fully efficient JI

Country	Unilateral reduction		Trade	Ex. post JI		
	Reduction (Mtonne)	Cost ($m)	Exp./Imp (Mtonne)	Reduction (Mtonne)	Cost ($m)	Net gain ($m)
1	2	3	4	5	6	7
Denmark	1.7	61	1.19	2.9	116	5.1
Finland	6.0	94	5.76	11.8	251	132.2
Norway	5.4	456	-4.4	1.0	40	194.5
Sweden	1.6	102	-2.55	-1.0	-51	25.1
Total	14.7	713	±6.95	14.7	356	356.9

If JI would take the form of trade on a perfectly competitive market (Table 16.2, columns 4-7), the equilibrium price would be $50.31 per tonne of emission reduction. Denmark and Finland would export 6.95 Mtonnes of emission reductions to Norway and Sweden at this price (see column 4). After trade, the total cost for the countries to reach their joint emission target would amount to $356 million, which is also the minimum cost. Compared to the case where each country unilaterally meets its target (Table 16.2, column 3), the total aggregate cost is lowered by $357 million, or by 50 per cent. It follows that this cost saving constitutes the maximum feasible aggregate gain from JI.

Table 16.3 describes the outcome if the two exporting countries (Denmark and Finland) would co-operate and manage to maximize their aggregate profit as a single monopoly using a uniform price. In this particular case, Finland would be the only country to actually sell emission reductions, i.e., to abate more than required by its emission target. Denmark's role would be to withhold supply. The monopoly price equals $64.02 per tonne of emission reduction. At this price Finland would export 4.52 Mtonne to Norway and Sweden. Some trade would also occur within the coalition itself in order to minimize costs. This trade, amounting to 0.44 Mtonne, would go from Finland to Denmark. Table 16.3 shows the separate profits for Norway and Sweden and the joint profits for Finland and Denmark.

Table 16.3 Monopoly solution

Country	Unilateral reduction		Trade	Ex. post JI		
	Reduction (Mtonne)	Cost ($m)	Exp./Imp (Mtonne)	Reduction (Mtonne)	Cost ($m)	Net gain ($m)
1	2	3	4	5	6	7
Denmark	1.7	61	-0.44	1.26	43.2	↓
Finland	6.0	94	4.96	10.96	214.2	168.6
Norway	5.4	456	-3.73	1.67	75.9	156.5
Sweden	1.6	102	-0.79	0.81	49.1	5.5
Total	14.7	713	±4.96	14.7	382	331

The cost savings from the trade in Table 16.3 amounts to $331 million. As can be seen by comparing the total net gains in Tables 16.2 and 16.3, the trade gains achieved under this monopoly solution amount to 93 per cent (331/357) of those achieved under perfect competition. In physical terms, 2.43 Mtonne or 35 per cent of the efficient trade does not materialize under the monopoly solution.

The seven trade agreements reached in the experiment are shown in Table 16.4 in chronological order.

Table 16.4 Sequence of trades

Trade No.	Seller	Quantity (Mtonne)	Price ($/tonne)	Buyer
1	Finland	1.0	55	Norway
2	Finland	0.5	55	Norway
3	Finland	1.0	52	Sweden
4	Finland	0.75	52	Norway
5	Finland	1.0	48	Sweden
6	Finland	0.75	50	Norway
7	Denmark	0.5	57	Norway

Total trades amounted to 5.5 Mtonnes, about one third of the emission reduction required. The average price of these contracts is $52.27 per tonne, which is slightly more than the perfectly competitive equilibrium price ($50.31 per tonne). By jointly implementing their emission reductions, the countries were able to reach their joint emission target at a cost which was $345 million, or 48 per cent, lower than if each country had fulfilled its emission target unilaterally. This means that 96.6 per cent of the maximum aggregate net gain is realized. In physical terms, around 1.45 Mtonne (or 21 per cent) of the efficient trade is not carried out. The outcome of the JI negotiations is shown in Table 16.5.

In Table 16.6 the costs savings achieved are expressed as percentages of the countries' unilateral abatement costs.

The countries' social marginal abatement costs as reported by the negotiating teams are shown in Figure 16.5. These curves are reproduced in Figures 16.1–16.3.

Table 16.5 Joint implementation among four countries (the fully efficient JI in parentheses)

Country	Unilateral reduction		Trade	Ex. post JI		
	Reduction (Mtonne)	Cost ($m)	Exp./Imp (Mtonne)	Reduction (Mtonne)	Cost ($m)	Net gain ($m)
1	2	3	4	5	6	7
Denmark	1.7	61	0.5 (1.19)	2.2 (2.9)	83 (116)	6.7 (5.1)
Finland	6.0	94	5 (5.76)	11 (11.8)	216 (25)	136 (132.2)
Norway	5.4	456	-3.5 (-4.4)	1.9 (1.0)	91 (40)	178 (194.5)
Sweden	1.6	102	-2 (-2.55)	-0.4 (-1.0)	-22 (-51)	24.4 (25.1)
Total	14.7	713	±5.5 (±6.95)	14.7 (14.7)	368 (356)	345 (357)

Table 16.6 Total cost savings

Country	Actual net gain ($million)	Unilateral abatement cost ($million)	Net gain relative to abatement cost (%)
Denmark	6.7	61	11
Finland	136.0	94	145
Norway	177.7	456	39
Sweden	24.4	102	24
Total	344.8	713	48

Figure 16.5 Social marginal abatement costs

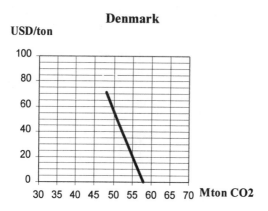

BAU (2000)   =   53.8   **Target (2000) =   52.1**

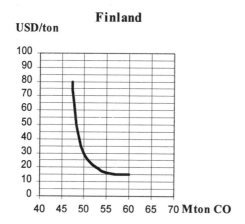

BAU (2000)   =   60.0   **Target (2000) =   54.0**

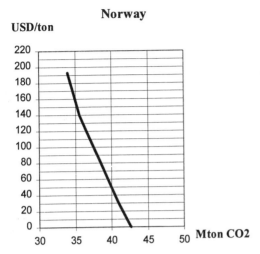

BAU (2000) = **41.0**   **Target (2000)** = **35.6**

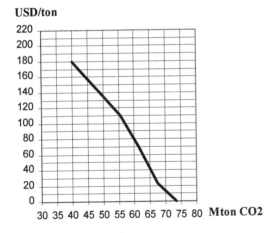

BAU (2000) = **62.9**   **Target (2000)** = **61.3**

NOTES

1 This chapter reports the results of an experiment carried out during September 1996. The experiment was commissioned by the Ad Hoc Group for Energy Related Climate Change Issues of the Nordic Council of Ministers. The members of the Group are Jørgen Abildgaard (Chairman), Olle Björk, Jon D. Engebretsen, Jón Ingimarsson, Seppo Oikarinen, Peter Molander, Lisbeth Nielsen and Camilla Rosenhagen. This is a reprint of the report 'Joint Implementation as Emissions Quota Trade: An Experiment Among Four Nordic Countries' (copyright: the Nordic Council of Ministers), excluding Appendix 3 which contains the instructions to the negotiating teams. The full report, NORD 1997:4, can be ordered from the Nordic Council of Ministers, Store Strandgade 18, DK-1255 Copenhagen K. I am grateful to Björn Carlén for his assistance in planning and running the pilot tests and in administering the final experiment, and to Scott Barrett, Jean-Charles Hourcade and Robert Stavins for their evaluation of the experiment (see Appendix 1). The members of the Ad Hoc Group who agreed to launch the experiment were instrumental in convincing their respective home ministries or government agencies to support the carrying out of this project and, in particular, to select representative members of the negotiating teams.

2 In the Kyoto Protocol the term Clean Development Mechanism is used for a concept similar to JI in this particular sense.

3 Some observers may even regard a couple of these countries as having in fact committed themselves to such a target or an even more stringent one. Thus, it may be mentioned that Denmark has committed itself to the more ambitious target of staying 20 per cent below its 1988 emission level by the year 2005.

4 The Danish Energy Agency, the Finnish Ministry of Trade and Industry, the Norwegian Ministry of Industry and Energy, and the Swedish Ministry of Industry and Trade.

5 The evaluation team consisted of Scott Barrett, London School of Economics, London, Jean-Charles Hourcade, CIRED-CNRS, Paris, and Robert Stavins, Harvard University, Cambridge, MA, all of whom are internationally recognized experts in the field. This is further acknowledged by their status as lead authors of the Second Assessment Report, Intergovernmental Panel of Climate Change (IPCC) Working Group III. The evaluation report is reproduced as Appendix 1 of this chapter.

6 The expected year 2000 business-as-usual (BAU) emissions for each country can also be taken to be widely known among the other three countries. In the experiment, the countries were required to make public among themselves their respective BAU estimates and told to base unilateral as well as negotiated emission reductions on these BAU levels. As can be seen from the report presented in Appendix 1, the evaluators point out as a circumstance that may influence the results that, in the real world, BAU estimates would not be known with certainty. This is a correct observation, of course, but probably not of decisive importance if, in the real world, governments would have to make up their minds before the negotiations are over what directives (in terms of BAU emissions and otherwise) to hand over to their negotiating teams.

7 The relevant range could in fact extend beyond the country's BAU emission level. Initially, the secretariat incorrectly indicated that the cost data to be delivered should *not* be beyond the country's BAU emission level. The first day of a maximum of six days of negotiations was wasted, and the agreements reached during that day had to be annulled, due to the fact that the secretariat had initially given the teams incorrect information on this point. They had been asked to deliver cost data starting from the BAU 2000 (where tax levels were taken to be at least equal to today's level) instead of the emission levels at

a zero domestic carbon tax level. The teams were able to provide the new information requested without much delay. The mistake had no serious consequences other than that Norway, which, as a result, lost a contract with Sweden, may have provided Sweden with undue information.

[8] The Instructions are available as Appendix 3 in the full report of this experiment; see note 1.

[9] This diagram was originally in colour. The black and white version does not allow countries to be distinquished.

REFERENCES

Ad Hoc Group on Energy Related Climate Issues (1995), *Joint Implementation as a Measure to Curb Climate Change: Nordic Perspectives and Priorities*, TemaNord 1995.534, Nordic Council of Ministers, Copenhagen.

Bohm, P. and B. Carlén (1997), 'Laboratory Tests of Joint Implementation Among Four Countries Taken to be Committed to Stringent Carbon Emission Targets', Working Paper 1997:3, Department of Economics, Stockholm University, Stockholm, (forthcoming in *Resource & Energy Economics*).

Hahn, R. and R. Stavins (1991), 'Incentive-Based Environmental Regulation: A new era from an old idea?', *Ecology Law Quarterly*, **18**.

Intergovernmental Panel on Climate Change (IPPC) (1996), Working Group III, *Climate Change 1995: Economic and Social Dimensions of Climate Change*, Cambridge University Press, Cambridge.

322 - 42

F18   925   423
           928

17. International tradable carbon permits as a strong form of joint implementation[1]

ZhongXiang Zhang and Andries Nentjes

1. INTRODUCTION

The concept of international tradable carbon permits has been discussed in scientific circles for over ten years. Since mid 1996, however, it has become a subject of more than just academic interest. The main reason for this change is to be found in the US Draft Protocol to the Framework Convention on Climate Change (FCCC), submitted by the US government on 17 January 1997. The US contribution to preparations for the third Conference of the Parties (COP3) to the FCCC, held in Kyoto in December 1997, represents the first concrete official proposal for an international emissions trading scheme. The European Union (EU) proposal for internal community burden sharing is also in line with the broad definition of emissions trading, although the individual country quotas are currently not transferable. These proposals clearly indicate that international trade in carbon dioxide (CO_2) emissions has turned into a politically relevant subject.[2]

In this chapter we use the term 'strong form' deliberately to distinguish a tradable carbon permit (TCP) scheme from a weak form of project level joint implementation.[3] We focus on discussing the following three aspects: (1) basic requirements for a TCP scheme; (2) a blueprint for designing national TCP schemes; and (3) constituting elements of an international TCP scheme. By discussing these aspects, the chapter indicates what a TCP scheme could look like and how it relates to joint implementation.

2. BASIC REQUIREMENTS FOR A TCP SCHEME

Greenhouse gases are uniformly mixed pollutants, i.e. one tonne of a greenhouse gas emitted anywhere on earth has the same effect as one tonne emitted

322

somewhere else. This means that it does not matter where reductions in greenhouse gas emissions take place; what is important is whether we are able to reduce the emissions effectively on a global scale. This provides the environmental rationale for TCP. Moreover, a TCP scheme is both economically efficient and environmentally effective, whereas other instruments are either not as effective (e.g. a carbon tax) or not as efficient (e.g. emission standards). Thus, an international TCP scheme is considered by many to be the most promising way to control CO_2 emissions (IPCC, 1996; UNCTAD, 1995). Then, what are the basic requirements for setting up a successful international TCP scheme?

First, there should be an international agreement or a protocol to the FCCC in which legally binding emission targets and timetables have been set. Countries that would wish to participate in an international TCP scheme should be committed to the binding obligations. This means that prospective participating countries are at least signatories to the FCCC. At the time of writing, a negotiating process towards such a protocol, in accordance with the Berlin Mandate adopted at the first Conference of the Parties to the FCCC in Berlin in April 1995, is well under way. It is likely that a protocol will be adopted at COP3 and that the new protocol will set emission targets and timetables (Dudek and Goffman, 1997; Matsuo, 1997; Mullins and Baron, 1997). The negotiated emission targets would then serve as a basis for determining the emission limits for individual countries in an international TCP scheme. Even though non-Annex I Parties to the FCCC (i.e. the developing countries) already have general commitments under the FCCC it is unlikely that the new protocol will commit these Parties to any specific emission targets. Given that binding emission limits are a necessary prerequisite for setting up a TCP scheme (Dudek and Goffman, 1997; Mullins and Baron, 1997), an international TCP scheme would be unlikely, at least initially, to include the developing countries.

Second, in this scheme emissions are transferred between sources in the countries involved. This condition should ensure that the scheme operates between entities that have the information and the incentives to secure the opportunities for lowering their costs of reducing carbon emissions by buying and selling carbon permits. In this respect the scheme should operate in a way that does not differ from international trades in any other commodity. This view of international carbon trade differs from some competing proposals which view the transfer of carbon quotas as the domain of governments negotiating with each other, where governments have to distribute their additional emissions or emission reductions among their national sources (legal entities). We think that allowing trading among individual emission sources could significantly improve cost-effectiveness because it would provide sources with strong incentives to exploit cost-effective abatement opportunities. By increasing the number of trades, it would also improve market liquidity and reduce the potential for abuse of market power. The latter might occur in governmental trading if one country or bloc holds a significant proportion of the total number of permits. Another major consideration is that national governments possess only global and imprecise information about CO_2 emission reduction options and their marginal cost. They can therefore make errors in their decisions of how many permits to buy or sell. Individual sources which have information on their technical options and costs can choose their efficient emission level by comparing marginal costs and the international permit price. Moreover, inter-source trading may lead to lower transaction costs than inter-governmental trading (Mullins and Baron, 1997). Finally, there is some suspicion that governments could lose their stance on domestic actions when facing political pressure to expand or contract purchases of permits abroad, just as there is pressure on central banks to set higher or lower interest rates (Palmisano, 1997).

However, we have to bear in mind that to make inter-source trading operational is not a simple matter. It can only be effective when complemented by stringent monitoring and vigorous enforcement by countries participating in the scheme. This brings up the issue of consistency in an international TCP scheme. It demands that the countries participating in the scheme have to first establish their national TCP schemes. Moreover, these national schemes should be compatible with each other.

The question arising from the requirement that an international TCP scheme should bring together countries with national TCP schemes is which preconditions should be fulfilled before a country could even consider to begin such a national scheme. We think that a basic requirement is that national environmental policy should have evolved to a stage of institutional maturity which ensures that the following conditions are satisfied.

First, governments should preferably have experiences with formulating national emission targets and timetables; not only as a paper exercise but as a binding emission obligation that has to be taken seriously and has to be translated into policies and measures to implement it.

Second, there should exist a reliable national registry of individual emission sources that could participate in a TCP scheme. Without such an inventory of sources and their present emission levels it would be impossible to design a scheme for permit allocation by means of grandfathering. Moreover, since countries (not sources) sign international agreements and it is the responsibility of governments to ensure that their countries are in compliance with the national emission limits, inter-source trading would have to be accounted for at the national level. This also underlines the need for such an inventory.

Third, there should be in place some system of monitoring emissions, either directly or indirectly. This is to ensure, among other purposes, that the emission permits sold by any source would represent real emission reductions from the allowed emissions levels. This, combined with the above requirement for accurate emission inventories, would provide certainty about the validity of permits traded, thus increasing confidence in the scheme and incentives for inter-source trading.

Fourth, there should be a tradition of effective enforcement; that is, detection of non-compliance and application of sanctions. Although enforcement is necessary for effective application of other instruments as well (e.g. charges and regulations), this requirement is of particular importance to TCP because under a TCP scheme firms which operate in a country without adequate enforcement can emit without handing over their permits. Consequently, they can sell their permits to firms in other countries, thus leading to increased emissions in those countries. By contrast, when charges or regulations are used, firms which defraud cannot sell permits to sources in other countries. Clearly, if enforcement was inadequate, it would be easy for a firm to sell permits or refrain from buying permits without taking adequate measures to reduce emissions. Consequently, a TCP scheme would lead to higher overall pollution levels compared with instruments like charges or regulations. Besides, enforcement at the international level often proves to be more difficult and less likely to be effective than at the national level because of the absence of an institution with the international jurisdiction to enforce policy. This further underlines the importance of national legal mechanisms for enforcement.

From the preceding discussion, it follows that a domestic TCP is bound to be a failure if the infrastructure defined by the four conditions does not exist. So where do countries now stand in this regard? For example, we notice that in the Netherlands, a country with a highly regarded environmental policy, the last four preconditions were not fulfilled 20 years ago; perhaps even not 10 years ago. A number of countries in the EU where environmental policy is less advanced do not meet the conditions at this very moment. The same holds for those countries with economies in transition, which are also listed in Annex I to the FCCC. They are still not ready yet for establishing national TCP schemes. This raises the question of whether the EU can participate as a whole in an international TCP scheme requiring high standards of compliance, a proposal put forward by the EU Council of Environment Ministers at their meeting in March 1997. Nevertheless this indicates that not all Annex I countries, and possibly not even all Annex II (OECD) countries, would qualify for engaging in emissions trading according to the above-specified conditions. This suggests that a TCP scheme might initially begin with only a handful of OECD countries, although this does not preclude its subsequent expansion to include other qualified countries. The narrow scope of participation would imply a smaller scope for efficiency gains than could be expected from wide participation beyond the OECD, but these are nevertheless larger than without emissions trading (IPCC, 1996; Richels et al., 1996). A major advantage of starting small and under optimal conditions is that such a 'demonstration project' would reduce uncertainties and accordingly increase confidence in the permit market. Moreover, since initial participating countries are all parties to the GATT/WTO, it might even be possible that enforcing an international TCP scheme can go beyond persuasion and adverse publicity by means of using trade measures, provided these do not violate the GATT/WTO rules. Besides, so far there has been limited international experience with tradable permits. While tradable permits have enjoyed some considerable success in various domestic contexts, this by no means guarantees their success in an international context (Tietenberg and Victor, 1994). Thus, such a scheme should initially be validated through more experience on a small rather than a large scale. In this regard, the initial experiment of implementing an international TCP scheme within a limited number of countries would serve the very important purpose of ensuring a smooth evolution of an international TCP scheme and providing opportunities for the various supporting administrative institutions to 'learn by doing' and for all potential participants to learn more about how such a scheme works (Tietenberg and Victor, 1994; Zhang, 1997). Thus, the phasing process is deemed necessary and can be an advantage rather than a disadvantage (Tietenberg, 1995; UNCTAD, 1995).

3. BLUEPRINT FOR DESIGNING A NATIONAL TCP SCHEME

Since a national TCP programme is the basis and precondition for a successful international TCP scheme we start by discussing the constituting elements of a national scheme. Attention is paid to: (1) the definition of the permits; (2) the issue of permits; (3) the initial distribution of the permits; (4) the permit market; (5) compliance with the scheme; and (6) its administrative cost.

3.1. Definition of the permits

For the time being, fuel saving and inter-fuel substitution are the major economically feasible options for reducing CO_2 emissions. For that reason and also for reasons of administrative efficiency and enforcement it makes sense to implement a policy of restricting CO_2 emissions by means of tradable permits for the carbon contained in fuels. The allowed national levels of carbon emissions can be based on the internationally agreed CO_2 emission targets and timetables. On this basis, a given number of tradable carbon permits are issued. A carbon permit is equivalent to a tonne of carbon, one carbon permit allowing the use of a quantity of fossil fuels which contains a tonne of carbon.

Within the jurisdiction where the carbon permit scheme applies, the permits are not limited in any way with regard to the period or place where they can be used. Restriction of place makes no sense because CO_2 is a uniformly mixed pollutant: its impact on climate is independent of the place where it is released. Restriction of time would be unnecessary since the greenhouse effect is caused by the accumulation of CO_2 and other greenhouse gases. Therefore, permit holders could be allowed to bank their unused permits to offset future emissions or to sell them to others. If property rights to permits are well defined, banking would encourage permit holders to go further with reducing emissions than their required emission limit in early years if it were more cost-effective for them to do so. Governments should not confiscate banked permits even if the latest scientific evidence suggests that further emission reductions are necessary. A more acceptable approach would be to reduce the issue of new permits proportionally from the year for which the stricter emissions cap applies. This suggests that a TCP scheme would have to be designed from the outset to be flexible enough to facilitate any changes that might be required in the overall emission limit.

3.2. Issue of the permits

The number of permits that can be issued annually is determined by the national emission targets. Each year a new vintage of permits can be made available. The carbon permits can be used from the year in which they are issued onwards. Put another way, the carbon permits are issued as an emissions budget that would allow permit holders to meet their target on average over a period of, for example, 3 to 10 years.

Since fossil fuels are an essential resource for the economy, a steady supply at a reasonable stable or steadily changing price is a necessary condition for economic stability. To avoid bottlenecks caused by a temporary lack of permits in the initial stage, the emission limit for the first stage should not be too strict, allowing permit holders to save or bank permits for later use. The US Acid Rain Program gives a good example of such an approach.

If a country starts with a strict limit on CO_2 emissions, bottlenecks could be prevented by allowing the borrowing of a limited amount of future permits provided that a premium is paid. By taking into account the turnover of capital stock, the prospect for low-carbon or carbon-free backstop technologies, and time discounting, borrowing would allow total abatement costs to be minimized while keeping to an overall emissions budget. Therefore, as with banking, borrowing is another way to increase flexibility and lower the cost of abating CO_2 emissions (Richels et al., 1996).

However, borrowing should be used with considerable caution because there are many problematic issues associated with it (Matsuo, 1997; Mullins and Baron, 1997). Borrowing would make it more difficult to check whether emission sources are in compliance with their emission limits. If borrowing is allowed, firms facing bankruptcy have an incentive to borrow without being able to meet their future commitments. Borrowing may tend to discourage trading among individual emission sources, thus reducing market liquidity. Borrowing may also undermine the incentive to search for cleaner technologies. To some extent, the delayed response will mean additional committed warming. All this suggests that safeguards should be developed to allow borrowing in such a way that it does not undermine the environmental objectives. Such safeguards may include:

- limiting the contribution of borrowing to meeting an emission target;
- restricting borrowed permits to own use, rather than sale to others;
- making the allowance of borrowing contingent on the stringency of overall emission limits (perhaps postponing its adoption until more stringent limits are agreed); and
- restricting how far into the future permits can be borrowed.

The last option depends on how often the Conference of the Parties to the FCCC is supposed to review the adequacy of commitments by the parties to the FCCC and on stability considerations. The former may favour shorter rather than longer budget periods; while the latter requires that emission targets and planned permit allocations should be formulated for long periods in order to reduce uncertainty for permit holders in planning their investment and fuel consumption. Clearly, a compromise needs to be reached between the desirability of allowing borrowing and its environmental effectiveness.

3.3. Distribution of permits

The initial distribution of permits among users can be organized as an auction (which implies that permits are sold to the buyers who make the highest bids), or permits could be distributed among fuel users for free, according to certain criteria. Auctioning of permits brings in revenue for the government, whereas grandfathering means distributing permits for free. As a basis the environmental authority can take the 'historical rights' of established polluters: existing sources receive an amount of permits which is a given fraction of their carbon consumption in a reference year.

With grandfathering, polluters can save considerable expenditures, since the individual source has to pay only for additional permits, if needed. Taken as a group, permit holders who receive permits for free will only have to make additional expenditure for reducing fuel use. Consequently, the political resistance of industry against the use of economic instruments to control CO_2 emissions can be overcome more easily with a system of tradable permits with grandfathering than with auctioned permits (Nentjes and Dijkstra, 1994). Moreover, a TCP scheme creates an asset of value to firms. So, even if a firm has to buy permits now to cover all of its emissions, it still can acquire the value of those additional permits by selling them in the future if its actual emissions are lower than what it is allowed to emit. This in turn creates an incentive for firms to comply with their caps. This scheme is also more attractive to firms than carbon taxes, because the latter scheme extracts revenues from firms without offering any compensation, let alone the political difficulties of introducing such taxes in countries such as the US.

Figure 17.1 shows a system for distributing carbon permits, which is a compromise between enhancing the political feasibility of tradable permits and keeping the administrative cost of grandfathering in check. It can be seen that a portion of the permits are grandfathered to fuel-intensive industries, while the other permits are auctioned by the government or its agency. Some of the auctioned permits are sold directly to end users, in particular to industry, and the rest are auctioned to fuel distributors who act as a purchaser for the smallest end users, including households and individual car owners.

Figure 17.1 Distribution of carbon permits

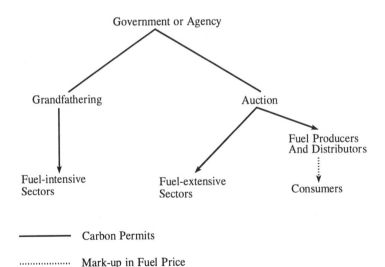

Carbon Permits

Mark-up in Fuel Price

Generally speaking, oil refineries, the chemical industry, basic metals, electricity producers, and freight transport are considered as fuel-intensive sectors. These would fall under the grandfathering regime. The remaining industrial sectors together with agriculture, households, services and (personal) transport can be taken as falling under the auctioning regime, either directly or indirectly (see below). The major argument for grandfathering permits is to exempt the fuel-intensive sectors from a considerable financial expenditure which would mobilize strong political opposition against a system of tradable permits. This is of particular importance in open economies where the fuel-intensive sectors have to compete on international product markets with those in countries that have made no hard commitments to reducing CO_2 emissions.

Grandfathering of tradable permits to small fuel users would entail high transaction cost, since it would be necessary to determine the carbon quota for each single user. Furthermore, experience in the Netherlands shows that it is easier to impose carbon taxes on small users like households and firms in fuel-extensive sectors than in fuel-intensive, export-oriented sectors. For this reason we envision a scheme in which permits are auctioned either directly to users with medium fuel use or to fuel distributors. If permits were awarded free to fuel distributors they would reap the rent of the higher fuel prices that would be necessary to reduce fuel use. This would not be accepted by other groups in society and therefore, in our view, it is not a politically feasible option. Under the auctioning regime, the distributors act on behalf of the groups with lowest fuel use, in particular households. For the Netherlands the most relevant examples are natural gas consumption of households and petrol and gasoline consumption of cars. Distributors sell fossil fuels to customers from these sectors, putting a mark-up on the fuel price which is equal to the price of the permits. With such a system small fuel users are exempted from the necessity (and transaction costs) of buying permits. Yet the rise in fuel price will motivate them to reduce fuel consumption or to switch from fuels with a high carbon content, such as coal, to fuels with a low carbon content such as natural gas.

3.4. The permit market

In the system outlined above two markets can be discerned. First, there is the auction of a portion of the permits by the government or its agency to fuel users, mainly the firms and fuel distributors that do not receive their permits for free. This market can be called the primary market. Next to that a secondary market will develop where firms with a surplus of permits trade with fuel users who have a shortage of permits. Arbitrage will equalize permit prices between the two markets.

The auction of carbon permits could be designed in such a manner that all bidders pay the price of the marginal buyer. Alternatively, it could be designed to conform to the example of the US Acid Rain Program.[4] In each case, the auction can be held once or twice a year. A fixed number of permits is offered, equivalent to carbon use for half a year or a full year. Potential buyers have to send in sealed orders, stating the number of permits they are willing to buy at a stated maximum price. The auctioneer then supplies permits beginning with the highest bidder until the excess supply is zero. The revenue from the auction is available for government expenditure or for a general or specific cut in taxes.

The number of potential actors on the secondary market is large. In the Netherlands, for example, there are more than 45,000 sources in industry alone. In addition to these, energy suppliers, such as gas distribution companies and power generators, can be expected to trade. Transaction costs may be relatively large for small fuel users. As we have seen, they can arrange for their fuel supplier to provide the carbon permits, complementary to the fuel. The supplier will pass on the permit cost as a mark-up on the fuel price.

3.5. Monitoring and enforcement

Monitoring of carbon use can be grafted onto the existing monitoring systems for levying taxes on fossil oil. For every tonne of fossil fuel that energy users purchase from distributors, they have to transfer an equivalent number of carbon permits. Distributors in turn can only obtain fuels from their suppliers in exchange for carbon permits. This way all permits will end up in the hands of producers and importers of fuel, including the permits purchased by distributors to cover their fuel supply to consumers and other small users that do not buy permits.

At the end of the year or the budget period, every fuel producer and importer has to report the type and quantity of fuels sold and the changes in fuel stocks. In addition, the fuel supplier has to show the enforcement agency that he has a sufficient number of permits on his account to cover the carbon equivalent of the fuel he has produced or imported. Following the example of the US Acid Rain Program, the firm can be granted a grace period (e.g. one month) to buy additional permits if necessary. If after this period for settling the account the firm does not comply with its cap, it has to pay a fine for each excess tonne of carbon. Such a fine for non compliance should be set high, say, five to ten times the average carbon permit price in the past year, for the following reasons. The first is consideration of the international implications of a domestic TCP scheme. By selling their emissions on an international TCP market, non-complying firms in one country would raise the overall supply of permits on the market and lower the value of the permits held by all the others, thus undermining the credibility of an international TCP scheme. Second, there are additional administrative costs in comparison with the US Acid Rain Program in which no reporting of domestic actions to any international organization is required. As required by the FCCC, Annex I countries in meeting their commitments to limiting greenhouse gas emissions have to deliver their national communications to the FCCC for review, and their governments as the parties to the FCCC would be accountable if their national emission limits were above the allowed levels. This requires these governments to take enhanced monitoring and enforcement efforts to ensure national compliance regardless of whether a TCP scheme is adopted.

On the other hand, the fines should not be too severe, at least in the initial stage of a TCP scheme during which it is very important to reveal the marginal abatement costs among emission sources. Otherwise risk-averse firms would hold surplus permits rather than sell them in order to avoid the risk of non-compliance. This will reduce trades and thus limit market liquidity and efficiency. Thus, there is a clear trade-off between environmental effectiveness and cost-effectiveness in setting the level of fines. Whatever levels are set, fines from non-compliance can be added to a 'Green Fund' for strengthening the research, development and diffusion of climate friendly technologies, or further enhancing governments' monitoring and enforcement efforts, or for assisting developing countries in reducing their greenhouse gas emissions, or for compensating oil exporting countries if fossil fuel uses are reduced as a result of actions taken to protect the global climate.

By focusing on producers and importers the number of firms that have to be monitored for compliance is relatively small. They have either received the permits from their customers or bought them at the auction to cover fuel consumption of non-permit holders. Figure 17.2 illustrates the system of monitoring. The advantage of supervising compliance with the tradable permit system in this way is that the existing institutions for levying excise duty on fossil fuels, which exist in most industrialized countries, can be used to enforce the TCP scheme.

Figure 17.2 Monitoring compliance

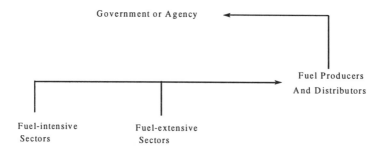

3.6. Administrative cost

Expenditure is required for preparing and initiating the system. In particular there are costs associated with collecting data on historic fuel use and with making decisions on the quota which firms will receive when permits are grandfathered.[5]

Recurrent annual costs consist of monitoring and enforcement and the cost of carbon permit trades. The first cost factor, monitoring and enforcement, will be comparable to that of implementing a charge on carbon in fossil fuels. Its cost per permit will not differ very much from the cost of the existing system for levying excise duty on fossil fuels. Since monitoring and enforcement concentrate on fuel producers and importers, registration can be restricted to their transactions. Other transaction costs, mainly brokers' costs, are directly borne by purchasers and sellers. In the US Acid Rain Program these are less than 5 per cent of transaction value (Klaassen and Nentjes, 1997). Since the number of sources in a TCP scheme is higher, we expect the transaction costs per permit to be lower.

4. CONSTITUTING ELEMENTS OF AN INTERNATIONAL TCP SCHEME

Once national permit markets are established, the next question is which elements should be added to extend them to an international market where a permit holder in country A can trade with a party in country B. For this, additional rules and agencies are required.

To ensure compatibility of linked national TCP schemes it is essential to have a rule that defines the type of permit that can be fully exchangeable internationally. Ideally the permit should be uniform. It can be defined as a tonne of carbon emissions when an emissions trading scheme only covers CO_2 emissions. If greenhouse gases other than CO_2 are involved, the permit can be defined in terms of 'tonnes of carbon equivalent emissions' as in the US Draft Protocol, or 'carbon equivalent units' as in Dudek and Goffman (1997), or something similar.

However, uniformity is not strictly necessary. A sufficient condition is that participating countries come to agree on conversion factors or fixed rates of exchange that would enable the translation of one permit of country A into an equivalent number of permits in country B.

As regards the other elements of national TCP schemes, which are mentioned in the previous section, we do not think they should necessarily be uniform. However, they should meet certain 'minimum quality' criteria, in particular with respect to monitoring and enforcement.

Next to that, two new international agencies have to be established by the

Conference of the Parties to the FCCC: 1) an international clearing house and 2) an international enforcement agency (IEA). The tasks of an international clearing (or administration) house, which might be a private agency, are the following:

- It keeps accounts of international permit trade (participation is compulsory for traders).
- It administers transfers of permits between legal entities.
- It registers the changes in permit holdings of each participating country.
- It informs the IEA by the end of each year about each country's TCP position.

An international enforcement agency has the following major tasks:

- It combines information on the agreed national emissions or fuel quota of countries and the information from the clearing house on TCP positions of countries (i.e. changes resulting from international permit transfers).
- It monitors compliance by countries; that is, it settles the accounts between countries by comparing permit holdings and emissions.
- It reports compliance by countries and assesses other relevant aspects.

An important issue is whether there has to be a uniform rule for initial allocation of permits or not. Should nations agree before starting trade on questions like:

- auctions or/and grandfathering?
- if grandfathering, then to which sectors?
- if grandfathering, what is the basis for initial allocation?

In answering these questions, it is important to bear in mind that grandfathering itself implies an opportunity cost for firms receiving permits (Nentjes et al., 1995). What matters here is not how you obtain your permits, but what you can sell them for – that is what determines opportunity cost. Thus, relative prices of products will not be distorted and substitution effects (switching towards the products of firms whose permits are awarded free) will not be induced by grandfathering. This makes grandfathering different from the exemptions from carbon taxes which may lead to substitution effects. For example, the Commission of the European Communities (CEC) proposal for a mixed carbon and energy tax provides for exemptions for the six energy-intensive industries (i.e. iron and steel, non-ferrous metals, chemicals, cement, glass, and pulp and paper) from coverage of the tax on grounds of competitiveness. This not only reduces the effectiveness of the tax in achieving its objective of reducing CO_2 emissions, but also helps the industries which are exempt from the tax to improve their competitive position in relation to those industries which are not. There will therefore be some switching of demand towards the products of these energy-intensive industries, which is precisely the reaction that such a tax should avoid (Zhang, 1997).

On the other hand, grandfathering gives implicit subsidies to some sectors, the value of which is independent of the behaviour of those sectors. This means that there is a distributional effect comparable to a lump-sum effect. An important question is: do the GATT/WTO rules permit differential treatment in this respect? To answer this question, we have to look at the underling GATT/WTO trade principles. There are two basic principles governing the GATT/WTO: namely the 'most-favoured nation' clause (Article I) and the 'national treatment or non-discrimination principle' (Article III). The principle of relevance here is the one of national treatment. This principle requires imported products to be accorded no less favourable treatment than domestic products. Although grandfathering gives advantages to some sectors, GATT/WTO appears not to reject such a differential treatment if domestic and imported fuels are treated equally in obtaining emissions permits.

Theory suggests that either grandfathering or auctions will ultimately result in a cost-effective allocation of permits among various polluters as long as they are all price-takers, transaction costs are low, and permits are fully transferable (Tietenberg, 1995). Moreover, studies of the effectiveness of policy instruments in other areas suggests that, whatever form international agreements take, domestic solutions should not be imposed on individual governments (UNCTAD, 1995).

Given rapid integration of the world economy, however, some express a concern that different allocation rules for permits among parties could distort international competitiveness, pointing out that a government that grandfathers permits to a firm could give it a competitive advantage over a similar firm in another country where permits are not awarded gratis. We think this is not necessarily the case, because even if a firm obtains emissions permits by auction, its government still can protect its international competitiveness by means of recycling the revenues raised through auctioned permits to lower other pre-existing distortionary taxes, such as taxes on labour and capital. Moreover, owing to national sovereignty considerations, it would not be feasible to set a uniform allocation rule. Given the fact that some governments are more touchy than others about national sovereignty, they may think that setting a uniform allocation rule will restrict their rights to select the option which is best suited to their own national circumstances. Take the above CEC proposal for a carbon/energy tax as an example. National sovereignty considerations to some extent explain why the CEC proposal for a carbon/energy tax failed to gain the unanimous support of its member states, partly because some member states opposed an increase in the fiscal competence of the Community and thus opposed the introduction at a European level of a new tax on grounds of fiscal sovereignty (Bill, 1997). This failure is also because some member states are loath to restrict themselves to the common CEC-specified framework of policies and measures to stabilize CO_2 emissions; they want the freedom to devise their own.

Given these theoretical and empirical findings, we conclude that individual governments should be left free to devise their own methods of allocating permits. The choice between grandfathering and auctions and the size of individual permit allocations will depend on a range of considerations. These may include: whether carbon taxes have been introduced; the importance of different sectors to the national economy; the bargaining power of each sector; the political and economic position of different fossil fuels; and the importance of minimizing transaction costs. For example, some Nordic countries have already introduced carbon taxes as a means of achieving their unilateral carbon abatement goals. These governments, if replacing carbon taxes by a TCP scheme, would need to raise revenue to compensate for the loss of abolishing carbon taxes. Kågeson (1991) suggests that 80 per cent of permits should be grandfathered and the remaining 20 per cent auctioned. Even for those receiving permits by grandfathering, we could envisage charging an annual fee, as is used in New Zealand in addition to tradable quotas to control over-fishing of selected species. Such a fee should be much lower than the auction price so that it would place a smaller financial burden on polluters than auctioning. The revenue from levying a low annual fee would then be used to further enhance governments' monitoring and enforcement efforts (Tietenberg, 1995; UNCTAD, 1995). With second-best considerations, some governments would also decide to auction permits, and the revenues generated through auctioned permits could then be used to reduce pre-existing distortionary taxes, thus generating overall efficiency gains. Parry et al. (1996), for example, show that the costs of reducing US carbon emissions by 10 per cent are four times larger under a grandfathered carbon permit scheme than under an auctioned scheme. This disadvantage reflects the inability to make use of the revenue-recycling effect in the former case. Besides, even without considering the revenue issue, governments may also decide to hold a small number of permits for auction in order to provide the market signals on current permit prices and to ensure permits are available for new sources, just as the US Acid Rain Program has set aside 2.8 per cent of the total allowance allocation for auctions and direct sales (Kete, 1992).

5. CONCLUSIONS

A TCP scheme can only be established if there are legally binding carbon emission limits. The EU has so far agreed to set a cap on overall emissions for the group as a whole and has worked out a specific cap for each member country. Although it has not proved easy for the EU to work out such an arrangement, it hopes that its 'bubble' approach to meeting commitments will gain recognition in terms of legal competence in the new protocol to the FCCC. As for the world's largest carbon emitter, the US is unlikely to agree to any targets unless it knows what degree of flexibility could be involved. Here flexibility includes the following: 1) would the carbon permits be issued as an emissions budget over a period? 2) can early-achievement be banked for future use and can under-achievement in the current period be fulfilled by the borrowed permits from a subsequent period? and 3) can emission reductions be achieved 'offshore' through emissions trading or joint implementation? Clearly, there is a 'chicken and egg' problem in setting the cap on carbon emissions. Given the ongoing tension over the responsibilities of different parties to the FCCC, if any concrete commitments and emission targets emerge from the upcoming COP3, they will only be the result of negotiation and agreement among the parties themselves.

Assuming that after lengthy negotiations CO_2 emission targets are internationally agreed and that emissions trading provisions are included in the new protocol as a long-term option, the details need to be worked out regarding the design of a feasible TCP scheme. From the discussion in this chapter, we think the following guidelines have to be considered in designing a feasible, effective, efficient and politically acceptable national TCP scheme.

- A permit should be defined as an allowance to use a tonne of carbon in fossil fuels.
- Carbon permits should be made available in quantities equal to the emission target for that year. These should be geared to clear and politically reliable timetables for reducing total CO_2 emissions. As a response to inevitable uncertainties and the latest scientific evidence, the number of permits may be subject to change but such changes should be scheduled in advance as far as possible to promote confidence in trading.
- Carbon permits should be issued as an emissions budget that would allow permit holders to meet the target on average over a period. The duration of a budget period needs to be carefully considered, weighting the economic efficiency of a longer budget period against the practical feasibility of doing so.

- No restrictions should be placed on the location where permits cán be used; no restrictions on ownership and no restrictions on trade apart from the application of anti-trust law.
- Banking and borrowing should be allowed in order to increase flexibility and lower the cost of abating CO_2 emissions. However, borrowing is only warranted if there are stringent emission targets and should be used with considerable caution. Safeguards should be developed to allow borrowing in such a way that it does not undermine the environmental objectives.
- Grandfathering of permits to fuel-intensive firms will foster political acceptability.
- Permits can be auctioned to other firms and to fuel distributors.
- Distributors should act as agents for small fuel users (e.g. households) and pass on their permit costs in a mark-up on the fuel price.
- Purchasers of fuels should hand over permits to sellers. At the end of the year or the budget period the government monitors the balance between carbon import and production, and permits that have been returned to fuel importers and fuel producers.
- Fines should be imposed for non-compliance. A trade-off between environmental effectiveness and cost-effectiveness should be one consideration in setting the levels of fines. Whatever levels are set, fines from non-compliance can be added to a 'Green Fund'.
- The government should be responsible for organizing the auctions; there is no special task for the government in organizing the secondary market. When property rights to permits are well defined and certain, a secondary market will develop 'spontaneously'.

For the design of an international TCP scheme, carbon permits should be defined in a homogeneous unit. The other above-mentioned elements of national TCP schemes, although not necessarily uniform, should meet certain 'minimum quality' criteria. Individual governments should be left free to devise their own ways of allocating permits. In addition, two new international agencies – an international clearing house and an international enforcement agency – have to be established by the Conference of the Parties to the FCCC in order to administer and enforce an international TCP scheme.

In this chapter, we have argued that a national TCP programme is the basis and precondition for an international TCP scheme. This demands that the countries participating in an international TCP scheme have to first establish their national TCP schemes. However, setting up a national TCP scheme requires that:

- governments have experience with formulating national emission targets and timetables;
- there is a reliable national register of individual emission sources that will participate in the scheme;
- there is an established system of emission monitoring, either direct or indirect; and
- there is a tradition of effective enforcement.

According to the above-specified conditions, not even all Annex II countries would so far qualify for engaging in emissions trading. This suggests that a TCP scheme might initially start with only a handful of OECD countries, although it does not preclude its subsequent expansion to include other qualified countries according to the rules of procedure agreed before trading begins. Such an expansion will: bring more emission sources into an international TCP scheme; reduce the leakage effects which occur when reduced greenhouse gas emissions in countries with caps are counteracted by increased emissions in countries without caps; lower the costs of abating emissions; and increase the scope for efficiency gains.

For some time to come, however, developing countries will not qualify for participation in an international TCP scheme. This promotes the concern: how can we encourage their participation in achieving the ultimate goal of the FCCC, given the fact that there are a great deal of low-cost abatement options there? One widely recognized option to bring the developing countries on board is by means of joint implementation (JI). Indeed many Annex II parties to the FCCC are keen to see JI as a key part of any protocol, although it is not without conceptual and operational problems (Zhang, 1997). However, the developing country stance on JI would be contingent on whether the North, particularly Annex II countries, have demonstrated once and for all that they are really taking the lead in significantly reducing their emissions within a short time-frame and are living up to their commitments to providing adequate transfers of financial resources, technology and expertise. This in turn raises the question of whether Annex I countries are able to reach an agreement on these issues at Kyoto and subsequent negotiations, which will acceptably draw the developing countries into the battle against global warming. If such an agreement can emerge, and if the four-year pilot phase of JI (referred to as activities implemented jointly) turns out to be a success, then an increasing number of the developing countries will become more positive about the concept of JI. Only then will there be a reasonable prospect of joint implementation of abating greenhouse gas emissions between developed and developing countries.

However, bringing the developing countries on board and integrating JI credit trading into an international TCP scheme promotes another concern about the credibility of the scheme. How can an international TCP scheme incorporate credits from JI projects and at the same time ensure that the confidence in the TCP scheme is not compromised? One option would be to restrict the amount of JI credits that could be bought by Annex I countries for compliance from non-Annex I countries. Another option, which is superior to the first option, would be to discount the credits awarded to JI projects. Such reduced crediting could provide an 'environmental bonus' and at the margin allow for the uncertainty about the reported emission reductions of JI projects. Moreover, we advocate a predetermined discount factor. In order to reflect the characteristics of a JI project and the differing quality of greenhouse gas monitoring and reporting infrastructures across countries, such a discount factor should differ both per type of project and per country and should be accordingly adjusted over time for those countries in order to reflect the improvement in their monitoring and reporting infrastructures. We think that a predetermined discounting approach is superior to a market-driven discounting approach, because the former would protect against the introduction of false credits into the TCP scheme, and provide non-Annex I countries with financial incentives to opt for binding commitments and develop stringent monitoring and reporting infrastructures.

In this chapter, we focus on designing a TCP scheme to control CO_2 emissions. However, it should be pointed out that the greenhouse effect is caused by the accumulation of not just CO_2 but also other greenhouse gases. Thus, some governments may commit to controlling all greenhouse gases in order to ensure that reductions in one gas do not lead to increases in another. Such a comprehensive coverage will also induce more cost-effective abatement options. Because of the difficulties in estimating and monitoring greenhouse gases other than CO_2, however, an international emissions trading scheme would initially begin with CO_2 emissions, although this does not preclude its subsequent expansion to include other greenhouse gases according to the rules of procedure agreed before trading begins. As for a national emissions trading scheme, its coverage of greenhouse gases could be wider than in an international scheme. Emissions trading could take place for each separate pollutant on the domestic markets; inter-pollutant trading would not be allowed unless global warming potentials that could be used to translate greenhouse gases into carbon equivalent units for trading could be internationally agreed.

NOTES .

[1] This study forms part of an ongoing project 'International Carbon Control Strategies: Tradable Permits'. The authors are grateful to the Netherlands Organisation for Scientific Research for financial support. The views expressed here are those of the authors. The authors bear sole responsibility for any errors and omissions that may remain.

2   Carbon will be used as shorthand for carbon dioxide throughout this chapter.

3   See Chapter 1 for definitions.

4   The US auctions differ from the first option described here in that participants pay the price that they bid, rather than that of the marginal buyer. The political reasons for this choice are described in Hausker (1992). While many expected that such a design would undermine the effectiveness of the auction, this does not appear to have been the case.

5   The size of these costs will depend on how politically contentious the distribution process is. Here we have abstracted from the political battles which precede and accompany the introduction of this new market based instrument.

REFERENCES

Bill, S. (1997), *European Commission's Experience in Designing Environmental Taxation for Energy Products*, European Commission, Brussels.

Dudek, D.J. and J. Goffman (1997*), Emissions Budgets: Building an Effective International Greenhouse Gas Control System*, Environmental Defence Fund, New York.

Hausker, K. (1992) 'The Politics And Economics Of Auction Design In The Market For Sulphur Dioxide Pollution', *Journal of Policy Analysis and Management*, **11**(4), 553–572.

IPCC (1996), *Climate Change 1995: Economic and Social Dimensions of Climate Change*, Contribution of Working Group III to the Second Assessment Report of the Intergovernmental Panel on Climate Change, Cambridge University Press, Cambridge.

Kågeson, P. (1991*), Economic Instruments for Reducing Western European Carbon Dioxide Emissions*, Swedish Environmental Advisory Council, Ministry of the Environment, Stockholm.

Kete, N. (1992), 'The US Acid Rain Control Allowance Trading System', in OECD, *Climate Change: Designing a Tradable Permit System*, Paris, pp. 78–108.

Klaassen, G. and A. Nentjes (1997), 'Sulphur Trading under the 1990 CAAA in the US: An Assessment of First Experiences', *Journal of Institutional and Theoretical Economics*, **153** (2), 384–410.

Matsuo, N. (1997), 'Key Elements Related to Emissions Trading for the Kyoto Protocol', Institute of Energy Economics, Tokyo.

Mullins, F. and R. Baron (1997), International GHG Emissions trading, 'Policy and Measures for Common Action' Working Paper No. 9, Annex I Expert Group on the UN FCCC, OECD, Paris.

Nentjes, A. and B. Dijkstra (1994), The Political Economy of Instrument Choice in Environmental Policy, in M. Faure, J. Vervaele and A. Weale (eds.), *Environmental Standards in the European Union in an Interdisciplinary Framework*, Maklu, Antwerpen, pp. 197–215.

Nentjes, A, Koutstaal, P. and G. Klaassen (1995), Tradable Carbon Permits: Feasibility, Experiences, Bottlenecks, NOP Report No. 410100104, Netherlands National Research Programme on Global Air Pollution and Climate Change (NOP), Bilthoven, the Netherlands.

Palmisano, J. (1997), Climate Change Economics, *Joint Implementation Fortnightly*, Update, No. 17.

Parry, Ian W.H., Williams III, R.C. and L.H. Goulder (1996), *When Can Carbon*

Abatement Policies Increase Welfare? The Fundamental Role of Distorted Factor Markets, Resources for the Future, Washington, DC.

Richels, R., Edmonds, J., Gruenspecht, H. and T. Wigley (1996), The Berlin Mandate: The Design of Cost-Effective Mitigation Strategies, in N. Nakicenovic, W.D. Nordhaus, R. Richels and F.L. Toth (eds.), *Climate Change: Integrating Science, Economics and Policy*, IIASA CP-96-1, International Institute for Applied Systems Analysis, Austria, pp. 229–248.

Tietenberg, T.H. (1995), 'Transferable Discharge Permits and Global Warming', in D.W. Bromley (ed.), *Handbook of Environmental Economics*, Blackwell, Oxford, pp. 317–352.

Tietenberg, T. and D.G. Victor (1994), 'Possible Administrative Structure and Procedures for Implementing a Tradable Entitlement Approach to Controlling Global Warming', in United Nations Conference on Trade and Development, *Combating Global Warming: Possible Rules, Regulations and Administrative Arrangements for a Global Market in CO_2 Emission Entitlements*, Geneva, pp. 1–60.

UNCTAD (1995), *Controlling Carbon Dioxide Emissions: The Tradable Permit System*, UNCTAD/GID/11, United Nations Conference on Trade and Development, Geneva.

Zhang, Z.X. (1997), *The Economics of Energy Policy in China: Implications for Global Climate Change*, New Horizons in Environmental Economics Series, Edward Elgar Publishing Limited, Cheltenham, England.

343-53

H23 Q2'
Q2f
F18

I selectil
countrol

18. Implementation issues in international CO$_2$ trading

Tim Denne

1. INTRODUCTION

A number of countries (including New Zealand and the US) have signalled their interest in the development of a tradable permit system in the context of the negotiation of a protocol under the Framework Convention on Climate Change (FCCC). This reflects a concern regarding the wide variation in mitigation costs between countries.

In the absence of trading, it is possible that equal emission targets for all countries will be achievable only at a high cost for some parties while the same targets are achievable as business as usual for others. Recognizing this, differentiated targets have been suggested by a number of parties but proposals have tended to slip rapidly into special pleading: any resulting formula is likely to reflect national circumstances, such as industrial structure and fuel mix, more than a measure of abatement effort to date. Furthermore, it is difficult to see how any formula could be developed that is demonstrably more equitable or more efficient than the status quo of equal emission targets; all formulae are to some extent arbitrary.

The principle of global least cost is an obvious goal around which, potentially, negotiating parties can rally in the search for an efficient and equitable solution. The obvious way of achieving this is through setting an equal price on emissions wherever they occur.[1]

In order to discuss the issues surrounding the operation of an international CO$_2$ trading scheme which would achieve this objective, this chapter first describes the possible operation of a domestic trading system.

343

2. A DOMESTIC SYSTEM OF CARBON TRADING

The key issues to be considered in designing a domestic system of carbon trading are: who trades; how is the initial allocation decided; and what form does the permit take?

2.1. Who trades?

There are two elements to the question of who trades:

- government or firms? And
- if firms, at what level in the economy?

It is perfectly feasible for governments to trade and Bohm gives an example of how this might occur (Bohm, 1997). However, for efficient trading it is necessary for governments to have a good understanding of the marginal costs of mitigation and therefore the value of permits. Many countries do not have cost curves and, for those that do, many do not believe them, partly because of the very wide range of possible mitigation options covering all sectors. Whereas it is possible to analyse the marginal cost of CO_2 mitigation, it is easier for the market to discover it. A domestic trading regime can achieve this and it is this connection of a domestic to an international trading system that enables the most efficient outcome.

Amongst firms, trading can be at more or less aggregated levels. Traditionally, permits for air pollutants have been traded amongst final emitters. For CO_2 the system can be simplified. The principle that 'carbon in' equals 'carbon out' can enable application of the same approach as is used for a carbon tax with permits applied to the introducers of carbon into the economy; that is, importers or producers of coal, oil and gas.

The advantage of this approach is that it simplifies the monitoring and verification requirement – the approach is the same that is used for measuring national inventories of greenhouse gases. In contrast, permits for final emitters would require measurement and monitoring of emissions including power plants and individual motor vehicles.

The disadvantage of this aggregate approach is that it reduces the number of potential traders in the system. Concerns with other permit trading systems have been over low levels of trading and the perceived need to maximize the number of traders. However, as is discussed below, the trading problem is often more related to the mechanism than the number of traders.

Assuming a competitive market, the level in the economy at which the permit obligation is established should make no difference to the price effect on final emitters. The permit price will be passed on to the extent that it can be, taking account of fuel price elasticities within the market. In the same way, a permit obligation on final emitters might result in fossil fuel wholesalers absorbing some of the costs if demand dropped.

2.2. The obligation

An effective and efficient permit system could result from a legal obligation on introducers of carbon into the economy to hold permits to cover the total quantity of fuel sold or used in any one year. Sources of industrial process emissions of CO_2 (e.g. cement manufacturers) would also be required to hold permits. The monitoring and verification issue is more complicated (and more costly) for these emissions but is in principle achievable.

2.3. Domestic allocation

It is often argued that initial allocation is unimportant because, through competitive trading, the actual emission reductions will occur where the marginal costs are lowest and thus an economically efficient outcome will result, with the effects being merely distributional. However, it is clear that grandparenting permits can significantly reduce the efficiency advantages of a permit system (Stavins, 1995).

- If permits are given away governments do not have a revenue stream which otherwise could be used to offset distortionary taxes and reduce overall costs to the economy.
- If transaction costs are positive, e.g. there is a cost associated with trading such as identifying potential trading partners, then achieving an efficient outcome is less likely than if there is an equal opportunity for all firms to obtain permits. This is especially an issue for new entrants to a sector which would need to purchase all their permits from current owners.

Auctions are regarded as a more efficient distribution mechanism but the detailed operation of this mechanism is not generally made clear. Permits could be made available via an open access system similar to the stock exchange or commodity exchange. In this scenario, the government would make a quantity of permits available on the market equal to the targeted quantity of emissions for any year, e.g. total 1990 emissions. National governments have an important role in establishing this trading system.

Ideally permits would trade freely and could be held by anyone. In an aggregate system, final emitters such as power companies may wish to hold permits to hedge against price fluctuations. These could then be exchanged with the fossil fuel supplier at the time that fuel was purchased. But it is the fossil fuel wholesalers who would be required to hold or surrender them at the end of the budget period. That said, it is unclear that power producers would choose to hedge against the risk of permit price fluctuation any more than other financial uncertainties.

2.4. The nature of the permit

Permits would need to be for a specified amount (e.g. one tonne of CO_2) and for a specified time period (e.g. permitting emissions in 2010). During any one year permits might be made available for both current and future years. In order to restrict the ability of firms to restrict market access, the number of future permits would need to be limited (see 'Banking and Borrowing' below).

2.5. The incentive

Fuel wholesalers would need to hold permits in order to cover their fuel sales. The tallying of sales and permit requirement might be made on an annual basis with heavy fines for non-compliance. Demand for permits between the different fuel wholesalers would determine the permit price.

End users of fossil fuels including power generators, industrial plants and car owners would be affected by permits in the form of an increase in fuel price. The permit system works, just as for a tax, through providing a price incentive for emission reductions. Total consumption of fossil fuels is restricted by the number of permits. Permit price and hence fossil fuel price will rise until demand falls to match supply. Ultimately, it is the cost of mitigation options at the margin which set the price of permits, although this will be limited by the value of any penalty introduced for failing to hold permits.

3. VARIANTS ON THE BASIC DOMESTIC SYSTEM

There are a number of possible variants on the basic system.

3.1. Capped permits

It is conceivable that governments may not want to meet their climate change targets at any cost. A limit might be set on the permit price by giving producers the option of holding a permit for their fuel use or paying a charge (a tax). The level of this charge would, in effect, set an upper limit on the price of the permit.

This arrangement works for a domestic system but would not for an international system as the country operating such a variation would set the international permit price ceiling and potentially gain revenue at the expense of the achievement of international targets.

3.3. Banking and borrowing

There is clear evidence from other permit systems and from analyses of the costs of reducing CO_2 emissions that mitigation costs can be reduced through spreading the emission limitations over time as well as over space (Manne and Richels, 1996). Doing less now and more later, particularly in step with the turnover of capital, allows total costs to be minimized while keeping to an overall emissions budget.

In practical terms this means that permits would need to be made available on the market for future years and that permits could be held in the current year if valid for current, future or previous years. A fuel wholesaler could purchase a portfolio of permits and hold them, covering current and future years in a way that balances costs of mitigation and the expected permit price. Borrowing involves purchasing 'future year' permits and using them now to cover current emissions, thus reducing the future availability of permits. This pushes up the price of future permits and would only be worthwhile if the permit price is expected to rise at less than the discount rate.[2]

Limits would need to be set on the availability of future permits and the period within which accounts need to be reconciled. Otherwise the clear incentive is to purchase permits for years in the distant future, and the availability of permits would reduce the current price whereby little mitigation action would be taken.

The possibility of borrowing from future years has been proposed by the US in the context of national targets under the FCCC and has met with a fairly hostile reaction (US Department of State, 1997). The primary issue of concern has been credibility – can we be sure that a country (or a firm) will limit future emissions if it is obviously increasing them now? Clearly this is more a political than a technical question.

An alternative and more politically acceptable arrangement might be to allow permit banking. This involves undertaking greater emission reductions now and making the surplus permits available for use in subsequent years. Banking would also enable firms to purchase additional current-year permits and sell them in future years when permit prices are higher. An arrangement of this type has precedents in the US Acid Rain Program and the US lead market. In both cases, standards are more stringent in later years. This creates an incentive to overachieve in the initial period, thereby increasing supply and reducing costs in future years. A disadvantage of banking is that it is consistent with, and may indeed encourage, rising emissions.

Systems designed to include trading over time have clear efficiency advantages over permit systems incorporating spatial efficiencies only. But the design needs to be carefully undertaken to ensure real emission reductions.

A related concept is that of a budget period. This introduces a time period within which all permits have equal validity. Given the concerns above, the length is best if it is fairly short. However, there is no obvious basis for the decision on budget period. For example, the length of the business cycle has been suggested by some analysts, but this assumes that all businesses turn over capital together and that it is of equal length for all sectors. It is inevitably an arbitrary choice.

3.3. Two-sided permits

Permits might apply both to emissions and to the creation of carbon sinks. Such a system allows firms to 'create' permits which could be sold on the market.

The system is more complex than for emission permits for several reasons:

- It requires that national targets are set on the basis of net rather than gross emissions. However, in order to ensure that permits have a positive value, international permit systems would require that emission targets were legally binding. The high degree of uncertainty surrounding estimates of absorption might auger against their inclusion within a legally binding target.
- There is a need for ongoing monitoring of the forest site registered for permit creation as, at the time of felling, it would be necessary for the forest owner to hold a permit to cover the associated emissions.[3]
- To cover all emissions, all forests would need to be covered by the system. Otherwise trees planted without earning permits would be felled without requiring a permit to be held, while at the same time new plantations would earn them; total net emissions would not be kept in balance.

There is also a large question mark over whether forest owners would trade. If permits will be required in order to fell in the future, the question over whether to sell now and buy in the future depends on the estimation of future trends in permit price. If permit price is likely to increase at a rate greater than the discount rate then they should not sell. This does of course leave open the option of firms investing in forest planting purely as a long-term carbon reservoir with no intention ever to fell the trees, if the costs are low enough.

3.4. Multi-gas permits

Permit systems might be extended to cover several greenhouse gases on the basis of Global Warming Potentials (GWPs). However, non-CO_2 greenhouse gases are more complicated to account for because there is not the same simple 'carbon in – carbon out' formula. Permit requirements would need to be at the level of the final emitter rather than the fuel sale in order to provide incentives for the full range of mitigation options. A further problem is that there is much greater uncertainty of emission estimates for non-CO_2 greenhouse gases in comparison with CO_2.

This may have important implications for the question of individual gas versus aggregate gas targets under the Convention. Whereas there is clearly a theoretical argument on least cost grounds for aggregate targets, such an approach is likely to make tradable permits more difficult to establish because of very different requirements for verification and greater levels of data uncertainty. Tradable CO_2 permits could be operated in the context of a multi-gas target but this would require countries to establish domestic and legally-binding CO_2 targets in addition to any multi-gas target.

In a sense there is a trade-off between two options for efficiency gain: international trading and inter-gas trading.

4. EXTENSION TO AN INTERNATIONAL SCHEME

It is relatively simple to see how a domestic permit scheme might be extended internationally so that permits might be sold between countries. Permits could be purchased by firms from the permit market in another country if the price is lower than in the domestic market. In this way an international market price is set by the lowest marginal cost mitigation options wherever they occur.

However, it is unlikely that several countries will establish such a domestic tradable permit system simultaneously. Rather, the development of an international permit scheme is more likely to evolve over time. An international permit scheme can be established from several different types of domestic policy mechanism, although none will be quite as efficient as a trading scheme.

4.1. Credit systems

An alternative system is for a country to estimate emission reductions relative to an emissions baseline and for the measured reduction 'credits' to be traded as equivalent to permits. This type of system is commonly termed 'baseline and credit' in contrast to the 'cap and allocate' system described above (Mullins and Baron, 1997).

Credit trading can occur in a number of ways (Mullins and Baron, 1997):

- *Government to firm* – the government of a country expecting to reduce emissions below a targeted level might make available emission reduction credits equal to the gap between actual and targeted emissions. These could be purchased by firms in the country operating a trading system and be registered as equivalent to permits for trading in the domestic market. This allows a government to participate in an international trading system while operating whatever domestic policy measures it wishes.
- *Firm to firm* – a government might recognize emission reductions made by firms and authorize the sale of those emission credits to firms operating within the permit market of another country.
- *Government to government* – governments might identify emission reductions associated with projects or a gap between actual and target emissions and trade these with a government that would otherwise fail to meet its targets.

In all cases, the country operating the credit system would need either to agree to meet their Convention commitments jointly with the other country or to formally arrange a credit in which emissions would be added to their inventory and subtracted from the purchasing country's emissions inventory. In either case a necessary requirement is that both countries are bound by a target under the Convention. Under this restriction there is no need for a complicated international auditing regime. Because the country operating the credit system is operating within the bounds of a binding target, there is a strong incentive for honesty in the calculation of emission reductions. And even if the estimates are wrong, the problem is limited to the two countries trading, so long as they are jointly bound by the target.

This is an important difference between the trading scheme and Joint Implementation (JI) as traditionally envisaged; that is, as a system for trading between OECD countries and either developing countries or economies in transition. While the OECD and economies in transition will be bound by emission targets, developing countries will not.[4] JI with a country that is not bound by an emission target requires international scrutiny of the emission reductions and of the baseline in order to ensure additionality. In reality this is impossible to prove. The most likely trading regime will therefore be amongst Annex I countries and particularly between the OECD and economies in transition.

The advantage of a tradable permit scheme over a credit scheme or JI is that there is no need to prove the counterfactual, i.e. to estimate what would have happened in the absence of the emission reduction project. For permit purposes, estimates of permit requirements are made in the same way as emissions are calculated – principally on the basis of fossil fuel consumption. But to demonstrate that an emission reduction has occurred for crediting purposes it is necessary to estimate what emission rates would have been in the absence of a specified action. Developing emission baselines is more complicated for CO$_2$ than for other pollutants where there is generally a more limited set of technological solutions for which standard emission reduction rates can be estimated. Nevertheless, if credit trading or JI is confined to Annex I countries then concerns over the counter-factual are purely domestic. Provided that a country is willing to identify and to sell an emission credit and still meet its emission target minus the emission reductions, then the overall system remains in balance. The important element is that the country is willing to be bound by the target.

JI also introduces a possible incentive for developing countries to be bound by emission limitation targets because emission reductions have an economic value. It requires agreement to be reached on acceptable and binding target levels but, if set, actual emission rates below the targeted level would result in a surplus that could be sold.

4.2. The problem of allocation

Internationally, the allocation of permits is equivalent to the setting of targets. Targets set the limit on the number of permits for a country; if additional permits are required they can be obtained through international trading, requiring that another country reduces emission rates below its target rate. Although the eventual outcome might be the same regardless of the initial allocation, there are clearly winners and losers. For example, if targets are set as now with a requirement to return to 1990 emission rates, the UK would be a winner, having permits (or credits) to sell, whereas most other EU member states would be losers, requiring to buy additional permits. However, what is clear is that the permit system would result in the UK reducing emissions further than it is currently projecting to because the cost of additional reductions are likely to be less than the value of those reductions as permit/credit equivalents, and other member states could meet targets more cheaply than in the absence of a permit system.

Having a permit system does not solve the current dilemma over the allocation of targets but it reduces the cost implications of any target agreed to.

5. CONCLUSIONS

Whatever eventual agreement is reached on emission limitation targets, there will be winners and losers. For all countries, tradable permits offer the potential for reducing the cost of emission reduction. They do not solve the problem of allocation of targets but mean that the costs of achieving any target is reduced globally and for individual countries, and that the implications of agreement on any specific formula are less significant.

An international permit scheme is best achieved through trading between countries with equivalent domestic schemes. However, a system could also develop country by country and include both countries with and without domestic permit schemes. Encouraging JI amongst Annex I parties, or with other countries willing to be bound by a target, would be a step towards a permit system.

It is unlikely that a fully functioning international permit trading system will be established in the near term but, at a minimum, it would be useful if negotiations over the next set of Convention commitments took account of the long term objective of international trading and ensured that the elements of any future protocol were compatible with a trading regime. Useful elements might include:

- Legally binding targets – without a legal obligation a permit has little value in exchange.
- Cumulative targets which require emissions to be limited within a multi-year period rather than targets for a single year. Otherwise the permits may trade at a very high price in the single target year since no firms have taken action to limit emissions in intervening years, thereby resulting in reduced economic activity in the target year rather than an ongoing incentive for efficiency improvement.
- The continuation of the option of achieving targets jointly with other parties which provides the basic legal framework for trading.
- Encouragement of economic instruments rather than regulatory requirements as part of any policies and measures component of the protocol.
- Single gas rather than aggregate targets as permit trading is more likely to be established initially for CO_2 alone and possibly be extended over time to other gases – the legal obligation has to match the permit system.

NOTES

[1] This is an efficient solution for CO2 emissions because the benefits of emission reduction are the same wherever they occur.

[2] In fact, in a competitive market the process might ensure that permit prices increase at the discount rate.

[3] The current methodology for estimating emissions from plantation forestry is to count emissions as occurring spontaneously at the time of felling. This approach is currently under review by the IPCC including an assessment of treatment of traded and long lasting goods. Any permit system would need to be compatible with the inventory methodology.

[4] OECD countries form Annex II of the FCCC, while the OECD and economies in transition together form Annex I. Only Annex I countries are required to negotiate binding targets.

REFERENCES

Bohm, P. (1997), *Joint Implementation as Emission Quota Trade: an Experiment Among Four Nordic Countries*, Nordic Council of Ministers, Nord 1997:4, Copenhagen.

Manne, A. and R. Richels (1996), 'The Berlin Mandate: the costs of meeting post 2000 targets and timetables', *Energy Policy*, **24** (3), 205–210.

Mullins, F. and R. Baron (1997), *International GHG Emissions trading*, Annex I Expert Group on the UNFCCC: Policies and Measures for Common Action, Working Paper 9.

Stavins, R.N. (1995), 'Transaction costs and tradable permits', *Journal of Environmental Economics and Management*, **29**, pp. 133–148.

US Department of State (1997), *Draft Protocol to the Framework Convention on Climate Change*, Bureau of Oceans and International Environmental and Scientific Affairs, 28 January.

354-79

[selected
contents]

92
428 H23

F18

19. Flexibility, emissions trading and the Kyoto Protocol

Jim Skea

1. INTRODUCTION

The UN Framework Convention on Climate Change (FCCC) represents the most ambitious effort ever to limit the human population's impact on the environment. If successful, the FCCC will result in the co-ordination of the activities of governments, companies and individuals across the globe for decades to come. Many varied policies and measures will be required. There is great interest in the potential of flexibility mechanisms in general, and greenhouse gas (GHG) emissions trading in particular, as a co-ordination mechanism.

Greenhouse gases make good candidates for emissions trading. Since climate change is a global problem, it does not matter where emissions arise. Prices established through market mechanisms could provide an effective means of transmitting information about the relative costs of reducing GHG emissions in different parts of the globe. Also, emissions of the main greenhouse gas, carbon dioxide (CO_2), are technically easy to measure and monitor. CO_2 emissions arise mainly from burning fossil fuels and emission levels are closely tied to the nature of the fuel (coal, oil, natural gas) used. Quantifying sources and sinks of carbon related to land use and emissions of other greenhouse gases is more problematic.

The protocol to the Framework Convention agreed at the third meeting of the Conference of the Parties (CoP-3) in Kyoto, Japan, in December 1997 is the bedrock on which future emissions trading regimes will be based (Conference of the Parties, 1998). However, the Kyoto agreement covers emissions trading in only the barest terms. A more specific agreement on the 'principles, modalities, rules and guidelines' for emissions trading was postponed until CoP-4 in Argentina in November 1998.

This chapter reviews the status of emissions trading and related mechanisms promoting flexible compliance within the international climate regime. It begins by analysing the flexibility mechanisms defined by the

354

Kyoto Protocol and the negotiations which led to their adoption. The chapter moves on to consider how the rules for emissions trading might be articulated more clearly. The discussion covers the problem of 'hot air', where emissions trading could allow countries to acquire rights to emit greenhouse gases which would not otherwise have been used. The chapter then considers the role which national governments, business, and non-governmental organizations (NGOs) could play in the establishment of an emissions trading regime. This is followed by a case study of how emissions trading might evolve at the national level, taking the UK as an example.

2. FLEXIBILITY AND THE KYOTO PROTOCOL

2.1. Kyoto commitments

The Kyoto Protocol commits Parties with developed economies (those referred to in Annex I of the Climate Convention) to a collective reduction in greenhouse gas emissions of 5.2 per cent during the *commitment period* 2008-2012 compared to 1990 levels. If the protocol is ratified by a sufficient number of parties, these emissions reductions will become legally binding. The political commitment to the Kyoto Protocol was established at the first meeting of the Conference of the Parties to the Climate Convention in Berlin in April 1995. Under the 'Berlin Mandate', the Parties to the Convention were to work towards a protocol which would 'strengthen the commitments' of Annex I countries (Conference of the Parties, 1995). The Berlin Mandate did not refer to developing countries.

The Kyoto Protocol is the result of a complex negotiation over a 30 month period. Nevertheless, agreement on many substantive issues came only in Kyoto itself. For example, the Clean Development Mechanism (CDM), which provides a key element of flexibility in the Protocol, was not part of any formal proposal prior to the conference itself. Inevitably, important technical issues were covered in a very compressed timescale or were postponed for later meetings.

The basis of the Kyoto agreement is a set of country-specific *quantified emission limitation or reduction commitments* (QELRCs) expressed as percentages of a baseline emissions level. Over the five-year commitment period 2008-2012, individual country emissions, after allowing for net trade in various credits obtainable through flexibility mechanisms, should be less than five times the baseline emission level times the quantified limitation/reduction commitment.

The commitments made by individual parties to the Convention are shown in Table 19.1. The EU and its Member States, along with three other

Western European countries, have committed to reducing greenhouse gas emissions by 8 per cent by 2008-2012. The US has committed to a 7 per cent reduction and Japan and Canada to 6 per cent. Other countries are allowed stabilization (New Zealand) or even emission increases (Norway, Australia and Iceland). These differentiated emission commitments reflect a simple fact: a given percentage emissions reduction does not reflect an equal burden in terms of compliance. The level of effort required depends on the structure of a country's economy, natural resource endowments, the balance of different gases in total GHG emissions, patterns of energy supply and demand and the effort expended prior to the 1990 base year.

Table 19.1 Quantified emission limitation or reduction commitments

OECD Countries	
Each individual EU Member State	92 per cent
EU collectively	92 per cent
Liechtenstein, Monaco, Switzerland	92 per cent
USA	93 per cent
Canada, Japan	94 per cent
New Zealand	100 per cent
Norway	101 per cent
Australia	108 per cent
Iceland	110 per cent
Countries with transition economies	
Bulgaria, Czech Republic, Estonia, Latvia, Lithuania, Romania, Slovakia, Slovenia	92 per cent
Hungary, Poland	94 per cent
Croatia	95 per cent
Russian Federation, Ukraine	100 per cent

Source: Kyoto Protocol to the UN Framework Convention on Climate Change

Apart from the Russian Federation and the Ukraine, each of the countries with economies in transition have committed to emission reductions. However, economic re-structuring in these countries since 1990 has led to a substantial reduction in emissions as output from heavy industries has fallen. The emission reduction commitments are therefore not as ambitious as they might at first appear. Russia's 'business-as-usual' emissions in 2008-2012 are likely to be below its commitment level. If these unused credits ('hot air') are transferred to other countries, then total emissions will be higher than they would otherwise have been.

2.2. Flexibility mechanisms

The range of flexibility mechanisms built into the Kyoto Protocol is extensive. The basic justification is that they can induce innovative searches for least-cost ways of reducing greenhouse gas concentrations in the atmosphere. However, they have been criticized because: a) they might allow developed countries to postpone necessary changes in activities; and b) unless tight rules defining their use are applied, then the protocol will be weakened. Three main types of flexibility are shown in Table 19.2:

Table 19.2 Summary of flexibility mechanisms in the Kyoto Protocol

'What' flexibility	
Six-gas basket	global warming potentials used to aggregate different gases
Sinks and sources	removals of greenhouse gases through sinks may be deducted from emissions
'Where' flexibility	
Joint fulfilment	Article 4 - *ex ante* (pre-ratification) approach to sharing emission commitments which would permit EU burden-sharing arrangements and a US 'trading umbrella'
Joint implementation	Article 6 - *ex post* provision of emission reduction units for 'additional' projects - a form of 'closed JI'
Clean development mechanism	Article 12 - *ex post* credit for 'additional' projects carried out in developing countries - a form of 'open JI'
Emissions trading	Article 17 - *ex post* trading according to as yet undefined rules
'When' flexibility	
5-year commitment period	evens out year-to-year variability in emissions due to weather, economic conditions etc.
Base year choice	base year for HFCs, PFCs and SF_6 may be 1990 or 1995; countries with economies in transition may use base years other than 1990
Emissions banking	unused emissions can be carried over to subsequent commitment period
Clean development mechanism	credits obtained in the period 2000-2007 can be used in the commitment period 2008-2012

Table 19.3 Fulfilling Kyoto commitments: the compliance scheme

	Emissions, sinks and credits	Protocol article	Flexibility mechanisms
A	Aggregate emissions of CO_2, CH_4 and N_2O in 1990[1]	3(7)	Flexibility across six greenhouse gases
B	Aggregate emissions of HFCs, PFCs and SF_6 in 1990 or 1995	3(7), 3(8)	
C	Removals from land use change[2]	3(7)	Allows for net CO_2 emissions
D	**Baseline emissions = A + B - C**	3(7)	
E	**Assigned amount for 2008-2012[3], derived from line D and QELRCs**	3(7)	
F	Adjustment between Parties jointly fulfilling commitments[4]	4(1)	Parties may share commitments as long as aggregate emissions do not exceed assigned amounts. Must: make agreement; specify emissions allocated to each Party; submit agreement at time of ratification
G	Net emission reduction units from 'closed JI' projects in Annex I countries[5]	3(10), 6(1)	Countries transfer or acquire emission reduction units resulting from relevant projects
H	Net emission reduction units obtained through trading[6]	3(10), 17	Undefined provision for emissions trading
I	Net certified emission reductions obtained from 'open JI' projects in developing countries under the clean development mechanism[7]	3(12), 12	Parties may acquire certified emission reductions by participating in project activities in developing countries which do not have quantified commitments. Reductions between 2000 and 2008 can be used
J	**Final assigned amount = F + G + H + I**	3(7)-3(12)	
K	**Aggregate GHG emissions 2008-2012 including net changes from forestry/land use since 1990**	3(1), 3(3)	Allows for net CO_2 emissions
L	Banked emissions, or difference between net emissions and assigned amount = J - K	3(13)	Emission credits from 2008-2012 can be 'banked' for use in a subsequent commitment period
M	Assigned amount second commitment period	3(9)	Negotiations to start in 2005

358

| N | Adjusted assigned amount, including banking = L + M | 3(13) |

Notes:

1. countries with economies in transition may use a baseline year other than 1990
2. only to be taken into account if CO_2 emissions from forestry/land use change exceed removals through sinks
3. line D times five times quantified commitments in Table 19.1
4. if joint agreement fails, each Party is responsible for the emissions assigned under the agreement.
5. projects must be: additional; subject to the approval of both Parties; supplemental to domestic action
6. must be supplemental to domestic action
7. must be: additional; on the basis of voluntary participation approved by each Party; have real, measurable, long-term benefits

Source: Author, based on the Kyoto Protocol to the UN Framework Convention on Climate Change

- 'what' flexibility relating to the coverage of gases, sources and sinks;
- 'where' flexibility allowing emission reductions or enhancement of sinks to be swapped between countries; and
- 'when' flexibility relating to the timing of emissions and emission reductions.

Table 19.3 shows how these different flexibility mechanisms together make up a complex scheme for compliance with quantitative commitments. The *assigned amount* of greenhouse gas emissions for 2008-2012 for each Party (line E of Table 19.3) is equal to five times the baseline emissions times the country-specific QELRCs in Table 19.1. The assigned amount is then adjusted to take account of the various forms of 'where' flexibility. 'Unused' emissions for the commitment period 2008-2012 may be 'banked' for use in a subsequent commitment period. Under Article 4(6) of the Protocol countries with economies in transition are to be allowed 'a certain amount of flexibility' in implementing their commitments.

'What' flexibility
Quantified commitments refer to aggregate emissions of six greenhouse gases:

- carbon dioxide (CO_2), arising mainly from fossil fuel use but also from land use change;
- methane (CH_4) arising from landfill, energy production and agriculture; and
- nitrous oxide (N_2O), sulphur hexafluoride (SF_6), perfluorocarbons (PFCs) and hydrofluorocarbons (HFCs) arising mainly from industrial processes.

Emissions of each of the gases are to be converted to CO_2-equivalents and aggregated using *global warming potentials* (GWPs) developed by the Intergovernmental Panel on Climate Change (IPCC). The ability to trade off emissions reductions between the six greenhouse gases represents a first form of flexibility.

The agreement also covers *net* emissions of CO_2. That is, CO_2 removed from the atmosphere through anthropogenic sinks may be deducted from CO_2 emissions. This second form of flexibility will allow afforestation projects carried out since 1990, for example, to contribute towards compliance. Sinks receive special treatment in calculating baseline emissions. Land use changes are to be included in the baseline *only if emissions from land use change and forestry exceed removals*. Countries in which land use sinks exceeded sources in 1990 will have higher baseline emissions, and hence easier compliance, than they otherwise would have had.

Joint fulfilment/emission bubbles

The first form of 'where' flexibility refers to a form of 'emissions bubble' established by two or more countries. Under Article 4 of the protocol, Parties are permitted to *jointly fulfil* their commitments (line F of Table 19.3) as long as their aggregate emissions do not exceed their assigned amounts. This is an *ex ante* form of flexibility where Parties must declare their hand before ratification. This provision will allow the EU to re-distribute emission commitments round its Member States according to an internal burden-sharing arrangement. However, the JUSCANZ[1] 'trading umbrella' involving other OECD countries may also want to make use of this provision. Parties must first re-assign their emissions so that overall commitments are met. The agreement must be communicated to the Conference secretariat when Parties ratify the protocol and must remain in place throughout the commitment period to which it refers. If the Parties collectively fail to meet their joint commitments, then individual Parties remain responsible for the emissions which have been re-assigned under the agreement.

Joint implementation

Under Article 6 of the protocol, Parties can acquire emission reduction units from any another Party by engaging in projects which reduce emissions or enhance removals by sinks (line G of Table 19.3). This type of project-level activity has generally been referred to as *joint implementation* (JI), though the term is not used in the protocol. Article 6 defines a form of 'closed JI' in that it is restricted to countries which have entered into quantitative commitments. It does not cover project activity in developing countries. The country which hosts a project must pass emission reduction units to the country which generates it. No additional emission 'rights' are created.

On the basis of experience under the FCCC pilot programme, activities implemented jointly (AIJ), Article 6 activities will probably cover projects in Central and Eastern Europe or in Russia where Western companies invest in low-cost emission reduction opportunities. Article 6 activities are bounded by various conditions:

- both Parties have to be fully in compliance with obligations relating to emissions inventories;
- both Parties must approve the project;
- the project must provide emissions reductions (or enhanced removal) which are additional to those which would otherwise have occurred;
- acquiring emission reduction units must be supplemental to domestic action, i.e. a Party cannot meet all of its obligations by gaining credits from other Parties.

Clean development mechanism
Developing countries are brought into the protocol under Article 12 (line I of Table 19.3) which defines a Clean Development Mechanism (CDM). This is intended: a) to help developed countries in 'achieving sustainable development and in contributing to the ultimate objective of the Convention'; and b) to help Annex I countries meet their quantified commitments by giving them credit for supporting relevant project activities. Unlike Article 6 JI, the CDM defines a form of 'open JI' in which additional emission rights are created for countries which generate projects. Certain conditions must be met:

- both countries must participate in a project voluntarily;
- there must be 'real, measurable, long-term' benefits relating to the mitigation of climate change; and
- emissions reductions must be additional to those which would have occurred in any case.

The potential difficulties associated with 'open' JI means that all emission reductions will have to be certified by bodies appointed by the Executive Board to the CDM. The CDM will help to arrange funding for certified projects. A proportion of the funding will be used to cover the costs of operating the mechanism and to help developing countries which are particularly vulnerable to climate change.

Annex I emissions trading
Under the five-line Article 17 of the protocol, emissions trading between Annex I countries will be permitted under 'principles, modalities, rules and guidelines' referring to verification, reporting and accountability (line H of Table 19.3). These rules are due to be developed at CoP-4 in November 1998. Emissions trading must be supplemental to domestic action. The protocol is no more explicit than this on how emissions trading might be defined or developed.

'When' flexibility
The protocol contains a variety of mechanisms allowing flexibility over time. The five year commitment period 2008-2012, as opposed to a single-year target, will reduce the significance of year-to-year variability in emissions due to weather and economic activity.

Under the CDM, emission reductions arising in the period 2000-2007 may be credited for the commitment period 2008-2012. This will ease compliance for Annex I countries and will accelerate the active involvement of developing countries.

The most important time flexibility mechanism relates to emissions banking. If a country's emissions over the period 2008-2012 are less than the assigned amount (line L of Table 19.3), the credit can be rolled over to meet subsequent commitments established under the Convention. This has environmental as well as flexibility advantages. Earlier greenhouse gas emission reductions will help to mitigate climate change.

Baseline emissions are also affected by time flexibility. Countries can choose 1990 or 1995 as the base year for the three 'minor' greenhouse gases, HFCs, PFCs and SF_6. Countries with economies in transition may nominate a base year other than 1990. Countries will inevitably select the base year which maximizes baseline emissions and eases compliance.

2.3. Timetables for flexibility

Much work on reporting, auditing, certification, verification, and accountability remains to make these flexibility mechanisms operational. Table 19.4 shows the key milestones. Defining the rules for emissions trading under Article 17 is the task of the Conference of the Parties to the Convention itself. Emissions trading rules will be addressed at CoP-4 in November 1998.

Most of the other tasks belong to Meetings of the Parties (MoP) to the Kyoto Protocol.[2] The MoP is not scheduled to meet until the first CoP after the protocol enters into force. This happens 90 days after at least 55 Parties have ratified the protocol, including developed countries accounting for at least 55 per cent of developed country CO_2 emissions in 1990.

In principle, the first MoP could take place by late 1999. In practice, ratifications are likely to come slowly, postponing the first meeting until the early years of next century. The first MoP has the task of: defining guidelines for verifying and reporting projects carried out under Article 6 of the protocol; and developing methods and procedures to ensure independent auditing and verification of the transparency, efficiency and accountability of the CDM.

This timetable presents problems. Under the CDM, Parties can earn certified emission reductions from the year 2000. But the MoP which defines the rules for the clean development mechanism will not have met by then. Some Parties may not want to ratify the protocol until flexibility rules are in place. On the other hand, the rules cannot be defined until a sufficient number of Parties ratify.

Table 19.4 Timetable for implementing the Kyoto Protocol

Date	Event	Article
11/1998	Fourth Conference of the Parties to the Convention: rules for emissions trading	17
3/98-3/99	Protocol open for signature. 35 countries, including the EU and its Member States had signed by April 1998	24
from 3/99	Protocol open for accession	25
after 2000	Protocol enters into force 90 days after 55 Parties have ratified, including Annex I countries accounting for 55 per cent of 1990 CO_2 emissions	
first CoP after Protocol enters into force	First Meeting of the Parties to the Protocol – rules for net emissions from land use change – guidelines on emission reduction units from JI projects – rules for clean development mechanism	3(4) 6(2) 12(7)
2005	Consider quantified commitments for a second period	3(9)
2005	Demonstrable progress towards commitments	3(2)
2006	Inventories in place	5(1)
2008	Start of first commitment period	

3. TRADING PHILOSOPHIES: THE ROAD TO KYOTO

3.1. Issues at stake

The political process through which the Kyoto Protocol was developed provides clues as to how trading rules and practices might develop. The key issues at stake were:

- the ambition of the protocol – how deep should emissions reductions be?
- differentiation – should all Parties have the same emissions reduction commitments or could these be different?
- to what extent should mechanisms for flexible implementation, through emissions trading for example, be included?
- should a 'net' approach to greenhouse gas emissions be used, where account is taken of removals of CO_2 from the atmosphere through emission sinks?
- how should developing countries participate?
- should the protocol reflect a 'common and co-ordinated' approach to policies and measures?

Issues such as ambition, differentiation and flexibility were traded off against each other during negotiations. A discussion of EU and US perspectives highlights the main points.

3.2. The EU

The EU's negotiating position was the most environmentally ambitious. It wanted a uniform 15 per cent reduction in emissions of the main greenhouse gases – CO_2, CH_4 and N_2O – by 2010 from a 1990 baseline for all developed countries. The credibility of this position was undermined by the EU's intention to re-assign its own 15 per cent reduction unevenly round the Member States. In March 1997, the EU developed a 'burden-sharing' arrangement for a 10 per cent reduction in GHG emissions which involved Germany and Denmark cutting emissions by as much as 25 per cent but Portugal being allowed to increase emissions by up to 40 per cent (EU Council of Ministers, 1997). Many countries, including Japan and the US, resented the EU's insistence on uniform emission reductions internationally while reserving the right to differentiate internally.

The EU was opposed to the use of emissions trading to meet Kyoto commitments because it believed that developed countries should be setting a lead by changing their own activities, rather than by undertaking measures overseas. The EU was opposed to the 'net' approach, because the measurement of greenhouse gas sinks is highly uncertain and it was likely to encourage investment in carbon sequestration activities overseas.

The EU wanted a reference to 'common or co-ordinated policies and measures' (CCPMs) in the Kyoto Protocol. The European Commission's own climate policy agenda included measures which might have significant impacts on global competitiveness. The most critical measure in this respect was a proposed carbon/energy tax. By establishing a process for considering CCPMs, the EU hoped to encourage the co-ordination of policies internationally, thus reducing competitiveness impacts.

3.3. The United States

The US allowed its Kyoto negotiating position to emerge gradually throughout 1997. A draft protocol text released in January 1997 highlighted the US emphasis on flexibility but did not quantify any of its proposals (US Department of State, 1997). The US proposed:

- multi-year commitment periods as opposed to single-year targets;
- two consecutive commitment periods, with banking of emissions from the first commitment period and the possible borrowing forward of emission budgets from the second period;
- a full basket of greenhouse gases going beyond the EU three-gas approach;
- a 'net' approach taking account of emission sinks;
- scope for emissions trading; and
- opt-ins through which developing countries could adopt quantified commitments and enter into trading arrangements.

The US was completely opposed to co-ordinated policies and measures. In October 1997, the US quantified the commitments it was willing to enter into, offering to stabilize its greenhouse gas emissions at 1990 levels by 2008-2012 and to negotiate on reductions for a second commitment period (White House, 1997). This was greeted with outrage by NGOs and the EU. The EU and US positions could not have been further apart, and remained so right up to the Kyoto Conference.

The US Administration's position was conditioned by strong internal opposition to any type of climate agreement. The US fossil fuel industries argued, through organizations such as the Global Climate Coalition, that fears about climate change were scientifically unfounded. In July 1997, the US Senate unanimously passed a resolution repudiating the Berlin Mandate and stating that it would not support a protocol which seriously harmed the US economy or which imposed commitments on developed countries without comparable limits on developing countries (105th Congress, 1997). Given the compromises which were necessary in Kyoto, the Senate as currently composed is unlikely to ratify the protocol. However, a different view may emerge before it is necessary to ratify the Kyoto Protocol as membership of the Senate changes.

The US Administration's strong support for the use of flexibility mechanisms can be attributed to four factors: a) familiarity with trading mechanisms as a result of experience with the Acid Rain Program (Chapters 2 and 3) and RECLAIM (Chapter 4); b) the fact that emissions trading could reduce the costs of complying with any given emissions commitment; c) opportunities for investment and markets in climate technology overseas;

and d) the prospect of engaging developing countries. These considerations could help to overcome internal US opposition to ratification of the Kyoto Protocol.

3.4. The Kyoto negotiations

The negotiations in Kyoto itself began with wide philosophical differences between the main players. In essence, the EU tried to maximize environmental ambition, while the US sought to maximize flexibility. Developing countries would not take on quantitative commitments and wanted to ensure that industrialized countries entered into commitments which reflected their historic responsibility for climate change.

The final set of quantified commitments (Table 19.1) sum to a reduction of 5.2 per cent in greenhouse gas emissions by 2008-2012. This appears mid-way between the US and EU starting positions. However, the precise way that the numbers are determined is critical. The US claims that only 3 per cent of its 7 per cent emission reduction is attributable to a change from its original negotiating position (US Environmental Protection Agency, 1998). One per cent is due to the fact that the baseline for SF_6, HFCs and PFCs can be 1995 rather than 1990 (line B of Table 19.3). The fact that carbon removals through sinks need only be deducted from the baseline emissions if emissions from land use change exceed removals through sinks (Note 2, Table 19.3) is said to be worth another 3 per cent.

As the EU pressed for ambitious emission reductions and resisting trading, the US established an informal 'trading umbrella' with Japan, Canada, Australia and New Zealand, colloquially referred to as JUSCANZ. This came to an understanding with Russia and the Ukraine about pooling emission commitments.

As a result, the US could envisage a more stringent emission commitment, as long as those of countries like Russia or the Ukraine were less ambitious. While underlying CO_2 emission trends 'without policies' in the US, Canada and Japan are upwards, they have each committed to a reduction in greenhouse gas emissions. The situation in Russia is the opposite (Table 19.5). In 1995, Russia's CO_2 emissions were more than 30 per cent below 1990 levels as a result of significant declines in economic output, especially in heavy industries (Grubb and Vrolijk, 1998). Future Russian CO_2 emissions are particularly uncertain, but it has been estimated that emissions in 2010 will be no more than 90 per cent of 1990 levels (Environmental Data Services, 1997). If this were so, Russia by itself would have at least 240 mtonnes of unneeded CO_2 to trade in international markets. This 'hot air' is equivalent to just over 3 per cent of 1990 emissions in the JUSCANZ 'trading umbrella' and could make a significant contribution to compliance in these countries. Such quantitative estimates can only be regarded as indicative, given uncertainties about emission inventories and projections for all six greenhouse gases.

Table 19.5 Commitments and CO_2 emission trends

	1990 CO_2 emissions (Mtonnes)	Projected 2000 CO_2 emissions	GHG reduction commitment
United States	4,957	5,163	7 per cent
Canada	457	510	6 per cent
Japan	1,173	1,200	6 per cent
Australia	289	333	plus 8 per cent
New Zealand	26	29	zero
Russia	2,389	1,930-2,026	zero

Source: Climate Convention Secretariat

One possible flexibility mechanism proposed by the US was pulled from the Kyoto Protocol at the last minute. This would have allowed developing countries to 'opt-in' to the group of countries with quantified emission commitments. This proposal was opposed by most developing countries, but its omission may make it more difficult for the US administration to persuade the Senate to ratify the Protocol.

4. DEVELOPING RULES FOR TRADING

The unfinished business of the Kyoto Conference with respect to emissions trading will be picked up at CoP-4 in November 1998 when 'principles, modalities, rules and guidelines' for emissions trading are due to be developed. The EU has already announced its intention of pressing for a 'concrete ceiling on the use of flexible mechanisms' (EU Council of Ministers, 1998).

Although the first commitment period under the Kyoto Protocol does not begin until 2008, a diverse group of organizations is beginning to establish *de facto* rules and procedures for operating flexibility mechanisms. Given the openness of the processes through which the Framework Convention operates and the need for expertise to inform negotiations, pro-active organizations can help to shape the formal regimes for emissions trading and clean development. First-mover advantages could result from being part of such a process from the beginning. The incentives for early action are many:

- credits from projects funded under the clean development mechanism can accrue from the year 2000 onwards;
- companies associated with domestic emissions trading in the US see substantial business opportunities at the global level, while non-US companies fear being left out of an emerging global market;
- trading will stimulate international markets for climate technologies;
- companies threatened by domestic climate policies see opportunities to invest in cheaper greenhouse gas mitigation measures overseas; and
- trading will create new tasks for international agencies eager to accept expanded responsibilities.

The two main issues relating to the development of flexibility rules are: a) verification; and b) the interpretation of the requirements for emission reduction units to be additional, supplementary to domestic action and to bring 'real, measurable and long-term benefits'.

Verification
Flexibility mechanisms can develop only as quickly as credible systems of verification (O'Connor et al., 1997). Verification concerns the measurement and/or estimation of emissions and emission reductions, institutional arrangements for ensuring that methodologies are transparent and consistent, independent corroboration of information, and communication to the Conference of the Parties. Not all greenhouse gases, sources and sinks can be covered by trading.

Many verification issues, for example measurement, are relevant whether or not flexibility mechanisms are employed. However, flexibility mechanisms will provide greater opportunities for non-compliance, especially in relation to 'open JI' under the CDM. Flexibility will raise pressures to improve best practice in measurement and the construction of emissions inventories.

A key technical issue is how accurately greenhouse gas emissions can be measured. Table 19.6 shows various estimates of uncertainties surrounding emissions and removals of the three main greenhouse gases (Corfee-Morlot, 1996). The greatest certainty is associated with energy-related CO_2 emissions, where a 10 per cent error is possible. N_2O emissions from agriculture and forestry are subject to errors of up to 100 per cent. The errors associated with CO_2 from forestry are between 20 and 35 per cent. Energy-related CO_2 will play an important role in early trading. Many groups have been opposed to afforestation/reforestation JI projects because of measurement difficulties, but the pressures are huge because of the large potential for low-cost carbon sequestration opportunities.

Table 19.6 Uncertainties for greenhouse gas inventories (+/- %)

	US	UK	Netherlands
CO_2 energy	<10	2-5	10
CO_2 deforestation	25	20	345
CO_2 other/forestry	25	20	25
CH_4 energy	10-25	20	30
CH_4 landfills	10	20	50
CH_4 animal husbandry	10	20	20
CH_4 rice	10-25	20	40-60
N_2O energy	25	25	50
N_2O agriculture/forestry	25	20	50-100

Source Corfee-Morlot, 1996

For flexibility mechanisms to be credible, all stakeholders must be clear that emissions, emissions trades and emissions reductions are being tracked accurately and consistently. Companies engaging in trading will have to report their activities to the relevant governments. The Parties to the Protocol must also be satisfied that the two countries involved in a trade are doing so correctly. This is particularly true in relation to the CDM where both parties may have an incentive to exaggerate the magnitude of emission reductions.

'Additional'
The concept of 'additionality', which applies to JI project activities and the CDM, concerns whether or not a project would have been carried out without a specific intervention aimed at climate change mitigation. Ensuring that projects are additional is particularly important under the 'open JI' defined under the CDM. Unless rigorous checks on additionality are made through the certification process, developed countries could secure additional emission units without corresponding emissions reductions in host countries.

Methodological issues have been explored in practical settings through the pilot programme on *activities implemented jointly* (AIJ) operated by the Climate Convention's Subsidiary Body for Scientific and Technological Advice (Conference of the Parties, 1997). To prove that emission reductions are additional, the global environmental benefits of a successful project must be measured against a credible and transparent baseline scenario which defines what would have happened had the project not been implemented. In constructing a baseline, consideration must be given to: system boundaries; time frames; stable baseline conditions which give certainty to investors; and verification by independent third parties. These methodological issues will need to be elaborated by MoP post-2000.

'Real, measurable and long-term'

AIJ projects are intended to bring 'real, measurable and long-term' benefits and again the pilot programme provides a foundation for the CDM. The following criteria have applied to AIJ projects:

- projects should support national environment and development strategies;
- projects should bring global benefits in cost-effectiveness terms;
- emission reductions should be verifiable and include baseline calculations; and
- financing should be additional to existing overseas development mechanisms.

Some countries involved in AIJ have applied additional criteria:

- projects should be initiated specifically to support climate change mitigation;
- emission monitoring is required;
- emission reductions should be sustainable and periodically re-assessed; and
- projects should be consistent with sustainable development principles and social and other (local) environmental impacts should be analysed.

Issues such as these may arise when flexibility rules are negotiated. Assessing these criteria would add to 'transaction costs' and inhibit project activity. Social and local environmental considerations could also come into conflict with global environmental goals. NGOs operating in developing countries are acutely concerned that, in their eagerness to make 'certified emission reductions', companies from the North may instigate projects which have negative impacts in local communities or which benefit specific social groups.

'Supplementary'

Articles 6 and 17 of the Kyoto Protocol require that JI project activities and emissions trading should be 'supplemental' to domestic action. This raises several issues:

- will the concept of supplementarity apply at the country level? If a country is manifestly engaged in a sufficient level of domestic action are all flexibility activities then acceptable?
- if a *company* wishes to engage in trading or project activities does it have to show that it is taking specific action at the domestic level?
- what level of domestic action is required to permit an entity - whether a government or company - to use flexibility mechanisms?

Another issue is the EU's desire to see 'concrete ceilings' on the use of flexibility mechanisms. A ceiling could be set on the quantity of emission reduction units acquired through flexibility mechanisms. But this raises many questions. Would the ceiling be expressed in tonnes of CO_2 equivalent, or as percentage of a country's baseline emissions? Could the ceilings be differentiated between countries? Would countries with quantified commitments greater than 1990 levels be allowed to acquire any emission reduction units at all? Would a ceiling cover all of the flexibility mechanisms? These difficult questions aside, 'concrete ceilings' are likely to face substantial opposition from the JUSCANZ group.

5. ACTORS IN A TRADING REGIME

5.1. National-international linkages

Companies and individuals, not governments, will implement climate mitigation measures on the ground. Companies will search out cost-effective measures under a flexible trading regime. But it is national governments which are committed by the Kyoto Protocol. Successful flexibility mechanisms will need to facilitate company activity. Deriving the benefits of flexibility mechanisms will require careful attention to institutional design in relation to international trading mechanisms, domestic policy and linkages between the two.

The following sections describe the roles which national governments, international agencies, private companies and NGOs could play in taking forward flexibility mechanisms.

5.2. National governments

As long as flexibility takes place through joint fulfilment (Article 4) or emissions trading (Article 17) then national governments could remain the only actors involved. On an *ex ante* basis, they could exchange commitments under Article 4. If policies were not proving adequate in one country but were 'over-achieving' in another, trading could then take place *ex post* under Article 17. However, to exploit these options fully and to make use of JI and the CDM, governments need to engage private companies much more closely.

Domestic policies would need to give companies credit for activities carried out overseas. This would be simplest if a domestic emissions trading regime analogous to that established under the US Acid Rain Program were used to implement international commitments. A company with a domestic greenhouse gas allowance could trade nationally or internationally. If it traded nationally, then the domestic tracking system would pick this up. There would be no need to adjust the 'assigned amount' allocated to the country under the Kyoto Protocol. If the company traded internationally, then it would gain credit under the domestic allowance system and a corresponding adjustment could be made to the country's assigned amount of emissions. These adjustments would need to be verified by an accredited body, accounted for in the country's emissions inventory and communicated to the Convention secretariat. A similar set of adjustments could be made if the company participated in JI or CDM activities.

Governments could set up or allow trading schemes in specific sectors with appropriate characteristics, perhaps even at an international level. For example, patterns of trade in the European electricity industry fluctuate from year-to-year because of weather-related changes in supply and demand. These fluctuations have a considerable impact on GHG emissions. European electricity trade is expanding as a result of market liberalization (Baron, 1998). A trading system within the European electricity sector could help meet protocol commitments in the context of a liberalized European market.

5.3. Private companies

Two main types of company are becoming interested in flexibility mechanisms: energy intensive businesses such as oil, coal and electricity; and those engaged in financial markets.

Energy-intensive companies could search out low-cost abatement measures overseas to meet domestic obligations. Two conditions would have to be met. First, they must be able to gain credit within the national policy framework. Second, they must be able to account for their GHG emissions in a transparent and verifiable way. Within Europe, larger sites will be obliged to report relevant data to national authorities under the 1996 Integrated Pollution Prevention and Control (IPPC) Directive (Skea and Smith, 1998). In addition, the movement towards corporate environmental reporting by larger companies provides another basis for trading activity. Independently audited corporate environmental reports containing quantitative data could also help to underpin trading mechanisms.

Multinational companies are showing great interest in flexibility mechanisms. BP, for example, has begun to develop an internal emissions trading system which would allow it to swap emissions between plants operating in different countries (Browne, 1998). BP is keen to participate in the international processes through which emissions trading rules are developed.

Voluntary agreements and negotiated agreements relating to energy efficiency or CO_2 emissions at the sector level have been established in several European countries. CEFIC for example, the European chemicals association, has developed a target of improving energy efficiency (energy use per unit output) by 20 per cent between 1990 and 2005 (CEFIC, 1997). The auditing procedures underlying such agreements may provide important lessons for verifying emission trades.

A number of financial companies have become involved in the development of international emissions trading activity. The prime example is Centre Financial Products of Chicago which has been heavily involved in the development of financial instruments such as futures markets under the US Acid Rain Program. Centre Financial Products has been closely associated with the UN Commission on Trade and Development (UNCTAD) in developing possible international trading mechanisms for greenhouse gases and stands to gain if substantial international markets develop (Sandor, 1997).

5.4. NGOs

NGOs might not appear at first to have a role to play in emissions trading. But, given widespread public doubts about the environmental benefits of trading, their participation has been sought in order to legitimize trading activity. BP has involved the US Environmental Defense Fund (EDF) in its creation of an internal emissions trading system (Browne, 1998). EDF has been a strong supporter of emissions trading and had staff seconded to the Environmental Protection Agency to help develop the US Acid Rain Program.

The Earth Council, a recently formed 'elite' NGO with membership drawn from the world's political, business and scientific communities, has established a new Policy Forum on Greenhouse Gas Emissions Trading in association with UNCTAD.

NGOs may also have a role to play in JI/CDM projects where wider issues concerning the social and local environmental aspects of sustainable development may arise.

5.5. International agencies

The OECD and its sister organization the International Energy Agency (IEA) have played a key role in developing guidelines for emissions inventories, supplying data and technical information and acting as fora for discussions between Parties to the Climate Convention on an unofficial basis. Given that measurement and verification will become even more critical under flexibility mechanisms, their role is likely to remain. IPCC has provided technical expertise on emission inventories and has a formal role to play in recommending the GWPs which will be used to aggregate emissions within the six-gas basket.

The Global Environmental Facility (GEF) is the designated funding mechanism for the FCCC and could be expected to have a major role in operating the CDM. GEF activities are managed through three implementing agencies, the World Bank, the UN Environment Programme and the UN Development Programme. The GEF has already acquired experience in applying concepts such as 'additionality'.

UNCTAD was cultivating a role for itself in relation to emissions trading even before the Climate Convention was agreed in 1992. In 1991, it began work with Centre Financial Products (see above) on the design of a system for tradable greenhouse gas emission allowances. As Kyoto approached, UNCTAD stepped up its activities by sponsoring a new Policy Forum on Greenhouse Gas Emissions Trading (Foster et al., 1997). UNCTAD sees a major role for itself in establishing and operating an international greenhouse gas emissions trading scheme.

6. FLEXIBILITY AT THE NATIONAL LEVEL: A UK CASE STUDY

6.1. The UK context

The take-up of flexibility mechanisms will depend on national circumstances and the nature of relationships between governments and the private sector. The UK provides an interesting case study because:

- the climate targets adopted by the incoming Labour government in 1997 are ambitious;
- the UK played a key role in negotiating the Kyoto Protocol on behalf of the EU;
- the UK has in the past opposed alternative 'market-based' mechanisms such as the proposed EU carbon/energy tax;
- previous attempts to introduce flexibility at the national level through a sulphur trading scheme failed (see Chapter 11); and
- the government is promoting a partnership relationship with industry.

Under the Kyoto Protocol the UK has accepted an 8 per cent reduction in GHG emissions. When the EU completed its internal burden-sharing exercise and re-distributed commitments around the Member States under Article 4 of the protocol, the UK emerged with a higher commitment of 12.5 per cent. The UK government has unilaterally committed itself to a 20 per cent reduction in CO_2 emissions by 2010 based on 1990 levels (Department of the Environment, Transport and the Regions, 1997). The latter commitment is not legally binding and could therefore be characterized as aspirational. A legally binding 12.5 per cent greenhouse emissions reduction could be achievable through cost-effective, win-win measures. However, the 20 per cent CO_2 target would involve a demanding set of policies and measures if implemented entirely through domestic action (Greene and Skea, 1997).

There has been speculation about how trading could reconcile the UK's legally binding Kyoto commitment and the 20 per cent aspirational target. If the UK were to reduce CO_2 emissions by 20 per cent through domestic action, could organizations contributing to this success sell emission reduction units on the global market? On the other hand, if only the legally binding commitment could be met by domestic action, would the UK be prepared to acquire additional emission reduction units in order to work towards its 20 per cent aspirational target? The government plans to publish first a consultation paper and then a climate strategy document during 1998. It signed the climate convention in April 1998, almost as soon as it was open for signature.

6.2. Business perspectives

In 1997, the UK government invited the business community, through the Advisory Committee on Business and the Environment (ACBE), to present its views on climate policy and to specify what contribution business might make to help the UK meet its commitments. ACBE was formed in 1991 to 'engage in a strategic dialogue' with government and is made up of the chief executives and chairpersons of major UK companies. ACBE supported the use of flexibility mechanisms as a means of meeting climate commitments at a lower cost (ACBE, 1998). Many ACBE companies, although British based, operate in global markets and will approach climate change from an international perspective, seeking out lower cost greenhouse gas mitigation options wherever they might arise. ACBE believed that the potential arising from flexibility mechanisms would be enhanced if business could participate directly in an international trading system.

ACBE also recommended that a domestic trading system be developed. The emerging IPPC system operated by the UK's Environment Agency could help to define the baseline from which trading takes place and emission reduction units are measured. However, there are possible tensions between IPPC, which is designed to regulate a wider range of environmental impacts in an integrated way at the site level taking into account local conditions, and the implementation of 'single-issue' environmental regimes represented by the Kyoto Protocol. If a site has an authorization to operate according to 'best available technique' criteria under IPPC, how could it then trade emissions without creating sub-optimal conditions as defined under IPPC?

Recognizing legal and operational difficulties, ACBE recommended that a further study should be undertaken to investigate how future trading arrangements could be designed. Such a study would have to address the scope of emissions trading (within sectors or between sectors) and how it might be coupled to the international regime. For example, could companies gain credit under IPPC for lower-cost projects undertaken overseas? The study would also have to address ACBE's related recommendations on voluntary agreements and negotiated, legally-binding sectoral agreements.

ACBE also recommended the establishment of a UK project office to support UK companies' involvement in JI/CDM activities. Like many European countries, the UK has not participated in pilot phase AIJ under the Climate Convention.

Activity has also taken place at the sectoral and company level. Detailed discussions have begun to take place about flexibility mechanisms through a wide range of trade associations, including those in the electricity and financial service sectors.

7. CONCLUSIONS

In principle, emissions trading and other flexibility mechanisms are ideally suited to dealing with climate change. Since it does not matter where GHG emissions arise, emissions trading could take place uninhibited by geographical constraints.

However, this potentially wide geographical scope raises major institutional and policy challenges. For almost the first time, emission trades could occur across national frontiers. This raises difficult questions about equity, technology transfer and trust between countries. Because the Kyoto Conference left unfinished business in terms of defining the rules for emissions trading, decisions about how to trade are now detached from decisions about environmental ambition. The more liberal the rules devised to accommodate emissions trading at CoP-4 in November 1998, the higher levels of greenhouse gas emissions will be. This problem is exacerbated by the existence of significant quantities of 'hot air', brought into being by Russia's generous allocation of GHG emissions for the commitment period 2008-2012.

But flexibility mechanisms still have advantages. Without the prospect of emissions trading, the Kyoto agreement might never have been agreed. Equally, if as expected, trading results in a relatively low price for GHG emission reductions, then political barriers to more ambitious commitments following the year 2012 will fall. The prospects for advancing a global climate strategy which truly grapples with the ultimate goals of the Framework Convention will have been enhanced.

Although there are major challenges, the conditions are in place for establishing a trading regime. It appears that the necessary 'winning coalition' of political support may already have formed. The US Administration and many developed countries - other than the EU - support trading. Some European countries, such as the UK, also appear to be leaning in favour of flexibility. The business sector, particularly multinational companies, favour the flexibility which trading could provide at a global level. International agencies ranging from UNCTAD to OECD are also interested in supporting trading activity. Finally, a number of influential environmental NGOs have lent support.

However, opposition to trading is based on profound moral beliefs and will not be easily forestalled. Big debates about the appropriateness of trading as well as intricate technical negotiations about 'principles, modalities, rules and guidelines' can be expected. Nevertheless, GHG emissions trading promises to be a major commercial activity in its own right. The existing activities described in other chapters of this book may turn out to be forerunners of an altogether larger market.

NOTES

[1]   Japan, US, Canada, Australia, New Zealand.

[2]   The annual Conference of the Parties to the Convention will act as the meeting of the Parties to the Kyoto Protocol. When this body meets as the Conference of the Parties to the Convention it is referred to as CoP; when it meets as the Parties to the Protocol, it is referred to as MoP.

REFERENCES

Advisory Committee on Business and the Environment (1998*), Climate Change: A Strategic Issue for Business*, DETR/DTI, London, March.

Baron, R. (1998), 'Evolution of Trading and Enforcement', Proceedings of the BIEE/RIIA/IAEE Conference *Climate after Kyoto: Implications for Energy*, Chatham House, London, 5–6 February.

Browne J. (1998), 'Climate after Kyoto: A Business Response', Proceedings of the BIEE/RIIA/IAEE Conference *Climate after Kyoto: Implications for Energy*, Chatham House, London, 5–6 February.

CEFIC (1997), *The European Chemical Industry's Voluntary Energy Efficiency Programme*, VEEP 2005, Brussels.

Conference of the Parties (1995), *The Berlin Mandate: Review of the Adequacy of Article 4*, FCCC/CP/1995/7/Add.1, 7 April.

Conference of the Parties (1997), *Activities Implemented Jointly under the Pilot Phase*, FCCC/SBSTA/1997/INF.3, 13 October.

Conference of the Parties (1998), 'Kyoto Protocol to the United Nations Framework Convention on Climate Change'. In: *Report of the Conference of the Parties on its*

Third Session held at Kyoto from 1 to 11 December 1997, FCCC/CP/1997/7/Add.1, 18 March.

105th Congress (1997), *Senate Record Vote Analysis: Conditions on 'Global Warming' Treaty*, Vote No 205, 25 July.

Corfee-Morlot, J. (1996), 'Emissions trading: design options and environmental performance'. In: M Grubb and D Anderson (ed.), *Proceedings of the conference controlling carbon and sulphur: international investment and trading initiatives*, RIIA, London.

Department of the Environment, Transport and the Regions (1997*), Historic Agreement Reached in Kyoto on Climate Change*, Press release 509/ENV, London, 11 December.

Environmental Data Services (1997), 'Climate change protocol', *The ENDS Report*, No 275, pp 16–20, London, December 1997.

EU Council of Ministers (1997*), EU Proposal for a Protocol to the UN Framework Convention on Climate Change*, Brussels, March.

EU Council of Ministers (1998), *Community Strategy on Climate Change: Council Conclusions*, Brussels, 23 March.

Foster, S., F. Joshua and M. Walsh (1997), 'UNCTAD and Earth Council launched Greenhouse Gas Emissions Trading Policy Forum in Chicago', *Global Greenhouse Emissions Trader*, Issue 2, September.

Greene, O. and J. Skea (eds) (1997), *After Kyoto: Making Climate Policy Work*, Special Briefing No 1, ESRC Global Environmental Change Programme, Brighton, November.

Grubb, M. and C. Vrolijk (1998), 'The Kyoto Protocol: specific commitments and flexibility mechanisms', Proceedings of the BIEE/RIIA/IAEE Conference *Climate after Kyoto: Implications for Energy*, Chatham House, London, 5–6 February.

O'Connor, M., S. Faucheux and S. Van den Hove (1997), *EU Climate Policy: Research Support for Kyoto and Beyond*, European Commission DG-XII/DG-XI, Brussels.

Sandor, R. (1997), 'Getting started with a pilot: the rationale for a limited-scale voluntary international greenhouse gas emissions trading program', testimony presented to the US Senate Energy and Natural Resources Committee, 30 September, Center Financial Products Ltd, Chicago.

Skea, J. and A. Smith (1998), 'Integrating Pollution Control'. In: P. Lowe and S. Ward (ed.), *British Environmental Policy and Europe: Politics and Policy in Transition*, Routledge, London.

US Department of State (1997), *Draft Protocol to the Framework Convention on Climate Change*, Washington DC, 28 January.

US Environmental Protection Agency (1998), *The Kyoto Protocol on Climate Change, Fact Sheet*, Washington DC, 15 January.

White House Office of the Press Secretary (1997), Remarks by the President on Climate Change, 22 October.

Index